THE I-9 AND E-VERIFY HANDBOOK

A GUIDE TO EMPLOYMENT VERIFICATION AND COMPLIANCE

THE I-9 AND E-VERIFY HANDBOOK

A GUIDE TO EMPLOYMENT VERIFICATION AND COMPLIANCE

Bruce E. Buchanan

Greg Siskind

ALAN HOUSE PUBLISHING

Produced in conjunction with Ramses House Publishing LLC. Requests for permission to make electronic or print copies of any part of this work should be mailed to the author at Siskind Susser PC, 1028 Oakhaven Road, Memphis, TN 38119.

Printed in the United States of America
First Printing: 2017

ISBN 978-0-9970833-7-8 (13-digit); 0-9970833-7-9 (10-digit)
Library of Congress Preassigned Control Number: 2017949317

Alan House Publishing
1028 Oakhaven Road
Memphis, TN 38119

Dedicated to my late mother, Meda Buchanan, for making me believe I can achieve anything I want if I work hard enough.

Bruce E. Buchanan

Dedicated to the women in my life: my wife, Audrey; my daughters Eden, Lily, and Noa; my law partner of 23 years, Lynn Susser; and my mother, Karen Siskind, all of whom have helped me accomplish so much.

Greg Siskind

ABOUT THE AUTHORS

Bruce E. Buchanan is a founding partner at Sebelist Buchanan Law PLLC with offices in Nashville and Atlanta. He represents employers and individuals in all aspects of immigration law, with a special emphasis on employer immigration compliance and employment/labor law matters. Additionally, he is Of Counsel to Siskind Susser PC regarding employer immigration-compliance matters.

Bruce authors a blog at *www.employerimmigration.com* on employer immigration compliance and is a regular contributor to *HR Professionals* magazine. He is also the editor of the Tennessee Bar Association's Immigration Law Section newsletter and past-chair of the association's Immigration Law Section.

Bruce has been interviewed by *Bloomberg BNA*, *Workcompcentral.com*, and WSMV-TV concerning various immigration-related stories. He has written articles for many publications, including LawLogix's blog, LexisNexis Legal Newsroom, the Society for Human Resource Management's website, *Bender's Immigration Bulletin*, Law360, *Employment Law Strategist*, and *The Tennessee Insurer* magazine.

For 20 years, Bruce served as senior trial specialist for the National Labor Relations Board. He also served for 12 years as adjunct professor at the William H. Bowen School of Law, University of Arkansas at Little Rock.

Bruce received his law degree from Vanderbilt University School of Law in 1982. He went into private practice in 2003 and was an attorney with Siskind Susser PC from 2012 to 2015, at which time he formed his own law firm and took Of Counsel status with Siskind Susser.

Greg Siskind is a founding partner of Siskind Susser PC (*www.visalaw.com*) and is one of America's best-known immigration attorneys. He founded Siskind Susser in 1994, and the firm represents employers across the country on immigration matters.

Because of Greg's expertise, he has authored many pieces of immigration-related legislation and has testified as an expert before the U.S. Congress's House of Representatives Immigration Subcommittee. He has authored several books, including *The Physician Immigration Handbook* (Alan House Publishing), the Society for Human Resource Management's *Employer's Immigration Compliance Desk Reference*, and LexisNexis' *J-1 Visa Guidebook*.

Greg has been interviewed by *USA Today*, the *Wall Street Journal*, the *New York Times*, *Time* magazine, the *Washington Post*, *NPR's All Things Considered*, *National Law Journal*, *Forbes*, *Modern Healthcare*, and *Bloomberg BNA*. *Who's Who in Corporate Immigration Law* listed Greg as one of its top 10 most distinguished lawyers in North America, and *Chambers and Partners* listed him as one of the top 25 immigration lawyers in the United States.

Greg is the current chair of the International Medical Graduate Taskforce (*www.imgtaskforce.org*), a physician immigration bar organization in the United States. He is one of the founders of Visalaw International (*www.visalawint.com*), a global alliance of immigration lawyers. Greg also serves on the Board of Governors of the American Immigration Lawyers Association (*www.aila.org*).

Greg is a man of many firsts. He created the first immigration law firm website in 1994 followed by the first lawyer blog in 1997. He also was the first immigration lawyer ever to grace the cover of the *American Bar Association Journal*.

Greg has been practicing law since 1990. He received his bachelor's degree from Vanderbilt University and his law degree from the University of Chicago.

SUMMARY TABLE OF CONTENTS

APPENDICES

PREFACE

Over the past 10 years, and since an earlier iteration of this book was published, immigration worksite enforcement has increased dramatically at both the federal and state levels. It began to increase at the federal level in 2007 after efforts to pass Comprehensive Immigration Reform failed in Congress. At that point, President George W. Bush's administration intensified immigration worksite enforcement.

During the first six years of President Barack Obama's administration, worksite enforcement increased to unprecedented levels. Although worksite enforcement efforts were diverted in 2015 and 2016, it has begun to increase under President Donald Trump. It would not be surprising to see worksite enforcement reach the highest level ever.

The situation for today's employers is much more complex than perhaps at any time, and it will only get more confusing. Employers have to, of course, comply with the Immigration Reform and Control Act (IRCA) of 1986's employer sanctions and anti-discrimination clauses. But now employers are being targeted for a variety of criminal sanctions, including harboring illegal aliens and money laundering, in addition to the criminal penalties contained in IRCA.

Employers may feel caught in the middle: abiding by the Form I-9 requirements enforced by U.S. Immigration and Customs Enforcement (ICE) while not being overzealous in those efforts because it might be viewed as violating the anti-discrimination laws as enforced by the Immigrant and Employee Rights Section (IER), Civil Rights Division of the Department of Justice (formerly Office of Special Counsel for Immigration-Related Unfair Employment Practices (OSC)).

Additionally, states have been passing a patchwork of new laws aimed at employers. By 2017, 23 states had passed employer sanctions laws. Of those 23 states, 8 states require all employers who meet jurisdictional standards to use E-Verify, while 12 states require contractors working with state or local governments to participate in E-Verify. And some companies are having their business licenses revoked and state contracts denied and/or revoked when they are found to have hired unauthorized employees.

If government enforcement is not enough, employers now need to worry about matters such as losing out on contracts with companies requiring their contractors to demonstrate immigration compliance, or inheriting an immigration mess in a merger or acquisition.

The I-9 and E-Verify Handbook will help human resource managers, immigration counsel, and others navigate these turbulent immigration waters. The array of compliance-related statutes and regulations are discussed in an easy-to-understand question-and-answer format with illustrations, flowcharts, checklists, and sample documents included, giving the reader tools that will help implement and improve their immigration compliance program.

The book is not intended to be an overall guide to the U.S. immigration system. Instead, it seeks to provide in-depth information on a topic that affects every employer in the country regardless of whether the company hires foreign employees.

We welcome your feedback on this book, particularly your suggestions for future editions. Please always feel free to e-mail us at gsiskind@visalaw.com or bbuchanan@visalaw.com or bbuchanan@sblimmigration.com.

Bruce E. Buchanan
Greg Siskind
September 2017

ACKNOWLEDGMENTS

Writing a book is rarely just the authors' endeavor, even if only two names are listed on the cover. This is certainly the case for this book. Many people are owed thanks for their help with this project, and we would like to thank our colleagues who have given us support on this project. They include Yvette Sebelist, Lynn Susser, Jennifer Pippin, and Ginger Clemence.

We owe a great debt of gratitude to Tatia L. Gordon-Troy of Ramses House Publishing for all of her work, including a much-needed push to the finish. We owe a good deal to the great white-collar criminal lawyer, Jonathan Marks, of the Law Firm of Jonathan Marks, P.C.

Finally, we wish to thank our families.

Greg: Thanks to my loving wife, Audrey, my daughters, Noa, Lily, and Eden, and my mother, Karen Siskind.

Bruce: I thank my daughter, Caroline, for her presence in my life and for always being there to listen and offer advice.

Bruce E. Buchanan
Greg Siskind
September 2017

DETAILED TABLE OF CONTENTS

Chapter 2

Chapter 3

Chapter 4

Chapter 5

Chapter 6

Chapter 7

Chapter 8

Chapter 9

Chapter 10

Chapter 12

Chapter 13

Chapter 14

Chapter 18

Chapter 19

APPENDICES

1

FORM I-9 GENERAL CONCEPTS

1.1   What is the basis for employment verification?

In 1986, Congress was debating many of the same questions still being debated today regarding illegal immigration and the best way to gain control of the border. The 1986 debate ended with the enactment of the Immigration Reform and Control Act (IRCA).

1

Central to IRCA is a section that creates an employer sanctions system that requires all employers in the United States to verify the identity and employment authorization of all employees hired since the law was passed in 1986. Employers have become a central part of the immigration enforcement process by taking over responsibility for verifying that their employees are legally in the country. Shortly after the law passed, the Immigration and Naturalization Service (legacy INS) created Form I-9, Employment Eligibility Verification, to document that the employer has met its Immigration Reform and Control Act (IRCA) obligations (see Appendix A). Employers are not permitted to "knowingly" hire unauthorized immigrants, and proper completion of the Form I-9 is the method for employers to demonstrate a lack of knowledge that a particular employee is ineligible for employment.

Coupled with the provisions sanctioning employers that fail to verify the employment authorization and identity of its employees are provisions barring certain immigration-related employment practices by the employer, including engaging in discrimination based on citizenship status, national origin, or requiring non–U.S. citizens to provide certain or more documents than U.S. citizens—unfair documentary practices (formerly referred to as document abuse). Employees also are protected from retaliation when they file a complaint using the anti-discrimination rules.

1.2   Which government agency regulates compliance with the employer sanctions rules under the Immigration Reform and Control Act?

Although the U.S. Department of Justice (DOJ) was responsible for enforcing compliance with the Immigration Reform and Control Act's (IRCA) employer sanctions rules when IRCA was passed, the responsibility was transferred to U.S. Immigration and Customs Enforcement (ICE) when the U.S. Department of Homeland Security (DHS) was created in 2002.

1.3   What is the Form I-9?

The Form I-9 is the two-page form, with a possible supplemental page as page 3 (see Appendix A), that employees and employers complete in order to verify the employees' identity as well as prove they are allowed to work in the United States. The form itself has three sections:

- Section 1 includes basic biographical information on the employee and also asks the employee to certify that he or she is a citizen, a noncitizen national, a permanent resident, or an individual authorized to work under another status.

- Section 2 is completed by the employer who must verify and attest, under penalty of perjury, which documents an employee presented to prove his or her identity and right to work, and that the paperwork was completed in a timely manner. Employees can refer to the "Lists of Acceptable Documents." For example, List A provides documents that prove both identity and authorization to work (such as a U.S. passport or a lawful permanent resident card). Or an employee can provide an identification document from List B (such as a driver's license or state identification) *and* a document from List C (such as an unrestricted Social Security card or birth certificate) that demonstrates employment authorization.

- Section 3 is reserved for employers that must periodically re-verify the Form I-9 if the employee is not authorized to work permanently in the United States. It also can be used for rehiring an employee under certain situations and updating an employee's name due to a name change (using this section for a name change is optional.).

The Form I-9 was updated on July 17, 2017, and all employers must use that version for new hires as of September 18, 2017. The July 17, 2017, version of the form does not change any content from the previous Form I-9 version (dated November 14, 2016). Rather, it adds one document to List C of Acceptable Documents—Consular Report of Birth Abroad (Form FS-240)—and lists it in combination with Form FS-545 and Form DS-1350. The July 17, 2017, Form I-9 also revises a couple of points in the instructions.

The previous Form I-9 (dated November 14, 2016) made some meaningful changes, including a third method of completing the form. Besides the paper and electronic methods, one can now complete what is called the "smart" Form I-9. See Chapter 2, section 2.1 for further discussion on the "smart" Form I-9.

Additionally, the November 14, 2016, version of the Form I-9 made these changes:

1. Replacing the "Other Names Used" field in Section 1 with "Other Last Names Used." This was an attempt to avoid having employees write their nicknames in this field;

2. Modifying Section 1 to request that certain employees enter either their I-94 number or foreign passport information, rather than both;

3. Requiring designation of whether the employee's number is an Alien (A) number or USCIS number, if using the smart form (although the numbers are the same; however, the more recent green cards refer to the number as USCIS);

4.   Requiring "N/A" be entered instead of leaving certain fields blank;

5.   Allowing an employee to use a P.O. Box for an address;

6.   Allowing use of a work or personal e-mail address (though either is still optional);

7.   Modifying the Form I-9 by adding a supplemental third page if using multiple preparers and/or translators; and

8.   Adding an area in Section 2 to enter additional information for temporary-protected-status (TPS) extensions, optional-practical-training (OPT) science-technology-engineering-math (STEM) extensions, and H-1B portability to avoid having to note this information in the margins of the Form I-9.

The 2013 Form I-9 (dated March 8, 2013), was a distinct departure from previous versions with the introduction of the two-page form. Additional changes included: (a) giving employees the option of providing an e-mail address (to directly notify an employee of a tentative nonconfirmation in E-Verify) and/or telephone number (which is optional as explained in the Form I-9 instructions but not on the Form I-9 itself); (b) clearer spaces for information in Sections 1 and 2; and (c) retitling Section 3 from "Updating and Reverification" to "Reverification and Rehires."

1.4   When must the Form I-9 be completed?

The Form I-9 (see Appendix A) process must start on the day an employee starts work or beforehand. The employee must complete the first section of the Form I-9 on the first day of employment and must provide the supporting documents noted on the "Lists of Acceptable Documents" attached to Form I-9 within three business days of the first day of employment (*e.g.*, if the employee's first day is Monday, Section 2 must be completed by Thursday). If the documents are not presented by that point, the employee must be removed from the payroll (though it is permissible to suspend the employee rather than to terminate the employee altogether). It is permissible to have the employee and employer complete the Form I-9 before the first day of employment. The U.S. Department of Homeland Security's *Handbook for Employers: Guidance for Completing Form I-9*, M-274 (see Appendix B), tells employers that the employee must have been *offered and accepted* the job and that the form should not be used to screen job applicants, lest there be a charge of national-origin and/or citizenship status discrimination. To the extent an employer chooses to have Forms I-9 completed before the date of hire, the forms should be requested only after a position has been offered and accepted.

The three-day requirement to produce the supporting documents also applies to recruiters and referrers for a fee, as well as to state employment agencies.

1.5   What if an employee is being hired for less than a three-day period?

Employees being hired for less than a three-day period must complete Section 1 of Form I-9 (see Appendix A) on the day of hire, and the employer needs to sign the verification attestation in Section 2 on the day of hire. Employees for jobs that are intended to last three days or less must, therefore, present their documents on the day of hire.

1.6   In a nutshell, what are an employer's Form I-9 requirements?

Employers, and others required to retain Forms I-9 (as described in Question 1.7), have six basic obligations:

1. Have employees fully and properly complete Section 1 of the Form I-9 no later than the date employment commences.

2. Review the required documents to provide identity and employment authorization to ensure that they appear genuine and that they apply to the person presenting them.

3. Properly complete Section 2 of the Form I-9, and sign and date the employer certification within three business days of the date that the employment commences (so-called Monday–Thursday rule).

4. Retain the Form I-9 for the required retention period.

5. Re-verify employment authorization for employees presenting a time-limited Employment Authorization Document (EAD) or other type of time-limited document.

6. Make the Forms I-9 available for inspection if requested by the U.S. Department of Homeland Security (DHS), U.S. Immigration and Customs Enforcement (ICE), the Immigrant and Employee Rights Section (IER) of the Civil Rights Division of the Department of Justice (formerly the Office of Special Counsel for Immigration-Related Unfair Employment Practices (OSC)), or the U.S. Department of Labor (DOL).

1.7   Are employers the only entities required to verify employment eligibility using Form I-9?

Aside from employers, agricultural associations and farm labor contractors must complete Forms I-9 for individuals recruited or referred for a fee. The terms "refer for a fee" and "recruit for a fee" do not include union halls that refer union members and nonunion members.

Recruiters and referrers for a fee are permitted to designate agents, including national associations and the actual employers of the employees, to handle the Form I-9 process. If the employer is designated to handle the process, the employer must provide the recruiter or referrer with a copy of the Form I-9, and the recruiter or referrer is still liable for Immigration Reform and Control Act (IRCA) violations.

Recruiters and referrers subject to the Form I-9 rules must abide by the timing and record-keeping requirements described in Question 1.4 and Chapter 4, and must make the Forms I-9 available to officers of U.S. Immigration and Customs Enforcement (ICE), the Immigrant and Employee Rights Section (IER) of the Civil Rights Division of the Department of Justice (formerly Office of Special Counsel for Immigration-Related Unfair Employment Practices (OSC)), or the U.S. Department of Labor (DOL). Fines and penalties applicable to employers apply to these recruiters and referrers as well.

Some state employment agencies also certify applicants they refer to employers. State employment agencies may elect to provide employees with certification of employment authorization, and if the agency refers a job seeker to an employer and sends a certification of employment eligibility within 21 days of the referral, the employer does not need to complete a Form I-9. Employers must still check the certification to make sure it refers to the person actually hired and must retain the certification as they would a Form I-9.

State agencies providing this service need to comply with the Form I-9 employment verification rules. One exception is that individuals may not present receipts for documents, such as for a replacement Social Security card, as they may in certain cases with Forms I-9 completed by employers.

When a state employment agency wants to refer an individual again after he or she has previously been certified, the state agency can rely on the prior Form I-9 if the individual remains authorized to be employed and the employee is referred to an employer within three years of completion of the initial Form I-9. State agencies must retain the Form I-9 for a period of at least three years from the date the employee was last referred and hired.

1.8   What is the employee's responsibility in completing the Form I-9?

Employees are required to complete Section 1 of the Form I-9 stating the employee's name, address, date of birth, and other names used, and whether they are a U.S. citizen or national, lawful permanent resident, or an alien with authorization to be employed. Additionally, the employees may provide his or her e-mail address, telephone number, and Social Security number (SSN), though if the employer uses E-Verify, the SSN is mandatory. If the employee is a permanent resident, he or she must provide an "Alien number." And if the employee is an alien with employment authorization, he or she must provide his or her alien or admission number and the expiration date of the employment authorization, if applicable, or the country of his or her foreign passport and number accompanied by a Form I-94/94A Arrival-Departure Record bearing the same name as the passport and containing an endorsement of the individual's nonimmigrant status and authorization to work for a specific employer along with the expiration date of the employment authorization. Employees must sign and date Section 1 of the Form I-9 attesting that the statements and documents are not false.

Employees also are required to present to the employer, recruiter, referrer for a fee, or referring state agency documentation from the "Lists of Acceptable Documents" demonstrating identity and employment authorization.

1.9   Are there any employees not required to complete the I-9 Form?

The Immigration Reform and Control Act (IRCA) requires all employers to have all employees hired after November 6, 1986, complete I-9 verification paperwork. The Form I-9 requirement applies to all employees, including U.S. citizens and nationals. Employees who are not hired do not need to complete Forms I-9, and employers who selectively choose who will and will not complete Forms I-9 could face penalties under anti-discrimination rules. Volunteers are not subject to Form I-9 rules because they receive no remuneration for their services. Independent contractors are not subject to the Form I-9 rules, but employers should note that if they outsource work to companies they know use unauthorized employees, they could also be held liable under IRCA. Persons transferring within a company are not required to complete a Form I-9. Employees rehired by a company need not complete a new Form I-9 as long as they resume work within three years of completing the initial Form I-9; however, an employer can legally decide to have a rehire complete a new Form I-9. Below are situations in which it is not necessary to complete a new Form I-9:

- After an employee completes paid or unpaid leave (such as for illness or a vacation).
- After a temporary layoff.
- After a strike or labor dispute.
- Gaps between seasonal employment.

1.10 What if an employee is a volunteer or is paid in ways other than with money? What if an employee receives a signing bonus prior to starting work?

U.S. Department of Homeland Security (DHS) regulations consider a person to be hired for purposes of the employer sanctions rules at the time of the "actual commencement of employment" for "wages or other remuneration."

> "Employment" is defined as service or labor performed by an employee for an employer.

Based on these definitions, employees who receive a signing bonus but who have not actually begun employment would not be required to complete a Form I-9 until actual work for the employer has commenced (see Appendix A).

True volunteer positions involve no receipt of pay, and the employee does not receive any other type of benefit in lieu of pay (such as food and lodging). Although it is possible Congress did not intend to include situations in which a charitable organization has provided meals and lodging to volunteers not receiving any pay for their labor, the rules do not seem to make an exception, and the charity should err on the side of completing Forms I-9 for the volunteers.

1.11 Is a new Form I-9 required for employees who are transferred within a company?

No. Promoted and transferred employees do not require a new Form I-9.

1.12 Do independent contractors need to complete a Form I-9?

No. Employees employed by an independent contractor are to be verified by the contractor. However, U.S. Immigration and Customs Enforcement (ICE) has targeted employers when they have been able to demonstrate that the employer deliberately used a contracting firm to circumvent the Immigration Reform and Control Act (IRCA) and knew that the contractor's employers were not employment authorized.

The U.S. Department of Homeland Security's (DHS) regulations define "independent contractors" to include individuals and entities that control their own work and are subject to control only as it pertains to the results. Employers should note that just because someone is called a contractor and is issued a Form 1099, or that an entity is paid and then pays the employee, does not mean that U.S. Immigration and Customs Enforcement (ICE) will consider the arrangement to be a contractor relationship as opposed to an employer-employee relationship. The agency will examine the nature of the relationship to determine whether it really should be classified as an employment relationship where employees should be completing the Form I-9.

According to Title 8 of the Code of Federal Regulations, section 274a.1(j), the following factors are considered in determining whether there exists a contractor relationship as opposed to an employer-employee relationship:

- Who supplies the tools or materials.
- Whether the contractor makes services available to the general public.
- Whether the contractor works for a number of clients at the same time.
- Whether the contractor has an opportunity for profit or loss as a result of the services provided.
- Who invests in the facilities for work.
- Who directs the order or sequence in which the work is to be done.
- Who determines the hours during which the work is to be done.

The regulation is not the only test applied by the Office of the Chief Administrative Hearing Officer (OCAHO) to determine independent status. Another test, developed by case law, uses the following factors:

- The independent nature of the worker's business.
- The worker's obligation to furnish tools, supplies, and materials.
- The worker's right to control the progress of the work.
- The time for which the worker is employed.

- Whether the worker is paid by the hour or by the job.
- The extent of relative investments.
- The degree of opportunity for profit or loss.
- The skill and initiative required.
- The permanency of the relationship.

1.13 Are domestic service employees (such as housekeepers, kitchen help, and gardeners) required to complete Forms I-9?

Sometimes. The term "employee" is defined by the U.S. Department of Homeland Security (DHS) to exclude those engaged in "casual domestic employment." Casual domestic employment includes individuals who provide domestic service in a private home that is "sporadic, irregular or intermittent."

The DHS *Handbook for Employers: Guidance for Completing Form I-9* (M-274), included as Appendix B, specifically notes, however, that "those who employ anyone for domestic work in their private home on a regular basis (such as every week)" are required to have the employee complete a Form I-9.

The M-274 handbook is not controlling law in and of itself but is merely interpreting the Immigration Reform and Control Act (IRCA). One could argue that certain domestic employees who show up every week at a private home are independent contractors meeting the tests described in the regulations and case law.

One way to determine if a domestic employee is an employee for Form I-9 purposes is whether the U.S. Internal Revenue Service (IRS) would consider an employer obligated to withhold taxes, pay Social Security, etc. If a tax specialist advises that withholding is required based on the nature of the relationship, then employment verification should occur. Even if this is not the case and even if an employee is paid in cash, it may still make sense to have the employee complete a Form I-9.

1.14 Under what circumstances would a returning employee <u>not be</u> required to complete a new Form I-9?

A returning employee does not need to complete a new Form I-9 in certain instances where he or she is considered to be continuing prior employment. These include the following:

- An individual is returning from an approved paid or unpaid leave of absence (on account of illness, pregnancy, maternity, vacation, study, family leave, union activities, or other temporary leave of absence approved by the employer).

- The individual is promoted or demoted or receives a significant raise.

- The individual is temporarily laid off for lack of work.

- The individual is out on strike or is in a labor dispute.

- The individual is reinstated after a finding of unlawful termination.

- An individual transfers units within the same employer (the Form I-9 may be transferred to the new unit).

- There is a merger, acquisition, or reorganization, and the new employer assumes the Form I-9 responsibilities from the prior employer.

- The employee is engaged in seasonal employment.

The employer claiming that the employee is continuing in prior employment must show that the employee expected to resume employment at all times and that the employee's expectation was reasonable. Factors to be considered include whether the:

- Employee was employed on a "regular and substantial basis."

- Employee complied with the employer's established policies regarding absence.

- Employer's history of recalling employees indicates the likelihood that the individual will be recalled.

- Position has not been taken over by another employee.

- Employee has not sought benefits like severance or retirement indicating that the employee would be leaving work permanently.

- Financial condition of the employer indicates an ability to resume employment.

- History of communications between the employer and employee indicates the intention to resume employment.

1.15 Are employees who return to work after a labor dispute required to complete a new Form I-9?

No. The U.S. Department of Homeland Security (DHS) regulations specifically state that employees returning after a labor dispute are considered to have been continuously employed.

1.16 Are seasonal employees required to re-verify their Forms I-9?

No, seasonal employees are not required to re-verify their Forms I-9. The U.S. Department of Homeland Security (DHS) regulations consider seasonal employees to be continuously employed.

1.17 Are there special rules for employer associations?

Yes. Agricultural associations that refer employees to individual employers are required to complete Forms I-9 for employees referred for a fee to employers. The association can in certain cases assign the task to the employer as well as to national associations. See also Question 1.7.

1.18 Do employers of part-time employees need to complete Forms I-9 for those employees?

Yes. There is no exemption from the verification requirements because an employee is not full time unless the employee is considered an independent contractor or the person is engaged in casual, nonregular domestic work in a private home.

1.19 Can an employer require job applicants to complete Forms I-9?

No, employers should not complete Forms I-9 for individuals applying for jobs. Only those individuals actually offered employment and who have accepted should be requested to complete the Forms I-9.

1.20 What privacy protections are accorded employees when they complete Forms I-9?

The U.S. Department of Homeland Security (DHS) regulations state that information contained on the Form I-9 may be used *only* to verify an individual's identity and employment eligibility and to enforce immigration law. Presumably, this regulation bars both the government as well as employers from using Form I-9 information for any other purposes.

Employers with electronic Form I-9 systems are required to implement a records security program that ensures that only authorized personnel have access to electronic records; that such records are backed up; that employees are trained to minimize the risk of records being altered; and that whenever a record is created, accessed, viewed, updated, or corrected, a secure and permanent record is created establishing who accessed the record.

1.21 Which foreign nationals are always authorized to work in the United States?

It helps to know which types of foreign nationals are entitled to work based on their status in the United States. The U.S. Department of Homeland Security (DHS) lists types of cases in which foreign nationals are entitled to work in the United States simply on the basis of their status:

- Lawful permanent residents (green-card holders).
- Persons admitted as refugees.
- Persons admitted as parolees.
- Persons in asylum status (note that the expiration date on the Employment Authorization Document does not mean the bearer's work authorization has expired).
- K-1 fiancé(e) visa holders.
- N-8 parents and N-9 dependent children processing for permanent residency on the basis of a family member working in the United States for an international organization.
- Certain citizens of the Federated States of Micronesia or the Marshall Islands.
- K-3 spouse visa holders.
- Individuals granted suspension of deportation or cancellation of removal for the period they hold that status.
- Certain persons granted voluntary departure by virtue of membership in a specific nationality group.
- Persons holding temporary protective status (TPS) for the period of time their country's nationals are granted that status.
- Individuals granted voluntary departure under the Family Unity Program of the Immigration Act of 1990 (IMMACT90).
- Persons granted Family Unity benefits under the Legal Immigration Family Equity Act (LIFE).

- Persons holding V visa status based on certain family-based green cards filed before 2001.
- Persons holding T visa status as victims of trafficking.
- Persons holding U visa status as victims of certain crimes.
- Persons granted deferred action under the Deferred Action for Childhood Arrivals (DACA) program.
- Persons granted deferred action or on an Order of Supervision.

Note that with the exception of permanent residents who show their Form I-551 or green card, the authorization to work in the other categories is demonstrated by an employment authorization card issued by U.S. Citizenship and Immigration Services (USCIS).

1.22 Which foreign nationals are sometimes authorized to work in the United States?

Certain individuals can live and work in the United States based on working for a specific employer and on meeting certain conditions. U.S. Citizenship and Immigration Services (USCIS) specifies that persons in the following categories are authorized to work on the basis of possessing a valid Form I-94 as opposed to an Employment Authorization Document:

- A-1/A-2 foreign government officials (individuals must work only for the sponsoring foreign government entity).
- A-3 personal employees of A-1 or A-2 visa holders.
- C-2/C-3 foreign government officials in transit (individuals must work only for the sponsoring foreign government entity).
- E-1/E-2 treaty investors and traders employed by a qualifying company.
- E-3 visa holders from Australia.
- F-1 students working on campus or engaged in curricular practical training (CPT); CPT employees must have a properly annotated Form I-20 Certificate of Eligibility.
- G-1/G-2/G-3 representatives of international organizations (individuals must work only for the sponsoring foreign governmental entity or international organization).
- G-5 personal employees of G-1/G-2/G-3 visa holders.
- H-1B /H-2A/H-2B/H-3 temporary employees and trainees.
- H-4 visa holders.

- I visa holders as representatives of foreign media organizations.
- J-1 exchange visitors (only within the guidelines set forth in the DS-2019 Certificate of Eligibility form).
- L-1 intracompany transferees.
- O-1/O-2 visa holders who have extraordinary ability in the sciences, arts, education, business, or athletics, and accompanying aliens.
- P-1/P-2/P-3 athletes, artists, or entertainers.
- Q-1 international cultural exchange visitors employed by the Q-1 petitioner.
- R-1 religious employees.
- NATO-1/NATO-2/NATO-3/NATO-4/NATO-5/NATO-6 employees of the North Atlantic Treaty Organization (NATO).
- NATO-7 personal employees of NATO employees.
- TN professionals from Canada and Mexico working pursuant to the North American Free Trade Agreement (NAFTA).
- A-3/E-1/E-2/E-3/G-5/H-1B/H-2A/H-2B/H-3/I/J-1/L-1/O-1/O-2/P-1/P-2/P-3/R-1/TN visa holders who have expired Forms I-94 but have timely filed for an extension (employment authorization continues for 240 days or until the application is denied).

Another group of visa categories allows individuals to apply for employment authorization:

- F-1 students seeking optional practical training (OPT) in their areas of study or because of severe economic hardship (after receiving support of the school's international student officer).
- Spouses and unmarried dependent children of A-1 and A-2 visa holders.
- Spouses and unmarried children of G-1, G-3, and G-4 international organization representatives.
- J-2 spouses and unmarried minor children of J-1 visa holders.
- L-2 spouses and unmarried minor children of L-1 visa holders.
- M-1 students seeking OPT in areas directly related to their courses of study as recommended by a school official on Form I-20.
- Dependents of visa holders classified as NATO-1 through NATO-7.
- Asylum applicants who have had their cases pending for more than 150 days.
- Applicants with a pending application for adjustment of status to lawful permanent resident.

- Certain applicants with pending suspension of deportation and cancellation of removal cases.

- Parolees admitted on public interest or emergency grounds.

- B-1 visitors who are personal or domestic servants of certain nonimmigrant work visa holders.

- Domestic servants of a U.S. citizen accompanying or following to join the U.S. citizen who has a permanent home or is stationed in a foreign country and who is temporarily coming to the United States.

- Employees of foreign airlines who would otherwise be entitled to E-1 visa status and who are precluded from E-1 status because they are not of the same nationality as the airline.

- Individuals under final orders of removal and who are released on an order of supervision because their home countries refuse to accept them (such cases are approved at the discretion of U.S. Citizenship and Immigration Services (USCIS)).

- Temporary protected status (TPS) applicants.

- Certain legalization applicants under the Immigration Reform and Control Act (IRCA) and the Legal Immigration Family Equity (LIFE) Act.

- Witnesses or informants in S visa status.

- Q-2 Irish peace process cultural and training program visitors.

- T-1 victims of trafficking and their immediate family members.

- U victims of crime and immediate family members who were included with the petition.

- Persons granted Deferred Action for Childhood Arrivals (DACA) or deferred action.

2

COMPLETING THE FORM I-9

RELEVANT APPENDICES:

APPENDIX A: SAMPLE FORM I-9, FORM I-9 SUPPLEMENT, AND FORM I-9 INSTRUCTIONS

APPENDIX B: U.S. DEPARTMENT OF HOMELAND SECURITY'S HANDBOOK FOR EMPLOYERS: GUIDANCE FOR COMPLETING FORM I-9, M-274

APPENDIX C: EXAMPLES OF CORRECT FORMS I-9

APPENDIX D: EXAMPLES OF INCORRECT FORMS I-9

APPENDIX F: CASE MANAGEMENT AND ELECTRONIC FILING SYSTEMS VENDORS

2.1   Where can I obtain a Form I-9 and what are the methods of completion?

U.S. Citizenship and Immigration Services (USCIS) makes the Form I-9 available for print on its website at www.uscis.gov. After printing the Form I-9, it can be completed in pen by the employee and employer. The form also can be ordered by telephone from the USCIS National Customer Service Center at 888-464-4218.

The second method is the electronically generated Form I-9. Various case management and electronic filing systems make the Form I-9 available (see Appendix A for a sample Form I-9 and Appendix F for a list of these companies and contact information). USCIS requires electronically generated Forms I-9 to be legible with no change to the name, content, or sequence of information and instructions.

In the Form I-9, dated November 14, 2016, USCIS introduced a third method of completion. This third method is referred to as the "smart" Form I-9, which can be completed on the computer screen using an Adobe Acrobat reader. The Form I-9 is then printed and signed by the employee and employer representative in the appropriate boxes.

2.2   Is the Form I-9 available in different languages?

U.S. Citizenship and Immigration Services (USCIS) makes Form I-9 available only in English and Spanish. Note also that the Spanish form may be used only for translation purposes and that the employer must retain the English language version of the form.

> **2.2: The lone exception to this rule is Puerto Rico where employers have a choice and can retain either the Spanish- or English-language versions of the form.**

2.3   Which version of the Form I-9 can an employer accept?

As of September 18, 2017, employers must use the version of the Form I-9 dated July 17, 2017 (with an expiration date of August 19, 2019). Re-verifications and rehires using Section 3 of the Form I-9 may be made on the previously completed version of the Form I-9 or the current version.

To determine the latest version of Form I-9, employers should check the U.S. Citizenship and Immigration Services (USCIS) website every three or four months, subscribe to or regularly read print and online publications on immigration and employment law, or use an electronic Form I-9 product from a reputable vendor that regularly updates the software for its subscribers. See Appendix F.

2.4 What documentation can an employee present that shows both identity and employment authorization?

Employees must present documentation of identity and work authorization and can present documents from a preset list included in the Form I-9's Lists of Acceptable Documents (see Appendix A). Some documents can prove both identity and work eligibility. Some documents prove only identity or work eligibility, and a combination of documents from Lists B and C must be presented to meet the Form I-9 requirements. Employers are not allowed to tell employees which documents from the list(s) they must present.

Documents showing both identification and employment eligibility are provided in List A in the Form I-9's instructions. They include the following:

- An unexpired U.S. passport or U.S. passport card.

- An unexpired permanent resident card (green card) or alien registration receipt card (Form I-551).

- An unexpired foreign passport with a temporary I-551 stamp.

- An unexpired Form I-766 Employment Authorization Document (EAD) that contains a photograph.

- An unexpired foreign passport with an unexpired Form I-94 Arrival/Departure Record with the same name as the passport and an endorsement showing the employee's nonimmigrant status and the individual's eligibility to work for the particular employer.

- Passport from the Federated States of Micronesia (FSM) or the Republic of the Marshall Islands (RMI) with Form I-94 or Form I-94A indicating nonimmigrant admission under the Compact of Free Association Between the United States and the FSM or RMI.

Section 2 of the Form I-9 actually provides three spaces for document numbers and expiration dates. The first purpose of this is to provide for situations in which a foreign passport is used and a Form I-94 is also needed to prove both identity and employment authorization. The passport number and expiration date and the Form I-94 number and expiration date can then be listed. The second purpose is when foreign students in F-1 status, who are participating in curricular practical training (CPT), present the following documents: (a) unexpired foreign passport, (b) Form I-20, and (3) a valid Form I-94 or Form I-94A. Otherwise, only one document would be listed by document number and expiration date.

2.5   What documentation can an employee present solely to prove the employee's identity?

Form I-9's List B itemizes documentation acceptable to prove identity, and a List B document may be provided with a List C document (see Appendix A). List B documents include the following:

- An unexpired driver's license or identification card issued by a state or outlying possession of the United States, provided it contains a photograph or information such as name, date of birth, gender, height, eye color, and address.

- An unexpired identification card issued by a federal, state, or local government agency or entity as long as the form contains a photograph or information such as name, date of birth, gender, height, eye color, and address.

- An unexpired school identification card with a photograph.

- An unexpired voter registration card.

- An unexpired U.S. military card or draft record.

- An unexpired U.S. Coast Guard Merchant Mariner card.

- An unexpired Native American tribal document.

- An unexpired driver's license issued by a Canadian government authority.

For persons under age 18 who cannot present one of the documents listed above, the following may instead be presented:

- A school record or report card.

- A clinic, doctor, or hospital record.

- A day care or nursery school record.

2.6   What documentation can an employee present solely to prove the employee's authorization to work?

Form I-9's List C itemizes documentation acceptable to prove employment eligibility, and a List C document may be provided together with a List B document (see Appendix A). List C documents include the following:

- A U.S. Social Security card issued by the Social Security Administration (other than a card stating that it is "not valid for employment" or "valid for work only with INS authorization" or "valid for work only with DHS authorization") or other agencies, such as the Department of Health, Education and Welfare.

- Certification of Birth Abroad issued by the U.S. Department of State (Forms FS-240, FS-545, or DS-1350).

- Original or certified copy of a birth certificate issued by a state, county, or municipal authority, or outlying possession of the United States bearing an official seal.

- Native American tribal document.

- U.S. citizen identification card (Form I-197).

- Identification card for use of Resident Citizen in the United States (Form I-179).

- Unexpired Employment Authorization Document (EAD) issued by the U.S. Department of Homeland Security (other than those listed under List A).

2.7   Where can an employer find illustrations of acceptable documents in Lists A, B, and C?

The U.S. Department of Homeland Security's *Handbook for Employers: Guidance for Completing Form I-9* (M-274) includes a number of illustrations. The M-274 handbook is included as Appendix B in this book.

2.8   May an employer specify which documents it will accept?

Employers may not tell employees which documents to supply. Rather, the employer must simply present the Lists of Acceptable Documents included on the latest Form I-9 instructions and must allow the employee to choose what will be presented. Employers must then accept the documentation provided as long as it appears genuine. Employers that violate this requirement risk being found liable for committing an unfair immigration-related employment practice that is in violation of the anti-discrimination rules of the Immigration Reform and Control Act (IRCA). This rule applies even when an employer writes down an "Alien number" in Section 1 of the Form I-9. Employees are not required to provide documentation to prove statements in Section 1 as long as proper documentation in Section 2 is provided.

> **2.8:** The one exception to this rule applies to employers using E-Verify, the government's electronic employment eligibility verification system. E-Verify employers may accept only List B documents with a photograph of the employee.

2.9   When will a Form I-20 presented by an F-1 student prove employment authorization?

Despite there being no reference to a Form I-20 on the Form I-9, F-1 nonimmigrant students may present a Form I-20 in two situations:

- First, if a student works on campus at the institution sponsoring the F-1 and the employer provides direct student services, the Form I-20 will serve as evidence showing employment eligibility. This also is the case for off-campus work at an employer that is educationally affiliated with the school's established curriculum or for employers contractually required to provide funded research projects at the postgraduate level in which the employment is an integral part of the student's educational program;

- Second, in cases when an F-1 student has been authorized by a designated school official (DSO) to participate in a curricular practical training (CPT) program that is an integral part of an established curriculum (for example, alternative work/study, internship, cooperative education, or other required internship offered by sponsoring employers through cooperative agreements with the school), the student must have a Form I-20 endorsed by the DSO, and the I-20 also must list the specific employer as well as the intended dates of employment.

In either case, the Form I-20 would be used only when an employee presents an unexpired foreign passport and a valid Form I-94.

2.10 When will a Form DS-2019 presented by a J-1 exchange visitor prove employment authorization?

J-1 nonimmigrant exchange visitors can sometimes work based on the terms of their visas. To document employment authorization, the J-1 visa holder can present a Form DS-2019 issued by the U.S. Department of State along with an unexpired passport and a Form I-94 as acceptable List A documentation.

2.11 Can a translator be used by an employee to assist with completing the form?

Yes. If an employee cannot fill out Section 1 of the Form I-9 (see Appendix A), he or she may receive the assistance of a translator or preparer. The preparer or translator would read the Form I-9 and instructions to the employee, help the employee complete Section 1 of the form, check the box for using a Preparer and/or Translator, complete the preparer/translator certification, and then sign the preparer/translator certification.

The Form I-9, dated November 14, 2016, introduced two boxes in the Preparer and/or Translator Certification (at the bottom of Section 1)—one stating "I did not use a preparer or translator" and a second stating "A preparer(s) and/or translator(s) assisted the employee in completing Section 1." Thus, one of the two boxes should be checked upon completion of each Form I-9.

A second addition to the Preparer and/or Translator Certification is a Form I-9 Supplement (possible third page to the Form I-9), which should be used when more than one preparer and/or translator is used in the completion of Section 1.

An employer may serve as translator as long as the translator block and employer verification section are signed.

2.12 May a company pre-populate data, through an electronic Form I-9 software program, in Section 1 of Form I-9?

The agencies involved, U.S. Citizenship and Immigration Services (USCIS), U.S. Immigration and Customs Enforcement (ICE), and the Immigrant and Employee Rights Section of the U.S. Department of Justice (formerly Office of Special Counsel for Immigration-Related Unfair Employment Practices (OSC)), have flip-flopped on this issue. In November 2016, in an E-Verify newsletter, USCIS stated Section 1 of Form I-9 could not be pre-populated. Pre-population involves the electronic inclusion of data about the employee in Section 1 by

Form I-9 software programs without the employee having to write the information in Section 1.

Currently, ICE holds no official position on the pre-population of Section 1 by electronic Form I-9 software programs. This is a change in past policy in which ICE stated pre-population could not be done by employers. On the other hand, in August 2013, the OSC stated that it discouraged the practice of pre-population because "it increases the likelihood of including inaccurate or outdated information."[1] Thus, the consensus is employers *may not* pre-populate Section 1 of Form I-9. However, this position of the agencies is subject to change.

2.13 May a company pre-populate data in Section 2 of Form I-9?

In November 2016, U.S. Citizenship and Immigration Services (USCIS) reaffirmed its position that an employer may pre-populate its business name and address in the certification portion of Section 2. However, it may not use a stamp for the employer representative's signature nor pre-populate data in Lists A, B, and C.

2.14 What if an employee states in Section 1 that he or she has a temporary work authorization but presents a List C document that does not have an expiration date?

An employer cannot specify that an employee provide documentation relating to the employee's temporary work authorization even if the employee has indicated in Section 1 that he or she has temporary work authorization. So if an employee has a valid List B document and a valid List C document without an expiration date, the employer is not allowed to request documentation regarding the temporary status of the employee, lest the employer be found guilty of immigration discrimination.

---

[1] *See* http://www.justice.gov/crt/about/osc/pdf/publications/TAletters/FY2013/169.pdf.

2.15 Are there employees who may properly check Box 3 in Section 1 indicating they are aliens without permanent residency in the United States but who do not have an expiration date for their status?

Yes. Refugees and asylees are two fairly large groups of individuals who would fit this description (see Chapter 19). Certain nationals of Micronesia, the Marshall Islands, and Palau are authorized to work in the United States by virtue of their statuses as nationals of those countries. If an employee fits into one of these categories, he or she can write "N/A" in the place in Section 1.

2.16 If an employee provides an "Alien number" or "USCIS number" in Section 1 but presents documents without the "Alien number" or "USCIS number," can the employer ask to see the document with the "Alien number" or "USCIS number"?

No, an employer cannot ask to see a document relating to the "Alien number" or "USCIS number" or otherwise specify to an employee which documents he or she is to provide. An employer is to only provide the employee with the Lists of Acceptable Documents.

2.17 What if an employee claims to be a U.S. citizen in Section 1 but presents a green card as documentation of identity and work authorization?

Employees who provide this sort of information often do not understand the question given that one cannot simultaneously be a U.S. citizen and a U.S. lawful permanent resident. The matter should be brought to the attention of the employee, and if a correction is needed, the employee should be able to change the Form I-9 and should initial any changes (see Appendix A).

2.18 What if a person claims to be a lawful permanent resident in Section 1 but provides a U.S. passport or birth certificate as documentation of status?

As with the answer to Question 2.17, employees who provide this sort of information often do not understand the question because one cannot simultaneously be a U.S. citizen and a U.S. lawful permanent resident. The matter should be brought to the attention of the employee, and if a correction is needed, the employee should be able to change the Form I-9 and should initial any changes.

2.19 May expired documents be accepted?

Expired identification documents *may not* be accepted in Lists A and B.

> 2.19: The only exceptions are in the case of temporary protected status (TPS) holders who have expired employment authorization documents (EADs) where the U.S. Department of Homeland Security (DHS) has granted an extension of 180 days through a *Federal Register* notice OR certain individuals who timely filed to renew an EAD in the same category as the previous EAD, and are in a category eligible for the extension (the following codes are eligible A03, A05, A07, A08, A10, A12, C08, C09, C10, C16, C20, C22, C24, and C31).

2.20 What types of Social Security Administration documents may be accepted?

Social Security cards that are marked "not valid for employment" or "valid for work only with the INS or "valid for work only with DHS authorization" may not be used as a List C document demonstrating employment eligibility. If an employee claims that he or she has become employment eligible without any limiting language on the Social Security card, the employee may have a new card issued from the Social Security Administration (SSA) or present another List C document or a List A document without a List B document.

Employees also are not permitted to use a printout from the SSA of the employee's particulars—such as name, Social Security number, and date of birth—as a substitute for an actual Social Security card.

2.21 Are receipts for documents acceptable?

In most cases, a receipt *will not* be acceptable. A common case is when an employee is waiting on an Employment Authorization Document (EAD) and has a receipt showing the application has been filed. A receipt for an initial grant of employment authorization or a renewal of employment authorization will not suffice for Form I-9 purposes unless it fits within the exceptions listed in 2.19.

> An exception is made in the case of a receipt for a replacement document when the document has been lost, stolen, or damaged. An employee may use the receipt to demonstrate work authorization for a 90-day period and then must present the replacement document.

A <u>Form I-94 issued with a temporary I-551 stamp</u> will serve as a valid receipt to replace a green card. The individual has until the expiration date of the I-551 stamp or one year from the date of the issuance of the Form I-94 if the I-551 stamp does not have an expiration date. Note that I-551 stamps are usually approved for one year anyway.

Finally, a <u>Form I-94 with an unexpired refugee admission stamp</u> may be used as a receipt for up to 90 days after an employee is hired. The employee would then need to present a valid document demonstrating work-authorization status.

When an employer does receive an acceptable receipt, the employer should record the document in Section 2 of Form I-9 (see Appendix A) with the annotation "receipt" and any document number in the place for such information. Once the actual document is presented, the employer will cross out the word "receipt" and the accompanying document number, and enter the number from the new document. The employer should date and initial the amendment.

2.22 Can an employee present photocopies of documents rather than original documentation?

An employee is *never* permitted to present a photocopy of a List A, List B, or List C document.

> 2.22: The exception to this rule would be a certified copy of a birth certificate.

2.23 What is the area entitled "Additional Information" in Section 2 to be used for?

This section is for recording pertinent information for TPS extensions, OPT STEM extensions, H-1B portability, and any other necessary information that cannot be recorded in Lists A, B, or C.

2.24 What should a lawful permanent resident present when he or she is still waiting on the actual permanent residency card?

An applicant waiting on a permanent resident card should present the specially issued Form I-94 or foreign passport with an I-551 immigrant visa stamp. The Form I-94 with the stamp is typically valid for one year.

2.25 What documentation should a refugee present to document authorization to work?

A refugee should present an Employment Authorization Document (EAD). However, if that application is being processed, the refugee can present a Form I-94 with a refugee admission stamp as long as the employment card is presented within 90 days.

2.26 What if the document presented by the employee does not look valid?

Being presented with invalid-looking documents is a tricky situation for employers. On the one hand, employers are not expected to be document experts. On the other hand, if a document is obviously a phony, an employer should not be expected to be off the hook. The U.S. Department of Homeland Security (DHS) requires employers to accept documents that "reasonably appear on their face to be genuine." Employers need to be careful, however, about being overzealous because they face the risk of being found to have committed an unfair immigration-related employment practice if they question the legitimacy of documents that do not reasonably appear to be genuine.

2.27 What if the name of the employee on the document is different from the name of the employee on the Form I-9?

If an employee presents a document with a name different from that stated in Section 1 of Form I-9 (see Appendix A), an employer would arguably have reason to believe that the documentation may not demonstrate employment eligibility. The employer should bring the discrepancy to the attention of the employee to see if there is a reasonable explanation (such as a legal name change by the employee).

2.28 What if the employee does not look like the person on the presented document or is different from the description of the person on the document (hair color, eye color, height, race, etc.)?

An employer is required to check that the presented documentation relates to the individual. If the individual presenting the document does not reasonably appear to be the same person in the identification document, then the employer can reject the documentation.

2.29 May an employer correct Forms I-9 after they are completed?

Yes, an employer may make changes. However, the employer should be careful to make changes in a way that makes it clear to an inspecting official that the form was corrected and also how the form was corrected. Blank fields should be completed, and incorrect answers should be lined through (so the original answer is visible) rather than erased or "whited out." Changes or additions in Section 1 should be initialed and dated by the employee, preparer, or translator in a differently colored pen. Changes or additions in Section 2 should be initialed and dated by the employer in a differently colored pen. Additionally, a memo should be attached to the corrected Form I-9 with an explanation.

2.30 Are employees required to supply a Social Security number on a Form I-9?

Employees are not required to supply a Social Security number (SSN) unless the employer participates in the E-Verify program. Employers using E-Verify may not ask an employee to provide a specific document with an SSN.

2.31 Are there special rules for minors?

Yes. Individuals under age 18 who are unable to produce a List A or List B document can present the following documents to establish identity:

- A school record or report card.

- A clinic doctor's or hospital record.

- A day care or nursery school record.

If a person under the age of 18 is not able to present a List A or List B document or one of the documents noted here, Section 1 of the Form I-9 should be completed by the parent or legal guardian, and the phrase "Individual under age 18" should be inserted in the employee signature space. The parent or legal guardian should then complete the "preparer/translator certification" block. Under List B, the phrase "Individual under age 18" should be stated.

2.32 Are there special rules for individuals with disabilities?

Yes. For individuals with disabilities unable to present a required identity document, who are being hired for a position in a nonprofit organization or association or as part of a rehabilitation program, a special procedure can be used.

Section 1 of the Form I-9 should be completed by the parent, legal guardian, or a representative from the nonprofit organization, association, or rehabilitation program placing the individual into a position of employment. The phrase "special placement" should be written in the employee signature space. The person completing the form would then complete the "preparer/translator certification" block. Under List B, the phrase "special placement" should be stated.

Qualifying individuals with disabilities include any person who:

- Has a physical or mental impairment that substantially limits one or more of the person's major life activities.

- Has a record of such impairment.

- Is regarded as having such impairment.

2.33 What are examples of various Form I-9 documents?

See Appendix B in this book: U.S. Department of Homeland Security's M-274 *Handbook for Employers: Guidance for Completing Form I-9*.

3

RE-VERIFICATION

3.1 What are the Form I-9 re-verification requirements?

If an employee is not a U.S. citizen, lawful permanent resident, or noncitizen national, he or she is likely working based on a status with a defined end date.

For these employees, the employer must note the expiration date of their documents on the Form I-9 (see Appendix A) and then must pull the employee's Form I-9 before the expiration date and re-verify that the employee's status has been extended. Employers should establish a reliable tickler system to prompt re-verification. Aside from complying with the re-verification rule, this system will also ensure that an employer that needs to extend a work visa for an employee will not forget to take care of this critical task (something that is, unfortunately, neglected by many employers and can result in an employee falling out of legal status). Green cards and passports with expiration dates do not need to be re-verified.

3.2   What if the re-verification section of the form has been completed from a prior re-verification?

In this case, an employer can complete and sign Section 3 of the new Form I-9 (see Chapter 1 and Appendix A). The employer should put the employee's name in Section 1 and retain the new Form I-9 with the original Form I-9.

3.3   Can an employee present a Social Security card to show employment authorization at re-verification when he or she had presented an expiring Employment Authorization Document or Form I-94 at the time of hire?

Yes, an employee may present a Social Security card to show employment authorization at re-verification as long as the Social Security card is not restricted with a statement such as "not valid for employment," "valid for work only with DHS [U.S. Department of Homeland Security] authorization" or "valid for work only with INS [Immigration and Naturalization Service] authorization." If the Social Security card has this language, it is not a valid List C document. This type of Social Security card must be accompanied by an Employment Authorization Document (EAD) to be valid. Employers may not specify which documents an employee may present either at the time of hire or at the time of re-verification. An employee may have become a lawful permanent resident or otherwise received employment-authorized status allowing the employee to obtain a Social Security card, absent the sponsorship of the employer, so the employer should not assume the employee is unauthorized.

3.4 What if a new Form I-9 comes out between the date the initial Form I-9 is completed and the time of re-verification?

If a new Form I-9 has been released between the date of hire and the date of re-verification, the employer should complete Section 3 of the new version of the Form I-9 and accept only documentation of employment eligibility from the Lists of Acceptable Documents in the Form I-9 instructions. However, the U.S. Department of Homeland Security (DHS) will accept use of Section 3 on the existing completed Form I-9 as long as it has not been previously completed for prior re-verification.

3.5 Do past employees resuming work with a company need to complete a new Form I-9?

Returning employees often do not need to complete a new Form I-9, but if that is not done, the employer needs to re-verify the employee's work authorization in Section 3 of the Form I-9, if the formerly listed work authorization has expired.

If a new version of the Form I-9 has come out since the last time the Form I-9 was completed, the employer may complete a new form or use Section 3 of the existing completed Form I-9. And if the form has been completed in Section 3 from a previous re-verification, the employer should complete Section 3 of a new Form I-9.

For an employee to be considered a "rehire," the employer must be rehiring the employee within three years of the initial hiring date of the employee, and the employee's previous grant of work authorization must not have expired. Employers must:

1. record the rehiring date;
2. if the formerly listed work authorization has expired, write the document title, number, and expiration date of any eligible document presented by the employee;
3. sign and date Section 3; and
4. if the re-verification is recorded on a new Form I-9, write the employee's name in Section 1.

Of course, it may be easier just to complete a new Form I-9, and an employer can certainly opt for this. Note that the rules on returning employees also apply to cases of recruiting or referring an individual.

3.6   What if a rehired employee is rehired after a new version of the Form I-9 is released?

If the Form I-9 has been modified since the form was completed on the date of hire, the employer may complete Section 3 of the existing completed Form I-9 or Section 3 of the new form and attach the old form.

3.7   What if an employee changes his or her name?

An employee's name change should be recorded by the employer in Section 3, although it is not mandatory to complete Section 3 for a name change. If an employee requests such, it is a best practice for the employer to request a document reflecting the name change, such as a marriage certificate or divorce decree.

3.8   What are examples of correctly completed Forms I-9?

See Appendix C.

3.9   What are examples of Forms I-9 with errors?

See Appendix D.

4

RECORDKEEPING

RELEVANT APPENDICES:

APPENDIX A: SAMPLE FORM I-9, FORM I-9 SUPPLEMENT, AND FORM I-9 INSTRUCTIONS

APPENDIX B: U.S. DEPARTMENT OF HOMELAND SECURITY'S HANDBOOK FOR EMPLOYERS: GUIDANCE FOR COMPLETING FORM I-9, M-274

4.1 What are the Form I-9 recordkeeping requirements?

Employers must keep Forms I-9 for all current employees, though the forms of certain terminated employees may be destroyed. In the case of an audit from a government agency, the forms must be produced for inspection. The forms may be retained in either paper or electronic format as well as in microfilm or microfiche format (*see Question 4.5 for more information on this subject*).

4.2   When can a Form I-9 be destroyed?

For terminated employees (the date employment ceased or ceased in the United States for employees transferred abroad), the form must be retained for at least three years from the date of hire or for at least one year after the termination date, whichever comes later.

Employers should note two dates when an employee is terminated. The first is the date three years from the date of the employee's date of hire. The second is the date one year from the termination date. The later date is the date until which the Form I-9 must be retained.

There is a different rule for recruiters or referrers for a fee. Those entities are required to maintain Forms I-9 for only a three-year period from the date of hire, regardless of whether the employee has been terminated.

In addition to establishing a reminder system to re-verify Forms I-9, employers should establish a tickler system to destroy forms no longer required to be retained.

4.3   Should recordkeeping be centralized at a company?

Keeping records in one location is generally advisable because it is easier to conduct internal audits to ensure the employer is complying with the rules of the Immigration Reform and Control Act (IRCA), and also to more easily prepare for a government inspection, given that having the forms at one location will allow more time for review. However, there may be situations in which keeping the records at each location is more convenient or practical.

The forms themselves can be kept onsite or at an offsite storage facility as long as the employer is able to produce the documentation within three days of an audit request from a federal agency.

4.4   Does an employer need to keep copies of the documents presented by the employee?

No, retaining copies of the supporting documents is voluntary except in certain circumstances when using E-Verify. Under E-Verify, if an employee presents a Permanent Resident Card, Employment Authorization Document, U.S. passport or passport card as the verification document, the employer must make a copy of that document and keep it on file with the Form I-9. Employers can retain copies of documents and must keep the copies with the specific Form I-9.

Although retaining copies of documents may leave an unnecessary paper trail for government inspectors, maintaining documentation could provide a good faith defense for an employer that needs to show it had reason to believe an employee was authorized even if the paperwork was not properly completed. Retaining copies of documents also makes it easier for an employer to conduct internal audits to ensure compliance; this allows the attorney or other auditor to see what documents were actually provided to the Human Resources representative responsible for completion of the Form I-9. Furthermore, if copies are retained and some data are missing in Lists A, B, or C, such as the issuing authority or expiration date, it is only a technical error, not a substantive one.

Whatever a company decides, however, it is important that the policy be consistently applied and to remember that simply having copies of the documents does not relieve the employer of responsibility for fully completing Section 2 of the Form I-9.

> Consistency is paramount. Employers should keep all the documents or keep none of them because keeping copies for only certain employees could open the employer up to charges of discrimination.

In Tennessee, for those employers with less than 50 employees, an employer must copy and maintain a certain designated document (such as an unexpired U.S. passport, permanent resident card, Employment Authorization Document, birth certificate, certificate of naturalization, or state-issued driver's license or identification) unless the employer uses E-Verify. Of course, E-Verify has its own rules on what documents must be retained. If the employer in Tennessee has 50 or more employees, it must utilize E-Verify, as of January 1, 2017.

In Louisiana, employers must retain an employee's picture identification and a copy of a U.S. birth certificate, certificate of naturalization, certificate of U.S. citizenship, or a Form I-94 with an employment-authorized stamp for all employees, unless the employer uses E-Verify.

4.5   Can a Form I-9 completed on paper be stored in another format?

Yes. In addition to paper, Forms I-9 may be retained in an electronic, microfilm, or microfiche format.

The U.S. Department of Homeland Security (DHS) suggests the following with respect to microfilm or microfiche:

- Use film stock that will last the entire retention period (which could exceed 20 years for some businesses).

- Use equipment that allows for a high degree of readability and that can be copied onto paper.

- For microfilms, place the index at the beginning or end of the series; and for microfiche, place the index on the last microfiche.

See Chapter 5 for further information on the requirements for electronic Form I-9 systems.

4.6 Should the Form I-9 records be kept with the personnel records?

Keeping Form I-9 records with personnel records is generally a bad idea. First, it could compromise the privacy of employees by allowing government inspectors to review items that are completely unrelated to the Form I-9. Employers that want to prevent this would have to manually go through the personnel records and pull the Form I-9 paperwork, something that could cost valuable time as the employer prepares for the government inspection. Keeping the Forms I-9 separate will make it easier to conduct internal audits to ensure compliance with the Immigration Reform and Control Act (IRCA) and to re-verify forms as needed.

5

ELECTRONIC FORM I-9 SYSTEMS

RELEVANT APPENDICES:

APPENDIX A: SAMPLE FORM I-9, FORM I-9 SUPPLEMENT,
AND FORM I-9 INSTRUCTIONS

APPENDIX F: CASE MANAGEMENT AND ELECTRONIC
FILING SYSTEMS VENDORS

Employers are eligible to file and store Forms I-9 electronically. As the national crackdown on employers of undocumented workers continues and a number of vendors now offer electronic Form I-9 products, employers are starting to weigh the benefits of ditching paper forms and going digital. This chapter discusses the applicable laws and regulations surrounding filing, and then reviews why companies would want to make the switch.

5.1   Can a Form I-9 be completed electronically?

In April 2005, a law took effect authorizing employers to retain Employment Eligibility Verification forms (Forms I-9) in an electronic format. U.S. Immigration and Customs Enforcement (ICE) issued rules setting standards for using electronic Forms I-9 in June 2006 (Code of Federal Regulations, Title 8, section 274a.2), and the agency is actively encouraging employers to store their Forms I-9 electronically.

5.2   Why would companies want to switch to electronic Form I-9 systems?

There are numerous reasons why companies would prefer electronic Form I-9 systems over paper-based systems:

- Most of the major vendors use a Web-based system, which means employers do not have to install software and only need Internet access and a Web browser.

- Employees are not able to complete the Form I-9 unless the data is properly entered. Many vendors offer systems that guide workers and Human Resource officials through proper completion of the forms.

- Some of the systems are "intelligent" and ensure that, based on answers provided in Section 1 of the Form I-9, only appropriate documents show up in Section 2.

- Some systems allow for certain information in Section 2 of the forms, that is, the same from applicant to applicant, to be prefilled to save time—such as the employer's name and address.

- The better electronic Form I-9 systems include "help" features that make it easier for Human Resource officials and employees to answer questions on the Form I-9.

- Employers with employees at multiple sites can more easily monitor I-9 compliance at remote locations.

- Re-verification is automated, and employers are less likely to incur liability due to an inadvertent failure to update an employee's I-9. Many systems send e-mail reminders.

- Employers can integrate the system with E-Verify or other electronic employment verification systems to minimize the chances that unauthorized workers end up employed.

- Using an electronic Form I-9 system reduces the risk of identity theft from stolen paper Form I-9 records (a recurring problem). By law, electronic Form I-9 software must have built-in security systems to protect the privacy of employees and the integrity of the data.

- Using an electronic Form I-9 system can make it easier to respond to U.S. Immigration and Customs Enforcement (ICE) audits. In addition to the audit trails required by regulation, some of the systems archive communications relating to the Form I-9.

- Electronic Form I-9 systems can integrate with payroll and employee database systems.

- Data from the electronic Form I-9 can be automatically uploaded to E-Verify. Several electronic Form I-9 vendors are federally approved E-Verify employer agents, thus allowing them to automate the entry of an employer's data in E-Verify.

- An electronic Form I-9 system allows for the automation of the purging of Forms I-9 for employees no longer with the employer, and for whom Forms I-9 may no longer be retained.

- Some of the systems contain instructions in multiple languages for employees who have difficulty understanding English.

- Employers can potentially achieve cost savings by storing Forms I-9 electronically rather than using conventional filing and storage of paper copies or converting paper forms to microfilm or microfiche.

- Electronically retained Forms I-9 are more easily searchable and, hence, are often a time saver for Human Resource personnel. The better systems produce a variety of reports that make monitoring Form I-9 compliance easier.

- Some of the systems also track visa and Form I-94 expiration dates.

5.3 Are there downsides to using an electronic Form I-9 system?

Some potential problems with using a digital system include the following:

- There are no 100 percent secure electronic systems (though the law requires electronic Form I-9 vendors and their employer customers to implement security measures).

- The electronic systems do not totally stop identity theft because an employee can present doctored identification and employment authorization paperwork, making it appear that the employee is another person (though E-Verify implemented a system in 2013 whereby it may "lock" a Social Security number if it is suspected to be compromised due to identity theft).

- A paper Form I-9 is free (aside from indirect costs like storage and training). Electronic systems typically charge a flat monthly fee or a per-employee fee (though the per-employee costs are usually no more than a few dollars with any of the major vendors).

- Most Forms I-9 are Internet dependent. When the Internet is not available, the Form I-9 may not be able to be completed (though an employer may be able to use a paper Form I-9 in such a case).

- If an electronic Form I-9 vendor goes out of business, the employer could be in a bind if precautions are not in place allowing easy retrieval of the employees' data (such as having backups on the employer's own computer system).

- Employers wanting to change electronic Form I-9 vendors should be aware of past litigation regarding the return of Form I-9 data to employers from the initial electronic Form I-9 vendors.

5.4   What requirements must electronic Form I-9 systems meet?

The June 2006 rules issued by U.S. Immigration and Customs Enforcement (ICE) set standards for completing forms electronically and also for scanning and storing existing Forms I-9. Since the change in the law, a number of software products have come on the market allowing for the electronic filing of Forms I-9. There are advantages to using such a system, including improving accuracy in completing forms and setting up automated systems to prompt employers to re-verify Forms I-9 for employees with temporary work authorizations.

The U.S. Department of Homeland Security (DHS) regulations require Forms I-9 generated electronically to meet the following standards:

- The forms must be legible when seen on a computer screen, microfiche, or microfilm or when printed on paper.

- The name, content, and order of data must not be altered from the paper version of the form.

- There are reasonable controls to ensure the accuracy and reliability of the electronic generation or storage system.

- There are reasonable controls designed to prevent and detect the unauthorized or accidental creation, deletion, or deterioration of stored Forms I-9.

- The software must have an indexing system allowing for searches by any field.

- There must be the ability to reproduce legible hard copies.

- The software must not be subject to any agreement that would limit or restrict access to and use of the electronic generation system by a government agency on the premises of the employer, recruiter, or referrer for a fee (including personnel, hardware, software, files, indexes, and software documentation).

- Compression or formatting technologies may be used as long as certain standards are met.

- There is a system to identify anyone who has created, accessed, viewed, updated, or corrected an electronic Form I-9 and also to see what action was taken.

Employers that know or should reasonably have known that an action or lack of action will result in loss of electronic Form I-9 records can be held liable under the Immigration Reform and Control Act (IRCA).

Employers may use more than one kind of electronic Form I-9 system as long as each system meets the standards noted above.

Employers using an electronic Form I-9 system also must make available, on request, descriptions of the electronic generation and storage systems, the indexing system, and the business process that create, modify, and maintain the retained Forms I-9 and establish the authenticity and integrity of the forms, such as audit trails. The Form I-9 software vendor should, of course, provide such documentation to the employer, though this is not a requirement in the regulations.

> **5.4:** Electronically stored Forms I-9 have special audit requirements, and those requirements are set out below in Section 5.8 of this chapter discussing the regulation of government inspections.

5.5 How is an electronic Form I-9 "signed" by an employee and employer?

The U.S. Department of Homeland Security (DHS) regulations require that electronic Forms I-9 be "signed" electronically through a system whereby the person providing the information will acknowledge that he or she has read the attestation.

The signature must be affixed to the document at the time the attestation is provided. The form must be printed and provided to the person providing the signature at the time the document is signed. This requirement applies to the employee as well as to the employer, recruiter, or referrer for a fee.

5.6   What are the Form I-9 record-keeping requirements for electronic Forms I-9?

Employers must keep Forms I-9 for all current employees, though the forms of certain terminated employees can be destroyed. In the case of an audit from a government agency, the forms must be produced for inspection. The forms may be retained in either paper or electronic format as well as in microfilm or microfiche format.

5.7   What privacy protections are accorded workers when they complete Forms I-9 electronically?

Employers with electronic Form I-9 systems are required to implement a records security program that ensures that only authorized personnel have access to electronic records, that such records are backed up, that employees are trained to minimize the risk of records being altered, and that whenever a record is created, accessed, viewed, updated or corrected, a secure and permanent record is created establishing who accessed the record.

5.8   How does an employer that uses an electronic Form I-9 system respond to an Immigration and Customs Enforcement audit?

Original Forms I-9 normally must be provided for inspection to U.S. Immigration and Customs Enforcement (ICE) examiners. If an employer retains Forms I-9 in an electronic format, the employer must retrieve and reproduce the specific forms requested by the inspecting officer as well as the associated audit trails showing who accessed the computer system and the actions performed on the system in a specified period of time. The inspecting officer must be provided with the necessary hardware and software, as well as access to personnel and documentation to locate, retrieve, read, and reproduce the requested Form I-9 documentation and associated audit trails, reports, and other related data.

Finally, an inspecting officer is permitted to request an electronic summary of all the immigration fields on an electronically stored Form I-9.

5.9 Can a company using an electronic Form I-9 system batch-load data to E-Verify?

Yes. The U.S. Department of Homeland Security (DHS) has a real-time batch method that requires a company develop an interface between its personal system or electronic Form I-9 system and the E-Verify database. Employers interested in more information about this method, including design specifications, should call U.S. Citizenship and Immigration Services (USCIS) at 800-741-5023.

5.10 Can employers convert existing Forms I-9 into an electronic format?

Yes. Many employers scan and index their current Forms I-9 and store them electronically using electronic Form I-9 software.

5.11 Where can I find out which companies offer electronic Form I-9 products and services?

A list of electronic Form I-9 vendors appears in Appendix F.

6

Knowledge of Unlawful Immigration Status

6.1 What if an employer knows an employee is not authorized to be employed even though the Form I-9 was properly completed?

An employer that knows the employee is not authorized to work, even though everything on the Form I-9 appears valid—is violating the Immigration Reform and Control Act (IRCA) because the employer is considered to have actual knowledge that an employee is not employment eligible. An employer that simply suspects an employee is ineligible to work should be extremely careful before terminating an employee, or even asking for additional documentation, unless the employer has a solid foundation for the belief. Taking an action after merely hearing from another employee that a particular employee is unauthorized to be in the United States is a recipe for a discrimination lawsuit because IRCA does not require employers to make inquiries under these circumstances. On the other hand, if an employee actually provides information to the employer regarding his or her immigration status, the employer would be considered to have knowledge. If the employer continues to employ this individual, it is a serious violation.

vould an employer be considered to ctive knowledge"?

...ment of Homeland Security (DHS) regulations hold employ-
...ot only when they have actual knowledge that an employee is unau-
...orized to work, but also when knowledge may be inferred through notice of certain facts that would "lead a person, through the exercise of reasonable care, to know about a certain condition." Code of Federal Regulations, Title 8, section 274a.1(e). This is called "constructive knowledge," and DHS lists several examples in its rules:

- The employer fails to complete or improperly completes the Form I-9.

- The employer has information that would indicate the alien is not authorized to work, such as a labor certification (this would generally apply only when an employee already was claiming to be a U.S. citizen or permanent resident on the Form I-9).

- The employer acts with reckless and wanton disregard for the legal consequences of permitting another individual to introduce an unauthorized employee into its workforce.[1]

This list is not exhaustive, and employers also need to be cognizant of the anti-discrimination rules. In addition, failing to re-verify a Form I-9 requiring reverification usually will be considered constructive knowledge.

A more difficult situation has arisen in cases where an employer received a no-match letter from the Social Security Administration (SSA) regarding an employee whose name did not properly match up with the Social Security number (SSN) he or she provided. There are no clear rules on how much follow-up is required on the part of the employer. Though some lawyers advise their clients not to terminate employees in no-match cases, given that the mismatch may be attributable to computer errors, typographical mistakes, or other issues, others have taken the position that an employee's failure to resolve the problem after a reasonable period of time could be construed to provide constructive knowledge. A more in-depth discussion of this topic can be found in Chapter 12.

A clearer situation is found when an employer receives a Notice of Suspect Documents (NSD) from U.S. Immigration and Customs Enforcement (ICE) that an employee has submitted fraudulent documentation. The courts generally have held that such a notification would provide an employer with constructive knowledge of a problem and that the employer would need to re-verify.

---

[1] *See* Code of Federal Regulations, Title 8, sections 274a.1(e)(i)–(iii).

6.3 What if an employee later presents a different Social Security number from when the Form I-9 was completed?

Because a person is assigned only one Social Security number (SSN) in his or her lifetime, an employee who comes to an employer with a number different from the one at the time of hire should be viewed with suspicion. The odds are that the employee used a false number to begin work and has somehow been able to obtain a valid SSN later (such as through a green-card application filed independently of the employer).

The same principle normally applies with an "A" or "Alien number." An employee should have only one "Alien number." The number does not change upon renewal of Permanent Resident card or moving from Employment Authorization card to Permanent Resident card. The authors know of only two occasions where an employee legitimately had two "Alien numbers" and that was when the employee failed to disclose the number to U.S. Immigration and Customs Enforcement (ICE) or U.S. Citizenship and Immigration Services (USCIS) before starting a new process. Having two different "Alien numbers" is a strong indication of unlawful status or previous unlawful status.

Employers will, of course, want to speak to employment counsel involving a violation of an employer's policies regarding making false statements during the hiring process. With respect to the Immigration Reform and Control Act (IRCA), the employer should inquire regarding the circumstances surrounding obtaining the new number. However, the employer is not required to terminate the employee even if the employee admits making a false statement; and the employer would be able to continue employing the employee if the employer had no knowledge of the employee's lack of work authorization. In this case, a new Form I-9 should be completed with the old Form I-9 attached with an explanation. The employer should correct the number with the Internal Revenue Service (IRS), so taxes are properly withheld.

However, if the employer has an honesty policy that states one can be terminated for lying on a company document and that policy has been followed, the employee must be terminated.

> **6.3:** California has a law preventing the discharge of an employee for providing updated personal information, i.e., name, Social Security number, "A" or "Alien number," "unless the changes are directly related to the skill set, qualifications, or knowledge required for the job."

6.4   Is an employer on notice that an employee is not authorized to work if the employee requests the employer to petition for the employee's permanent residency?

The U.S. Department of Homeland Security (DHS) regulations list an employer being requested to file a green-card application through labor certification as an example of a situation in which there may be constructive knowledge that the employee is not eligible to work. This would be the case, for example, when the employer is requested to file a green-card application for an employee who stated on the Form I-9 that he or she was a U.S. citizen or lawful permanent resident. There are situations, however, in which an employee may request that an employer file for permanent residence that would not indicate a problem.

The obvious example is when an employee is on a nonimmigrant work visa sponsored by the employer. But it also may happen when an employee is in a status that allows for employment, but not for actual permanent residency. This may be the case if, for example, an employee is in a temporary protected status (TPS) or asylum status or has a green-card application pending through another petition, and the employee wants to have a backup strategy to gain permanent residency.

6.5   What if the employee states in Section 1 that he or she is a permanent resident or U.S. citizen but then presents an employment document with an expiration date?

The employer in this situation should ask the employee if he or she properly understood the question in Section 1 regarding status, because the document presented is facially inconsistent with the status claimed. Perhaps the employee has a pending permanent residency petition and has an Employment Authorization Document (EAD) associated with that application. If the employee erred, then he or she should both correct and initial the attestation or present documents that are consistent with the claim of being a permanent resident (including documents that do not show permanent residency but that do show identity and work authorization, such as a driver's license and a Social Security card without annotations). The employee also may complete a new Form I-9. If the employee states that he or she is in fact a U.S. citizen or permanent resident, then the employer should not accept an EAD because the document directly contradicts the employee's stated status.

6.6 Should an employer re-verify a Form I-9 for an employee who is subject to a Social Security no-match letter?

The rules regarding Social Security Administration (SSA) letters telling an employer that an employee's name and Social Security number (SSN) do not match were not in place at the time of the publication of this book.

In August 2007, the U.S. Department of Homeland Security (DHS) promulgated a regulation that would require an employer to re-verify a Form I-9 after going through a series of set procedures in a specified timeframe. The rule was to take effect in September 2007. However, a coalition of business and labor groups sued to overturn the regulation and succeeded in convincing a court to issue an injunction blocking the regulation from taking effect. In August 2009, the 2007 rule was rescinded. Since then, the SSA has stopped issuing no-match letters, though it is unclear if this change is permanent.

If the no-match letters return, lawyers differ over the meaning of "receiving" one. Does the letter itself mean an employer has knowledge that an employee's Social Security number (SSN) is suspect? Because there are many reasons why a letter from the SSA may have nothing to do with an employee's immigration status, an employer cannot assume that the employee is improperly documented.

The employer should initially check to make sure that an error has not been made on the employer's part. After the employer establishes that the problem is not its fault, the employer should notify the employee. Beyond that, it is not clear under current law what an employer should do. The no-match letters in the past have stated that they are not to be construed by the employer as being a statement about an employee's immigration status. And a case out of the U.S. Court of Appeals for the Ninth Circuit held that the mere receipt of a no-match letter by an employer does not equate to the employer having constructive knowledge that an employee is unauthorized to work.[2]

A December 23, 1997, legacy Immigration and Naturalization Service (INS) opinion letter indicated that receiving a no-match letter does not alone constitute notice that an employee is ineligible to work. However, the letter did indicate that a Social Security number (SSN) with the following characteristics might lead to a duty to re-verify, including the following:

- The number has more than nine digits.
- The number has fewer than nine digits.

---

[2] *See Collins Food International, Inc. v. INS*, 948 F.2d 549 (9th Cir. 1991).

- The number's first three digits are "000."
- The number's first digit is "8" or "9."
- The middle two digits are "00."
- The last four digits of the number are "0000."

A no-match letter regarding an SSN with these characteristics would be a reasonable indication that the employee's SSN is falsified.

A later April 12, 1999, opinion letter from the General Counsel of legacy Immigration and Naturalization Service (INS) stated that receiving a no-match letter in and of itself put an employer on notice that an employee is not authorized to work. The 1999 letter, however, warns employers: "We emphasize that although it is incorrect to assume that an SSA discrepancy necessarily indicates unauthorized status, it would be equally incorrect for an employer to assume that in all cases it may safely ignore any possible INA [Immigration and Nationality Act] relevance or consequence of SSA discrepancies."[3]

The letter then noted that a Social Security Administration (SSA) no-match letter in combination with other information the employer receives regarding the employee may be enough to put the employer on notice that an employee's status is not valid for work authorization. The letter specifically warned employers that INS would likely consider the employer to have violated the Immigration Reform and Control Act (IRCA) if the employer had given an employee the opportunity to explain and reconcile a reported discrepancy with Social Security Administration (SSA) records and the employee had failed to do so satisfactorily. In other words, an employer starting to make inquiries into Social Security number (SSN) discrepancies and then ignoring the findings is worse than not making the inquiry at all.

6.7   What if an employer receives a U.S. Department of Homeland Security notice that there is a problem with a document presented in connection with a Form I-9?

The U.S. Department of Homeland Security's (DHS) requires an employer to take specific steps in a prescribed timeframe when it receives notification from DHS that a document presented by an alien for employment verification purposes is invalid, fraudulent, or cannot be authenticated. The main uncertainty surrounds how quickly an employer would need to respond and to what extent.

---

[3] General Counsel, INS HQCOU 90/10.15-C (April 12, 1999).

An employer that receives this type of notice (known as a Notice of Suspect Documents, or NSD) would not violate the anti-discrimination rules of the Immigration Reform and Control Act (IRCA) if it requests that an employee provide additional documentation. The courts have held that U.S. Immigration and Customs Enforcement (ICE) need not provide irrefutable proof that the employee is ineligible to work. It is enough that ICE provides information that arouses suspicion. As for timing, an employer must act within 10 days of ICE's notice, although it is debatable as to what action the employee must take within 10 days. It may be that the employer must notify the suspect employee or it may be that the employer must discharge the employee if he or she does not provide any new work authorization or ICE has rejected the new documents. Certainly, it must be reasonable under the circumstances.

Another type of notice from U.S. Immigration and Customs Enforcement (ICE) is called a Notice of Discrepancies. It advises the employer that based on a review of the Forms I-9 and documentation submitted by the employee, ICE has been unable to determine the employee's work eligibility. The employer should provide the employee with a copy of the notice and give the employee an opportunity to present ICE with additional documentation to establish his or her employment eligibility.

When an employer follows up with an employee, the question also arises regarding what action must be taken. Clearly, the employer must provide the new documentation to ICE, which will determine the new documentation's validity. What if the employee provides new, valid documentation that does not include the suspect document? In this case, the employer would have a defense against a later charge of knowingly employing an unauthorized employee.

6.8 What if an employee tells the employer that another employee is unauthorized?

The employer should not consider a mere tip from another employee to constitute knowledge that an employee is out of status. An employer acting on such a tip alone could be vulnerable to being found to have violated anti-discrimination laws.

According to a U.S. Immigration and Customs Enforcement (ICE)/Office of Special Counsel (OSC) December 2015 guidance, "tips concerning an employee's immigration status may lead to the discovery of an unauthorized employee, tips and leads should not always be presumed to be credible. An employer is cautioned against responding to tips that have no indicia of reliability, such as unsubstantiated, retaliatory, or anonymous tips. Heightened scrutiny of a particular employee's Form I-9 or the request for additional documentation from the

unreliable tips may be unlawful, particularly if the tip was
....ation, the employee's national origin, or perceived citizen-

....ther hand, an April 12, 1999, opinion letter from legacy Immigration
....aturalization Service (INS) general counsel noted that if an employer re-
....ives a tip from another employee indicating that an employee is not authorized
to be employed, and the employer later receives a Social Security no-match letter, the employer would likely have constructive knowledge based on a "totality
of the circumstances."

6.9   Is an employer liable if it uses a contractor and knows the contractor's employees are not authorized to work?

Yes. The U.S. Department of Homeland Security (DHS) regulations state that
any person who uses a contract, subcontract, or exchange to obtain the labor or
services of a foreign employee in the United States, knowing that the employee
is unauthorized to work, should be considered to have hired the employee for
purposes of determining if a person has violated the Immigration Reform and
Control Act (IRCA).

6.10   May an employer be deemed to have constructive knowledge when it failed to complete a Form I-9 for an employee or when the form is completed improperly?

Yes. In various cases, employers have been held to have had constructive
knowledge that an employee was unauthorized to work even if the employer had
no direct knowledge of the employee's employment status. Courts have held that
employers are not excused simply because there is a Form I-9, if the form itself
was not properly completed. A court would look to the circumstances surrounding the particular form and use a standard of what is reasonable to determine if
an employer should have known that an employee was likely not authorized.

6.11 May an employer be deemed to have constructive knowledge when it fails to re-verify a Form I-9?

Yes. Courts have found that an employer that fails to re-verify a Form I-9 when such re-verification is required will usually have constructive knowledge that an employee is unauthorized to work. The more complicated question is what to do when the employee presents documentation that does not relate to the expired document presented at the time of hire. U.S. Immigration and Customs Enforcement (ICE) and the courts have held that an employer has an obligation to make an inquiry regarding the continuing employment authorization. This would seem to violate the anti-discrimination rules in the Immigration Reform and Control Act (IRCA) that bar employers from specifying which documents an employee may submit. However, Congress addressed this issue in Section 421 of the Illegal Immigration Reform and Immigrant Responsibility Act (IIRAIRA), which punishes employers for making inquiries regarding continuing work authorization only when such inquiries are made for the purpose or with the intent of discriminating against an individual.

7

UNFAIR IMMIGRATION-RELATED EMPLOYMENT PRACTICES

7.1   What are the Immigration Reform and Control Act's anti-discrimination and unfair documentary practices (document abuse) rules?

Although employers need to be diligent about complying with the employment verification rules of the Immigration Reform and Control Act (IRCA), they should not be so overzealous that they end up penalizing qualified employees. IRCA has anti-discrimination rules that can result in an employer facing stiff sanctions. Employers of more than three employees are covered by IRCA anti-discrimination rules (as opposed to the 15 or more employees required by Title VII of the Civil Rights Act). IRCA protects most U.S. citizens, permanent residents, temporary residents, asylees, and refugees from discrimination on the basis of national origin or citizenship status if the person is authorized to work. Aliens illegally in the United States are not protected.

Under Immigration Reform and Control Act (IRCA), employers may not refuse to hire someone because of his or her national origin or citizenship status, and they may not discharge employees on those grounds either. The employer is also barred from requesting specific documents in completing a Form I-9 and cannot refuse to accept documents that appear genuine on their face. But note that an employer must be shown to have had the intent to discriminate. However, the issue of intent is highly debatable with the Immigrant and Employee Rights Section of the U.S. Department of Justice (formerly known as the Office of Special Counsel for Immigration-Related Unfair Employment Practices (OSC)), and the Office of the Chief Administrative Hearing Officer (OCAHO) taking the position in *Life Generations Healthcare* (2014) that intent could be proven with "statistical or evidence," which appears contrary to OCAHO's decision in *Diversified Technology & Services* (2003).

In December 2016, the Department of Justice, where the Immigrant and Employee Rights Section is located, promulgated a new regulation on the definition of "discriminate." Under the new regulation, the word, "discrimination," in the context of Title 8 of the U.S. Code, section 1324b: Unfair Immigration-Related Employment Practices, and in the context of completing the Form I-9, means the act of:

> *intentionally treating an individual differently from other individuals because of national origin or citizenship status, regardless of the explanation for the differential treatment, and regardless of whether such treatment is because of animus or hostility.*

According to the Immigrant and Employee Rights Section, this regulation merely incorporates the intent requirement contained in the amended statutes and case law. It agrees that under section 1324b, a violation cannot be established under a strict liability standard or a disparate impact theory.

Employers can be separately sanctioned based on laws enacted in 1990 if they request more or different documents than required by the Form I-9 rules. Employers originally were held strictly liable for violations under this category, but in 1996, a law was enacted requiring a showing that employers intended to discriminate. Thus, one must determine whether non–U.S. citizens are treated differently than U.S. citizens.

7.2   Who may file a complaint under the Immigration Reform and Control Act against an employer for violations of the employer sanctions rules?

Any person having knowledge of a violation or potential violation of the Immigration Reform and Control Act (IRCA) may submit a signed, written complaint in person or by mail to the local U.S. Department of Homeland Security (DHS) office having jurisdiction over the employer.

7.3   How is enforcement responsibility split between the Immigrant and Employee Rights Section of the U.S. Department of Justice and the U.S. Equal Employment Opportunity Commission?

The Immigrant and Employee Rights Section and the U.S. Equal Employment Opportunity Commission (EEOC) split jurisdiction over "national-origin" discrimination charges.

The EEOC handles matters involving employers with 15 or more employees, whereas the Immigrant and Employee Rights Section has responsibility for smaller employers with between 4 and 14 employees. The Immigrant and Employee Rights Section covers "national origin" claims involving intentional acts of discrimination with respect to hiring, firing, and recruitment. The EEOC has broader jurisdiction under Title VII of the Civil Rights Act.

The Immigrant and Employee Rights Section has exclusive jurisdiction to rule on "citizenship and immigration status" discrimination claims against employers with four or more employees. The Immigrant and Employee Rights Section also has jurisdiction over unfair documentary practices claims for employers with four or more employees.

7.4   What is "national origin" discrimination?

"National origin" discrimination refers to when a person or entity discriminates against any individual (other than an unauthorized immigrant) with respect to the hiring, recruitment, or referral for a fee of the individual for employment, or the firing of the individual from employment because of the individual's national origin.

7.5   What is "citizenship or immigration status" discrimination?

"Citizenship or immigration status" discrimination refers to when a person or entity discriminates against any individual (other than an unauthorized immigrant) with respect to the hiring, recruitment, or referral for a fee of the individual for employment, or the firing of the individual from employment because of the individual's citizenship or immigration status.

7.6   What is "unfair documentary practices"?

Unfair documentary practices (formerly referred to as "document abuse") refers to discriminatory practices related to the verification of employment eligibility in the Form I-9 process. Employers that treat individuals differently based on national origin or citizenship commit unfair documentary practices when they engage in one of four following types of activity:

1. Improperly requesting that employees produce more documentation than is required to show identity and employment authorization.

2. Improperly asking employees to produce a particular document to show identity or employment eligibility.

3. Improperly rejecting documents that appear to be genuine and belonging to the employee.

4. Improperly treating groups of applicants differently (for example, based on looking or sounding foreign) when they complete Forms I-9.

All individuals authorized to be employed can file a claim under the document abuse rules if an employer has four or more employees.

7.7   What are examples of prohibited practices?

The following are examples of prohibited practices when they are based on an employee's "national origin' or "citizenship or immigration status":

- Setting different employment eligibility verification standards or requiring different documents based on national origin or citizenship status. (One example would be requiring non–U.S. citizens to present U.S. Department of Homeland Security–issued documents, like green cards).

- Requesting to see employment eligibility verification documents before hire and completing the Form I-9 because an employee appears foreign or the employee indicates that he or she is not a U.S. citizen.

- Refusing to accept a document or to hire an individual because an acceptable document has a future expiration date.

- Requiring an employee during re-verification to present a new unexpired Employment Authorization Document (EAD) if the employee presented an employment document during the initial verification. (Note that this appears to contradict earlier legacy Immigration and Naturalization Service (INS) statements and the outcome of at least one court case holding that an employer may have a responsibility to ask an employee whether employment authorization has been extended. An employer should consult with counsel in such situations.)

- Limiting jobs to U.S. citizens, unless a job is limited to citizens by law or regulation.

- Asking to see a document with an employee's "Alien" or "Admission number" when completing Section 1 of Form I-9.

- Asking a lawful permanent resident to re-verify employment eligibility because the person's green card has expired.

7.8   How does Title VII of the Civil Rights Act provide employees additional protections?

Title VII of the Civil Rights Act bars employment discrimination based on national origin, race, color, religion, and sex. Only employers with 15 or more employees for 20 or more weeks in the preceding or current calendar year are covered. Title VII covers discrimination in any aspect of employment.

7.9   What is the basis for regulating immigration-related unfair employment practices?

Section 274B of the Immigration and Nationality Act (INA) specifically prohibits discrimination based on national origin or citizenship status.

7.10   Can employers discriminate against employees requiring visa sponsorship?

Nonimmigrant aliens (whether work-authorized or not), aliens not in legal status in the United States, and other individuals requiring visa sponsorship are not protected by the anti-discrimination provisions in the Immigration Reform and Control Act (IRCA). However, Title VII of the Civil Rights Act offers some protections to these individuals, insofar as employers that appear to be inconsistent in whom they consider for sponsorship and in whom they do not, may be found to have engaged in "national origin" discrimination under that law.

7.11 Can employers discriminate against employees with an expiring Employment Authorization Document?

No. The existence of a future expiration date should not be considered in determining whether a person is qualified for a position, and considering a future employment authorization expiration date may be regarded as employment discrimination. In other words, employers may not refuse to hire a person only because he or she has temporary employment authorization. This does not, of course, preclude re-verification upon the expiration of employment authorization.

7.12 Are employees protected from retaliation if they complain about discrimination?

Yes. Employers cannot retaliate against employees who file a charge with the U.S. Department of Justice's Immigrant and Employee Rights Section or the U.S. Equal Employment Opportunity Commission (EEOC). Employees also are protected if they are a witness or participate in an investigation or prosecution of a discrimination complaint, or if the employee asserts rights under the Immigration Reform and Control Act's (IRCA's) anti-discrimination provisions or under Title VII of the Civil Rights Act.

7.13 Who is a "protected individual" under the Immigration Reform and Control Act, and can an employer discriminate against individuals not included?

A "protected individual" under the anti-discrimination rules of the Immigration Reform and Control Act (IRCA) includes anyone who is a U.S. citizen as well as individuals who fit the following categories:

- Recent lawful permanent residents (LPRs) or green-card holders—meaning individuals who have not held LPR status for no longer than six months beyond becoming eligible to naturalize.
- Refugees.
- Certain beneficiaries of the 1986 legalization program (only a few of these people have not become green-card holders at this point).
- Asylees.

Employers are not required to consider applicants who are outside of this list under IRCA's anti-discrimination rules. Employers should be careful, however, to be consistent in applying their policies so as to avoid a finding that a particular group has been disparately treated. Such inconsistency could lead to a finding of "national origin" discrimination under Title VII of the Civil Rights Act.

7.14 What information can be requested of an individual prior to the commencement of employment?

Employers that require applicants to complete Forms I-9 prior to the beginning of employment need to be careful because of the possibility of "national origin" discrimination. The employer *always* should wait until an offer has been extended and accepted before requesting completion of the Form I-9. After that, the employer can start the Form I-9 process. Having a uniform policy regarding completion of the Form I-9 is a smart practice, and if an exception is made, there should be a rational reason.

7.15 Can an employer maintain a policy of employing only U.S. citizens?

No, an employer may not maintain a policy of employing only U.S. citizens unless the employer is governed by a law or regulation stating the employee must be a U.S. citizen. Discriminating against protected individuals under the Immigration Reform and Control Act (IRCA) would be considered unlawful discrimination.

7.16 Can an employer require employees to post indemnity bonds against potential liability under the Immigration Reform and Control Act?

No. Such a practice is specifically prohibited under U.S. Department of Homeland Security (DHS) regulations, including any other type of indemnification required by an employer against potential liability arising under the Immigration Reform and Control Act (IRCA). However, the regulations do say that an employer may require an employee to agree to a "performance clause" stating an employee unable to perform the job duties may be held accountable to the employer. Whether such a clause is enforceable is a question of contract and employment law, of course, and counsel should be consulted.

7.17 Can an employer not sure whether documents are valid for a new hire request U.S. Department of Homeland Security verification of the status of the employee?

Only employers participating in E-Verify can validate the status of an employee through the U.S. Department of Homeland Security (DHS) (see Chapter 11 for more information). Employers are permitted, however, to contact DHS if they have a reason to believe that an employee's documentation is suspicious. If DHS believes the matter to be worth pursuing, U.S. Immigration and Customs Enforcement (ICE) may investigate the matter. An employer that contacts DHS about documents it believes to be invalid would not be liable for discrimination if it genuinely believed the documents to be potentially invalid and if the employer was not singling out an employee on the basis of appearing or sounding foreign.

Employers can contact the Social Security Administration (SSA) to verify the validity of a Social Security number (SSN). Information regarding this online service can be found at www.ssa.gov/bso/services.htm.

7.18 How is a complaint filed for an Immigration Reform and Control Act anti-discrimination violation?

The U.S. Department of Justice's Immigrant and Employee Rights Section accepts charges filed by individuals or their representatives who believe they have been the victims of employment discrimination. The U.S. Department of Homeland Security (DHS) officers also may refer matters, especially based on data-gathering through E-Verify.

Discrimination charges must be filed within six months of the alleged discriminatory acts. After the claim is filed, the Immigrant and Employee Rights Section has 10 days to notify the employer and then will either file a complaint with an administrative law judge (ALJ) within 120 days or notify the charging party that it will not file a complaint. The charging party may independently file a complaint within 90 days of receiving this notice from the Immigrant and Employee Rights Section. The Immigrant and Employee Rights Section may reverse its decision and file a complaint within this 90-day period. The ALJ will then conduct a hearing and issue a decision, or the parties may independently reach a settlement agreement.

7.19 What is the procedure to file a complaint under the Immigration Reform and Control Act against an employer for violation of the anti-discrimination rules? What about a complaint under Title VII of the Civil Rights Act?

The complaint must detail the allegations, identify the parties, and list the relevant dates of the alleged violations. The complaint must be filed within 180 days of the alleged discriminatory act.

Individuals who believe they have been the victim of discrimination prohibited by the Immigration Reform and Control Act (IRCA) can call the U.S. Department of Justice's Immigrant and Employee Rights Section employee hotline at 800-255-7688 or e-mail the Immigrant and Employee Rights Section at ier@usdoj.gov. The Immigrant and Employee Rights Section also has a telephone intervention program allowing employers and employees to speak with a representative and attempt to resolve a matter without resorting to the formal complaint process. The employer telephone number for this service is 800-255-8155.

The Immigrant and Employee Rights Section also may file a complaint based on an investigation that its office initiated—such as a referral from U.S. Citizenship and Immigration Services (USCIS)—up to five years after the date of alleged discrimination.

Individuals seeking to file a complaint under Title VII of the Civil Rights Act can call the U.S. Equal Employment Opportunity Commission (EEOC) at 800-669-4000, visit www.eeoc.gov, or e-mail info@eeoc.gov.

7.20 How does the Immigrant and Employee Rights Section investigate complaints?

First, the U.S. Department of Justice's Immigrant and Employee Rights Section must determine if the claim has merit. If the Immigrant and Employee Rights Section decides to investigate a complaint, it will notify the employer in writing about the opening of an investigation, and it will request in writing information and documentation relating to the complaint. The documents may be subpoenaed if an employer refuses to cooperate.

The Immigrant and Employee Rights Section has 120 days to determine if the charge is true and whether to bring a complaint. It also can send a letter to the complaining party during that 120-day period indicating it will not file a complaint.

The charging party may file a complaint directly with the chief administrative hearing officer within 90 days of receiving the notification from the Immigrant and Employee Rights Section that it will not pursue the case.

7.21 How many complaints to the Office of Special Counsel for Immigration-Related Unfair Employment Practices resulted in a monetary settlement in 2015?

In 2015, the Office of Special Counsel for Immigration-Related Unfair Employment Practices (OSC) (now known as the U.S. Department of Justice's Immigrant and Employee Rights Section) reached a settlement with 15 employers on document abuse or citizenship discrimination. The settlements resulted in civil penalties of approximately $1.5 million, with the largest civil penalty being $445,000 and back pay due to individuals of approximately $250,000.

In 2016, the OSC reached a settlement with 17 employers on document abuse or citizenship discrimination. The settlements resulted in civil penalties of more than $1.1 million, with the largest civil penalty being $200,000 and back pay due to individuals of approximately $116,000.

8

PENALTIES AND OTHER RISKS

8.1 What penalties does an employer face for Form I-9 violations?

Employers can face stiff penalties for Immigration Reform and Control Act (IRCA) violations that include substantial fines and debarment from government contracts. Penalties can be imposed for knowingly hiring unauthorized employees as well as for simply committing paperwork violations even if all employees are authorized to work. Fines for knowingly hiring unauthorized employees amount to anywhere from $548 to $21,916 per employee, depending on the prior history of violations. Employers also can be barred from competing for government contracts for one year if they knowingly hire or continue to employ unauthorized employees. Furthermore, there is the possibility of criminal prosecution for a pattern or practice of hiring or employing undocumented workers.

Paperwork violations can result in significant fines. Each Form I-9 with a substantive error—mistake or missing item—can result in a penalty from $220 to $2,191 per form for the first offense. The level of the penalty is based on the percentage of I-9 errors. The revised matrix on the exact amount of penalty at each of the levels stated above was not issued at the time of publication. The following is an educated estimate:

- 0–9%: $220;
- 10–19%: $545;
- 20–29%: $873;
- 30–39%: $1202;
- 40–49%: $1,530; and
- 50% and above: $1,859.

For second offenses, the matrix starts at approximately $871 and goes up to $2,191, depending on the percentage of violations. For a third offense, each error costs $2,191.

An employer, for example, that has 100 employees and has substantive errors on 50 Forms I-9 might face a fine of about more than $100,000. U.S. Immigration and Customs Enforcement (ICE) investigators have considerable discretion in assessing fines. All of these fines increased to the dollar amounts stated in 2016, pursuant to a new regulation.

> **Employers should be cautioned that knowingly accepting fraudulent documents from employees is a different kind of violation that can be criminally prosecuted under other immigration laws.**

Aside from federal violations, many states have passed laws that penalize employers violating their immigration laws and the Immigration Reform and Control Act (IRCA), including barring such employers from state contracts and revoking their business licenses. Civil and criminal penalties are as follows for IRCA violations:

Hiring or continuing to employ unauthorized aliens

Fines will vary depending on past violations:

- First offense: $548 to 4,384 for each unauthorized employee.
- Second offense: $4,384 to $10,957 for each unauthorized employee.
- Subsequent offenses: $10,957 to $21,916 for each unauthorized employee.

Failing to comply with the Form I-9 requirements

The fine is $220 to $2,191 per individual employee for each substantive and uncorrected technical error—failing to properly complete, retain, or make available for inspection Forms I-9. U.S. Immigration and Customs Enforcement (ICE) will consider the following factors in mitigating or aggravating the fine by 5 percent per factor:

- Business's size.
- Employer's good faith.
- Seriousness of the violation.
- Whether the individual was, in fact, unauthorized to work.
- History of violations by the employer.

Injunctions

If the U.S. Attorney General has reasonable cause to believe that an employer is engaged in a pattern of unlawful employment, recruitment, or referral activities, the Attorney General may bring a civil action in the appropriate U.S. district court requesting relief, such as a temporary or permanent injunction, restraining order, or other order against an Immigration Reform and Control Act (IRCA) violator.

Criminal Penalties

Employers can be criminally sanctioned for Immigration Reform and Control Act (IRCA) violations. Employers, and their representatives, that engage in a practice or pattern of hiring or continuing to employ unauthorized employees face fines of more than $3,000 per employee and imprisonment of up to six months.

Indemnity Bonds

Employers that require employees to post a bond or indemnify the employer against Immigration Reform and Control Act (IRCA) violations can be fined up to $2,191 per violation and subjected to an order to return the money to the employee.

Document Fraud

Employers that assist in the production and use of false documents for employees to use to document employment eligibility are, not surprisingly, subject to penalties. Fines range from $452 to $9,054 per document depending on whether it is an employer's first offense. Criminal penalties may be imposed on persons who fail to disclose that they have prepared or assisted in the preparation of false documents. Fines and imprisonment of up to five years may be imposed for a first offense, and subsequent offenses may result in 15 years of imprisonment.

Other Criminal Sanctions

For an extensive discussion of sanctions an employer may face, see Chapter 14.

8.2   What are the penalties for unlawful discrimination?

IRCA

The U.S. Department of Justice's Immigrant and Employee Rights Section can seek several remedies when an employer has been found to have engaged in prohibited discriminatory practices under the Immigration Reform and Control Act (IRCA). The Immigrant and Employee Rights Section has the power to seek an order requiring an employer to:

- Hire individuals adversely affected with or without back pay (if back pay is ordered, there is a limit of two years).
- Pay to the U.S. government civil penalties, which can be significant.
- Post notices to employees about their rights and the employer's obligations.
- Educate all personnel involved in IRCA compliance about IRCA's anti-discrimination rules.

- Remove (in applicable cases) a false performance review or false warning from a personnel file.

- Lift (in applicable cases) restrictions on an employee's assignments, work shifts, or movements.

> **Unfair documentary practices (document abuse) comes with a separate monetary penalty of $181 to $1,811 for each individual subjected to discrimination.**

Penalties for immigration-related employment discrimination range from $452 to $3,621 per individual for a first offense to $5,432 to $18,107 per individual for the third or greater offense.

Title VII

Employers found to have violated Title VII of the Civil Rights Act may be ordered to do one or more of the following:

- Hire, reinstate, or promote with back pay and retroactive seniority the individual subjected to discrimination.

- Post notices for employees regarding their rights and the employer's obligations.

- Remove false or derogatory information from an employee's personnel file.

Financial penalties also may be imposed under Title VII of the Civil Rights Act for financial losses and mental anguish as well as for punitive damages for employers that act with malice or reckless indifference.

Finally, under either Immigration Reform and Control Act (IRCA) or Title VII of the Civil Rights Act, the prevailing party may be ordered to pay attorney's fees. Under IRCA, reasonable attorney's fees may be awarded if the losing party's argument is without reasonable foundation in law and fact. IRCA states that the U.S. government cannot be held liable for attorney's fees, so this effectively means only the employer would pay this cost. However, under Title VII, a judge may award reasonable attorney's fees (including expert fees) to either prevailing party, and the U.S. government may be held liable for costs the same as the employer.

8.3   Can employers that tried in good faith to comply avoid penalties?

Yes. If an employer has complied with the Form I-9 requirements in good faith but has been found to have hired an unauthorized employee, the employer would have a good-faith defense. The government would need to show the employer had actual or constructive knowledge that the employee was unlawfully present. For paperwork violations that are technical, employers that have made a good-faith attempt to comply may be excused. This good-faith provision will not apply if the U.S. Department of Homeland Security (DHS) has notified the employer of problems and the employer has not corrected the problems within 10 days. This good-faith provision also does not apply to employers that have been engaged in a pattern or practice of violations.

8.4   What is the process for imposing penalties?

If U.S. Immigration and Customs Enforcement (ICE) investigates and determines that a violation of the employer sanctions rules has occurred, it may issue a Notice of Intent to Fine (NIF) or, in the alternative, a Warning Notice. A Warning Notice must contain a statement of the basis for the violations and which sections of the law have been violated.

If a NIF is issued, the notice must contain the basis for the charge, the sections of the law violated, and the penalty to be imposed. It also must advise the employer of the right to counsel, that any statement given by the employer may be used against the employer, and that the employer is entitled to a hearing before an administrative law judge (ALJ).

If an employer wants to challenge the fine, it must file for a hearing in front of an ALJ within 30 days of being served with the notice. If no appeal is filed, U.S. Immigration and Customs Enforcement (ICE) will issue a final order 45 days from the issuance of the NIF. If an appeal is filed, the employer may negotiate for a lower fine. If unsuccessful in reaching an agreeable resolution, the employer may litigate the matter before the ALJ.

8.5   Are entities at a company liable in addition to the one division targeted for penalties?

When an order is issued against a specific entity in a family of distinct corporations, separate entities in the corporate family that do their own hiring are not considered subject to the order.

8.6 How does U.S. Immigration and Customs Enforcement decide which cases to investigate?

U.S. Immigration and Customs Enforcement (ICE) may investigate cases on its own initiative and need not have received a complaint. When ICE does receive a complaint, it has the discretion to decide whether the complaint has a reasonable probability of validity and whether to investigate (Code of Federal Regulations, Title 8, section 274a.9(b)).

8.7 Must U.S. Immigration and Customs Enforcement provide advance notice of a Form I-9 audit?

U.S. Immigration and Customs Enforcement (ICE) is required to provide three days' notice before it can inspect Forms I-9. The forms must be made available by the employer at the location requested by ICE.

8.8 In what format must Forms I-9 be provided to U.S. Immigration and Customs Enforcement auditors?

The original forms must be provided for inspection, except that recruiters or referrers for a fee who designate an employer to handle Form I-9 completion may present copies of the Forms I-9.

If an employer retains Forms I-9 in an electronic format, the employer must retrieve and reproduce the specific forms requested by the inspecting officer as well as the associated audit trails showing who accessed the computer system and the actions performed on the system in a specified period of time. The inspecting officer must be provided with the necessary hardware and software as well as access to personnel and documentation to locate, retrieve, read, and reproduce the requested Form I-9 documentation and associated audit trails, reports, and other related data.

Finally, an inspecting officer is permitted to request an electronic summary of all the immigration fields on an electronically stored Form I-9.

8.9   What if records are kept at a different location from where the U.S. Immigration and Customs Enforcement agents will be visiting?

If forms are stored at a location other than the worksite, the employer must inform the inspecting officer where they are kept and cooperate with the inspector in making the forms available either at the location where they are kept or at the office of the government agency conducting the inspection.

8.10   Can an employer be penalized if it properly completed a Form I-9, but the employee turns out to be unauthorized?

No. Employers that follow the rules of the Immigration Reform and Control Act (IRCA) will have a good-faith defense against any penalties that might be imposed for knowingly hiring an unauthorized employee. This assumes, of course, that the employer did not otherwise have knowledge, actual or constructive, that the employee is not authorized to work.

8.11   How much in fines was paid by employers in 2014 for Form I-9 violations?

In 2014, employers were assessed over $16 million in fines on 642 final orders. In comparison, in 2013, there were 637 final orders with penalties of more than $15.8 million. The statistics for 2015, 2016, and 2017 are unavailable—although U.S. Immigration and Customs Enforcement (ICE) stated that there were approximately 1,200 inspections in 2016; that number should be about the same in 2017. However, anecdotal evidence suggests the number of inspections in 2017 has substantially risen from 2016.

8.12   Aside from penalties under the Immigration Reform and Control Act, are there other risks associated with not properly completing Forms I-9?

Yes. There are a number of other reasons why an employer needs to be diligent in complying with the Form I-9 requirements of the Immigration Reform and Control Act (IRCA). They include:

- Qualifying to do business with large employers that now require contractors to be in compliance.

- Qualifying for government contracts with local, state, and federal agencies that require compliance.

- Avoiding problems in a merger or acquisition where an employer's Form I-9 records are requested as part of a due-diligence review (see Chapter 13 for more information on immigration issues in mergers and acquisitions).

- Avoiding liability under state laws that penalize employers for Form I-9 violations (including revoking business licenses and barring access to state contracts).

- Avoiding lawsuits filed by employees who have faced immigration problems as a result of an employer's errors (particularly when such errors might have been identified if an employer re-verified an employer's Form I-9 and such re-verification failed to take place).

9

IMMIGRATION REFORM AND CONTROL ACT COMPLIANCE TIPS

9.1 What are the best ways to prevent being prosecuted for Form I-9 employer violations?

Employers can minimize the chances for being found to have violated the employment verification rules of the Immigration Reform and Control Act (IRCA) by undertaking several steps:

- Appoint an immigration compliance officer.

- Establish an immigration compliance policy regarding Forms I-9 and other immigration compliance issues.

- Conduct a preventive internal audit of the Form I-9 files to see if there are violations requiring correction. Such an audit should be conducted by, or under the close supervision of, an immigration attorney familiar with IRCA.

- Establish a regular training program for human resource professionals regarding Form I-9 compliance rules. The training should be conducted by an immigration attorney familiar with IRCA rules.

- Establish uniform company policies regarding Forms I-9. Should copies of documents be retained or not? What kinds of questions can be asked about national origin and citizenship status before the date of hire? Are employees all treated the same when there is a Social Security no-match letter?

- Establish a re-verification tickler system to ensure Forms I-9 are checked in a timely manner.

- Centralize the Form I-9 recordkeeping process.

- Establish a process for human resource professionals to check quickly with counsel when there are any problems in the verification process.

- Establish a backup system to ensure timely compliance with Form I-9 rules when a human resource professional is out of the office.

- Segregate Forms I-9 from personnel records.

- Consider using an electronic Form I-9 product to automate the collection of information, to speed up the production of information in the case of a government audit, to ensure timely re-verification of Forms I-9 and reduce errors.

9.2   What are the best ways to avoid immigration-related employment discrimination?

The U.S. Department of Justice's Immigrant and Employee Rights Section suggests that employers take the following 10 steps to avoid liability under the anti-discrimination rules of the Immigration Reform and Control Act (IRCA):

1. Treat all people the same when announcing a job, taking applications, interviewing, offering a job, verifying eligibility to work, hiring, and firing.

2. Accept documentation presented by an employee if it establishes identity and employment eligibility, is included in the List of Acceptable Documents.

3. Accept documents that appear to be genuine. Employers are not expected to be document experts, and establishing the authenticity of a document is not their responsibility.

4. Avoid "citizen only" or "permanent-resident only" hiring policies unless required by law, regulation, or government contract. In most cases, it is illegal to require job applicants to be U.S. citizens or to have a particular immigration status.

5. Give out the same job information over the telephone to all callers, and use the same application form for all applicants.

6. Base all decisions about firing on job performance or behavior, not on the appearance, accent, name, or citizenship status of employees.

7. Complete the Form I-9, and keep it on file for at least three years from the date of employment or for one year after the employee leaves the job, whichever is later. This means that employers must keep Forms I-9 on file for all current employees. Employers must also make the forms available to government inspectors on request.

8. On the Form I-9, verify that employers have seen documents establishing identity and work authorization for all employees hired after November 6, 1986, including U.S. citizens.

9. Remember that many work authorization documents must be renewed. On the expiration date, employers must re-verify employment authorization and record the new evidence of continued work authorization on the Form I-9. Employers must accept any valid document employees choose to present, whether or not it is the same document provided initially. Individuals may present an unrestricted Social Security card to establish continuing employment eligibility. Permanent-resident cards should not be re-verified. Identity documents (for example, driver's licenses) should not be re-verified.

10. Be aware that U.S. citizenship, or nationality, belongs not only to persons born in the United States but also to individuals born to a U.S. citizen, and those born in Puerto Rico, Guam, the U.S. Virgin Islands, the Commonwealth of Northern Mariana Islands, American Samoa, and Swains Island. Citizenship is granted to legal immigrants after they complete the naturalization process.

9.3   Should a company have an immigration compliance officer?

Yes. Employers should ensure that an official at the company is thoroughly trained in the Immigration Reform and Control Act's (IRCA) employer sanctions and anti-discrimination rules and is able to supervise all persons charged with handling Forms I-9. The officer should be responsible for the following additional functions:

- Ensuring that Form I-9 records are properly retained.

- Ensuring that a reliable system is in place to re-verify Forms I-9.

- Acting in concert with employees, managers, subcontractors, customers, recruiters, and others to ensure that the company's immigration compliance policy is followed.

- Working with outside counsel to ensure that regular Forms I-9 preventive audits are conducted.

- Working with outside counsel to conduct regular training programs for human resource professionals and others at a company charged with hiring employees.

- Consulting with counsel to properly respond to Social Security no-match letters, if they are reinstituted.

- Working with outside counsel to establish an action plan should the company be the subject of an audit or investigation by the U.S. Department of Homeland Security (DHS), U.S. Immigration and Customs Enforcement (ICE), the U.S. Department of Labor (DOL), or the U.S. Department of Justice's Immigrant and Employee Rights Section.

- Ensuring that contractors supplying labor are properly screened to ensure IRCA compliance.

- Overseeing the company's immigration compliance policy to ensure it is readily available and periodically updated by counsel.

9.4   Should a company have an immigration compliance policy?

Yes. Employers should establish an immigration compliance policy that is included with the company's personnel policies and materials. The immigration compliance policy should:

- Name the company's immigration compliance officer.

- Advise on complying with the employer sanctions and anti-discrimination rules of the Immigration Reform and Control Act (IRCA).

- Contain rules for working with outside contractors.

- Set training requirements for employees completing the Forms I-9.

- Have a zero-tolerance policy for the employment of individuals who cannot comply with IRCA's employment verification rules.

- Determine whether copies of documents should be retained.

- Determine whether the company should use E-Verify.

- Determine if the company is required by state law to use E-Verify.

- Determine if the company is covered by Federal Acquisition Regulation (FAR) E-Verify.

- Establish the timing and procedures for regular internal Form I-9 audits.

- Contain rules on who has access to Form I-9 records.

- List procedures for using E-Verify.

- Set protocols for interacting with government officials in connection with IRCA compliance.

- Outline re-verification procedures.

- Determine what questions can be asked about national origin and citizenship status before a job offer.

9.5   Should companies have Form I-9 policies for dealing with outside contractors?

U.S. Immigration and Customs Enforcement (ICE) is increasingly targeting companies that use contractors employing unauthorized employees. The Immigration Reform and Control Act (IRCA) specifically states that a person or entity who uses a contract to obtain the labor of an alien knowing that the alien is unauthorized to work will be considered to have hired the alien for employment in the United States.

This principle was the basis of the government's targeting of Wal-Mart in 2005. ICE raided 60 Wal-Mart stores and 245 unauthorized employees were discovered working as night janitors and cleaners. The employees were employed by a contracting firm, and the government argued that Wal-Mart was responsible for the contractor's actions. The retail giant eventually paid an $11 million fine to resolve the dispute. In response, Wal-Mart has now established a compliance program that is considered one of the most rigorous in the country.

Employers are also, as noted above in the Wal-Mart case, sometimes held to be the responsible employer of unauthorized employees as opposed to the contractor that ostensibly employs them. The lesson is that employers may very well need to focus on IRCA compliance by its contractors.

9.5: Given the risks associated with using contract labor, many companies are beginning to demand that their contractors adhere to IRCA and attest to their compliance of a Form I-9 audit through a written statement or certification by a qualified individual, such as an immigration compliance attorney. Publix Super Markets is an example of an employer with this type of policy.

9.6   How do mergers, acquisitions, and other major changes affect Form I-9 requirements?

Though a closing may be a cause for celebration at a company, it also can be the cause of a nightmare for a company, given that the closing can instantly render all completed Forms I-9 for an acquired company invalid. An employer that continues to employ some of or a previous employer's entire workforce in cases involving a corporate reorganization, merger, or sale of stock or assets may accept the Forms I-9 previously prepared by the predecessor company. However, the Forms I-9 should be checked in the due-diligence process to ensure that the acquired forms are in compliance, as any errors or omissions on the adopted forms become the responsibility of the acquiring employer. Employers should consider adding Forms I-9 to a merger checklist and have all employees of the combined company complete new forms on the day of closing or beforehand. In any case, an immigration compliance attorney should be consulted in any merger, acquisition, or divestiture to ensure that the transaction does not result in immigration problems. (For an in-depth discussion of the immigration consequences of mergers and acquisitions, see Chapter 13.)

9.7   Can an employer that does not wish to assume an acquired company's liability for Form I-9 violations re-verify the entire workforce?

Yes. In such a case, the succeeding employer may have all employees complete new Forms I-9. The benefit of this action is that employers will have the opportunity to correct past problems and ensure compliance. Also, if any employees require a visa transfer as a result of the merger or acquisition, the employer will have an additional chance to discover the issue.

9.8 Are there U.S. Immigration and Customs Enforcement best hiring practices?

Yes. The best hiring practices of U.S. Immigration and Customs Enforcement (ICE) include the following:

- Use E-Verify for all hiring.

- Use the Social Security Number Verification Service (SSNVS) for wage reporting purposes. Verify the names and Social Security numbers of the current workforce, and work with employees to resolve any discrepancies.

- Establish an internal compliance and training program covering Form I-9 compliance, detecting fraudulent identity documents, and using E-Verify and SSNVS.

- Ensure that only trained employees complete Forms I-9 and use E-Verify.

- Establish a secondary review process to ensure that one person cannot subvert the process.

- Establish a written hiring and employment eligibility verification policy.

- Conduct an annual internal Form I-9 audit.

- Establish self-reporting procedures to inform ICE of violations or deficiencies.

- Set protocols for responding to Social Security Administration no-match letters.

- Establish a tip line for employees to report activity that relates to the employment of unauthorized workers, and create a protocol for responding to credible employee tips.

- Report immediately to ICE the discovery of credible information of suspected criminal misconduct in the employment eligibility verification process.

- Ensure that contractors and subcontractors establish procedures to comply with employment eligibility verification requirements. Encourage contractors and subcontractors to incorporate ICE's IMAGE (Mutual Agreement between Government and Employers) best practices, and, when practicable, incorporate the use of E-Verify in subcontractor agreements.

- Establish and maintain appropriate policies, practices, and safeguards to ensure that authorized workers are not treated differently with respect to hiring, firing, or recruitment. Further, ensure equal treatment during referral for a fee or during the Form I-9, E-Verify, or SSNVS processes because of an employee's citizenship status or national origin.

- Maintain copies of any documents accepted as proof of identity and employment authorization with the Form I-9 for all new hires.

9.9 What is some useful contract language for contractors?

Here is an example of sample language for contractors:

CONTRACTOR represents and warrants that all necessary visa or work authorization petitions have been timely and properly filed on behalf of any employees requiring a visa stamp, Form I-94 status document, employment authorization document, or any other immigration document necessary for such employees to legally work in the United States.

CONTRACTOR has complied in all respects with the provisions of the Immigration Reform and Control Act of 1986, including properly completing, retaining, and re-verifying Forms I-9. CONTRACTOR has complied in all respects with any state or local laws relating to employers that knowingly or intentionally hire unauthorized immigrants. There are no claims, lawsuits, actions, arbitrations, administrative or other proceedings, governmental investigations, or inquiries pending or threatened against the CONTRACTOR relating to the CONTRACTOR'S compliance with local, state, or federal immigration laws and regulations.

There have been no letters or other correspondence received from the U.S. Department of Homeland Security or other agencies regarding the employment authorization of any employees of CONTRACTOR. If the CONTRACTOR operates in a state, or has contracts with a state or federal agency, that requires or provides a "safe harbor" if an employer participates in the U.S. Department of Homeland Security's E-Verify electronic employment verification system, the CONTRACTOR has been participating in E-Verify for the entire period such participation has been required or available as a "safe harbor" or as long as the company has been operating in such state or contracting with such agency.

CONTRACTOR agrees to conduct a self-audit on an annual basis of its personnel records to ensure compliance with the Form I-9 requirements in the Immigration Reform and Control Act (IRCA). CONTRACTOR agrees to certify annually to [Company Name] that it does not knowingly employ any unauthorized workers, is in compliance with all immigration laws and requirements, and is not being investigated by any government agency with respect to compliance with immigration law. CONTRACTOR shall provide [Company Name] with a copy of its immigration compliance policy and procedures.

CONTRACTOR agrees to indemnify and hold harmless [Company Name] from any liability for CONTRACTOR's failure to comply with any U.S. immigration law or regulation.

[*Note*: Language should be included reciting that the relationship is an independent contractor relationship and listing factors showing this is the case. Furthermore, your legal counsel should review and approve the language.]

10

CONDUCTING AN I-9 SELF AUDIT

10.1 Which questions should be asked when preparing for a Form I-9 audit?

To assess Immigration Reform and Control Act (IRCA) compliance practices, the auditor (preferably an immigration compliance attorney) should interview the employer to determine the following:

- Are Forms I-9 completed by a single office in the organization? If not, how is the responsibility divided (for example, by department or branch)?

- If the responsibility for the forms is centralized, how many people are responsible? Identify all individuals with this responsibility.

- Has each person who is responsible for Forms I-9 received training in immigration compliance and immigration-related anti-discrimination rules?

- Does the employer have a manual or electronic Form I-9 system? If the latter, which system is used, and when was it implemented?

- Where are the employee files kept, and are they in good physical order?

- Are Forms I-9 consistently completed on the date of hire? If they are ever completed earlier than the date of hire, is the form ever completed before the employee has been offered the position and has actually accepted an offer of employment?

- Does the employer ever instruct employees which documents to present?

- Has the employer ever revoked a job offer or terminated an employee because of an upcoming expiration date in Section 1 of the Form I-9?

- Prior to signing Section 2 of the Form I-9, do employees responsible for Forms I-9 actually review the original Lists A, B, and C documents to determine whether the documents reasonably appear to be genuine and whether they relate to the employee in question?

- Does the employer have a system to identify and destroy Forms I-9 for terminated employees that are no longer required to be maintained?

- Does the company keep copies of Section 2 documents in all cases? In none? If the answer is only sometimes, why the inconsistency?

- Does the employer have a tickler system to re-verify work authorization and to complete Section 3 of forms requiring such re-verification? Describe the system.

- When was the last time an audit was conducted? What was its scope (full or partial)? What were the findings? Provide a copy of the audit.

- Has the employer had previous immigration violations or been previously audited regarding any immigration matters? If so, what were the results?

- Has the employer ever received a Social Security no-match letter?

- Does the employer use E-Verify?

- Does the employer have contracts with government agencies? If so, which government agencies? If so, does the employer use Federal Acquisition Regulation (FAR) E-Verify?

- Is the employer compliant with all state laws on immigration compliance?

10.2 Should employers prepare a spreadsheet for a Form I-9 audit?

Yes. The spreadsheet should include the following information:

- The names of all current employees hired since the company opened or since November 8, 1986, whichever is later.
- The date of hire of each employee.
- The names of all former employees terminated in the last three years.
- The date of termination for each employee no longer employed.
- Dates of rehire and termination if an employee's period of employment has been periodic.
- Whether a Form I-9 has been located for the current employees identified by payroll records as having been employed by the company since the company opened or since November 8, 1986, whichever is later.
- For terminated employees in the last three years, whether Forms I-9 are retained.
- Do Forms I-9 need to be retained for all employees terminated in the past three years?
- For terminated employees' Forms I-9 that no longer have to be retained, have those Forms I-9 been purged?
- Whether an employee fits in any of the following categories: the employee is under age 18, has a disability, is returning from a layoff or labor dispute, or has had employment authorization verified by a state employment service, or the employer is not required to receive a Form I-9 because the employer is part of a qualifying employer association.

Depending on the size, budget, immigration history, and overall vulnerability of an employer, either all Forms I-9 records or a random selection for current employees should be pulled for review. If a random selection is chosen, the selection should be varied in terms of departments, type of employee, dates of hire, and whether the employee's form must be re-verified. The same should be applied for former employees terminated in the past three years, although a random selection is more likely to be acceptable than such a sample of current employees.

> **10.2:** The number of Forms I-9 included in a random selection should be large enough to be a statistically close representation of the actual situation at the company to meaningfully estimate the liability exposure (i.e., 25 percent).

10.3 Should employers use an audit checklist?

Yes, employers should consider using the following:

Section 1. Employee Information and Verification

1.	Yes	No		Is the employee's name correct, and does it exactly match the employer's records and the supporting documents?
2.	Yes	No		Is the employee's Social Security number properly stated?
3.	Yes	No		Is the date of birth properly stated?
4.	Yes	No		Is the employee's address properly stated?
5.	Yes	No		Is one of the boxes checked stating that the employee is a U.S. citizen, foreign national, lawful permanent resident, or employment-authorized alien?
6.	Yes	No		In the previous box, if the employee has indicated that he or she is a lawful permanent resident or an employment-authorized alien, has the applicable "Alien" or "Admission number" been included and is there an expiration date?
7.	Yes	No		In the box above, if the employee has indicated that he or she is an employment-authorized alien, has the expiration date of the employment authorization been stated?
8.	Yes	No		Has the employee signed his or her name?
9.	Yes	No		Has the employee dated the signature on or before the first date of employment?
10.	Yes	No		If a translator or preparer has been used, has that person signed and dated the attestation, printed his or her name, and provided his or her address?

| 11. | Yes | No | | If a translator or preparer was not used, did the employer check the appropriate box that no preparer or translator was used? |

Section 2. Employer Review and Verification

List A (complete only if applicable)

1.	Yes	No		If a List A document is used, has a proper document been referenced?
2.	Yes	No		If a List A document is used, has the issuing authority been listed?
3.	Yes	No		If a List A document is used, has a document number been provided?
4.	Yes	No		If a List A document is used, has the document expiration date been provided?
5.	Yes	No	N/A	If a receipt for a List A document is provided in lieu of showing the actual document, has the original document been presented within 90 days of presenting the receipt?
6.	Yes	No		If a List A document is provided, has the employer left blank all information in List B and List C?

List B (complete only if applicable)

7.	Yes	No		If a List B document is used, has a proper document been referenced?
8.	Yes	No		If a List B document is used, has the issuing authority been listed?
9.	Yes	No		If a List B document is used, has a document number been provided?
10.	Yes	No		If a List B document is used, has the document expiration date been provided?
11.	Yes	No	N/A	If a receipt for a List B document is provided in lieu of showing the actual document, has the original document been presented within 90 days of presenting the receipt?
12.	Yes	No		If a List B document is provided, has the employee left blank all information in List A and provided information in List C?

List C (complete only if applicable)

13.	Yes	No		If a List C document is used, has a proper document been referenced?
14.	Yes	No		If a List C document is used, has the issuing authority been listed?
15.	Yes	No		If a List C document is used, has a document number been provided?
16.	Yes	No		If a List C document is used, has the document expiration date been provided?
17.	Yes	No	N/A	If a receipt for a List C document is provided in lieu of showing the actual document, has the original document been presented within 90 days of presenting the receipt?
18.	Yes	No		If a List C document is provided, has the employer left blank all information in List A and provided information in List B?

Documentation

19.	Yes	No	Are copies of the List A or List B/List C documents included in the Form I-9 file, and do they appear genuine?
20.	Yes	No	If documents were not provided on the date of hire, was Section 2 completed and the documents shown no later than the third business day after the first day of employment?
21.	Yes	No	Do the documents presented appear consistent with the status described in Section 1 (for example, a lawful permanent resident card is shown, but the applicant claims to be a U.S. citizen)?

Employer Certification

22.	Yes	No	Has an authorized representative of the company completed this portion of the form?
23.	Yes	No	Has the authorized representative properly listed the date he or she examined the documents?
24.	Yes	No	Has the authorized representative signed within three days of the first day of employment?

25.	Yes	No		Has the authorized representative signed the form?
26.	Yes	No		Has the authorized representative printed his or her name?
27.	Yes	No		Has the authorized representative listed his or her title?
28.	Yes	No		Has the employer's name and address been properly stated?
29.	Yes	No		Has the authorized representative dated the form?

Section 3. Employer Rehire and Reverification (complete only if applicable)

1.	Yes	No		If the employee provided an expiration date for work authorization in Section 1, has Section 3 been completed before the expiration date listed in Section 1?
2.	Yes	No	N/A	If the employee's name has changed, has the new name been provided?
3.	Yes	No	N/A	If the employee is a rehire, has the rehire date been provided?
4.	Yes	No		If re-verification is needed, has a proper document been presented demonstrating continuing employment authorization?
5.	Yes	No		If a rehire, does the prior documentation need re-verification?
6.	Yes	No		Has a document title been properly stated?
7.	Yes	No		Has the document number been properly stated?
8.	Yes	No		Has the new expiration date been properly stated?
9.	Yes	No		Has the authorized representative of the company properly signed Section 3?
10.	Yes	No		Has the authorized representative dated Section 3?

Additional notes:

_____

_____

_____

11

E-Verify, IMAGE, and the Social Security Number Verification Service

RELEVANT APPENDIX:

APPENDIX E: E-VERIFY MEMORANDA OF UNDERSTANDING (MOUs)

11.1   What is E-Verify?

E-Verify, originally known as the Basic Pilot Program, is a free Internet-based system that employers may use to confirm the legal status of newly hired employees. The system compares the following to an employee's name and other Form I-9 information to confirm employee matches: Social Security number (SSN) data, information in the U.S. Department of Homeland Security's (DHS) immigration databases, passports, and data from driver's license records in a few states (Arizona, Idaho, Iowa, Florida, Maryland, Mississippi, Nebraska, North Dakota, Wisconsin, and Wyoming). If an employee's information does not match up, U.S. Citizenship and Immigration Services (USCIS) will notify the employer of the tentative nonconfirmation. The average response time in E-Verify is less than one minute.

11.2   How many employees are typically run through E-Verify in one year?

As of October 2016, more than 673,000 employers were using E-Verify. During fiscal year 2016, over 16 million cases were made in the E-Verify system while over 8 million have been made in the first quarter of fiscal year 2017. That number has increased dramatically, as many states plus federal contractors are requiring that E-Verify be used by some or all the states' employers. Just under 99 percent of verification queries are verified within 24 hours.

11.3   Who administers E-Verify?

E-Verify, a partnership of the U.S. Department of Homeland Security (DHS) and the Social Security Administration (SSA), is administered by U.S. Citizenship and Immigration Services (USCIS).

11.4   How does E-Verify work?

Employers submit information provided on an employee's Form I-9 to the E-Verify website. The E-Verify system will return one of four results:

1. "Employment authorized": The employee is employment authorized.

2. "SSA Tentative Nonconfirmation" (TNC): The employee's name and Social Security number (SSN), as listed on the Form I-9, do not match the records in the Social Security Administration (SSA) database.

3. "DHS Tentative Nonconfirmation" (TNC): The employee's name on the Form I-9 does not match the name listed in the U.S. Department of Homeland Security (DHS) database.

4. "DHS Verification in Process": DHS will usually respond within 24 hours, though it may be up to three federal government workdays, with a reply of "Employment Authorized," "DHS Case in Continuance," or "DHS Tentative Nonconfirmation."

If an employee shows up as "employment authorized," the employer will attach the E-Verify authorization document to the employee's Form I-9 or record the system-generated verification number on the Form I-9. In the author's opinion, the best practice is to attach the authorization document to the Form I-9.

If an employer receives a tentative nonconfirmation (TNC) response, the employer must promptly provide the employee with information about how to challenge the TNC, and the employee can then contest the determination and resolve the matter with the Social Security Administration (SSA) or the U.S. Department of Homeland Security (DHS). The document is called a "Further Action Notice" (FAN), and if the employee provided his or her e-mail address on Form I-9, U.S. Citizenship and Immigration Services will provide the FAN to the employee by e-mail.) The employee will have eight federal government workdays to contact the SSA or DHS to resolve the issue. The employer may not terminate, suspend, or take any other adverse employment action against the employee for the TNC while the matter is being contested, unless the employer obtains independent information of an employee's unauthorized status. If the employee contests the TNC, the SSA or DHS has 8 federal government workdays from the employer's referral to resolve the matter unless the SSA or DHS determines it needs additional time.

If the employee does not contest the finding, the determination is considered final, and the employer should terminate the employee and resolve the case.

Employers are required to post a notice in an area visible to prospective employees that the company is an E-Verify participant.

And the employer must post an anti-discrimination notice issued by the Immigrant and Employee Rights Section (IER) of the Civil Rights Division of the Department of Justice (formerly known as Office of Special Counsel for Immigration-Related Unfair Employment Practices (OSC)) in an area visible to prospective employees. These posters must be posted in at least two languages, English and Spanish. If applications for employment are taken online, these posters must be on the website where the application process occurs or with the online application. These posters are invaluable tools to deter undocumented individuals from applying for employment.

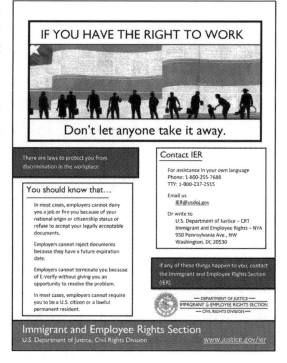

11.5   How does E-Verify handle H-1B portability cases?

According to an advisory e-mail, E-Verify does not check who the employer sponsor is, and the new employer can use the employee's Form I-94 information from the previous employer in an H-1B portability situation.

11.6   What computer requirements are necessary to use E-Verify?

Users need an Internet-capable computer and a Web browser (Internet Explorer 6.0, Firefox 3.0, Chrome 7.0, or Safari 4.0, or the latest version of each).

11.7   Can a company batch-load data to E-Verify?

Yes. The U.S. Department of Homeland Security (DHS) has a real-time batch method requiring that a company develop an interface between its personal system or electronic Form I-9 system and the E-Verify database. Employers interested in more information about this process, including design specifications, should call 800-741-5023.

11.8   What is the required timetable for using E-Verify?

An employer can complete E-Verify any time after an offer of employment is accepted and after the Form I-9 is completed. This can be before the start date (as long as an employer is not prescreening applicants), but in no case later than three business days after the new employee's actual start date. If the employee does not have a Social Security number (SSN), the employer should wait until the number is available (see Question 11.12 regarding employees without SSNs). A query may be submitted before the actual start date, but the employer needs to be careful not to prescreen applicants and may not delay training or an actual start date based on a tentative nonconfirmation; the employee may not face adverse consequences as a result of the employer's use of E-Verify unless a query results in a nonconfirmation. The employer cannot accelerate a start date for an employee because employment authorization is confirmed. Employers must always be consistent in the timing of a query to avoid discrimination.

11.9   Does E-Verify tell an employer anything about the immigration status of a new hire?

No. The system only verifies an employee's authorization to work and not his or her immigration status.

11.10 What is E-Verify's photo-matching tool?

The E-Verify photo tool enables matching of an employee's photo to the photo that U.S. Citizenship and Immigration Services (USCIS) has on file for that employee. The photo to be used could be on an employee's Employment Authorization Document (EAD), a permanent-resident card (green card), U.S. passport, or U.S. passport card. The E-Verify photo tool enables detection of instances of document fraud.

The photo-matching step happens automatically when an employer creates a case for an employee who has presented a U.S. passport, U.S. passport card, permanent-resident card, or an EAD for Form I-9 completion. When the employee presents one of these documents, employers must copy the document and retain it with the employee's Form I-9. If the employee's Form I-9 information matches records available to the U.S. Department of Homeland Security (DHS), E-Verify displays the employee's photo from the document presented.

The E-Verify process will then ask if the photos match. The employer answers yes—the photo on the employee's actual document or a copy matches the photo displayed by E-Verify—or no—the photo on the employee's actual document or a copy does not match the photo displayed in E-Verify.

After a selection is made, one of the following case results will appear:

- "Employment authorized."
- "DHS Tentative Nonconfirmation" (TNC).
- "SSA Tentative Nonconfirmation" (TNC).

11.11 What information does an employer need to supply for each employee?

After an employee completes a Form I-9 (see Appendix A), the employer must submit a query that includes:

- The employee's name and date of birth.
- The Social Security number (SSN).
- The status the employee attests to.
- An "Alien" or "Admission number" or Form I-94 number, if applicable.
- The type of document provided on the Form I-9 to establish work authorization status.
- Proof of identity and its expiration date, if applicable.

11.12 What about employees who do not have Social Security numbers yet?

E-Verify cannot be used for employees who do not yet have Social Security numbers (SSNs). The Form I-9 still needs to be completed, and after the SSN is received, the query needs to be filed with E-Verify. If an employee otherwise meets the requirements to begin work without the SSN, the employee should be permitted to work until the SSN is received and the employee has received a negative response from the U.S. Department of Homeland Security (DHS) on the name check.

11.13 What happens if E-Verify issues a Social Security Administration or a U.S. Department of Homeland Security tentative nonconfirmation finding?

Social Security Administration

If the employer receives a tentative nonconfirmation (TNC) from the Social Security Administration (SSA), the employer must print out the "Further Action Notice" (FAN) and provide it to the employee, so the employee can decide whether to contest the finding. (Additionally, if the employee provided his or her e-mail address on the Form I-9, U.S. Citizenship and Immigration Services will notify the employee by e-mail of the TNC.) If the employer erred in the data input, the employer should attempt to refile with E-Verify.

The employer must then record the case verification number, review the data input in the system to make sure there was no error, and confirm whether the employee will contest.

If the employee wants to contest the TNC, E-Verify will provide the employer with a FAN, concerning referring employees to SSA field offices. The employer shall provide the FAN to the employee with instructions that the employee must seek to resolve the matter within eight federal government workdays.

After eight federal government workdays from the referral, the employer will re-query E-Verify to obtain a confirmation or a final nonconfirmation, unless the SSA instructs otherwise.

U.S. Department of Homeland Security

If the employer receives a tentative nonconfirmation (TNC) from the U.S. Department of Homeland Security (DHS), the employer must print out the "Further Action Notice" (FAN) and provide it to the employee, so the employee can decide whether to contest the finding. (Additionally, if the employee provided his or her e-mail address on the Form I-9, U.S. Citizenship and Immigration Services will notify the employee by e-mail of the TNC.) If the employer erred in the data input, the employer should attempt to refile with E-Verify.

If the employee wants to contest the TNC, the employer will print out the FAN, and the employee must phone DHS within eight federal government workdays to attempt to resolve. DHS will provide the results within eight federal government workdays of the referral unless it determines it needs more time.

11.14 Can employers selectively choose which employees are verified in the electronic system?

No. Employers must verify *all* newly hired employees, including both U.S. citizens and noncitizens. Employers may not choose which employees are put through the verification system.

11.15 Can an employer prescreen job applicants through E-Verify?

No. The employer needs to be careful not to prescreen applicants and may not delay training or an actual start date based on a tentative nonconfirmation, and employees may not face adverse consequences as a result of the use of E-Verify unless a query results in a nonconfirmation. An employer cannot accelerate a start date for an employee because employment authorization is confirmed. Employers must always be consistent in the timing of a query to avoid discrimination.

11.16 Is E-Verify voluntary?

For most employers, E-Verify is voluntary. However, some states require E-Verify for all employers. Others limit the requirement to state agencies and employers with state or local government contracts. (A full discussion of state laws is included in Chapter 16.)

Furthermore, all companies that contract with the federal government on contracts of $150,000 or greater, and subcontractors on those related contracts that are $3,000 or greater, must use E-Verify (called FAR E-Verify for federal contractors) to verify work authorization of all new hires and all employees (existing and new) assigned to the contract. Additionally, a contractor or subcontractor using FAR E-Verify may opt to verify the work authorization on all employees, regardless of whether they are assigned to the contract or length of employment.

11.17 What if a company does not have a computer or Internet access? Can a third-party agent be used to manage E-Verify filings?

Employers can outsource to a third-party agent the ability to submit employment eligibility verification queries. E-Verify–designated agents must register online and sign one or two memoranda of understanding (MOU)—E-Verify

Employer Agents or Web Services E-Verify Employer Agents; agents may represent multiple clients. Employers still need to separately register and complete an MOU, and they will have a unique client number. Designated agents can track their client's reporting, billing, and compliance. Attached as Appendix E is the MOU for E-Verify Employer Agents.

11.18 What is an E-Verify corporate administrator?

An employer can designate an employee as a corporate administrator who has management authority over an employer's hiring sites participating in E-Verify. This person generally would not conduct the actual inquiries, but after registering, would be able to register company sites, add and delete users at company sites, and view reports generated by company sites.

11.19 How does an employer sign up for E-Verify?

To participate in E-Verify, an employer must register online at the U.S. Department of Homeland Security (DHS) E-Verify page and accept the applicable electronic memorandum of understanding (MOU) that details the responsibilities of the Social Security Administration (SSA), DHS, and the employer. There are six different MOUs, which vary depending on whether an employer or employer agent is using E-Verify and the access method for E-Verify. Attached as Appendix E are three MOUs — one for an employer, one for an employer agent, and the MOU for the E-Verify Program for Employment Verification.

The remaining four MOUs can be found online at https://www.uscis.gov/e-verify/publications/memos/publications-memorandums.

The enrollment page for E-Verify is at www.uscis.gov/e-verify/e-verify-enrollment-page.

11.20 What are the government's obligations with regard to privacy and data security?

In the memorandum of understanding (MOU), the Social Security Administration (SSA) agrees to safeguard the information provided by an employer and limit access to individuals responsible for the verification of Social Security numbers (SSNs) and for the evaluation of E-Verify. The U.S. Department of Homeland Security (DHS) agrees to safeguard the information provided by the employer and to limit access to individuals responsible for the verification of alien employment eligibility and for the evaluation of E-Verify. Information can be used only to verify the accuracy of SSNs and employment eligibility, to enforce the Immigration and Nationality Act (INA) and federal criminal laws, and to ensure accurate wage reports to the SSA.

11.21 What are the employer's obligations under the memorandum of understanding?

The employer must agree to the following:

- Display the two notices supplied by the U.S. Department of Homeland Security (DHS).

- Provide DHS with the names and contact information for the employer representatives responsible for E-Verify.

- Comply with the most recent E-Verify manual.

- Ensure that any employer representative takes the E-Verify tutorial before attempting to file an E-Verify case and takes refresher tutorials when requested to do so.

- Comply with Form I-9 rules except that List B documents proving identity must have a photograph; also, if an employee presents a U.S. passport or U.S. passport card, a Form I-551 permanent-resident card, or a Form I-766 Employment Authorization Document (EAD), the employer must keep a copy of the document.

- Print the screenshot with the case verification number and attach it to the employee's Form I-9, or record the case verification number on the Form I-9.

- Notify U.S. Department of Homeland Security (DHS) of any employee the employer continues to employ after a final nonconfirmation. (The employer is liable for fines of between $763 and $1,527 for each failure.)

- Not use E-Verify to engage in pre-employment screening or to support any unlawful employment practice.

- Not use E-Verify to selectively check only some employees as opposed to all new hires.

- Not use E-Verify to re-verify employees with Forms I-9 requiring re-verification or run existing employees through E-Verify.

- Follow the rules with respect to dealing with tentative nonconfirmations.

- Not to terminate or take any adverse employment action against an employee until a final nonconfirmation is received from DHS unless an employer gains actual knowledge that an employee is not work-eligible.

- Comply with the Section 274B anti-discrimination rules of the Immigration and Nationality Act (INA).

- Safeguard the information provided to and received from E-Verify under subject of criminal penalties and notify DHS of any security breaches to E-Verify personal data.

- Permit DHS and the Social Security Administration (SSA) to make periodic visits to the employer for the purpose of reviewing E-Verify records.

11.22 Can a large employer have a controlled rollout of E-Verify instead of including every location? Can a large employer change the sites participating?

Yes. An employer with multiple sites has flexibility. The employer can have one of its sites verify new hires at all of its sites, or it can have each site perform its own verification inquiries. Whether one site or multiple sites are handling queries, each site must sign a separate memorandum of understanding (MOU), although a single MOU may be used by employers with more than 1,000 employees and multiple sites. Employers with multiple sites should select "multiple site registration" and give the number of sites per state it will be verifying. An employer also can choose to include only some of its sites and can control the rollout of E-Verify across an organization. However, at each worksite, all new hires for that site must be verified.

11.23 What are the benefits of participating?

Employers are presumed not to have violated the employer sanctions rules in the Immigration and Nationality Act (INA) Section 274A with respect to the hiring of any individual if it obtains confirmation of the identity and employment eligibility in compliance with the terms and conditions of E-Verify. The U.S. Department of Homeland Security (DHS) does not consider using E-Verify to provide a "safe harbor" from worksite enforcement. However, some states, such as Tennessee, do consider the use of E-Verify to be a "safe harbor" from violation of the state's own law. A violation of this state law can lead to the revocation of a business license for an employer knowingly hiring unauthorized immigrants.

Additionally, the use of E-Verify removes some of the burden of determining whether an employee's documents are genuine. Finally, E-Verify should reduce the number of undocumented workers employed by an employer because it does a much better job of detecting fraudulent work-authorization documents.

11.24 Are there risks associated with participating in E-Verify?

An employer will have a rebuttable presumption that it knowingly employs someone ineligible to work if it continues to employ someone after receiving a final nonconfirmation through E-Verify. If an employer believes E-Verify is incorrect, the employer will have a strong incentive to terminate an employee, given that an employer acting in good faith on information received from E-Verify is immunized from civil and criminal liability.

Employers must agree to permit U.S. Department of Homeland Security (DHS) and Social Security Administration (SSA) officials to visit their worksites to review E-Verify records and other employment records related to E-Verify. And DHS and SSA may interview an employer's authorized agents or designees regarding the employer's experience with E-Verify for the purpose of evaluating E-Verify.

Around 2013, the Monitoring and Compliance branch of U.S. Citizenship and Immigration Services (USCIS) began making a number of referrals to the U.S. Department of Justice's Immigrant and Employee Rights Section to investigate potential discrimination. It has done so based on the improper use of Form I-9, determined through E-Verify activity data.

11.25 Can an employer verify existing employees as well as new hires?

No. E-Verify may not be used retroactively to go back and check employees hired before the company signed the memorandum of understanding (MOU) or to re-verify employees who have temporary work authorizations. However, if an employer falls under Federal Acquisition Regulation (FAR) E-Verify, it must verify existing employees working on the federal project, as well as new hires, and may opt to verify all existing employees and new hires.

11.26 Can an employer quit using E-Verify?

Yes, an employer may stop using E-Verify, assuming state or Federal Acquisition Regulation (FAR) E-Verify law does not require its use.

Employers that have "buyer's remorse" and choose to stop using E-Verify must continue using the program for 30 days after giving written notice to U.S. Citizenship and Immigration Services (USCIS) that it wants to stop using the system.

11.27 Is an employer protected from an investigation if it uses E-Verify?

No. Worksite enforcement is still permitted, but an employer using E-Verify is presumed not to have knowingly hired unauthorized workers.

11.28 What can employees do when they feel they have been subject to discrimination?

Employees who think they have been subject to discrimination because of their national origin, citizenship, or immigration status with respect to hiring, firing, recruitment, or referral for a fee through an employer's use of E-Verify, or when completing I-9 forms should contact the U.S. Department of Justice's Immigrant and Employee Rights Section at the telephone number, 1-800-255-7688, or online at www.justice.gov/crt/immigrant-and-employee-rights-section.

Employers may not take any adverse action against an employee because the employee contests a tentative nonconfirmation (TNC). Adverse actions include firing, suspending, withholding pay or training, or otherwise infringing on the employee's employment.

11.29 Which states require E-Verify?

A complete list of states that require E-Verify for all or some of a state's employers can be found in Chapter 16.

11.30 How reliable is E-Verify in accurately identifying unauthorized employees?

The statistics published by U.S. Citizenship and Immigration Services (USCIS) as of September 2016 are as follows:

- 98.92 percent of employees are automatically confirmed as authorized to work ("work authorized") either instantly or within 24 hours, requiring no employee or employer action.

- 1.08 percent of employees receive initial system mismatches:
    - 0.16 percent of employees are confirmed as work authorized after contesting and resolving the mismatch.
    - 0.92 percent of employees are not confirmed as work authorized.

- Of the 0.92 percent of employees not confirmed as work authorized:
    - 0.61 percent of employees receive initial mismatches and do not contest the mismatch, either because they choose not to or are unaware they can contest. As a result, they are not found work authorized.
    - .01 percent of employees receive and contest initial mismatches and are not found work authorized.
    - 0.30 percent of employees receive initial mismatches that remain unresolved because employees closed the cases as "self-terminated" or as "requiring further action" by either the employer or employee.

11.31 How do federal contractors know of the necessity of using FAR E-Verify?

The contract between the contractor and the federal government is required to have a Federal Acquisition Regulation (FAR) E-Verify clause.

11.32 How do subcontractors know of the necessity for using FAR E-Verify?

A subcontractor's agreement with the contractor should include a Federal Acquisition Regulation (FAR) E-Verify clause. Even if it does not, it is incumbent upon the subcontractor to determine whether FAR E-Verify applies to the underlying contract.

11.33 Does the receipt of federal grants by a company mean FAR E-Verify applies?

In almost all cases, the answer is no. However, employers should make sure by reviewing the federal grant.

11.34 Can the requirement to include the E-Verify clause in federal contracts be waived?

In exceptional circumstances, the head of the contracting activity at an agency may waive the requirement for Federal Acquisition Regulation (FAR) E-Verify. This authority may not be delegated.

11.35 Are any contracts exempt from FAR E-Verify?

Yes, the following types of contracts do not require inclusion of the Federal Acquisition Regulation (FAR) E-Verify clause:

- Contracts for commercial off-the-shelf (COTS) items as well as items that would be classified as COTS items but for minor modifications.
- Prime contracts that have a value less than $150,000 and subcontracts under those contracts that have a value of less than $3,000.
- Contracts waived based on exceptional circumstances by the head of contracting authority at the agency.
- Contracts that are less than 120 days in duration.
- Contracts for work that will be performed outside the United States (the 50 states, the District of Columbia, Guam, Puerto Rico, and the U.S. Virgin Islands).

11.36 How much time does a federal contractor employer have to start running employees' names through the FAR E-Verify system?

There are a few key timelines to watch in complying with the regulation. For an employer not yet enrolled as a federal contractor in E-Verify:

- An employer has 30 calendar days to enroll as a federal contractor in E-Verify after a contract is awarded.
- Within 90 calendar days of enrollment in E-Verify, the employer must begin verifying employment eligibility for all new hires working in the United States.
- For all employees assigned to the contract, the employer must begin verification within 90 calendar days of enrollment in E-Verify or within

30 calendar days of the employees' assignment to the contract, which-ever date is later.

For an employer already enrolled as a federal contactor in E-Verify when the contract is awarded, the following timelines apply:

- For an employer already enrolled for 90 calendar days or more, the employer must indicate verification of all new hires within three business days after date of hire (except certain universities, state and local government employers, and federally recognized Indian tribes).

- For an employer enrolled for less than 90 calendar days, the employer must initiate verification of all new hires within 90 calendar days after enrollment as a federal contractor.

- For each employee assigned to the contract, the employer must begin verification within 90 calendar days after the date of the contract award or within 30 days after assignment to the contract, whichever date is later. The 90-day clock starts on the date the contract is awarded instead of 90 days from the date of enrollment, as would be the case for employers enrolled less than 90 days when the contract is awarded.

11.37 Which types of employers need to verify only employees assigned to work on the federal contract?

The following types of employers must verify *only* employees assigned to work on the federal contract:

- Institutions of higher education.
- State and local governments.
- Federally recognized Indian tribes.
- Sureties performing under a takeover agreement entered into with a federal agency pursuant to a performance bond.

11.38 Can an employer verify all existing employees under FAR E-Verify as opposed to just employees working on the contract?

Yes. Employers can choose to verify all of its employees in the Federal Acquisition Regulation (FAR) E-Verify. If this option is exercised, the employer must notify the U.S. Department of Homeland Security (DHS) and must initiate verifications for the contractor's entire workforce within 180 days of notice being given to DHS. To notify DHS that the entire workforce will be verified, the employer should update its company profile through the "Maintain Company" page on E-Verify.

11.39 Does a company already enrolled in E-Verify need to re-enroll to comply with FAR E-Verify?

No. However, an employer does need to update its profile on E-Verify's "Maintain Company" page. Once the federal contractor option is selected, employees and employers must take a brief federal contractor tutorial that explains the new policies and features that are unique to contractors. Once the federal contractor option is selected, an employer will not be able to verify new employees until it takes the refresher tutorial.

11.40 What are a company's obligations under FAR E-Verify once the contract is over?

After the contract is over, the company should update its "Maintain Company" page to reflect the revised status. After that, existing employees may not be run through E-Verify. If the company chooses to terminate participation in E-Verify, it can select "request termination" in the E-Verify system.

11.41 How does FAR E-Verify treat commercially available off-the-shelf contracts?

Federal Acquisition Regulation (FAR) E-Verify does not apply to contracts to supply commercially available off-the-shelf (COTS) items.[1] The term "COTS items" applies to items of supply that are commercial items sold in substantial quantities in the commercial marketplace and that are offered to the government, without modification, in the same form in which they are sold in the commercial marketplace. FAR E-Verify also does not apply to contracts to supply bulk cargo such as agricultural products and petroleum products. Contracts for items that would be COTS items but for minor modifications are also not covered. The

---

[1] *See* www.uscis.gov/sites/default/files/USCIS/verification/E-Verify/Federal%20Contractors/e-verify-FAR-presentation.PDF.

preamble to the rule specifically notes that food is an item of supply, so most agricultural suppliers will not be affected by the rule.

Services related to supplying the COTS items that are procured at the same time the COTS items are procured, and supplied by the same employer providing the COTS items, are also not subject to the rule. The services must be typical or normal for the COTS provider.

11.42 Which employees associated with work on a contract must be verified under FAR E-Verify?

Federal Acquisition Regulation (FAR) E-Verify covers employees hired after November 6, 1986, who are directly performing work in the United States under the contract. An employee is not considered to be directly performing work under the contract if the employee:

- Normally performs support work, such as indirect or overhead functions.

- Does not perform any substantial duties applicable to the contract.

The rule exempts employees who hold an active security clearance status of confidential, secret, or top secret: employees for which background investigations have been completed and credentials issued pursuant to the Homeland Security Presidential Directive (HSPD) 12: Policy for a Common Identification Standard for Employees and Contractors, issued August 27, 2004.

11.43 Under FAR E-Verify, how should an employer treat a Form I-9 for an existing employee who is not a current Form I-9?

Employers may use a previously completed Form I-9 as the basis for initiating E-Verify verification of an assigned employee as long as that Form I-9 complies with the E-Verify documentation requirements and the employee's work authorization has not expired, and as long as the employer has reviewed the Form I-9 with the employee to ensure that the employee's stated basis for work authorization has not changed. If the Form I-9 does not comply with the current E-Verify requirements, or if the employee's basis for work authorization has expired or changed, the employer should complete a new Form I-9.

11.44 Are subcontractors also responsible for participating in FAR E-Verify?

Yes. Any subcontractor furnishing commercial or noncommercial services or construction under a prime contract or a subcontract covered by the rule must participate in Federal Acquisition Regulation (FAR) E-Verify. The value of the contract must be more than $3,000, and the work to be performed must be in the United States.

11.45 What is the plain language of the FAR E-Verify regulation?

The following is the language set forth in the Federal Acquisition Regulation (FAR) E-Verify regulation:

> Employment Eligibility Verification
> (a) Definitions. As used in this clause —
> Commercial available off-the-shelf (COTS) item:
> (1) Means any item of supply that is —
> (i) A commercial item (as defined. in paragraph (1) of the definition at 48CFR 2.101);
> (ii) Sold in substantial quantities in the commercial marketplace; and
> (iii) Offered to the Government, without modification, in the same form in which it is sold in the commercial marketplace; and
> (2) Does not include bulk cargo, as defined in section 3 of the Shipping Act of 1984 (46 U.S.C. App. 1702), such as agricultural products and petroleum products. Per 46 C.F.R. Section 525.1 (c)(2), "bulk cargo" means cargo that is loaded and carried in bulk onboard ship without mark or count, in a loose unpackaged form, having homogenous characteristics. Bulk cargo loaded into intermodal equipment, except LASH or Seabee barges, is subject to mark and count and, therefore, ceases to be bulk cargo.
> Employee assigned to the contract means an employee who was hired after November 6, 1986, who is directly performing work, in the United States, under a contract that is required to include the clause prescribed at 22.1803. An employee is not considered to be directly performing work under a contract if the employee —
> (1) Normally performs support work, such as indirect or overhead functions; and
> (2) Does not perform any substantial duties applicable to the contract.
> "Subcontract" means any contract, as defined in of 48 CFR 2.101, entered into by a subcontractor to furnish supplies or services for the performance of a prime contract or a subcontract. It includes purchase orders, and changes and modifications to purchase orders.
> "Subcontractor" means any supplier, distributor, vendor, or firm that furnishes supplies or services to or for a prime Contractor or another subcontractor.

"United States," as defined in 8 U.S.C. Section 1101 (a)(38), means the 50 states, the District of Columbia, Puerto Rico, Guam, and the U.S. Virgin Islands.

(b) Enrollment and reverification requirements. (1) If the contractor is not en-rolled as a Federal Contractor in E-Verify at time of contract reward, the Contractor shall —

(i) Enroll. Enroll as Federal Contractor in the E-Verify program within 30 calen-dar days of contract award;

(ii) Verify all new employees. Within 90 calendar days of enrollment in the E-Verify program, begin to use E-Verify to initiate verification of employment eligi-bility of all new hires of the Contractor, who are working in the United States, whether or not assignment to the contract, within 3 business days after the date of hire (but see paragraph (b)(3) of this section); and

(iii) Verify employees assigned to the contract. For each employee assigned to the contract, initiate verification within 90 calendar days after date of enrollment or with-in 30 calendar days of the employee's assignment to the contract, whichever date is later (but see paragraph (b)(4) of this section)

(2) If the contractor is enrolled as a Federal Contractor in E-Verify at the time of contract award, the Contractor shall use E-Verify to initiate verification of employment eligibility of —

(i) All new employees. (A) Enrolled 90 calendar days or more. The Contractor shall initiate verification of all new hires of the Contractor, who are working in the United States, whether or not assigned to the contract, within 3 business days after the date of hire (but see paragraph (b)(3) of this section); or

(B) Enrolled less than 90 calendar days. Within 90 calendars days after enroll-ment as a Federal Contractor in E-Verify, the Contractor shall initiate verification of all new hires of the Contractor, who are working in the United States, whether or not as-signed to the contract, within 3 business days after the date of hire (but see paragraph (b)(3)of this section); or

(ii) Employees assigned to the contract. For each employee assigned to the contract, the Contractor shall initiate verification within 90 days after the date of contract award or within 30 days after assignment to the contract, whichever date is later (but see paragraph (b)(4) of this section).

(3) If the Contractor is an institution of higher education (as defined at 20 U.S.C. 1001(a)); a State or local government of a federally recognized Indian tribe; or a surety performing under a takeover agreement entered into with a federal agency pur-suant to a performance bond, the Contractor may choose to verify only employees as-signed to the contract, whether existing employees or new hires. The Contractor shall follow the applicable verification requirements at (b)(1) or (b)(2) respectively, except that any requirements for verification of new employees applies only to new employees as-signed to the contract.

(4) Option to verify employment eligibility of all employees. The Contractor may elect to verify all existing employees hired after November 6, 1986, rather than just those employees assigned to the contract. The Contractor shall initiate verification for each existing employee working in the United States who was hired after November 6, 1986, within 180 calendar days of —

(i) Enrollment in the E-Verify program; or

(ii) Notification to E-Verify Operations of the Contractor's decision to exercise this option, using the contact information provided in the E-Verify program Memorandum of Understanding (MOU).

(5) The Contractor shall comply, for the period of performance if this contract, with the requirements of the E-Verify program MOU.

(i) The Department of Homeland Security (DHS) or the Social Security Administration (SSA) may terminate the Contractor's MOU and deny access to the E-Verify system in accordance with the terms of the MOU. In such case, the Contractor will be referred to a suspension or debarment official.

(ii) During the period between termination of the MOU and a decision by the suspension or debarment official whether to suspend or debar, the Contractor is excused from its obligations under paragraph (b) of this clause. If a suspension or debarment official determines not to suspend or debar the Contractor, then the Contractor must re-enroll in E-Verify.

(c) Website. Information or registration for and use of the E-Verify program can be obtained via the Internet at the Department of Homeland Security website: www.dhs.gov/E-Verify.

(d) Individuals previously verified. The Contractor is not required by this clause to perform additional employment verification using E-Verify for any employee:

(1) Whose employment eligibility was previously verified by the Contractor through the E-Verify program;

(2) Who has been granted and holds an active U.S. government security clearance for access to confidential, secret, or top secret information in accordance with the National Industrial Security Program Operating Manual; or

(3) Who has undergone a completed background investigation and been issued credentials pursuant to Homeland Security Presidential Directive (HSPD) 12: Policy for a Common Identification Standard for Federal Employees and Contractors.

(e) Subcontracts. The Contractor shall include the requirements of this clause, including this paragraph (e) (approximately modified for identification of the parties), in each subcontract that —

(1) Is for — (i) Commercial or noncommercial services (except for commercial services that are part of the purchase of a COTS item (or an item that would be a COTS item, but for minor modifications), performed by the COTS provider, and are normally provided for that COTS item); or

(ii) Construction;

(2) Has a value of more than $3000; and

(3) Includes work performed in the United States.

11.46 What is the ICE Mutual Agreement between Government and Employers (IMAGE)?

U.S. Immigration and Customs Enforcement's (ICE) Mutual Agreement between Government and Employers (IMAGE) is a joint government and private-sector initiative designed to "combat unlawful employment and reduce vulnerabilities that help illegal aliens gain such employment."[2] The initiative is basically designed to improve employer self-compliance.

Under the IMAGE program, employers receive education and training from ICE on proper hiring procedures, fraudulent document detection, use of E-Verify, and anti-discrimination procedures. To participate in IMAGE, employers must submit to a Form I-9 audit by ICE and verify all their employees through E-Verify.

After completing the program, an employer will be deemed "IMAGE Certified." ICE believes that this will become an industry standard.

11.47 Will participating in IMAGE guarantee that an employer will not be found liable in an enforcement action?

No. However, U.S. Immigration and Customs Enforcement (ICE) does waive potential fines if substantive violations are discovered on less than 50 percent of the required Forms I-9; and if over 50 percent of the Forms I-9 are in violation, it will mitigate the fines to the statutory minimum of $110 per violation. Furthermore, an ICE official stated it has waived fines even if the employer has more than 50 percent of the Forms I-9 in violation.

11.48 What obligations do IMAGE participants face?

All U.S. Immigration and Customs Enforcement (ICE) Mutual Agreement between Government and Employers (IMAGE) participants must meet the following requirements:

- Enroll and participate in the E-Verify program within 60 days.

- Establish a written hiring and employment eligibility verification policy that includes internal Form I-9 audits at least once per year.

---

[2] *See* www.ice.gov/image.

- Submit to a Form I-9 inspection by ICE (but the employer will not be subject to another inspection for two years.).

11.49 Does the IMAGE program offer best employment practices?

Yes. The best employment practices for the U.S. Immigration and Customs Enforcement (ICE) Mutual Agreement between Government and Employers (IMAGE) program include the following:

- Participate in E-Verify to verify the employment eligibility of all new hires.

- Use the Social Security Number Verification Service (SSNVS) for wage reporting purposes. Verify the names and Social Security numbers (SSNs) of the current workforce, and work with employees to resolve any discrepancies.

- Establish an internal compliance and training program covering Form I-9 compliance, detecting fraudulent identity documents and using E-Verify and SSNVS.

- Ensure that only trained employees complete the Form I-9 and use E-Verify.

- Establish a secondary review process to ensure that one person cannot subvert the process.

- Establish a written hiring and employment eligibility verification policy.

- Conduct an annual internal Form I-9 audit.

- Establish self-reporting procedures to inform U.S. Immigration and Customs Enforcement (ICE) of violations or deficiencies.

- Set protocols for responding to no-match letters.

- Establish a tip line for employees to report activity that relates to the employment of unauthorized workers and create a protocol for responding to credible employee tips.

- Report immediately to ICE the discovery of credible information of suspected criminal misconduct in the employment eligibility verification process.

- Ensure that contractors and subcontractors establish procedures to comply with employment eligibility verification requirements. Encourage contractors and subcontractors to incorporate IMAGE best practices, and, when practicable, incorporate the use of E-Verify in subcontractor agreements.

- Establish and maintain appropriate policies, practices, and safeguards to ensure that authorized workers are not treated differently with respect to hiring, firing, or recruitment. Further, ensure equal treatment during referral for a fee or during the Form I-9, E-Verify, or SSNVS processes based on citizenship status or national origin.

- Maintain copies of any documents accepted as proof of identity and employment authorization with the Form I-9 for all new hires.

11.50 What is the Social Security Number Verification Service (SSNVS)?

The Social Security Number Verification Service (SSNVS) was created in 2006 by the Social Security Administration (SSA) to allow employers to verify SSNs via a website. It is a free service available to any employer.

SSNVS can be used by employers and payroll services to verify only that a Social Security number (SSN) matches a particular name and only for the purpose of completing a Form W-2. SSNVS will not tell employers whether an employee is authorized to work in the United States.

Employers can verify up to 10 names at a time and receive results instantly. They also can upload files with up to 250,000 names and obtain a response in one business day.

The SSA has posted a detailed tutorial on using SSNVS online at www.ssa.gov/employer/SSNVS.pdf.

11.51 What restrictions are placed on employers seeking to use the SSNVS?

The following restrictions are placed on employers' use of the Social Security Number Verification Service (SSNVS):

- Employers cannot use the system to prescreen applicants.

- Employers cannot use the system by itself to take punitive actions against an employee whose name does not match.

- Employers must establish policies that are applied consistently to all employees.

- Privacy must be protected by ensuring that third-party use of the SSNVS is limited to organizations that handle annual wage reporting responsibilities under contract to the employer.

- The SSNVS should not be used by third-party companies that conduct identity verification, background checks, or nonwage reporting purposes.

11.52 What special E-Verify rules apply to student visa holders?

In April 2008, U.S. Citizenship and Immigration Services (USCIS) released a new rule allowing for certain F-1 students to acquire an additional 17 months of optional practical training (OPT) on top of the currently available 12 months, if an employer participates in E-Verify. This benefit is seen as highly useful given the extreme demand for H-1B visas. Eligible students will now have additional opportunities to try for success in the annual H-1B lottery.

> In March 2016, USCIS promulgated a new rule lengthening the STEM OPT extension to 24 months. However, under the new rule, there are some additional requirements, including the employer implementing a formal training program to augment the student's academic learning and completing a Form I-983 Training Plan for STEM OPT students.

F-1 students—students who have degrees in science, technology, engineering, or mathematics (STEM) and who are already in a period of approved post-completion OPT—can apply to extend that period by up to 24 months (for a total of 29 months of OPT) if the student has accepted employment with an employer registered and in good standing with E-Verify.

Students already working for an employer need not be run through E-Verify because the system is only for new employees. Also, U.S. Citizenship and Immigration Services (USCIS) currently takes the position that the location where the student is working must be using E-Verify.

USCIS also takes the position that all employers employing students under the curricular practical training (CPT) program must use E-Verify for CPT students. According to USCIS, because E-Verify cannot automatically check a student's Form I-20 to produce an automatic confirmation of employment eligibility, students under CPT will be sent to secondary verification. But employment eligibility should still be confirmed within 24 hours, provided the student's record can be located within the Student Exchange Visitor Information System (SEVIS).

11.53 What do the U.S. Department of Homeland Security E-Verify Memoranda of Understanding state?

See Appendix E for three of the six E-Verify Memoranda of Understanding (MOUs). The remaining MOUs can be found at https://www.uscis.gov/e-verify/publications/memos/publications-memorandums.

12

SOCIAL SECURITY NO-MATCH LETTERS

In August 2007, a long-awaited, no-match letter regulation from U.S. Immigration and Customs Enforcement (ICE) was released. Quickly challenged in court, the regulation was barred from taking effect by a federal district court. Eventually, in 2009, the U.S. Department of Homeland Security (DHS) rescinded the regulation. Furthermore, the Social Security Administration (SSA) stopped sending no-match letters until April 6, 2011. However, these no-match letters were not under the 2007 regulation; thus, failure to act on the letter was not constructive knowledge. These no-match letters from the SSA were short-lived as they were discontinued on August 29, 2011, for budgetary reasons and have not resumed to date.

The rescinded regulation described the obligations of employers when they receive no-match letters from the SSA or receive a letter regarding employment verification forms from DHS. The regulation also provided "safe harbors" that employers could follow to avoid a finding that the employer had constructive knowledge that an employee referred to in the letter was an alien not authorized to work in the United States. Employers with knowledge that an immigrant worker is unauthorized to accept employment are liable for both civil and criminal penalties.

Though the regulation is *not* in effect, many immigration law compliance attorneys expect that a no-match regulation eventually will come into force and that it will resemble the regulation as originally released. Therefore, this chapter is included to educate readers on what to expect if and when DHS succeeds in its efforts.

12.1   Why did the court block the regulation from taking effect?

The regulation was challenged in court prior to it taking effect, and a judge issued a preliminary injunction on three grounds:

- The U.S. Department of Homeland Security (DHS) failed to supply a reasoned analysis justifying what the court thought was a change in the DHS position, that is, that a no-match letter may be sufficient, by itself, to put an employer on notice that its employees may not be work authorized.

- DHS exceeded its authority (and encroached on the authority of the U.S. Department of Justice) by interpreting anti-discrimination provisions of the Immigration Reform and Control Act (IRCA).

- DHS violated the Regulatory Flexibility Act (RFA) by not conducting a regulatory flexibility analysis.

12.2   Why did U.S. Immigration and Customs Enforcement issue this regulation?

All employers in the United States are required to report Social Security earnings for their workers. Those Form W-2 reports listing an employee's name, Social Security number (SSN), and the worker's earnings are sent to the Social Security Administration (SSA). In some cases, the SSN and the name of the employee do not match. In some of these cases, the SSA sends an employer a letter informing the employer of the no-match.

In some cases, the no-match is the result of a clerical error or a name change. In other cases, it may indicate that an employee is not authorized to work.

U.S. Immigration and Customs Enforcement (ICE) issues similar letters to employers after it conducts audits of an employer's employment eligibility verification forms (Forms I-9) and finds evidence that an immigration status document or employment authorization document does not match the name of the person on the Form I-9.

There had been considerable confusion and debate over an employer's obligations after receiving a letter like this as well as whether an employer would be considered to be on notice that an employee is not authorized to work. This regulation attempted to clarify both issues, albeit in a way that is unfriendly to employers and workers.

The U.S. Department of Homeland Security (DHS) cited *Mester Manufacturing Company v. U.S. Immigration & Naturalization Service*, 900 F.2d 201 (9th Cir. 1990) to remind employers that if they have "constructive" knowledge that an employee is out of status, they are in violation of the Immigration Reform and Control Act (IRCA), the statute that punishes employers for knowingly hiring unlawfully present workers or for violating paperwork rules associated with the Form I-9 employment verification form.

12.3   How was the definition of "knowing" going to change in the regulation?

Two additional examples of "constructive knowledge" were added to the list of examples of information available to employers indicating an employee is not authorized to work in the United States. First, an employer receives a written notice from the Social Security Administration (SSA) that the name and the Social Security number (SSN) do not match SSA records. And second, an employer receives written notice from the U.S. Department of Homeland Security (DHS) that the immigration document presented in completing the Form I-9 was assigned to another person or that there is no agency record that the document was assigned to anyone.

However, the question of whether an employer has "constructive knowledge" will "depend on the totality of relevant circumstances."[1] So the proposed regulation was just a "safe harbor" regulation telling how an employer can avoid a constructive knowledge finding, but not guaranteeing that an employer will be deemed to have constructive knowledge if the "safe harbor" procedure is not followed.

12.4   What steps should an employer take if it receives a no-match letter?

First, an employer should check its records to determine if the error was a result of a typographical, transcription, or similar clerical mistake. If there is an error, the employer should correct it and inform the appropriate agency—either the U.S. Department of Homeland Security (DHS) or the Social Security Admin-

---

[1] Code of Federal Regulations, Title 8, section 274a.1(j).

istration (SSA), depending on which agency sent the no-match letter. The employer should then verify with that agency that the new number is correct and internally document the manner, date, and time of the verification. U.S. Immigration and Customs Enforcement (ICE) indicated in the preamble to the regulation that 30 days is an appropriate amount of time for an employer to take these steps.

If these actions do not resolve the discrepancy, the employer should request that an employee confirm the employer's records are correct. If they are not correct, the employer needs to take corrective actions, which would include informing the relevant agency and verifying the corrected records with the agency. If the records are correct according to the employee, the reasonable employer should ask the employee to follow-up with the relevant agency (such as by visiting an SSA office and taking original or certified copies of required identity documents). Thirty days is a reasonable period of time for an employer to take this step.

> The regulation provided that a discrepancy is only resolved when the employer has received verification from the U.S. Department of Homeland Security (DHS) or the Social Security Administration (SSA) that the employee's name matches the record.

When 90 days have passed without a resolution of the discrepancy, an employer should undertake a procedure to verify the employee's identity and work authorization. If the process is completed, an employer will not be deemed to have constructive knowledge that an employee is work unauthorized if the system verifies the employee (even if the employee turns out *not* to be work authorized). This assumes that an employer does not otherwise have actual or constructive knowledge that an employee is not work authorized.

Under the proposed regulation, if the discrepancy is not resolved and the employee's identity and work authorization are not verified, the employer must either terminate the employee or risk DHS finding the employer had constructive knowledge of the employee's lack of employment authorization.

12.5 What is the procedure to re-verify identity and employment authorization when an employee has not resolved the discrepancy as described above in 12.4?

Sections 1 and 2 of the Form I-9 would need to be completed within 93 days of receiving the no-match letter. So if an employer took the full 90 days to try to resolve the problem, the employer would then have three more days to complete the new Form I-9. And an employee may not use a document containing the disputed Social Security number (SSN), the "Alien number", or a receipt for a replacement of such a document. Only documents with a photograph may be used to establish identity.

12.6 Does an employer need to use the same procedure to verify employment authorization for each employee who is the subject of a no-match letter?

Yes, the anti-discrimination rules require the employer to apply these procedures uniformly. The U.S. Department of Homeland Security (DHS) also reminds employers about the document abuse provisions that bar employers from failing to honor documents that, on their face, appear reasonable. But employers, under the proposed regulation, have the "safe harbor" stating that this provision does not apply to documents that are the subject of a no-match letter.

DHS notes that if employers require employees to complete a new Form I-9, the employer must not apply this requirement discriminatorily. It should require a Form I-9 verification for all employees who fail to resolve the Social Security Administration (SSA) discrepancies and apply a uniform policy to all employees who refuse to participate in resolving discrepancies and in completing new Forms I-9. Employees hired before November 6, 1986, are not subject to this rule.

12.7   What if the employer has learned that an employee is unlawfully present from some source other than the Social Security Administration or the U.S. Department of Homeland Security?

Employers with *actual* knowledge that an alien is unauthorized to work are liable under the Immigration and Nationality Act (INA) even if they have complied with the Form I-9 and no-match regulations. But the government has the burden of proving actual knowledge. The U.S. Department of Homeland Security (DHS) also notes that constructive knowledge still may be shown by reference to other evidence.

12.8   Will following the procedures in this proposed regulation protect an employer from all claims of constructive knowledge, or just claims of constructive knowledge based on the letters for which the employer followed the "safe harbor" procedure?

An employer that follows the "safe harbor" procedure will be considered to have taken all reasonable steps in response to the notice, and the employer's receipt of the written notice will not be used as evidence of constructive knowledge. But if other independent evidence exists that an employer had constructive knowledge, the employer is not protected.

12.9   What were the timeframes required under the regulation to take each necessary action after receiving the no-match letter?

The timeframes were as follows:

- The employer checks its own records, makes any necessary corrections of errors, and verifies corrections with the Social Security Administration (SSA) or the U.S. Department of Homeland Security (DHS) *(0–30 days)*.

- If necessary, the employer notifies the employee and asks him or her to assist in the correction *(0–90 days)*. (*Note that under the March 2008 proposed regulation, employers would have five days to notify employees of the no-match if the employer conducts its internal review.)*

- If necessary, the employer corrects its own records and verifies the correction with the SSA or DHS *(0–90 days)*.

- If necessary, the employer performs a special Form I-9 procedure *(90–93 days)*.

12.10 May an employer continue to employ a worker throughout the process noted above in Questions 12.4 to 12.8?

Yes. The only reason an employer would have to terminate prior to 93 days would be if the employer gained actual knowledge of unauthorized employment. The U.S. Department of Homeland Security (DHS) notes that it does not require termination by virtue of this regulation; rather, it is just providing a "safe harbor" to avoid a finding of constructive knowledge. Employers may be permitted to terminate based on information in their own personnel files, including an employee's failure to show up for work or an employee's false statement to the employer. Employers are advised to consult employment and immigration compliance counsel before terminating employees for such reasons during the no-match process.

Employers also may terminate if they notify an employee of the no-match letter and the employee admits that he or she is unauthorized to work.

12.11 Does it matter which person at the place of employment receives the no-match letter?

No. The U.S. Department of Homeland Security (DHS) will not allow an employer to designate a specific person to receive no-match letters, despite concerns raised about a no-match letter not making it to the appropriate party. DHS has noted that an employer can designate an office within a company to be the recipient of all mail from DHS and the Social Security Administration (SSA).

12.12 Does verification through systems other than those described in this proposed regulation provide a "safe harbor"?

No, and this includes instances in which the Social Security Administration (SSA) provides options for Social Security number (SSN) verification in addition to E-Verify. But the U.S. Department of Homeland Security (DHS) notes that it may choose to use prosecutorial discretion when employers take such steps.

12.13 Does an employer have to help an employee resolve the discrepancy with the Social Security Administration or the U.S. Department of Homeland Security?

No. An employer merely needs to advise the employee of the timeframe to resolve the discrepancy. Employers are not obligated to help resolve the question or share any guidance provided by the Social Security Administration (SSA).

12.14 If a new Form I-9 is prepared based on this regulation, does that affect the amount of time the Form I-9 must be retained?

No. The original hire date remains the same even though the "safe harbor" procedure is used. For example, if an employee was hired several years ago, completes the Form I-9 again, and then moves on to a new employer, the original date of hire applies for purposes of determining the one-year retention requirement.

12.15 Will an employer be liable for terminating an employee who turns out to be work authorized if the employer receives a no-match letter?

If the employee is authorized to work and an employer does not go through the various "safe harbor" steps in the regulation, then the employer might be liable for unlawful termination.

12.16 What if the employee is gone by the time the no-match letter arrives?

An employer is not obligated to act on a no-match letter for employees no longer employed by it.

13

MERGERS AND ACQUISITIONS

13.1 Generally speaking, how does immigration law factor into mergers, acquisitions, or other major corporate transactions?

Though U.S. immigration laws have been a factor in corporate transactions for decades, a massive increase in the enforcement of immigration laws and the proliferation of new regulations certainly should have raised the profile of this subject among lawyers handling major corporate transactions. But to survey transactional lawyers regarding how many of them address immigration issues in their due-diligence inquiries, including adding immigration provisions in their agreements and dealing with immigration in their due-diligence and pre-closing activities, is likely to elicit less than 50 percent of responses.

Perhaps the lack of attention to immigration issues by many attorneys is the result of in-house legal departments lacking immigration lawyers in their offices to educate them on the immigration issues. It also could be that most immigration lawyers, even those at large law firms, focus their practices on filing visa petitions and they simply lack a background in corporate law.

Lawyers working on these deals need to quickly educate themselves and be prepared to address these immigration issues if they are to avoid an immigration

133

"train wreck." Inheriting immigration problems is no longer a mere inconvenience for a company. Consider these developments:

- At the federal level, employers are being aggressively targeted by the U.S. Department of Homeland Security (DHS) for Form I-9 audits and inspections, which can result in significant fines.

- At the state level, new laws allow authorities to revoke business licenses and access to state contracts if employers are found to have immigration law violations.

- Employees on work visas are now suing companies for negligence in handling their immigration matters when actions of the company result in employees having problems pursuing permanent residency, potentially facing bars on returning to the United States, and falling out of legal status.

- Major companies, like Wal-Mart, now include strong immigration compliance provisions in their vendor contracts, and having a history of immigration law violations can jeopardize doing business with such firms.

- Immigration is a major topic being covered by the media, and any companies with immigration law violations risk facing front-page coverage.

In some cases, companies pick up immigration problems that occurred prior to closing. In other instances, the actual closing of the deal triggers the immigration violations that create exposure. In other words, at the moment the transactional documents are signed, employees may find themselves converted to an illegal status and subject to deportation. And, unfortunately, these consequences are ticking time bombs that are frequently not discovered until long after the celebration of the closing has occurred; then, it is too late to reverse the damage.

If these concerns are not enough to convince the corporate attorney of the need to routinely deal with immigration in corporate transactions and to warn clients of the immigration consequences, perhaps the threat of being found liable for legal malpractice will.

13.2 What are the major immigration risks associated with mergers, acquisitions, or other major corporate transactions?

First, the visas or pending applications of the employees potentially could be affected by the deal. Do petitions need to be transferred prior to closing? Are amendments required? Are any employees no longer eligible in the category under which they were petitioning?

Second, all employers in the United States are, of course, barred from hiring unauthorized employees and are required to maintain documentation (Form I-9) demonstrating that each of their employees is legally permitted to work in the United States. Companies also may be required to file new paperwork regarding the status of all employees, and this paperwork may need to be completed on the actual day of closing or before.

13.3 What corporate changes typically have immigration consequences?

Corporate changes that typically have immigration consequences are stock or asset acquisitions, mergers, consolidations, initial public offerings, spin-offs, corporate name changes, changes in payroll source, and the relocation of an employer or its employees.

Acquisitions involve the purchase of assets or stock. In an asset acquisition, the purchaser may not accept the liabilities of the seller. In a merger, two or more legal entities combine all their assets in what is called the "surviving entity." Other entities, which are called the "merged entities," cease to exist. The surviving entity assumes all their liabilities. In a consolidation, however, two or more legal entities combine all their assets to form a new entity. The new entity assumes their liabilities, and they cease to exist. An initial public offering (IPO) changes the ownership structure of a corporation, similar to an acquisition. A spin-off involves the creation of a new company from a divestiture of shares or assets of an existing company.

There is no "one size fits all" approach to advising clients regarding the effect of a transaction on the immigration consequence of a merger or acquisition. Rather, there are a number of important questions to ask as the due-diligence process begins. They include:

- How is the deal to be structured? Is it a merger or spin-off in which employees will have a new employer with a different taxpayer identification number? Is it a stock purchase? Is it an asset acquisition where no liabilities are being assumed (or where just immigration liabilities are assumed)? Or a successor-in-interest where liabilities are to be assumed?

- What are the timing issues in the case? Is there enough time to file new petitions? Are employees going to suffer adverse consequences as a result of the timing? Is it possible to lease employees to the successor entity until the necessary transfer paperwork can be filed? Can filings be deferred until after the closing without a penalty or risk?

- For Form I-9 and E-Verify filings, will the documentation of the post-transaction entities survive? And, if so, does the convenience of not being required to have employees prepare new I-9 forms or have to refile in E-Verify outweigh the risk of assuming liabilities associated with the former employer's prior filings?

These questions initially should be addressed in the due-diligence request and in early discussions between the lawyers involved in the transaction. In most cases, immigration is not addressed in due diligence, and many lawyers may not know where to begin in requesting documentation. See Figure 13a, which provides a sample immigration due-diligence checklist.

The impact of a corporate change will vary from employee to employee, depending on the type of visa or status the employee has and on what stage he or she is in in the immigration process.

One goal of the due-diligence process will be to determine whether the company that is the subject of the due diligence has complied with immigration laws and the scope of any potential liability. Another will be to identify what pre-closing and post-closing activities are required to ensure a smooth transition.

To meet those objectives, the due-diligence review will cover the visa history of employees potentially affected by the transaction. The review also will test the Form I-9 compliance of the company that is the subject of the due diligence. This may take the form of a full review of the I-9 forms or a sample audit if a full review is not practical. If a sampling determines that many problems exist, a full audit may be warranted.

Figure 13a: Immigration Due Diligence and Boilerplate Language

Below is a sample due-diligence query that can be included with a request in a merger, an acquisition, or other major corporate transaction.

1. Provide a list of all employees who are not U.S. lawful permanent residents or citizens. The list should show each employee by visa category, work authorization expiration date, number of years in a particular visa category, the employee's worksite, and whether any nonimmigrant visa applications, extension petitions, or permanent residency petitions are pending or promised. Also note any changes in job duties, location, or salary that will occur as a result of the transaction.

2. For all employees listed in the first step, provide a copy of all documents relating to each employee's immigration status, including the following:

   a. Nonimmigrant visa applications and extension petitions.

   b. Employment authorization documents.

   c. Forms I-9.

   d. Labor certification and immigrant visa applications and supporting documentation.

   e. Approval notices and correspondence with any government agencies.

   f. Forms I-94 (Arrival/Departure Record) and passport visa stamps.

   g. Visa documentation for each employee's spouse and minor children.

   h. H-1B public access files.

3. Provide copies of all correspondence with the Social Security Administration (SSA) relating to the mismatch of Social Security numbers (SSN) for any employees.

4. Provide copies of any correspondence with agencies of the U.S. Department of Homeland Security (DHS), the U.S. Department of Labor (DOL), the U.S. Department of Justice (DOJ), or the U.S. Department of State regarding compliance with U.S. immigration laws.

5. Provide a copy of all Forms I-9 required to be kept by the employer. Provide a list of all employees of the company employed since November 7, 1986. Counsel will select _____ employees from the list and request that their Forms I-9 be provided.

13.4   What visa categories typically are impacted by corporate changes?

In order to understand how corporate changes can impact foreign employees, let's review a few basic immigration and corporate law concepts.

Immigrant and Nonimmigrant Status

Employees coming to the United States for employment normally hold either nonimmigrant or immigrant status. Nonimmigrant employees at corporations normally are in the H-1B, L, E, and TN visa categories, as well as on training tied to J-1 and F-1 visas. Immigrant visas are held by individuals who have obtained lawful permanent residency (green-card holders). In the corporate transaction context, only nonimmigrant visa holders are considered because the transaction will not affect the status of green-card holders. However, employees in various stages of green-card processing short of completion could be affected.

Employers also are federally mandated to verify the employment eligibility of all their employees via the Form I-9. The Form I-9 must be completed on the day of hire, and employees are required to present documents from an official list of documents deemed to demonstrate one's identity and employment authorization. Some employers also participate in the E-Verify system, through which an employee's work authorization is verified electronically by the U.S. Department of Homeland Security (DHS). Finally, some employers have received no-match letters from the Social Security Administration (SSA) when the Social Security number (SSN) and employee name do not match. All of these topics are covered elsewhere in this book.

Visa Categories

The most common employment visa, the H-1B, is used for an "alien who is coming to perform services in a specialty occupation" in the United States.

L visas are used for intracompany transferees who enter the United States to render services "in a capacity that is managerial, executive, or involves specialized knowledge."

E-1 and E-2 visas are used for "treaty traders and investors," and E-3s are used by Australians working in specialty occupations.

The TN category includes "Canadian and Mexican citizens seeking temporary entry to engage in business activities at a professional level," as listed in the North American Free Trade Agreement (NAFTA).

F-1 visas are held by students, many of whom are entitled to employment authorization for periods of up to one year, and possibly for an extension of 24 months if in a STEM category, during and after completion of their studies.

J-1 visas are held by exchange visitors in many categories, including one that permits internship and training opportunities of 12 and 18 months' duration.

13.5 How are H-1B visas affected by mergers and acquisitions?

In an H-1B visa case, the questions to analyze are whether a corporate change results in a new employer and, if so, to what extent the interests of the target corporation are being assumed.

An H-1B visa requires separate applications to the U.S. Department of Labor (DOL) and U.S. Citizenship and Immigration Services (USCIS). A petitioner must first submit an approved Labor Condition Application (LCA) from DOL, and then must have its Form I-129, Petition for a Nonimmigrant Worker, approved by USCIS.

Under rules adopted on December 22, 2000, a new LCA is not required merely because a corporate reorganization results in a change of corporate identity, regardless of whether there is a change in Employer Identification Number (EIN), provided that the successor entity, prior to the continued employment of the H-1B employee, agrees to assume the predecessor's obligations and liabilities under the LCA with a memorandum to the "public access file" kept for LCA purposes.

Material changes in the employee's duties and job requirements and in the relocation of the employee require a new LCA. Therefore, if employees are relocated due to a merger or sale, new LCAs will be required for H-1B employees under the below circumstances.

In *Matter of Simeio Solutions, LLC*, 26 I&N Dec. 542 (AAO 2015), the USCIS Administrative Appeals Office (AAO) held that an H-1B employer must file an amended or new H-1B petition when a new LCA for Nonimmigrant Workers is required due to a change in the H-1B worker's place of employment to a new geographical area outside the existing Standard Metropolitan Statistical area (SMSA). This is considered a material change. This action must be taken, placing an H-1B employee at a new place of employment not covered by an existing, approved H-1B petition. Once the H-1B employer properly files the amended or new H-1B petition, the H-1B employee immediately can begin to work at the new place of employment, provided the requirements of §214(n) of the Immigration and Nationality Act (INA) are otherwise satisfied.

> DOL uses the standard metropolitan statistical area, or SMSA, as criteria in determining the need for a new LCA or labor certification. If the employee is relocated outside the SMSA, then a new filing is required. But a simple name change will not trigger the need for a new LCA.

The rules governing when a new Form I-129 (Petition for a Nonimmigrant Worker) must be filed are similar to the LCA, but not identical. The need to file a new Form I-129 can be a fairly expensive requirement. For each new employment petition, the employer must pay the American Competitiveness and Workforce Improvement Act fee, which is $1,500 for companies with more than 25 employees and $750 for smaller companies. Couple this with the $500 fraud fee, a $460 base filing fee, and a $1,225 premium processing fee for fast adjudication,[1] and the company will be paying over $3,600 per employee.

The INA contains an exemption from filing a new Form I-129 in cases of corporate structuring in which the new employer is a successor-in-interest that assumes the interests and the obligations of the prior employer. This is a restatement of the existing U.S. Citizenship and Immigration Services (USCIS) policy stating that if an employer, for H-1B purposes, "assumes the previous owner's liabilities which include the assertions the prior owner made on the labor condition application," then there is no need for a new or amended petition. If a new or amended petition is not needed, the employer may wait until filing an extension petition for the employee to notify USCIS.

One potential pitfall involving H-1B employees relates to the "dependency" provisions in the H-1B statute. Employers with over a certain number or a certain percentage of H-1B employees are considered "H-1B dependent," and such companies face tight restrictions in terms of documenting recruiting efforts and hiring H-1Bs before and after layoffs. The numbers will need to be recalculated for a company after a transaction, and the result could dramatically affect a company's bottom line. Companies that are H-1B dependent should be a signal for further scrutiny because it may be the result of being found to have had prior H-1B violations, and this could mean a company may be inheriting a poor history of compliance.

An issue likely to affect only a small number of employers (particularly in the health care sector) involves loss of eligibility for cap-exempt status. If an employer's status as exempt from the quota limitations on H-1B visas was the basis for an employee's H-1B status, the corporate practitioner will want to examine

---

[1] As of the time of publication, premium processing for H-1B visas had been suspended.

whether cap-exempt status is lost after the closing. This may happen, for example, when a nonprofit entity is replaced by a for-profit entity as a sponsoring employer. A loss of H-1B cap-exempt status could make it impossible for an employee to continue being employed by the succeeding entity as an H-1B status holder.

13.6 What impacts do mergers, acquisitions, and other major corporate transactions have on TN visas?

Because Labor Condition Applications (LCAs) are not required for obtaining a TN visa or status for a citizen of Canada or Mexico, a basic successor-in-interest analysis is required to determine how to proceed here. If the new company is successor-in-interest of the prior company, new petitions are not required. The fact that a company may change nationality will not matter in these cases because the TN visa is tied to the employee's nationality, not to the company's nationality.

13.7 How are L-1 intracompany transfers affected by mergers, acquisitions, and other major corporate transactions?

For an L-1 visa, the law requires a qualifying relationship between the U.S. entity and the foreign entity from which the employee will be transferring. This relationship must be within the definitions of a "parent, branch, affiliate or subsidiary" as defined by U.S. Citizenship and Immigration Services (USCIS). Obviously, changes in the ownership structure of either one of the entities, through a corporate change, may terminate the qualifying relationship and, consequently, invalidate the underlying L visas. However, if the petitioner, after a corporate change, can document that a qualifying relationship survives, then only an amended petition will be necessary.

The foreign entity that actually employed the L-1 transferee does not have to remain in existence as long as there is another foreign entity that has a qualifying relationship with the U.S. entity.

For affiliated companies, if the ownership breakdown of the overseas entity and the U.S. entities changes, the qualifying relationship may no longer exist. Also, if the U.S. company is sold to another international company, the L-1 may survive even if the original foreign entity is no longer part of the corporate family. The key will be whether the company still maintains an overseas office.

Finally, companies will want to look at issues pertaining to the "blanket L." Blanket L-1s are available to companies that prequalify with USCIS and can show they are large multinational operations with a large volume of L-1 filings. A transaction may render a company too small or suddenly large enough to qualify for a blanket L filing. From a strategic point of view, if a company can qualify for a blanket L under a merged entity's qualification after a transaction, it may be possible to add the new entity, and then employees can be covered under the blanket.

13.8   How are E visas affected by mergers, acquisitions, or other major corporate transactions?

Under the E-1 and E-2 visas, certain investors and traders may be admitted to the United States and be employed therein, if a "treaty-qualifying" company petitions and obtains status for them. A company is qualified based on its nationality. A corporate change may alter a corporation's nationality, and, therefore, result in the termination of the qualification. U.S. Citizenship and Immigration Services (USCIS) regulations specifically state that prior USCIS approval must be obtained when there has been a "fundamental change" in a company's characteristics, including in the case of a merger, acquisition, or sale.

The E-3 visas for nationals of Australia are similar in many respects to the H-1B, including in the requirement for the filing of a Labor Condition Application (LCA). The same considerations applicable to the H-1B apply here. E-3 status is tied to the nationality of the employee, not to the company's nationality. In that respect, it is similar to the TN visa because it is not affected per se by a change or by a company's nationality.

13.9   How are permanent residency applications affected by mergers, acquisitions, and other major corporate transactions?

A lawful permanent resident (LPR) application normally consists of three steps. First, the employer must usually prove that despite reasonable recruitment efforts, it has not been able to find a domestic employee to fill the alien's position. This is called a PERM labor certification and is handled through the U.S. Department of Labor (DOL). Second, the employer files a Form I-140, Immigrant Petition for Alien Worker, with U.S. Citizenship and Immigration Services (USCIS). After the Form I-140 petition is approved, the employee files a petition with USCIS for the adjustment of his or her immigration status to the status of a lawful permanent resident.

DOL takes a liberal view of when a new PERM labor certification petition must be refiled. If after an acquisition, a new owner remains the employee's employer and has assumed all of the past owner's obligations, the new owner should qualify as a "successor-in-interest," and a PERM labor certification will survive.

In lawful permanent resident (LPR) cases, USCIS traditionally has used a stricter version of the successor-in-interest theory, permitting an employer to continue with the prior employer's petition, only if the new employer assumed all the prior employer's liabilities. Without successorship, a new Form I-140 petition may be necessary even when an adjustment-of-status application already is pending.

The lawful permanent resident (LPR) adjustment process may take a couple of years, and in the past, unless the case fit under certain exceptions, beneficiaries of immigrant petitions were not able to change employers until the completion of the entire process. Therefore, corporate changes that created a new employer potentially caused further delays. Legislation now makes it possible in many instances to change employers while an adjustment application is pending. An adjustment application pending six months or more will survive if an employee finds new employment in the same or a similar occupation. The sponsoring employers may, in some cases, want to consider leasing an employee to the new entity for a period of time to ensure that the "portability" rule is available.

Unfortunately, because of long green-card backlogs, many applicants are not in a position to file a Form I-485 adjustment-of-status application. Hence, the applicant may find that a petition becomes worthless if the original job offer disappears.

Aside from labor certification cases, some employees pursue permanent residency through an intracompany transfer–based Form I-140 petition. In these cases, a labor certification is not required. Many of the same issues regarding maintaining a qualifying relationship that apply in an L-1 case will arise. However, if a case has advanced far enough, the portability rule noted above may apply as well.

Some permanent residency petitions are based on self-sponsorship by an applicant. These include national interest petitions and EB-1 extraordinary ability cases. These matters are normally not affected by a major transaction, except that in some cases, an employment relationship is how an applicant demonstrates that he or she will work in the field on approval of permanent residency. If the transaction will result in an employee losing the position, this could, in theory, affect qualification for EB-1 or EB-2 status.

13.10 How are Forms I-9 affected by mergers, acquisitions, or other major corporate transactions?

A successor-in-interest assumes the Form I-9 liabilities of a corporation. Failure to comply with Form I-9 requirements may result in costly sanctions running into the thousands of dollars per employee. Therefore, before a corporate restructuring, the transition team should examine the Form I-9 compliance of the entity by performing either a sample Form I-9 audit or a review of the alien employees' Forms I-9.

If a company does not assume the liabilities of the acquired corporation, Forms I-9 are generally required of all employees, and in the case of a merged entity that is completely new, Forms I-9 may be needed for all employees of both entities.

The good news here may be that a successor-in-interest can assume that the Forms I-9 are in place at the time of closing. But many companies will want to consider requiring all employees of an acquired or merged entity to complete new Forms I-9 on the date of closing. This approach ensures that past violations are not continued, and also the company tracks which employees have a temporary employment authorization document that will require re-verification at a later time. Of course, the employer needs to require all employees to complete a new Form I-9 and not single out some employees.

13.11 What are some general tips for employers going through mergers, acquisitions, or other major corporate transactions?

The following are tips for employers:

- Ensure visas are transferred to a new employer prior to closing when a closing will affect the visas' validity.
- File amendments before or shortly after closing (unless regulations specifically require filing before closing).
- Move employees to new visa categories before the closing when they will no longer be eligible in a particular category post-closing.
- In cases where a closing will void a visa status, employ an employee in a leasing arrangement to continue the employer-employee relationship.
- Start green-card processing early to minimize the number of nonimmigrant visas requiring attention.

Immigration queries should be incorporated into the due-diligence inquiry, and representations and warranties (see Figure 13b) addressing immigration issues should be incorporated into the transaction documents.

Figure 13b: Contract Representation and Warranty

Below is sample language that can be adapted for inclusion in agreements associated with a merger, an acquisition, or other major corporate transaction.

Immigration. All necessary visa or work authorization petitions have been timely and properly filed on behalf of any employees requiring a visa stamp, Form I-94 status document, employment authorization document, or any other immigration document to work legally in the United States. All paperwork retention requirements with respect to such applications and petitions have been met. No employees have ever worked without employment authorization from the U.S. Department of Homeland Security (DHS) or any other government agency that must authorize such employment, and any employment of foreign nationals has complied with applicable immigration laws. Forms I-9 have been timely and properly completed for all employees hired since the establishment of the company or the effective date of the Immigration Reform and Control Act, whichever is earlier. Forms I-9 have been lawfully retained and re-verified. There are no claims, lawsuits, actions, arbitrations, administrative or other proceedings, governmental investigations, or inquiries pending or threatened against [Company Name] relating to [Company Name]'s compliance with local, state, or federal immigration regulations, including, but not limited to, compliance with any immigration laws except for employees named in schedule __.

There have been no letters received from the Social Security Administration (SSA) regarding the failure of an employee's Social Security number (SSN) to match his or her name in the SSA database. There have been no letters or other correspondence received from DHS or other agencies regarding the employment authorization of any employees. If [Company Name] operates in a state or has contracts with a state or federal agency that requires or provides a "safe harbor" if an employer participates in DHS's E-Verify electronic employment verification system, [Company Name] has been participating in E-Verify for the entire period such participation has been required or available as a "safe harbor" or as long as the company has been operating in such state or contracting with such agency.

14

CRIMINAL LAW AND EMPLOYER IMMIGRATION LAW COMPLIANCE[*]

RELEVANT APPENDIX:

APPENDIX G: WORKSITE ENFORCEMENT OPERATIONS

In fiscal year 2008, U.S. Immigration and Customs Enforcement (ICE) began to greatly expand its Form I-9 inspections of employers. It increased inspections to thousands of inspections each fiscal year through 2014. These inspections are expected to substantially increase under the Trump administration. With the increase in inspections, the total amount of civil penalties paid by employers has dramatically increased. But employers who unlawfully employ unauthorized immigrants and violate U.S immigration laws can be subject not only to civil penalties, but to criminal investigation, arrest, and penalties. Criminal investigations may result in employers facing charges beyond unlawful employment.

---

[*] Updated by Jonathan L. Marks.

Managers, officers, and owners, and even the company itself can be held criminally responsible. Every employer should appreciate that under certain circumstances, unlawful employment activity raises serious risks of criminal investigation and prosecution, and thus should respond to such issues with appropriate diligence and commitment to compliance.

14.1   Which agency is responsible for worksite enforcement operations?

U.S. Immigration and Customs Enforcement (ICE) is primarily responsible for employer enforcement actions. Depending on the facts of the case, enforcement actions also involve the U.S. Department of Justice (DOJ) and local U.S. Attorney's offices, the Internal Revenue Service (IRS), the Social Security Administration (SSA), the U.S. Department of Labor (DOL), other federal agencies, various state agencies, and local law enforcement.

14.2   On what grounds are criminal arrests being made and criminal charges being brought in worksite enforcement operations?

Companies and company officials can be charged under a variety of statutes in an immigration enforcement case. They include:

- Criminal sections of the Immigration Reform and Control Act (IRCA).
- Criminal sections of the Immigration and Nationality Act (INA).
- Racketeer Influenced and Corrupt Organizations (RICO) Act.
- Statutes that prohibit false statements and false identity documents.
- Mail fraud and wire fraud.
- Money laundering.
- Tax evasion charges.
- Charges for structuring of monetary transactions.

14.3   What types of employers are more likely to be targeted?

Any employer may be targeted for worksite enforcement. However, factors that may increase the odds of being the subject of a criminal or administrative action include whether:

- The employer has previously been the subject of an audit.

- The employer provides services in an area connected to "critical infrastructure" or national security. Critical infrastructure and national security sites include military bases, defense facilities, nuclear power plants, chemical plants, airports, and ports.

- The employer is in an industry known to have a high rate of employing unauthorized immigrants (for example, construction trades, restaurants, and warehouses).

- The employer engages in egregious violations of applicable statutes.

- The employer mistreats or exploits workers.

- The employer engages in other criminal conduct such as identity or benefit fraud, money laundering, or human smuggling or trafficking.

- The employer employs significant numbers of unauthorized immigrants or utilizes unauthorized workers as a business model.

14.4   What is the difference between detention and a criminal arrest?

Detention in the immigration context refers to the detaining of an individual on suspicion of being an unauthorized immigrant. The detained individual may be issued a Notice to Appear in administrative removal (deportation) proceedings. A criminal arrest can result in criminal charges; if the charges result in conviction, can lead to prison sentences, supervised release (the equivalent of probation), fines, and forfeiture of assets and proceeds.

14.5   Are employees of a company who are not owners potentially liable for criminal violations?

Yes. Nonowners have been held liable, including Human Resource managers, plant managers, and corporate officers. Also, the company itself can be held criminally liable.

14.6   What is the offense of "unlawfully employing illegal aliens"?

The Immigration Reform and Control Act (IRCA) makes it unlawful "to hire, or to recruit or refer for a fee, for employment in the United States an alien knowing the alien is an unauthorized alien." It is also unlawful to continue to employ someone if an employer learns that an employee is unauthorized.

14.7   What are the penalties for "unlawfully employing illegal aliens"?

Violators can be punished with criminal penalties and injunctions. Unlawfully employing illegal workers is considered a misdemeanor, as opposed to a felony. Anyone engaging in a "pattern or practice of violations" can be fined up to $3,000 for each unauthorized worker and imprisoned up to six months.

14.8   What defenses may be available to the charge of "unlawfully employing illegal aliens"?

Employers may avoid criminal liability under the Immigration Reform and Control Act (IRCA) if they can demonstrate that they lacked knowledge that an employee was unauthorized to work or that they acted in a good-faith manner to comply with IRCA requirements.

14.9   What is the crime of "bringing in and harboring" unauthorized immigrants?

The Immigration and Nationality Act (INA) makes it a crime for anyone who:

- Knowing that a person is an unauthorized immigrant, brings to or attempts to bring to the United States the person at a place other than a designated port of entry regardless of whether the alien previously received authorization to enter the United States.

- Knowing or in reckless disregard of the fact that an immigrant has come to the United States illegally, transports such unauthorized immigrant within the United States in furtherance of such violation of the law.

- Knowing or in reckless disregard of the fact that an immigrant has come to the United States in violation of the law, "conceals, harbors, or shields from detection" such unauthorized immigrant in any place, including any building or any means of transportation.

- Encourages or induces an immigrant to come to, enter, or reside in the United States knowing or in reckless disregard of the fact that the person has not received prior official authorization to enter or reside in the United States.

- Knowing or in reckless disregard of the fact that an immigrant has not received prior official authorization to enter or reside in the United States, brings to or attempts to bring to the United States such unauthorized immigrant.

In some circumstances, individuals who conspire with, aid, or abet others in committing these offenses can be charged as well. In addition, charges can be brought for attempting these prohibited acts depending on the situation. Employers can be guilty of these offenses if they had actual knowledge of an employee's immigration status or, depending on the situation, if they "recklessly disregarded" the fact that the person was an unauthorized immigrant. Reckless disregard has sometimes been construed to mean circumstances in which an employer is aware, but consciously disregards facts and circumstances that the person is an unauthorized immigrant.

14.10   What are the potential penalties for "bringing in and harboring" unauthorized immigrants?

- For anyone bringing someone into the United States illegally, the penalty is up to 10 years' imprisonment, a fine of up to $250,000, or both.

- For transporting, concealing, harboring, shielding from detection, or encouraging or inducing, the penalty is up to five years' imprisonment or a fine of up to $250,000, or both. If a person is found guilty of any of these offenses and it was done "for the purpose of commercial or private financial gain," the maximum prison sentence increases to 10 years.

- For aiding and abetting any of these kinds of offenses, the maximum prison sentence is five years or a fine of up to $250,000, or both.

- For conspiring to commit any of these offenses, the maximum prison sentence is 10 years or a fine of up to $250,000, or both.

- If anyone is seriously injured or anyone's life is endangered, the maximum jail sentence will increase to 20 years. If someone is killed, the penalty can be up to life in prison or death.

- If a person is found guilty of bringing or attempting to bring into the United States a person who has not received prior official authorization to enter or reside in the United States, the maximum penalty is one year. But if that act is committed "for the purpose of commercial advantage or private financial gain," a sentence of three to 10 years for a first or second violation may be imposed, and five to 15 years for subsequent violations.

Maximum jail times for each of these offenses can be increased by another 10 years if the offense was part of an ongoing commercial organization, immigrants were transported in groups of 10 or more, the immigrants were transported in a dangerous manner, or the immigrants presented a life-threatening health risk to people in the United States.

Punishment also can include the forfeiture of the proceeds stemming from the violation.

14.11   What is the penalty for hiring more than 10 unauthorized immigrants?

Violators can be punished by up to five years' imprisonment, a fine, and forfeiture of the proceeds stemming from the violation.

14.12   What crimes involving false statements have been used to charge employers in cases involving unauthorized immigrants?

It is a crime to knowingly and willfully make a materially false statement or representation in any matter within the jurisdiction of any branch of the U.S. government. It is also a crime to make or use in such matters a document knowing that the document contains any materially false statements. Additionally, it is a crime to falsify, conceal, or cover up by any trick, scheme, or device a material fact in such matters. A statement has been considered material if it has the tendency to influence or is capable of influencing a governmental entity. Though this prohibition is not uniquely applied to instances of unauthorized immigrants, it has been used by the government to charge employers in connection with information communicated or presented to the government.

14.13   What is the penalty for making false statements?

Violators can be imprisoned for up to five years and fined up to $250,000, or both.

14.14 What fraud and identity theft offenses potentially apply to employers of unauthorized immigrants?

It is a federal crime to:

- Knowingly and without lawful authority produce an identification document.

- Knowingly transfer such a document knowing it was stolen or produced without lawful authority.

- Possess such a document with the intent that it will be used to defraud the United States.

- Possess an identification document of the United States knowing that the document was stolen or produced without lawful authority.

It is also a crime to knowingly transfer, possess, or use without lawful authority another person's identification with the intent to violate federal law, commit a felony under state or local law, or aid and abet such wrongdoing. The prohibition applies to documents issued by the United States or, if the offense involves or affects interstate commerce, documents issued by a state or political subdivision of a state.

Employers in several cases around the country have been accused of violating these provisions, including circumstances in which employers assisted employees in obtaining false documents. Such employers can be viewed as assisting workers in making it appear that an employee is authorized.

States also have document fraud and identity theft laws, and employers could face prosecution under these rules as well.

14.15 What penalties may be imposed on employers convicted of document fraud and identity theft?

Employers violating these rules may be imprisoned for up to five years and fined up to $250,000, or both. The potential penalty increases up to 15 years if the offense involved a fraudulent identification document that is a federal document (for example, a passport, birth certificate, driver's license, or personal identification card); the production or transfer of five or more documents; or the transfer, possession, or use of a document with the intent to violate federal law or to commit a felony under state law, and the offense resulted in obtaining anything of value worth $1,000 or more.

14.16   What is the crime of mail fraud?

It is a crime for a person to devise, or participate in, a scheme to defraud, or to obtain money or property by false representations, if the person does so with the intent to defraud and if, for the purpose of carrying out or attempting to carry out the scheme or misrepresentation, the person used or caused another person to use the U.S. mails or a commercial interstate carrier (for example, Federal Express). The item mailed or sent by interstate carrier need not itself be fraudulent as long as the use of the mails or interstate carrier furthered the wrongdoing.

14.17   What is the crime of wire fraud?

It is a crime for a person to devise, or participate in, a scheme to defraud, or to obtain money or property by false representations, if the person does so with the intent to defraud and if, for the purpose of carrying out or attempting to carry out the scheme or misrepresentation, the person transmitted or caused another person to transmit by wire, radio, or television in interstate commerce some communication. As with mail fraud, the communication sent by interstate wire need not itself be fraudulent as long as the use of an interstate wire transmission furthered the wrongdoing.

14.18   What are the potential penalties for mail fraud and wire fraud?

Violators of either the mail fraud or wire fraud statutes can be imprisoned for up to 20 years and fined up to $250,000, or both. If a violation of these statutes affects a financial institution, the penalties can be increased to 30 years' imprisonment and a $1 million fine, or both.

14.19   What is the crime of money laundering and how does it apply to employers?

The federal crime of money laundering punishes a person who conducts a financial transaction with property that represents the proceeds of "specified unlawful activity" with the intent to promote the carrying on of "specified unlawful activity." It is also a crime to conduct a financial transaction with property that represents the proceeds of specified unlawful activity, knowing that the transaction was designed to conceal or disguise the nature, the location, the source, the ownership, or the control of the proceeds of specified unlawful activity. Money laundering also involves a person knowingly engaging in a monetary transaction with property derived from specified unlawful activity and having a value of more than $10,000. Specified unlawful activity includes the crimes of harboring unauthorized workers, employing 10 or more unauthorized workers, mail fraud, and wire fraud. Thus, for example, if an employer were to knowingly employ 10 or more unauthorized workers and such employment generated funds, the employer could be guilty of money laundering if the employer engaged in a financial transaction with those funds with the intent to carry on the crime of employing unauthorized workers or to hide the source of the funds. Similarly, an employer could be charged with money laundering if that employer engaged in a monetary transaction involving more than $10,000 derived from employing 10 or more unauthorized workers.

The government can and has brought money-laundering charges in enforcement cases under a theory that employers who knowingly employ unauthorized immigrants are often using the money gained from such illegal employment to further a criminal enterprise that continues to illegally hire such employees.

14.20   What are the penalties for money laundering?

Depending on which money-laundering statute is charged, violators can be imprisoned for up to 10 years or fined up to $250,000, or both, or be imprisoned for up to 20 years and fined up to $500,000, or twice the value of the property involved in the transaction. Additionally, the government can seek forfeiture of any property involved in the offense or any property traceable to such offense.

14.21   What is the crime of fraud and misuse of visas and permits?

It is a federal crime to use or attempt to use, possess, obtain, accept, or receive a forged immigrant or nonimmigrant visa, permit, border-crossing card, alien registration receipt card, or other document prescribed for entry into the United States or for employment in the United States, knowing that the document is forged, altered, or obtained by fraud. It is also a federal crime to, under oath, knowingly subscribe as true any false statement about a material fact in any application or other document required by the immigration laws or regulations or to knowingly present such a document that contains a false statement. Also criminal would be for a person to use an identification document, knowing or having reason to know, that the document was not lawfully issued or that the document is false, for the purpose of meeting the employee verification requirements under the Immigration and Nationality Act (INA).

14.22   What are the penalties for fraud and misuse of visas and permits?

Violators of these provisions can be fined up to $250,000 or, depending on which provision is involved, imprisoned for up to five years or 15 years, or both.

14.23   What is "misuse of a Social Security number"?

It is unlawful for any person to falsely represent, with intent to deceive, that a Social Security number (SSN) assigned to one person is, in fact, assigned to another person. It is also a crime to use an SSN obtained with false information.

14.24   What is the penalty for "misuse of a Social Security number"?

Anyone found to have unlawfully misused a Social Security number (SSN) can be fined up to $250,000 or imprisoned for up to five years, or both.

14.25   What is the Racketeer Influenced and Corrupt Organizations Act?

The Racketeer Influenced and Corrupt Organizations (RICO) Act was originally enacted to address organized crime, though it has been used in a wide variety of circumstances to punish repeated criminal acts typically carried out through an entity, organization, or group. Thus, it is criminal for any person employed by or associated with an enterprise to conduct or participate in the conduct of the affairs of that enterprise through a pattern of racketeering activity. An "enterprise" can include a partnership, a corporation, an association, or other legal entity, or even a group of associated individuals. A "pattern of racketeering activity" typically involves two or more violations of certain identified laws. Among the offenses that can lead to RICO charges are repeated acts of harboring unauthorized immigrants, employing 10 or more unauthorized workers, mail fraud, and wire fraud.

14.26   What are the penalties for violation of the Racketeer Influenced and Corrupt Organizations Act?

Persons convicted of criminal Racketeer Influenced and Corrupt Organizations (RICO) Act violations can be fined up to $250,000, imprisoned for up to 20 years, and subject to civil forfeiture of property.

14.27   What types of penalties are typically being imposed on employers convicted in connection with unauthorized immigrants?

Although the statutes under which employers are charged usually set a maximum term of incarceration, judges imposing sentences have greater flexibility, and sentences are almost always considerably below the maximum.

A sampling of prison terms imposed reflects sentences ranging from two months to five years, with an average sentence of two years in cases in which a prison term was actually imposed. Terms of imprisonment are often followed by a term of supervised release, which is similar to probation. Some cases, however, have involved supervised release rather than imprisonment.

A sampling of terms of probation in cases in which supervised release rather than imprisonment was imposed reflects terms from one to five years, with an average of two years. Forfeiture of assets and fines are also imposed. There have been instances of fines as high as $200,000 and of forfeiture of assets as high as $12 million.

14.28   What is "seizure and forfeiture"?

Employers found to be liable for certain criminal offenses can be subject to the seizure of any assets deemed to be the fruits of such wrongdoing. Whereas Immigration Reform and Control Act (IRCA) fines typically have not amounted to more than $200,000, seized assets in harboring and money-laundering cases have involved millions of dollars.

14.29   Is it more likely U.S. Immigration and Customs Enforcement will pursue a worksite enforcement charge or a criminal investigation?

Since 2008, there has been a greater chance of an administrative fine than a criminal charge. In fiscal year (FY) 2014, there were 642 final orders for Form I-9 penalties totaling over $16.2 million. In FY2013, ICE issued 637 final orders for Form I-9 penalties with over $15.8 million in assessed fines. In FY2012, there were 495 final orders for payment of Form I-9 penalties totaling over $12.4 million.

Criminal arrests of employers' representatives on immigration-related violations between 2010 and 2014 have averaged around 200 per year, with 196 arrested in 2010, 221 in 2011, 240 in 2012, 179 in 2013 and 172 in 2014. Statistics since 2014 were unavailable at the time of publication. Nevertheless, criminal investigations and charges remain a risk. In guidance issued in 2009, the U.S. Department of Homeland Security (DHS) identified "criminal prosecution of employers [as] a priority of [Immigration and Customs Enforcement's] worksite enforcement ... program and interior enforcement strategy," stating that it "must prioritize the criminal prosecution of the actual employers who knowingly hire illegal workers because such employers are not sufficiently punished or deterred by the arrest of their illegal workforce." As the Trump administration is changing priorities in favor of more enforcement, the use of criminal law to address unauthorized employment could result in an increase in arrests and heightened exposure for employers.

14.30   What should an employer do if a U.S. Immigration and Customs Enforcement agent arrives at its place of business in connection with an investigation of immigration violations?

There is no "one size fits all" answer to this question; to some extent, the answer depends on whether the investigator is seeking to conduct an onsite inspection immediately, where the employer's Forms I-9 are kept, how careful the company has been with respect to Form I-9 compliance, whether the U.S. Immigration and Customs Enforcement (ICE) officer has a Notice of Inspection and Subpoena or a search warrant, and other factors. The best approach is to consult with immigration counsel and develop a set of protocols for reacting to such a visit or raid ahead of time. Employers always have three days to produce the

Forms I-9 unless waived. There is no strategic advantage to waiving the three days.

Here are some basic items to add to the protocol list:

- Instructing employee who has first contact with government official to immediately contact a designated manager or company official and inform him or her which agency is conducting the inspection.
- Contacting immigration counsel immediately.
- Trying to note the names of officials and any comments made, including any references to alleged violations.
- Not consenting to a search until counsel has been consulted.
- Not destroying or tampering with Forms I-9 or any other records.
- Not consenting to the removal of Forms I-9 or the copying of Forms I-9 by ICE officials without consulting with counsel.
- Insisting on three days' notice for an inspection as required by law.
- Designating one person to communicate with an inspector or government official.

15

LAYOFFS AND DOWNSIZING

RELEVANT APPENDIX:

APPENDIX B: U.S. DEPARTMENT OF HOMELAND
SECURITY'S HANDBOOK FOR EMPLOYERS: GUIDANCE FOR
COMPLETING FORM I-9, M-274

15.1 What are the immigration-related consequences of layoffs on foreign employees in nonimmigrant status?

For employers that employ foreign nationals, the company's foreign work-force consists of two separate groups of employees: nonimmigrant workers and immigrant workers. Nonimmigrant workers usually fall under the H-1B, L, E, and TN temporary visa categories. The most common nonimmigrant employ-ment visa, H-1B, is used for an "alien who is coming to perform services in a specialty occupation" in the United States. L visas are used for intracompany transferees who enter the United States to render services "in a capacity that is managerial, executive, or involves specialized knowledge," whereas E visas are used for "treaty traders and investors" as well as for Australian specialty occupation workers. Finally, the TN category includes "Canadian and Mexican citizens seeking temporary entry to engage in business activities at a professional level," as listed in the North American Free Trade Agreement (NAFTA). As compared to nonimmigrant workers, immigrant workers are those who have obtained or are in the process of obtaining lawful permanent residency (green-card holders).

Nonimmigrant work visas are generally issued for the specific purpose of employment with a particular employer. Thus, a nonimmigrant residing in the United States under one of the temporary work visa categories is legally authorized to remain in the United States only as long as he or she is employed with the particular employer noted in the employee's visa application. If the employee is laid off, he or she immediately loses his or her visa status. As a result, employers that lay off nonimmigrant employees with little or no notice place these individuals in the difficult situation of having to quickly find an alternative visa status to legally remain in the United States. If the nonimmigrant employee cannot secure an alternative status, he or she must choose between remaining in this country illegally or leaving everything behind and returning to his or her home country to possibly seek a new visa status from abroad.

However, under new 2017 regulations, individuals in these statuses—E-1, E-2, E-3, H-1B, H-1B1, L-1, O-1, or TN classification—who are laid off, terminated, or otherwise lose their jobs, shall be provided up to 60 consecutive days or until the end of the authorized validity period, whichever is shorter, to remain in the United States in lawful status and seek sponsorship by another employer. This may occur only once during each authorized validity period. The U.S. Department of Homeland Security (DHS) may eliminate or shorten this 60-day period as a matter of discretion. One's dependents also may remain during this grace period. Except for H-1B visa holders, in most cases, the nonimmigrant visa holder cannot work until the new employer's petition is approved.

Securing an alternative visa status without notice, or with little notice, is not easy, but the employee needs to act quickly once he or she learns of the termination. Even if the nonimmigrant is fortunate enough to secure an alternate employment offer, he or she will not be permitted to begin work for the new employer under most nonimmigrant work visa categories until a new visa petition is actually approved, something that could take up to several months. An exception is available to employees working under the H-1B visa category. Those workers normally may start work for a new employer immediately upon filing a new visa petition.

An employee also may file for a change to visitor status. This strategy will allow the worker to remain legally in the United States, though not authorized to work. As long as the application is filed while the worker remains employed, the worker will remain in status for up to 240 days while the visitor change-of-status application is pending. The worker must also file a new nonimmigrant application once a new position has been found.

For individuals filing for a new H-1B visa who previously held H-1B status, H-1B "portability" remains available in most cases, and work for the new employer can begin immediately upon filing the new H-1B change-of-status petition. One additional good piece of news for H-1B visa holders is that if a worker was counted against the H-1B cap for the prior position, the worker should not need to be counted again, and the new employer does not need to go through the H-1B lottery.

L-1, E-1, and E-2 applicants often need to find a new visa category to remain in the United States. Because L-1s are intracompany transfers and must be working for an employer that employed them for one year outside the United States within the prior three years, the odds are pretty low that they will qualify to work for a different employer in the same status. So changing to another nonimmigrant category will likely be necessary. E-1 and E-2 statuses are tied to working for an employer with the same nationality as the employee. To remain in the E-I or E-2 status, the worker must find another employer from his or her home country and be employed in a managerial, executive, or essential skills position. Like the L-l employee, a laid-off E-1 or E-2 worker probably will need to switch to another nonimmigrant visa category. TN and E-3 workers are in better shape because if they can find a job in the same occupation and, in the case of an E-3, are paid the prevailing wage, their statuses can continue with a new employer.

In situations where the nonimmigrant remains in the United States in a visa category that prohibits employment or while an employment-based visa is pending, the individual is generally not eligible to collect any type of unemployment compensation under most states' laws because unemployment statutes usually require that an individual must be available to work and be authorized to accept work to be eligible for unemployment compensation.

15.2 What should a nonimmigrant employee do if he or she falls out of legal status?

If the nonimmigrant employee is unable to secure a legal visa status after being laid off, and the 60-day grace period expires, any time spent out of status has the potential to create significant future problems that the nonimmigrant often does not realize. Even minor periods of time spent out of legal status can render the nonimmigrant ineligible for certain immigration benefits. For example, in the final stage of the green-card process, an individual usually has the choice of completing the process from within the United States (referred to as adjustment of status) or at the U.S. consulate located in his or her home country. However, individuals who have spent any period of time out of status are potentially not eligible to adjust status and must endure the disruption of having to return home to complete their green-card process. Furthermore, U.S. Citizenship and Immigration Services (USCIS) has begun cracking down on workers who engage in any unlawful employment even after an adjustment application has been filed. Adjustment applicants must therefore be careful to make sure that they have a valid employment authorization card just in case they lose their nonimmigrant work status.

> Under immigration law, individuals who are unlawfully present in
> the United States for a period of six months to one year are
> barred from reentering the United States for three years.
> Individuals unlawfully present in the United States
> for over one year are barred for 10 years.

Individuals who spend longer periods of time out of status are faced with considerably more serious consequences. A person in this situation may be able to convince an examiner to exercise discretion and approve a late-filed change-of-status petition based on extraordinary circumstances beyond the control of the immigrant. But a prudent person should assume the petition may be denied and should be cognizant of the fact that the longer a person remains out of status, the harder it will be convince a consular officer to approve a visa.

15.3 Is there a grace period for an H-1B worker to find a new position without being considered out of status?

Yes. Under the 2017 regulations, H-1B workers terminated from their positions have a 60-day grace period to remain in the United States in lawful status and seek sponsorship by another employer. There is a 10-day grace period following the expiration of the admission period noted on the Form I-94 (Arrival/Departure Record), but this would not apply to prematurely terminated workers.

Even before the 2017 regulations, when employees are given a notice of termination from employment, but the employee continues to receive salary and benefits after the employee is no longer returning to the place of employment, the rules are more liberal. For example, under the Worker Adjustment and Retraining Notification Act (WARN Act), some employees are given 60 days of notice prior to a layoff or plant closing. The salary may appear on the pay stub as a lump sum paid up front, but it is based on a pro rata salary until a future date.

According to an American Immigration Lawyers Association/U.S. Citizenship and Immigration Services (USCIS) liaison meeting on February 25, 2009, if an employee finds a new position and the new employer files an H-1B petition after the worker has stopped returning to the first employer, the employee would be considered to still be in status. The employee would need to provide pay statements with documentation from the previous employer documenting the employee's final date of pay and benefits.

15.4 What are the immigration-related consequences of layoffs on foreign employees with pending green-card applications?

For employees with pending green-card applications, a layoff can present different problems. Often, after having an opportunity to evaluate an employee's skills and future potential, an employer will agree to sponsor the foreign employee for lawful-permanent-resident (LPR) status, commonly referred to as green-card status. An LPR application generally consists of three steps:

- First, through a process called labor certification or PERM (Program Electronic Review Management), the employer must prove to the satisfaction of the U.S. Department of Labor (DOL) that it has not been able to find a domestic employee to fill the foreign employee's position.

- Second, after the labor certification is complete, the employer files an immigrant petition with U.S. Citizenship and Immigration Services (USCIS).

- Finally, after the immigrant petition is approved, the employee files a petition with USCIS for the adjustment of his or her immigration status to the status of an LPR. The entire LPR process may take several years.

The LPR process is predicated on the idea of granting a foreign worker permanent work authorization to work for a particular employer in a particular position. Thus, foreign employees who are laid off during the first two steps of the LPR process cannot continue with their applications, and must restart the entire process with another employer if they remain interested in securing LPR status. Foreign employees laid off during the third step of the process may or may not be able to continue the LPR process, depending on their situations.

Historically, foreign employees could not switch employers before their statuses were adjusted without risking invalidation of their underlying immigrant petitions. However, under a law passed in October 2000, a foreign employee whose adjustment-of-status application has been pending for over six months can now switch employers without invalidating his or her immigrant petition as long as he or she will be working in a position similar to the position noted in his or her labor certification and immigrant petition. Obviously, during a recession, finding work in one's occupation may not be easy, and if a worker accepts employment in a field not closely related to the field that served as the basis for the green-card application, adjustment portability may not be available. The worker must be working in the new position at the time the adjustment petition is adjudicated.

15.5 What are the immigration-related consequences of layoffs on foreign employees who are already lawful permanent residents?

For foreign workers who already have secured lawful permanent resident (LPR) status, the impact of being laid off is not much different from that of a U.S. worker. The green-card holder would continue to be in LPR status while he or she looks for new employment. Many immigrants who recently have obtained their green-card status may be rightfully concerned about leaving their positions too quickly after gaining permanent residency. U.S. Citizenship and Immigration Services (USCIS) sometimes accuses an individual of not having appropriate intentions when he or she was awarded lawful permanent residency. However, an involuntary termination of employment will not trigger that type of problem because the applicant presumably did not intend to leave the employer. Also, depending on the applicable state law, the LPR might be eligible for unemployment compensation because he or she is lawfully present in the United States and is available and authorized to accept employment.

15.6 What are the immigration-related consequences of layoffs on employers employing foreign nationals?

When downsizing includes laying off a company's foreign workers, the employer must be cognizant of its affirmative duties under immigration law with respect to those workers. For most employment-related visa types, the employer has an affirmative responsibility to notify U.S. Citizenship and Immigration Services (USCIS) when a foreign worker's employment has been terminated so that USCIS can revoke the individual's visa. In the case *Administrator, Wage & Hour Div. v. Help Foundation of Omaha, Inc.*, ARB No. 07-008 (ARB Dec. 31, 2008), the Administrative Review Board held that an employer was liable for back wages to a worker when the employer failed to notify USCIS of the termination in employment. With respect to H-1B employees, the employer also must provide the H-1B worker return transportation to his or her home country at the employer's expense.

In the H-1B context, these affirmative responsibilities are particularly important because employers that do not comply with these obligations run the risk of being subject to continuing wage obligations for the H-1B employee. Under the anti-benching provisions of the H-1B regulations, an employer must continue to pay an H-1B employee his or her normal wages during any time spent in nonproductive status "due to the decision of the employer."

In a layoff situation, the employer's payment obligation ends only if there has been a "bona fide" termination of the employment relationship, which the U.S. Department of Labor (DOL) will deem to have occurred when:

(1) The employer notifies USCIS of the termination; (2) The H-1B petition is canceled; and (3) The return fare obligation is fulfilled.

In addition to complying with its affirmative immigration obligations when laying off foreign workers, an employer must be aware of other possible consequences of its downsizing strategy, particularly with respect to the H-1B visa program. One possible issue that could arise in a layoff scenario concerns severance benefits provided by the employer. Under H-1B regulations, all employers employing H-1B workers are required to provide them with fringe benefits equivalent to those of its U.S. workers. Though DOL has not said whether severance benefits would fall under the definition of "fringe benefits," DOL could possibly interpret the failure to provide similar severance benefits to both U.S. and H-1B workers as a violation of the H-1B regulations.

Another possible issue that may arise with downsizing relates to how the resulting change in the employer's workforce affects its calculation of "H-1B dependency," a concept outlined in the final H-1B regulations issued by U.S. Department of Labor (DOL) in December 2000. Under these regulations, an employer with 25 or fewer employees is considered H-1B dependent if it has more than seven H-1B employees. An employer with between 26 and 50 employees is considered H-1B dependent if it has more than 12 H-1B employees. And, finally, an employer with over 50 employees is H-1B dependent if more than 15 percent of its employees are H-1B visa holders.

When an employer lays off significant numbers of workers, regardless of whether they are U.S. or H-1B workers, the employer should recalculate to determine if it is an H-1B dependent employer. Nondependent employers that become dependent will become subject to myriad legal requirements applicable to H-1B–dependent employers, such as additional recruiting requirements. Likewise, an H-1B–dependent employer could become nondependent following a downsizing, thus relieving itself from many burdensome obligations.

For H-1B–dependent employers, downsizing can present even more issues to consider. Under immigration law, H-1B–dependent employers filing a visa petition must attest under oath that they have not "displaced" a U.S. worker for a period of 90 days before and 90 days after the petition was submitted.

> A "displacement" occurs when an employer lays off a U.S. worker
> from a job essentially equivalent to that offered
> to the H-1B worker.

A U.S. worker who accepted an offer of voluntary retirement is not considered to have been laid off. Also, a layoff does not result when the employer offers the U.S. worker a similar employment position at equivalent or higher terms in lieu of termination. To comply with these anti-displacement provisions, H-1B–dependent employers are required to keep detailed records relating to all layoffs affecting U.S. workers.

H-1B–dependent employers that place their H-1B employees with secondary employers where there are "indicia of employment" between the secondary employer and the H-1B worker also can sustain displacement liability when the secondary employer lays off U.S. workers. Under the H-1B regulations, U.S. workers at secondary employers are protected from displacement by H-1B workers. Thus, if an H-1B–dependent employer is placing an H-1B employee with a secondary employer, the H-1B–dependent employer must use due diligence to make sure the secondary employer has not placed any U.S. workers in a position equivalent to that offered to the H-1B worker for a period of 90 days before and after filing the H-1B petition. Secondary employers that lay off workers are not subject to any liability, so the H-1B–dependent employer is obliged to make inquiries as to the secondary employer's layoffs and cannot ignore constructive knowledge that the layoffs have occurred.

Employers that violate either the primary or secondary employer displacement prohibitions can be subject to monetary penalties and be barred from using the H-1B program. This being the case, H-1B–dependent employers that have laid off U.S. workers or placed employees with secondary employers who have laid off U.S. workers must be extremely careful when hiring new H-1B employees.

Employers that lay off workers could jeopardize permanent residency applications pending for the company's workers. With U.S. Citizenship and Immigration Services (USCIS) and U.S. Department of Labor (DOL) examiners now regularly searching the Internet for information on petitioners and beneficiaries, practitioners are reporting more and more denials of PERM and immigrant visa petitions based on examiners finding media reports of downsizing at the employer. Employers will need to be prepared to document that the sponsored worker is not employed in an occupation in which U.S. workers have found themselves terminated.

15.7 What are some proactive strategies for preventing negative immigration consequences for employers and employees during downsizing?

With careful planning, employers can protect themselves and their employees from most of the immigration problems associated with corporate downsizing discussed in this chapter. Here are some general guidelines employers should keep in mind when developing their companies' layoff strategies:

- Employers should try to provide as much advance notice as possible to foreign employees who will be laid off. With advance notice, foreign employees are in a better position to take steps to secure an alternate visa status, allowing them to remain legally in the United States without having to spend time out of status or being required to leave the country. Also, employers should try to fully understand each individual's immigration situation. Often, employers may learn through this exercise that by keeping a foreign employee employed for a few more weeks or months, the employee can secure immigration benefits that would take several years to reprocess if the employee had to start over. Employers that do not fully understand the immigration issues facing their foreign employees should work with an immigration attorney to develop a comprehensive transition plan.

- Some progressive employers will provide laid-off workers with access to an immigration attorney to assist the workers in maintaining status. The cost associated with this may be offset for some workers by not having to reimburse the workers for transportation costs to their home country given that proper counseling may result in the workers remaining in the United States legally.

- Employers should remind laid-off workers to be careful not to allow themselves to fall out of status even for a day. If a new work status application cannot be filed before being terminated or during the 60-day grace period, the worker should consider filing an application to change to visitor status. Interviewing for a new job is an acceptable visitor visa activity.

- Employers should ensure they are aware of all the affirmative immigration-related obligations that apply to them based on the types of foreign employees being laid off. Different visa categories have different requirements when terminating employment, and a failure to comply with these requirements could result in considerable financial liability on the part of the employer.

- As layoffs occur, employers should reassess whether the resulting changes in the makeup of their workforces affects the H-1B dependency determination. A change in a company's classification could result in a substantial increase or decrease in legal compliance obligations.

- H-1B–dependent employers should consider carefully how layoffs at their companies, or at companies where they place their employees, affect the prohibition against displacing U.S. workers.

16

STATE EMPLOYER IMMIGRATION LAWS

At the time of the publication of this book, 23 states had enacted employer sanctions laws that impose additional restrictions on employers (depending on number of employees) beyond federal requirements. Of the 23 states, 8 states require all employers who meet jurisdictional standards to use E-Verify, while 12 states require contractors with state or local governments to participate in E-Verify. This chapter's state law summaries contain an overview of the states with employment-related immigration laws.

16.1 Which states have enacted employment-related immigration laws and compliance requirements?

Below is a listing of state laws and requirements. If a state is not covered, it means that state does not have employment-related immigration laws and compliance requirements.

ALABAMA

The Alabama Taxpayer and Citizen Protection Act (ATCPA), which is one of the strictest state immigration laws, requires all Alabama employers to enroll in and use E-Verify. The ATCPA prohibits any employer doing business in the state of Alabama from "knowingly" hiring, employing, or continuing to employ unauthorized "aliens" in Alabama. An employer that has "complied in good faith" with E-Verify will have an affirmative defense that it did not knowingly hire or employ an unauthorized alien.

AL.1 Are there different provisions of the law concerning a private employer and an employer contracting with the state of Alabama or its political subdivision?

Yes, Section 9 of the Alabama Taxpayer and Citizen Protection Act (ATCPA) covers contractors and subcontractors that contract with the state of Alabama and any political subdivision, and Section 15 covers private employers.

AL.2 What are the penalties for a private employer violating the Alabama Taxpayer and Citizen Protection Act?

For a first violation, the following penalties apply:

1. A court order to terminate the employment of every unauthorized worker.

2. A three-year probationary period throughout the state, during which time the employer must file quarterly reports with the local district attorney for each new employee hired.

3. A court order to file a signed, sworn affidavit with the local district attorney within three days after the order is issued by the court stating that the employer has terminated the employment of every unauthorized worker and that the employer will not knowingly or intentionally employ an unauthorized worker in Alabama.

4. Suspension of any state or local business licenses and permits for a period not to exceed 10 business days specific to the business location where the unauthorized employee performed work.

5. An employer's license or permit will not be reinstated until the employer files a signed, sworn affidavit with the local district attorney stating that employer is in compliance with the law, including registering with and using E-Verify and providing a copy of the E-Verify Memorandum of Understanding (MOU).

For a second violation, the penalties are increased to include the permanent revocation of the business license or permit specific to the business location where the unauthorized employee performed work.

For a third violation, the penalties are increased to include the permanent revocation of the business license or permit throughout the state of Alabama.

AL.3 What are the penalties for a contractor or subcontractor that contracts with the state of Alabama or its political subdivision for violating the Alabama Taxpayer and Citizen Protection Act?

For a first violation, the following penalties apply:

1. Contractor's or subcontractor's contract terminated.

2. The contractor or subcontractor may be barred from doing business with any political subdivision.

3. The Alabama attorney general may sue to suspend business licenses and permits for up to 60 days.

4. The employer is required to file a signed, sworn affidavit with the local district attorney within three days after the order is issued by the court stating that the employer has terminated the employment of every unauthorized worker and that the employer will not knowingly or intentionally employ an unauthorized worker in Alabama.

5. An employer's license or permit will not be reinstated until the employer files a signed, sworn affidavit stating it is in compliance with the law, including being registered with and using E-Verify and providing a copy of the E-Verify Memorandum of Understanding (MOU).

For second and subsequent violations, the penalties are increased to the permanent revocation of the business licenses statewide.

AL.4 Which entity enforces the law?

The enforcement provisions in the employment provisions of the Alabama Taxpayer and Citizen Protection Act (ATCPA) include the Alabama attorney general, local district attorneys, and state courts.

AL.5 Is a contractor liable for a subcontractor's violations of the law?

No, unless the contractor knew of the subcontractor's violations.

AL.6 Are there any other penalties for employers violating the Alabama Taxpayer and Citizen Protection Act?

Yes, an employer cannot claim as a deductible business expense for any state income or business tax purposes wages, compensation (whether in money, in kind, or in services), or remuneration of any kind for the performance of services paid to an unauthorized worker. Any employer that knowingly violates this provision will be liable for a penalty equal to 10 times the business expense deduction claimed.

ARIZONA

Arizona was the first state to enact mandatory E-Verify participation for all employers in a state. The Legal Arizona Workers Act took effect on January 1, 2008. The law was upheld by the U.S. Supreme Court in *Chamber of Commerce v. Whiting*, 131 S. Ct. 1968 (2011).

The law requires the Arizona attorney general or the county attorney to investigate employers that "knowingly employ an unauthorized alien." Also, all employers are required to verify employment eligibility of their employees using the federal government's E-Verify program. All Arizona employers participating in E-Verify will be publicly listed on a state website.

AZ.1 How are complaints investigated in Arizona?

Complaints are investigated by the Arizona attorney general (AG) or a county attorney (CA). The AG is required to create a complaint form for alleging violations. Complaints also will be accepted that are not on the prescribed form, and the complaints may be submitted anonymously. Complaints made using the form must be investigated. Complaints made not using the form may be investigated at the discretion of the AG.

Complaints submitted to a CA must be submitted to the CA in the county where the alleged unauthorized employment occurred. The CA may be assisted in the investigation by the county sheriff or any other local law enforcement agency.

The AG or the CA must check with the federal government to determine if the employee is an unauthorized alien. State, county, and local officials are not to independently attempt to verify employment authorization. Persons who knowingly file false complaints can be charged with a misdemeanor.

Complaints made solely on the basis of race, color, or national origin are expressly barred. Also under that law, the AG must determine that a complaint is not false as well as not frivolous.

If the AG determines the complaint is not frivolous, the AG or the CA must notify U.S. Immigration and Customs Enforcement (ICE), local law enforcement, and the appropriate CA. The CA will then bring an action against an employer.

AZ.2 What are the penalties if an employer is found to have violated the Arizona law?

For a first violation in which an employer is guilty of a "knowing violation," the court:

- Will order the employer to terminate the employment of all unauthorized aliens.

- Will order the employer to be subject to a three-year probation period in which the employer will file quarterly reports with the county attorney (CA) on all new hires (at the business location where the unauthorized employee performed work).

- Will order the employer to file a signed sworn affidavit with the CA within three business days after the order has been issued stating that the employer has terminated all unauthorized aliens in Arizona and that the employer will not intentionally or knowingly employ any unauthorized aliens in Arizona.

- May, depending on the severity of the violations and all the factors in the case, order the appropriate agencies to suspend the business license of the employer for up to 10 business days for the business location that is the subject of the complaint (unless the employer does not hold a license specific to that location). The license must be reinstated as soon as the employer signs the affidavit noted above.

The court may consider the following factors in determining whether to suspend the business license:

- The number of unauthorized employees.

- Prior misconduct.

- The degree of harm caused by the violation.

- Whether the employer made good-faith efforts to comply.

- The duration of the violation.

- The role of the directors, officers, or owners in the violation.

- Any other factors the court deems appropriate.

For a second violation occurring during a probationary period, the court will order the appropriate agencies to permanently revoke the business license specific to the business location where the unauthorized employment occurred (unless the employer does not hold a license specific to that location).

Employers that are found to be violators are to have their names listed on the Arizona attorney general website.

AZ.3 Are there any "safe harbors" in the bill?

Yes. If an employer has complied in good faith with the federal Form I-9 rules, the employer will have an affirmative defense that it did not knowingly employ an unauthorized alien. This includes technical violations that are isolated, sporadic, or accidental.

Employers also benefit from a rebuttable presumption that they did not knowingly employ an unauthorized alien if they have verified the status of an employee using the U.S. Department of Homeland Security's (DHS's) E-Verify electronic work authorization program.

There is a "voluntary enhanced employer compliance program" for companies not already in a probationary period. The program has a sunset date in 2018. Employers participating in this voluntary program will not be subject to the state's employer sanctions penalties. Program participants must submit a signed affidavit to the Arizona attorney general (AG) stating the employer will perform the following in good faith:

- Verify new employees in E-Verify.

- Run each employee's Social Security number (SSN) through the Social Security Number Verification Service (SSNVS).

- Provide the AG with documents indicating that employees have been run through E-Verify or SSNVS.

Participants in the voluntary program will be listed on a publicly available state website.

AZ.4 How does Arizona define "knowingly"?

The state law uses the same definition of "knowingly" as federal law. Federal law defines "knowing" to include both actual and constructive knowledge. Because constructive knowledge triggers liability, employers need to be careful that the actions of managers and supervisors are monitored because their knowledge of violations can be imputed to the whole company.

"Knowing" is not actually defined in Title 8 of the U.S. Code (U.S.C.), section 1324a, but the U.S. Department of Homeland Security (DHS) has regulations. Under Code of Federal Regulations, Title 8, section 274a.1(e), "constructive knowledge" may be fairly inferred through notice of certain facts and circumstances that would lead a person, through the exercise of reasonable care, to know about a certain condition. Constructive knowledge may include situations in which an employer fails to properly complete Forms I-9, has information that would indicate the alien is not authorized to work, or has reckless and wanton disregard for the legal consequences of permitting an unauthorized worker into its workforce.

AZ.5 Who is an "an unauthorized alien"?

Arizona states that an unauthorized alien includes an alien who does not have the legal right under federal law to work in the United States as described in U.S. Code (U.S.C.), Title 8, section 1324a(h)(3). This is the section of the U.S. Code containing the Form I-9 rules.

AZ.6 Is an employer liable for work performed by independent contractors?

The statute states that when contract labor is used, "the employer" means the independent contractor and not the entity using the contract labor. Whether an organization is actually an independent contractor is determined based on several factors, including:

- Who supplies the tools or materials.
- Whether the services are available to the general public.
- Whether the contractor works for a number of clients at the same time.
- Whether the contractor can actually make a profit as a result of the labor.
- Whether the contractor invests in the facilities for work.
- Who directs the order or sequence in which the work is done.
- Who determines when the work is finished.

However, an employer is still liable if it knows that the contract employees are not authorized to work.

AZ.7 Do existing employees need to be run through E-Verify to satisfy the Arizona law?

No. Only employees hired on or after January 1, 2008, need to be run through E-Verify.

AZ.8 What steps can a company take to reduce the likelihood of being found to have violated the Arizona law?

Aside from using E-Verify, companies should consider the following actions:

- Conduct regular Form I-9 training for employees responsible for the function.
- Centralize Form I-9 recordkeeping.
- Establish a nondiscriminatory system to re-verify Forms I-9 with expiring work authorization documents.
- Switch from a paper-based Form I-9 system to an electronic one.

- Purge Forms I-9 that employers are legally permitted to purge.

- Have an immigration compliance attorney conduct an internal Form I-9 audit to identify and remediate violations before a government audit occurs.

- Develop a government audit response plan and thoroughly train employees in how to respond to a surprise audit.

AZ.9 What are the changes to the state's identity theft rules that relate to the employment of unauthorized employees?

Using a false identity to obtain or continue employment as one of the elements that may constitute identity theft is a felony in Arizona. It is also a crime to hire a person knowing that the person is providing false identification and using that identification information to meet the employment authorization requirements of the Immigration Reform and Control Act (IRCA). Trafficking in false identification documents to enable someone to obtain or continue employment is a felony as well.

AZ.10 What penalties do employers receiving economic development incentives face for violating the Arizona sanctions laws?

The law specifies that an employer receiving economic development incentives must show proof to the agency providing the incentive that it is registered in E-Verify. Employers not participating will be required to repay all monies received under the incentive.

AZ.11 What are Arizona's special sanctions rules for employers paying employees in cash?

Employers with two or more employees that pay their employees in cash are required to comply with income tax withholding rules, employer reporting laws, employment security law, and workers' compensation rules. The law is not specific to employers of unauthorized immigrants, but such employers are included in the sanctions law because many employers of unauthorized employees pay such employees with cash to keep them off the books and to avoid complying with the Immigration Reform and Control Act (IRCA). Employers violating this rule are subject to triple damages or $5,000 for each employee, whichever is greater. Fines will be used to help the state offset monies appropriated for education and health care expenses for unauthorized aliens. Note that this does not mean penalties under other statutes would be waived.

AZ.12 How does Arizona regulate government procurement contracts for employers with Immigration Reform and Control Act violations?

Government agencies in Arizona are not permitted to award contracts to any contractors or subcontractors that are not registered in E-Verify. Contractors and subcontractors are required to certify their compliance with federal immigration laws and are required to include contract language that states that such violations will be considered a material breach of contract. The contract also must state that the contractor agrees to allow the government agency to inspect the documents of the contractor to ensure compliance with federal immigration laws and to be subject to random audits by the government agency.

ARKANSAS

In 2007, legislation passed in Arkansas prohibiting state agencies from contracting with businesses that employ "illegal immigrants."

AR.1 What does the Arkansas law bar?

No state agency may enter into or renew a public contract for services with a contractor that knows that the contractor or a subcontractor employs or contracts with an illegal immigrant to perform work under the contract.

AR.2 Who is an "illegal immigrant" under the law?

An illegal immigrant is any person who is not a U.S. citizen and who has:

- Entered the United States in violation of federal immigration laws.

- Legally entered the United States but is not authorized to work.

- Legally entered the United States but has overstayed the time limit on his or her status.

AR.3 Who is a contractor under the Arkansas law?

"Contractor" includes any person having a public contract with an Arkansas state agency for professional services, technical and general services, or any category of construction.

AR.4 Are all contracts covered?

All "professional service contracts" where there is a relationship between the contractor and state agency are independent contractor relationships and not employee relationships. The services offered must be professional in nature, and the state may not exercise direct managerial control of the day-to-day activities of the individual providing the services. The contract must specify the results expected from the rendering of the services, and the services are rendered to the state agency itself or to a third-party beneficiary. Contracts must have a total value of $25,000 or more to be covered by this law.

AR.5 Are all agencies in Arkansas covered?

"Covered agencies" include any agency, institution, authority, department, board, commission, bureau, council, or other agency of the state supported by state or federal funds.

Some institutions are exempt from the law, including all constitutional departments of the state, the elected constitutional offices of the state, the General Assembly and its supporting agencies, the Arkansas Supreme Court and related courts.

AR.6 How do contractors show they have not hired unauthorized employees?

Before signing a public contract, a prospective contractor must certify—in a manner that does not violate federal law—that the contractor, at the time of certification, does not employ or contract with an illegal immigrant.

AR.7 What if it is determined that a contractor has hired unauthorized employees?

If a contractor violates the law, the state must give a contractor 60 days to remedy the violation. If the violation is not remedied by that point, the state is to terminate the contract. The contractor will then be liable to the state for actual damages for violating the contract.

AR.8 Does it matter if a contractor is using the services of individuals hired by a subcontractor?

If a contractor uses a subcontractor, the subcontractor must certify that it does not employ or contract with an illegal immigrant, and it must submit the certification within 30 days of execution of the subcontract. Contractors that learn that a subcontractor is violating the rule may terminate the contract and not be liable for a breach of contract.

AR.9 Does the law require employers that have contracts with the state to use E-Verify?

No, the Arkansas law does not require employers contracting with the state to use the E-Verify electronic employment verification system.

CALIFORNIA

California prohibits state, city, and county governments from mandating the use of E-Verify "except as required by federal law or as a condition of receiving federal funds."

COLORADO

Colorado has passed four separate pieces of legislation affecting employers. They are the following:

- H.B. 06-1343, which requires employers contracting with the state to use E-Verify.

- H.B. 06S-1001, which bars employers from receiving access to state economic development incentives if they are not complying with the Immigration Reform and Control Act (IRCA).

- H.B. 06S-1015, which requires the state to set up an employment verification website that will enable a person to access a database to determine the validity of a taxpayer identification number.

- H.B. 06S-1020, which bars employers that cannot verify an employee is a legal U.S. resident from claiming an employee's wages as a deductible business expense.

CO.1 What does H.B. 06-1343 bar?

H.B. 06-1343 bars state agencies and local government agencies from entering into or renewing public contracts for services with contractors that "knowingly" employ or contract with an "illegal alien" to perform work under the contract or with contractors that contract with subcontractors that knowingly employ or contract with an "illegal alien" to perform work under the contract.

CO.2 Who is an "illegal alien" under the law?

Unlike other state laws, "illegal alien" is not defined under the Colorado statute.

CO.3 Who is a contractor under the Colorado law?

A "contractor" is a person having a public contract for services with a state agency.

CO.4 Are all contracts covered?

No. Only public contracts are covered. These are agreements between a state agency and a contract for the provision of services (as opposed to the provision of goods). "Services" covers the furnishing of labor by a contractor or subcontractor and not the delivery of goods.

CO.5 Are all agencies in Colorado covered?

Yes. There are no exemptions provided in the statute from complying with the Colorado rule.

CO.6 How do contractors show they have not hired unauthorized employees?

Contractors are required to include language in their contracts with the state certifying that they do not knowingly employ illegal aliens and that the contractors participate in E-Verify.

CO.7 What if it is determined that a contractor has hired illegal aliens?

If a contractor violates this law, a state agency may terminate its contract with the contractor. The contractor would be liable for any damages to the state agency. The state agency must inform the secretary of state of the breach. The secretary of state will keep a list, including the name of the contractor and the state agency that terminated the public contract, and will not remove the contractor until two years have passed. And the list must be made available to the public.

CO.8 Does the law require employers contracting with the state to use E-Verify?

Yes. Employers are required to include a provision in their contracts with state agencies that certifies that they participate in E-Verify.

CO.9 Does it matter if a contractor is using the services of individuals hired by a subcontractor?

Yes. First, if a contractor obtains actual knowledge that a subcontractor performing work under a public contract knowingly employs an illegal alien, the contractor must notify the subcontractor and the contracting agency within three days of gaining actual knowledge. And the contractor must terminate the subcontract if the subcontractor does not stop employing or contracting with the illegal alien unless the subcontractor shows that it has not knowingly employed an illegal alien.

CO.10 If an employer is found to have violated the law, how long will the employer remain on the list of employers barred from doing business with the state?

Two years.

CO.11 What type of investigative authority does the state have under this law?

The state's Department of Labor and Employment (DLE) has the authority to investigate whether a contractor is complying with the terms of a public contract. It may conduct onsite inspections where a public contract is being performed. The DLE receives complaints of suspected violations and has the discretion to determine which complaints, if any, are to be investigated.

CO.12 What does H.B. 06S-1001 require?

Employers must be in compliance with the rules of the Immigration Reform and Control Act (IRCA) to be eligible to receive a grant, loan, or performance-based or other economic development incentive offered by the Colorado Economic Development Commission (CEDC).

CO.13 How does the Colorado Economic Development Commission determine that an employer is in compliance with the Immigration Reform and Control Act?

The Colorado Economic Development Commission (CEDC) has the discretion to determine when to verify that an employer is in compliance with the Immigration Reform and Control Act (IRCA).

CO.14 What happens when the Colorado Economic Development Commission determines an employer is out of compliance?

When the Colorado Economic Development Commission (CEDC) determines that an employer is out of compliance or the employer cannot prove compliance, the CEDC will notify the employer of noncompliance, and the employer must repay the total amount of money received as an economic development incentive within 30 days of receipt of notice. Furthermore, employers will be barred from receiving an economic development incentive for five years after the date that the employer has repaid the CEDC in full.

CO.15 Do employers have any right to argue against the determination of the Colorado Economic Development Commission?

Yes. Employers can appear at a hearing before the Colorado Economic Development Commission (CEDC) and present proof that the employer is in compliance with the Immigration Reform and Control Act (IRCA).

CO.16 What does H.B. 06S-1015 do?

The law requires Colorado to create a "work eligibility verification portal" that will enable a person to access a database to verify whether a taxpayer identification number is valid. Employers providing a Form 1099 to persons who fail to provide a valid taxpayer identification number are required to withhold state income taxes presumably because it is assumed that undocumented immigrants are not as likely to pay taxes on their own.

CO.17 What does H.B. 06S-1020 do?

It bars employers from taking a state income tax deduction for wages greater than $600 paid to unauthorized aliens if the business knew of the unauthorized status of the alien.

CO.18 Are there exceptions to the law?

Yes. It does not apply to individuals hired before the effective date of the bill. It does not apply to persons who hold and presented a valid license or identification card issued by the Colorado Department of Revenue. And it does not apply in cases in which the individual being paid is not directly compensated or employed by the taxpayer.

FLORIDA

Governor Rick Scott signed an Executive Order concerning E-Verify in 2011.

FL.1 What does the Executive Order state?

The Executive Order contains the following provisions:

- All agencies under the direction of the governor must verify the employment eligibility of all new agency employees through the E-Verify system.

- All agencies under the direction of the governor are to include, as a condition of all state contracts, an express requirement that contractors use the E-Verify system to verify the employment eligibility of:

- All persons hired during the contract term by a contractor to perform employment duties within the state of Florida.

- Employees hired by subcontractors during the contract term.

GEORGIA

In 2011, Georgia passed the Illegal Immigration Reform and Enforcement Act, which requires all employers with more than 10 employees to enroll in and use E-Verify. Previously, in 2006, Georgia had enacted the Georgia Security and Immigration Compliance Act, which requires public employers and employers doing business with state agencies to enroll in and participate in E-Verify.

GA.1 Do all employers in Georgia have to enroll in E-Verify?

No, the employer must have more than 10 employees.

GA.2 Is there a minimum number of hours that an employee must work to be counted toward the more-than-10-employee threshold?

Yes. The employee must work at least 35 hours per week.

GA.3 Is the threshold of more than 10 employees based on employees employed in the state of Georgia or nationwide?

Nationwide.

GA.4 How does an employer notify the state of Georgia that it is enrolled in and using E-Verify?

Employers must sign an affidavit stating they are enrolled in and using E-Verify.

GA.5 When does the employer have to provide this affidavit, and to whom is it provided?

Employers must provide the affidavit to counties and municipalities when applying for or renewing a business license, occupational tax certificate, or other document required to operate a business.

GA.6 What is the penalty for a private employer failing to enroll in and use E-Verify?

If a company fails to submit an affidavit certifying that it is enrolled in and using E-Verify or that it is exempt (because of 10 or fewer employees), the county or municipality where the employer is seeking a business license, occupational tax certificate, or other document required to operate a business must deny the business license or its renewal.

GA.7 Where do employers obtain the affidavits?

The affidavits are available on the state's website, law.ga.gov/immigration-reports.

GA.8 Is it a violation to make a false or misleading statement in the affidavit?

Yes.

GA.9 What is the penalty for making a false or misleading statement in the affidavit?

The individual is subject to a fine of up to $1,000 and possible imprisonment for one to five years. Furthermore, an employer is prohibited from bidding or receiving a public contract for 12 months.

GA.10 Who enforces the Georgia state immigration laws?

The Georgia attorney general has the authority to investigate and bring criminal or civil actions.

GA.11 Are all public contractors, even those with 10 or fewer employees, mandated to enroll in E-Verify because of a contract with state or local government?

Yes, if the contract is for $2,500 or more for labor or services.

GA.12 Do contractors with a contract with the state of Georgia or a local government agency face penalties for failure to comply with state law?

Yes. For a first violation, there is public disclosure on a state website. For a second violation, contractors face debarment for 12 months.

GA.13 Are subcontractors and sub-subcontractors covered by the same E-Verify law as contractors on projects with the state or local government?

Yes.

GA.14 Are public contractors and subcontractors responsible for contractors below them?

Contractors and subcontractors are required to obtain E-Verify affidavits from all subcontractors and sub-subcontractors. These affidavits must be forwarded to the contracting entity within five business days of receipt, and the primary contractor must submit all affidavits to the public employer within five business days of receipt.

GA.15 Can public contractors or subcontractors be held liable for the failure of a subcontractor to enroll in and use E-Verify?

Yes, however, contractors and subcontractors are excluded from civil or criminal liability if they "unknowingly or unintentionally" accept bids violating law.

GA.16 Does a contractor or subcontractor that does not have any employees and does not plan to have any employees face any requirements under state law?

Yes, the contractor or subcontractor must provide a state driver's license or identification card of each independent contractor employed in the completion of a public contract.

GA.17 Are contractors subject to common audits?

Yes, public contractors can be audited by the Georgia Department of Labor.

GA.18 What does the bill do with respect to deduction of wages paid by employers to unauthorized employees?

Employers that pay more than $600 to an employee may not deduct the amount if an individual is not an authorized employee. Independent contractors receiving a Form 1099 are covered by this provision as well. Individuals hired before January 19, 2008, are not covered, nor are individuals not directly compensated or employed by an employer. And individuals who present a valid license or identification card issued by the Georgia Department of Driver Services are exempted.

GA.19 What does the bill state with respect to withholding state income tax?

Employers must withhold state income tax at the rate of 6 percent for individuals receiving a Form 1099 if the individual has failed to provide a taxpayer identification number or an IRS-issued taxpayer identification number for non-resident aliens, or has provided an incorrect taxpayer identification number. Employers failing to withhold will be liable for the taxes.

IDAHO

In 2009, Idaho Governor C. L. "Butch" Otter signed Executive Order No. 2009-10 addressing the subject of illegal immigration. This executive order superseded E.O. 2006-40.

ID.1 What does the executive order do?

The executive order requires that all workers employed by state contractors be verified as legal employees and that state agencies must participate in the E-Verify system. Penalties for violations include cancellation of contracts and civil penalties.

ILLINOIS

Illinois passed the Right to Privacy in the Workplace Act, which creates a website, sponsored by the Illinois Department of Labor (IDOL) that tracks the E-Verify program's accuracy and provides information for employers to understand their obligations and their employees' rights under the federal program. Another state law (H.B. 1743) provides state-level protections for employees from employers that discriminate.

IL.1 Are employers in Illinois prevented from using E-Verify by either law?

No.

IL.2 Do companies using E-Verify in Illinois have to meet any state requirements?

Yes. E-Verify enrollees must attest, under penalty of perjury, to the Illinois Department of Labor (IDOL) the following:

The company has received the E-Verify training materials from the DHS [U.S. Department of Homeland Security] and all employees who will administer the program have completed the computer-based tutorial training provided by the E-Verify program; and the company must keep the signed original attestation and computer-based tutorial training certificates for inspection and copying by the IDOL. 820 ILCS 55/12(b).

IL.3 Are there any causes of action for employers that discriminate against its employees by not following E-Verify's procedures?

Yes, there is a cause of action for employees and prospective employees to file a charge of discrimination against employers that discriminate on the basis of hiring, discharging, or taking any other adverse employment action by not following E-Verify's procedures.

IL.4 What are H.B. 1743's anti-discrimination rules?

H.B. 1743 creates a series of new state civil rights violations for discrimination against employees. These include:

- Employers that refuse to hire, segregate, or otherwise treat employees adversely on the basis of unlawful discrimination or citizenship status.

- Employers that impose restrictions on a language (excluding slang or profanities) being spoken by an employee if the communication is unrelated to the employee's duties.

- Employment agencies that refuse to accept or refer applicants, or that make or have the effect of making unlawful discrimination or discrimination on the basis of citizenship status a condition of referral.

- Unions that limit membership or employment opportunities on the basis of unlawful discrimination or citizenship status.

IL.5 What types of immigration-related practices does H.B. 1743 bar?

Employers are barred from requiring more or different documents than required in the Form I-9 rules. Employers participating in E-Verify are barred from refusing to hire, segregate, or act with respect to recruitment, hiring, promotion, renewal of employment, selection for training or apprenticeship, discharge, discipline, tenure, or other privileges without following the E-Verify rules. Employers that follow the rules of the Immigration Reform and Control Act (IRCA) are not considered to be violating H.B. 1743.

IL.6 Did Illinois previously have a law prohibiting participation in the E-Verify program?

Yes, but that law is no longer in effect.

INDIANA

Indiana passed an E-Verify statute, effective July 1, 2011, wherein contractors that enter into contracts with state and local governments in Indiana must enroll in and use E-Verify for all new hires. The law also requires Indiana state and local governments to enroll in and use E-Verify for all new hires.

IN.1 How is the law enforced?

The law authorizes state agencies or local governments to terminate a public contract, without penalty, if the contractor knowingly employs "illegal immigrants."

IN.2 What actions must a contractor take to be in compliance with the state law?

Contractors must enroll in and use E-Verify as well as provide an affidavit that the contractor does not knowingly employ unauthorized workers. Contractors must submit their E-Verify verification numbers before work begins on a public work project.

IN.3 Are there any provisions related to subcontractors?

Yes. If subcontractors are employed under a public contract, the subcontractor must certify to the contractor that it uses E-Verify and does not knowingly employ illegal immigrants.

IN.4 What are the penalties for violating the law?

The state will terminate the contract and damages will be owed if a contractor does not remedy the violation within 30 days. If the state determines that termination of the contract would be detrimental to the public interest or to public property, it may allow the contract to remain in effect until a new contractor is in place. If a contractor determines that a subcontractor is in violation of the law, it may terminate the contract with the subcontractor.

IN.5 Is there a "safe harbor" for employers using E-Verify?

Yes, an employer may not be found to knowingly employ an unauthorized alien if the employer verified the employee through E-Verify.

IN.6 Does the law apply to any other companies besides those contracting with state and local governments?

Yes, the law applies to business entities that receive a grant of more than $1,000 from a state agency or state political subdivision. These companies must sign and show documentation that they use E-Verify and do not knowingly employ unauthorized workers.

IN.7 Who has authority to enforce the law?

The local prosecuting attorney has the authority to file a cause of action against a company for violation of the law.

IN.8 Are there any provisions in the law related to business expenses?

Yes. The law prohibits business owners who knowingly hire unauthorized workers from deducting expenses associated with those employees in the calculation of their state income taxes.

IOWA

Iowa has a statute stating that businesses receiving economic development assistance are subject to contract provisions mandating that new and retained jobs must be filled by people who are U.S. citizens or individuals otherwise authorized to work in the United States. Employers may be required by the state to provide "periodic assurances" that employees are authorized to work in the United States.

LOUISIANA

Louisiana has two E-Verify laws. One law requires the employer to use the E-Verify system *or* to retain an employee's picture identification and a copy of a U.S. birth certificate, certificate of naturalization, certificate of U.S. citizenship, or a Form I-94 with an employment-authorized stamp for all employees. The second law requires all private contractors doing business with a state or local public entity in Louisiana to use E-Verify.

LA.1 Are all employers in Louisiana required to enroll in and use E-Verify?

No, under Louisiana's law, it is not mandatory for private employers that do not contract with state or local government to enroll in and use E-Verify.

LA.2 Are there penalties under Louisiana law for employers that employ unauthorized workers?

Yes. A first violation is a fine of up to $500 per "illegal immigrant" employee, and a second offense results in a fine of up to $1,000 per illegal employee. For a third and subsequent offenses, a business faces the immediate suspension of its work permit or license for 30 days to six months and a fine not to exceed $2,500 per illegal immigrant.

LA.3 Do the penalties apply equally to health care facilities?

No, if a business is licensed by the Louisiana Department of Health and Hospitals, such as a nursing home or a medical clinic, that agency will determine the penalties based on applicable licensing statutes and rules.

LA.4 If a contractor bids on a project with state or local governments, are there specific provisions that the contractor must follow?

Yes. Any bidder seeking a public contract must file a sworn affidavit as part of the bid package, binding the firm to use E-Verify at the start of the contract and for all new workers hired.

LA.5 What are the penalties for violation of the law concerning contracting with state or local governments?

Failure to enroll in and use E-Verify could result in the cancellation of the contract and a possible three-year ban on the contractor receiving other public contracts. If a contract is cancelled, the private company "shall be liable for any additional costs incurred" by the public body in awarding a new contract or for delays in the project.

LA.6 Do prime contractors have any responsibility toward their subcontractors?

The prime contractor must require all subcontractors to use E-Verify to confirm the legal status of their workers.

LA.7 Is there a "safe harbor" for employers using E-Verify or for retaining one of the applicable documents, such as a U.S. birth certificate, naturalization certificate, or permanent resident card?

Yes, an employer may not be found to knowingly employ an unauthorized alien if the employer verified the employee through E-Verify or retained one of the applicable documents.

MASSACHUSETTS

Massachusetts Governor Deval L. Patrick signed Executive Order No. 481 in 2007 regarding the use of undocumented employees on state contracts.

MA.1 What does Executive Order No. 481 do?

Under the order, all state agencies are prohibited from using "undocumented workers" in connection with the performance of state contracts.

MA.2 Are employers subjected to any new requirements under Executive Order No. 481?

Yes. Employers must certify, as a condition to receiving Massachusetts government funds, that they must not knowingly use undocumented workers in connection with the performance of the contract and that they have lawfully verified the immigration status of all workers assigned to the contract. Also, employers must certify that they have not knowingly or recklessly altered, falsified, or accepted altered or falsified documents from any workers.

MA.3 What provisions must be added to contracts between employers and state agencies?

All contracts must now specify that a breach of the immigration terms of the agreement may be regarded as a material breach and that the employer will be subject to sanctions, monetary penalties, withholding of payments, contract suspension, or termination.

MICHIGAN

MI.1 How does Michigan regulate state government contractors?

On October 31, 2007, Michigan's governor signed Public Act No. 127, which orders state agencies to consider a business's use of employees, contractors, subcontractors, or others that are not citizens of the United States, legal resident aliens, or individuals with valid visas in determining whether to contract with that business. If contracting with such an employer would be detrimental to the people of Michigan, that fact may be considered when deciding to contract with the employer.

MI.2 Are any employers required to enroll in and use E-Verify?

Yes, but only in limited circumstances. Contractors and subcontractors contracting with the Michigan Department of Transportation for the performance of construction, maintenance, and engineering services must enroll in and use E-Verify.

MINNESOTA

A 2011 law requires employers, including contractors and subcontractors, entering into contracts with the state that are valued at more than $50,000 to participate in the E-Verify program.

MN.1 What are the penalties for violation of this law?

The state may cancel the current contract and debar the contractor from future contracts.

MISSISSIPPI

Mississippi's law mandates use of E-Verify for all employers in the state and the revocation of business licenses of employers violating immigration laws, and creates a felony for persons illegally accepting employment.

MS.1 What is the law regarding employing workers unauthorized to work?

Employers in Mississippi are permitted to hire only employees who are legal citizens of the United States or are "legal aliens." Legal aliens are those lawfully present in the country at the time of employment and for the duration of employment.

MS.2 What is the state's E-Verify mandate?

All employers, both public and private, must enroll in and use E-Verify, the electronic employment verification system.

MS.3 What penalties do employers face for violating the Mississippi law?

Employers are subject to the cancellation of any state or public contract and face a bar of up to three years on accessing state contracts. Employers also face the loss of any license, permit, certificate, or other document granted by any agency in Mississippi. This includes a business license, and the revocation of the license may be for up to one year. The Mississippi Department of Employment Security, state tax commission, Mississippi secretary of state, the Mississippi Department of Human Services, and the attorney general have the authority to seek penalties for noncompliance.

MS.4 Are there any "safe harbors" for employers?

Yes. Employers in the following circumstances are exempted from liability:

- Employers hiring employees through a state or federal work program requiring verification of the employee's Social Security number (SSN) and verifying employment authorization.

- Any candidate referred by the Mississippi Department of Employment Security (MDES) if the MDES has verified the SSN and verified employment authorization.

- Individual homeowners who hire workers on their private property for noncommercial purposes unless required by federal law to do so.

MS.5 What are the obligations of out-of-state employers that send workers into the state?

All employers employing workers in Mississippi are required to register to do business in Mississippi with the Mississippi Department of Employment Security (MDES) before placing employees into the workforce in Mississippi.

MS.6 How are U.S. citizen workers affected by the law?

Mississippi law states it is a discriminatory practice if an employer discharges a U.S. citizen or permanent resident employee and replaces him or her with an employee not authorized to work. Employers using E-Verify are protected from liability. Employees that can demonstrate they were unlawfully terminated have the right to sue an employer for damages.

MS.7 What is the felony provision in Mississippi applicable to those accepting unauthorized employment?

Mississippi law makes it a felony for any person to accept employment if the employee knows he or she is unauthorized. Violators are subject to imprisonment from one to five years and a fine of between $1,000 and $10,000.

MISSOURI

In 2008, Missouri enacted H.B. 1549, an employer sanctions bill. The governor also issued Executive Order 87-02, wherein the Missouri Housing Development Commission (MHDC) must prohibit owners of a project that receives federal or state tax credits from using "undocumented workers" in the construction of MHDC-funded projects.

MO.1 What does the law in Missouri say generally with respect to hiring "unauthorized aliens"?

H.B. 1549 bars business entities and employers from knowingly employing, recruiting, hiring for employment, or continuing to employ unauthorized aliens.

MO.2 What is a "federal work authorization program" under H.B. 1549?

A "federal work authorization program" is an electronic employment verification system run by the U.S. Department of Homeland Security as authorized by the Immigration Reform and Control Act (IRCA). Currently, E-Verify is the only one.

MO.3 What is a "public employer"?

Every department and agency in the state or any political subdivision of the state is a "public employer."

MO.4 How does H.B. 1549 affect public employers?

Public employers are required to enroll in a federal work authorization program.

MO.5 How does H.B. 1549 affect employers contracting with state agencies?

As a condition to any contract worth more than $5,000, employers are required to certify and document that it is enrolled in a federal work authorization program. The certification is limited to employees working in connection with the contracted services. Businesses also must certify that they do not knowingly employ unauthorized aliens in connection with contracted services.

MO.6 Is there a "safe harbor" in H.B. 1549?

Yes. Employers that enroll in a federal work authorization program have an affirmative defense against claims under H.B. 1549 related to hiring unauthorized aliens.

MO.7 Are businesses liable for the actions of contractors and subcontractors?

No, as long as the contract with the contractor or subcontractor states that the contractor or subcontractor has not hired unauthorized aliens and that it is enrolled in a federal work authorization program. A sworn affidavit stating that the contractor or subcontractor's workers are not unauthorized aliens is also acceptable.

MO.8 How are complaints filed and handled under H.B. 1549?

Any state official, business entity, or resident of Missouri can file a written complaint alleging the actions constituting the violation as well as the date and location of the violation. Complaints based on national origin, race, or ethnicities are invalid. Within 15 days, the Missouri attorney general (AG) will request identity information from the employer, and if the employer fails to respond, the AG will direct the municipality or county to suspend the employer's licenses or permits.

Once the AG receives the identifying information, he or she will check the names with the federal government to determine if the workers are authorized to be employed. If the federal government says the workers are authorized or that it is unable to make a determination, then the AG will drop the investigation. State officials are not to make independent determinations of work authorization status, and the law explicitly states that only the federal government can make such a determination.

If the federal government indicates that an employee is not work authorized, the AG will bring an action in a court.

MO.9 What penalties may a court impose when the attorney general brings an action under H.B. 1549?

If an employer did not knowingly violate the law against hiring unauthorized aliens, the employer will have 15 business days to terminate the unauthorized alien or to obtain new documentation that the employee is authorized. The employer will provide an affidavit swearing that the violation has ended and that the employer has enrolled in a federal work authorization program.

If the employer knowingly violated the law, the applicable municipality or county will suspend any license or permit held by the employer for 14 days or 1 day after the employer provides an affidavit that it no longer has unauthorized workers and that it is enrolled in a federal work authorization program.

Municipalities and counties that fail to suspend a license or permit as directed by the court will be considered "sanctuary cities" and subject to penalties.

Second violations will result in a one-year suspension of a license or permit. Subsequent violations will result in a permanent revocation.

Businesses contracting with the state that are found to have hired unauthorized aliens will be deemed to be in breach of the contract, and the state may break the contract and debar the employer from doing business with the state for up to three years for first violations. The debarment may be permanent for subsequent violations. The state may also withhold up to 25 percent of the money due the employer under the contract.

MO.10 What happens if someone files a frivolous complaint?

Anyone who submits a frivolous complaint will be liable for actual, compensatory, and punitive damages to the alleged violator.

MO.11 How are employer tax deductions for the wages paid to unauthorized aliens affected?

Employers are not allowed to deduct wages paid to unauthorized aliens.

MO.12 Does the law contain transporting provisions?

Yes. It is a state crime to knowingly move or transport an illegal alien for the purposes of employment, and violators will be subject to jail for not less than one year and at least a $1,000 fine.

MO.13 What does the executive order do?

Owners of Missouri Housing Development Commission (MHDC)-funded projects must require their contractors to obtain a Form I-9 from each employee and must also require that contractors, in turn, require subcontractors to obtain a Form I-9 from their employees. The owner is required to collect copies of these Forms I-9, to keep the Forms I-9 at the project site, and to have the owners require their contractors to assemble a list of all employees completing Forms I-9 (and to update the list regularly). Each month, the owner must provide the MHDC with a list of all employees employed by the contractor or subcontractor. Violators are subject to sanctions, though they are not specified in the order.

NEBRASKA

L.B. 403, enacted in 2009, states contractors performing work for public employers in Nebraska are required to use E-Verify to determine the employment eligibility of all newly hired employees. The law also applies to state and local government agencies in Nebraska. The law does not apply to private employees who are not contracting with the state of Nebraska or with a local government agency.

NE.1 Which entities must use E-Verify in Nebraska?

Public contractors performing work for public employers in Nebraska and state and local government agencies are required to use E-Verify.

NE.2 What is the definition of a "public contractor"?

Public contractors are defined as "any contractor or his or her subcontractor who is awarded a contract by a public employer for the physical performance of services within the State of Nebraska. Neb. Rev. Stat. 4-114 (1)(b). Every contract between a public employer and contractor must contain a provision requiring the contractor to use E-Verify to determine the employment eligibility of new employees.

NE.3 Are there tax incentives for employers using E-Verify?

Yes.

NE.4 What are the penalties for violating L.B. 403?

The contractor may be disqualified or the contract terminated if lawful presence cannot be verified.

NEVADA

In 2007, Nevada enacted Assembly Bill 383, which regulates various aspects of immigration in Nevada. The bill has an employer sanctions provision.

NV.1 How does Nevada regulate employer compliance?

Assembly Bill 383 permits the Nevada Tax Commission to impose administrative fines on employers with business licenses that "willfully, flagrantly or otherwise egregiously" engage in the unlawful hiring or employment of an unauthorized alien in violation of federal law. Employers are permitted to submit proof that they have attempted to verify the Social Security number (SSN) of the unauthorized alien within six months from the date on which the unauthorized alien was allegedly employed. The proof may include a printout from the Internet. The statute does not specify the amount of the fines.

The law also contains a provision penalizing harboring of unauthorized aliens, a charge that has been used against employers at the federal level.

NEW HAMPSHIRE

NH.1 How does New Hampshire regulate employer compliance?

Since 1976, New Hampshire has had a law in force (N.H. Rev. Stat. Ann. Section 275-A:40a) that bars employers from employing any alien whom the employer knows is not a U.S. citizen and is not in possession of either a permanent resident card or other documentation showing the individual is authorized to work. Employers violating this provision are subject to fines of up to $2,500 per day.

NORTH CAROLINA

In 2011, North Carolina passed H.B. 36, which requires employers to verify the work authorization of new employees through E-Verify. Previously, in 2006, North Carolina passed S.B. 1523, requiring all public employers in the state to use E-Verify.

NC.1 Does H.B. 36 apply to all employers in North Carolina?

An employer must employ 25 or more employees in North Carolina for an employer to be required to enroll in and use E-Verify.

NC.2 What is the definition of an employee?

An "employee" excludes those individuals hired to work for less than nine months in a calendar year. This provision is meant to exclude temporary agricultural employees.

NC.3 How can a complaint be filed?

Any person with a good faith belief that an employer is violating or has violated the law may file a complaint with the North Carolina commissioner of labor.

NC.4 What are the penalties for violating H.B. 36?

For a first violation, the commissioner of labor will order the employer to file a signed, sworn affidavit with the commissioner within three business days after the order is issued. The affidavit must state with specificity that the employer has, after consultation with the employee, requested a verification of work authorization through E-Verify. If an employer fails to timely file an affidavit required by this subsection, the commissioner will order the employer to pay a civil penalty of $10,000.

For a second violation, the commissioner will order the employer to pay a civil penalty of $1,000, regardless of the number of required employee verifications the employer failed to make.

For a third violation, the commissioner will order the employer to pay a civil penalty of $2,000 for each required employee verification that the employer failed to make.

NC.5 Are there any provisions related to contracting with state or local governments?

City, county, and state government agencies and boards are barred from entering into contracts with contractors that are not enrolled and participating in E-Verify. Also, these government contractors and subcontractors are required to include an E-Verify provision in their contracts.

OKLAHOMA

In 2007, the Oklahoma Taxpayer and Citizen Protection Act (OTCPA) was enacted and includes requiring public contractors and subcontractors to enroll in and use E-Verify.

OK.1 What are the Oklahoma Taxpayer and Citizen Protection Act's E-Verify provisions?

All contractors and subcontractors entering into contracts with public employers in Oklahoma must enroll in and use E-Verify to verify the work authorization of all new employees.

No public employer may enter into a contract for the performance of services within the state unless the employer participates in E-Verify. All public employers are required to enroll in and use E-Verify to verify the work authorization of all new employees.

OK.2 What is the Oklahoma Taxpayer and Citizen Protection Act's unfair trade practices provision?

A situation in which an employer fires a U.S. citizen or permanent resident alien employee at the same time it employs an unauthorized immigrant is considered an unfair trade practice. Fired employees have a private right to sue for such an unfair trade practice. This only covers situations, however, in which the terminated employee is working in a job category requiring equal skill, effort, and responsibility and which is performed under similar working conditions.

OK.3 Is there a "safe harbor" provision under the Oklahoma law?

Yes. Employers using E-Verify for employees hired after July 1, 2008, are exempt from liability.

OK.4 What are the Oklahoma Taxpayer and Citizen Protection Act's transporting and harboring provisions?

The Oklahoma law makes it unlawful for any person to transport, conceal, harbor, or shelter from detection in any place, including any building or means of transportation, any alien who is in violation of the law. This provision could be used against employers knowingly employing unauthorized immigrants.

OK.5 What are the penalties for violating the transporting and harboring provisions?

Violating these provisions constitutes a felony punishable by one year in jail and a fine of not less than $1,000, or both.

PENNSYLVANIA

Pennsylvania S.B. 637, effective January 1, 2013, states that employers that enter into contracts with the state, or any of its political subdivisions, any authority created by the state assembly, or any instrumentality or agency of the state, for a public works contract must use E-Verify and confirm the same using the verification form.

Pennsylvania H.B. 2319, passed in 2006, bars employers from knowingly employing the labor services of an illegal alien on any project. The law requires employers that receive any state grants or loans to repay such grants or loans if they are found under federal law to have knowingly used labor provided by an "illegal alien." Employers can avoid liability if they can show that contractors that provided the labor to the employer provided a certification regarding compliance with the Immigration Reform and Control Act (IRCA).

PA.1 What is the definition of "public work" under S.B. 637?

"Public work" is defined as "construction, reconstruction, demolition, alteration and/or repair work other than maintenance work, done under contract and paid for in whole or in part out of the funds of a public body where the estimated cost of the total project is in excess of $25,000, but shall not include work performed under a rehabilitation or manpower training program. 43 Penn. Cons. Stat. Section 165-5.

PA.2 Does the law apply to both contractors and subcontractors of public work?

Yes.

PA.3 Are there any preconditions for a contractor being awarded a public contract?

A contractor must provide the government with a verification form (provided by the state) that certifies that the information contained in the form is true and correct and that the individual signing the form understands that submission of false or misleading information subjects the individual and the contractor to sanctions.

PA.4 What are the penalties for violating the law?

Violating the law results in the following penalty stages:

- First violation for failing to enroll in and use E-Verify: warning and posting on the state website.
- Second violation: debarred from public work for 30 days.

- Third violation: debarred from public work for 180 days to one year.

PA.5 What penalties apply to willful violators?

Willful violators are debarred from public work for three years.

PA.6 What are the penalties for providing a false statement?

Employers that make a false statement or misrepresentation with respect to the verification form are subject to a civil penalty of $250 to $1,000 for each violation.

PA.7 Which government agency investigates complaints?

The Pennsylvania Department of General Services must investigate credible complaints and conduct audits to ensure compliance.

SOUTH CAROLINA

In 2008, the South Carolina legislature passed the South Carolina Illegal Immigration Reform Act (SCIIRA). In 2011, the law was amended to require all employers in South Carolina to enroll and participate in E-Verify, effective January 1, 2012.

In FY2014, South Carolina performed audits of 3,214 employers with 4.6 percent of the companies in violation of the law. At the time of this publication, no newer statistics are available.

SC.1 Are all private employers required to enroll in and use E-Verify?

Yes. All private employers must enroll in and use E-Verify to confirm employment authorization of new employees.

SC.2 What obligation does the law impose on government employers?

All public employers are required to register and participate in E-Verify.

SC.3 How are complaints against employers investigated and violations punished?

After the director of the South Carolina Budget and Control Board receives a written complaint against a private employer, or the state begins its own investigation based on good cause or under random auditing, the director must conduct an investigation. If the director believes "substantial evidence exists" to support a finding of a violation of the South Carolina law, the director must notify U.S. Immigration and Customs Enforcement (ICE) and local and state law enforcement agencies enforcing state immigration laws.

SC.4 What are the penalties for an employer failing to verify a new employee?

If an employer fails to verify a new employee through E-Verify within three business days of the hire, the employer is placed on probation for a period of one year and is required to submit quarterly reports to the South Carolina Department of Labor, Licensing and Regulation (LLR) demonstrating compliance with the law. A subsequent violation within three years results in a business's license being revoked from 10 to 30 days. Additionally, if the employee was not verified, the employer must discharge the employee.

SC.5 What are the penalties for an employer "knowingly" employing an unauthorized alien?

The penalties are the following:

- The employment license will be suspended for 10 to 30 days for a first offense of "knowingly" employing an unauthorized alien, and the employer may not employ any workers during the suspension period. After the period of suspension, the private employer's license may be reinstated if the employer demonstrates that the unauthorized employee has been terminated and pays a reinstatement fee equal to the cost of investigating and enforcing (not to exceed $1,000).

- For a second offense, the suspension of the employment license will be for 30 to 60 days with reinstatement being permitted based on the same terms as those for a first offense.

- For a third or later offense, the employment license will be revoked, and the employer may seek a provisional license only after 90 days. The employer must provide quarterly reports to the director of the South Carolina Budget and Control Board demonstrating compliance and proving that unauthorized employees have been terminated. Also, a reinstatement fee must be paid.

- If an employer engages in business or employs a new employee during the suspension period, the employer is subject to a revocation of the employment license, and reinstatement will not be permitted for at least five years.

The director of the South Carolina Budget and Control Board maintains a list of violators and publishes it on the agency's website.

SC.6 What is the "employment license" created by the law?

All private employers in South Carolina on or after July 1, 2009, are deemed to have an employment license that permits the employer to employ a person in the state. The employer may not employ a person in South Carolina unless the employment license is in effect and is not suspended or revoked. The employment license will remain in effect only as long as the employer is in compliance with the law.

SC.7 Is there a "safe harbor" for employers in the law?

Yes. Employers complying with E-Verify may not be sanctioned under the law.

SC.8 Are there penalties for employers filing false complaints?

Employers convicted of making false reports will be found guilty of a felony and will be imprisoned for up to five years.

SC.9 What is the transporting bar contained in the law?

It is a state-law felony to transport, shelter, harbor, or conceal unauthorized individuals knowingly or in reckless disregard of the fact that the person is illegally present in the United States. Fines range from $3,000 to $5,000, and guilty parties may be subject to imprisonment for up to five years. Also, persons convicted under the law are barred from receiving a professional license in South Carolina.

SC.10 What does the law change with regard to identity theft?

Individuals who engage in identity theft for the purpose of working in the United States must pay restitution to the state for any benefits received under any state programs, and individuals suffering any harm as a result of such identity theft may now bring a private cause of action and seek triple damages and attorney's fees.

SC.11 Does the law give any rights to discharged U.S. workers?

Yes. Employees who are replaced by unauthorized workers, when the employer knows the replacement worker is unauthorized, have a civil right of action for wrongful termination. The replacement must have occurred within 60 days of the termination, the replacement worker must not have been authorized at the time of the replacement, the employer must have known the replacement worker's status, and the replacement worker must perform the same duties and have the same responsibilities as the terminated employee. Employees successful in such a lawsuit can seek reinstatement in the position, actual damages, and attorney's fees. The claim must be made within one year of the date of the alleged violation.

TENNESSEE

In 2016, Tennessee amended the Tennessee Lawful Employment Act (TLEA) with an effective date of January 1, 2017. Pursuant to the amended law, employers with 50 or more employees must utilize E-Verify for new hires.

The original law, enacted in 2011, continues to be in force for those employers with six to 49 employees. Under this part of the law, employers are required to enroll in E-Verify or copy and retain a state-issued driver's license or identification, unexpired U.S. passport, permanent resident card, employment authorization card, birth certificate, certificate of naturalization, or a few other forms of identification.

Previously, in 2008, Tennessee enacted a new version of T.C.A. Section 50-1-703 permitting the Tennessee commissioner of labor and workforce development to order the suspension of a business license of any employer found to "knowingly employ, recruit or refer for a fee for employment, an illegal alien."

In 2006, Tennessee enacted Public Chapter No. 878, which bars state agencies from contracting with employers that have knowingly hired "illegal aliens."

TN.1 Are all employers covered under the Tennessee Lawful Employment Act?

Employers with five or fewer employees are exempt from the law.

TN.2 How does an employer violate the Tennessee Lawful Employment Act?

An employer violates the law by failing to receive E-Verify confirmation, to request and retain a copy of one of the specified identification documents, or to utilize E-Verify (for those employers with 50 or more employees).

TN.3 Is there a "safe harbor" for employers under the Tennessee Lawful Employment Act?

An employer has a "safe harbor" and cannot be found to have violated the law by employing an employee without work authorization if the employer used E-Verify and received a confirmation or if the employee appealed the tentative nonconfirmation and the appeal has not been resolved. This "safe harbor" is not available for employers that copy and retain an employee's identification document if the employee is found to be without employment authorization.

TN.4 What are the penalties under the Tennessee Lawful Employment Act?

The penalties are as follows:

1. First offense: $500 penalty plus $500 per employee or nonemployee not verified or without a copy of documentation retained.

2. Second offense: $1,000 penalty plus $1,000 per employee or nonemployee not verified or without a copy of documentation retained.

3. Third offense: $2,500 penalty plus $2,500 per employee or nonemployee not verified or without a copy of documentation retained.

Additionally, an employer, who fails within 45 days to abide by a state order under this law, will be fined $500 per day of the continued violation.

TN.5 How does the commissioner of labor and workforce development determine when to go after a company?

For an investigation to occur into an alleged violation of the new law, a complaint must be filed.

TN.6 Who can file a complaint and with whom?

Any "lawful resident" of Tennessee or any federal agency employee may file a complaint with the Tennessee Department of Labor and Workforce Development, which will investigate complaints providing "satisfactory evidence" of a violation. Additionally, the Department may conduct its own audit if the employer is inspected or under investigation by the Tennessee Department of Labor and Workforce Development.

TN.7 How does Tennessee define "knowingly"?

The law requires actual knowledge that a person is an illegal alien or, importantly, having a "duty imposed by law" to determine the immigration status of an illegal alien and failing to perform such duty.

So aside from the obvious example of simply hiring someone an employer knows is out of status, an employer arguably could be found to have knowingly employed an illegal alien if the employer did not follow immigration law in determining the immigration status of an employee. This could mean failing to complete a Form I-9 for an employee, failing to examine the identity and work authorization documents associated with the Form I-9, and failing to re-verify employment authorization on Forms I-9 for employees with expiring work documents.

TN. 8 Who is an "illegal alien"?

Although the definition may seem obvious, the definition in the bill is broad. All persons who are neither permanent residents nor authorized to work are "illegal aliens." So someone legally in the United States who is not a permanent resident would be considered an illegal alien under the law. This might include a nonimmigrant like a student, a legally admitted refugee, or a person with a pending adjustment application who is awaiting green-card status and is legally allowed to remain in the United States while he or she waits. The catch is that if such a person is not authorized to work, for purposes of the law, they are illegal aliens. This is because the law is designed to prevent employers from hiring individuals barred from working in the United States, not just those who are out of status.

TN. 9 If the commissioner of labor and workforce development determines there is evidence that T.C.A. Section 50-1-103 has been violated, what is the process that occurs before a company's business license is affected?

If the commissioner of labor and workforce development determines that there is evidence of a violation, then the commissioner shall issue a notice and initial order with findings and determinations. Such order may be appealed.

TN.10 If the business license is revoked, how can it be reinstated?

For a first violation, the commissioner of labor and workforce development can order the revocation of the business license only "until the person shows to the satisfaction of the commissioner that the person is no longer in violation of subsection (b). If the case is focused on the employment of a single individual and the individual is terminated, then the business license would presumably be reinstated. Furthermore, if an investigation determined that there may be numerous employees working illegally at the company because a company has been lax with respect to its Forms I-9 and other immigration recordkeeping, the commissioner might choose to conduct an audit to determine that a company has no other employees illegally working for it.

TN.11 What happens if a subsequent violation is found to have occurred?

If an employer is found to have committed a second or subsequent violation within three years of the first order, the business license will be suspended for one year.

TN.12 Is there an appeals process?

The statute does not provide for an appeals process.

TN.13 Is an employer liable for work performed by independent contractors?

No, as long as employment law does not consider the work to be true employment for which a Form W-2 must be filed for an employee.

TN.14 Are there any "safe harbors" under Section 50-1-103?

Yes. If an employer has received a Form I-9 from an employee within 14 days of hire and the information provided by the person was later determined to be false, an employer will not be found to have violated the new law. Federal law requires that such a form be received by an employee on the first day of employment and the documentation proving work authorization within three days of thereafter.

TN.15 What steps can a company take to reduce the likelihood of being found to have violated T.C.A. Section 50-1-103?

Companies should consider the following actions:

- Conduct regular Form I-9 training for employees responsible for the function.
- Centralize Form I-9 recordkeeping.
- Establish a nondiscriminatory system to re-verify Forms I-9 with expiring work authorization documents.
- Switch from a paper-based Form I-9 system to an electronic based one.
- Purge Forms I-9 that employers are legally permitted to purge.
- Have an outside law firm conduct an internal Form I-9 audit to identify and remediate violations before a government audit occurs.
- Develop a government audit response plan, and train employees thoroughly in how to respond to a surprise audit.

TN.16 Are there other Tennessee laws covering employers and immigration?

The main, additional law was passed in 2006 and is Public Chapter No. 878. It bars employers that knowingly use the services of illegal immigrants in the performance of a contract from access to contracts with Tennessee state agencies. Employers also are required to sign an attestation that they will not knowingly use the service of illegal immigrants in the performance of the contract. Firms found to have used illegal employees in the performance of a state contract will be barred from contracting with the state for a one-year period.

TN.17 What limits does Public Chapter No. 878 impose on state agencies?

The state is barred from contracting to acquire goods or services from any person who knowingly uses the services of "illegal immigrants" in the performance of a contract for goods or services. Employers that employ "illegal immigrants" are barred from supplying goods or services to the state. Under the law, employers must first sign an attestation promising not to knowingly employ illegal immigrants.

TN.18 What happens if a contractor is found to have employed an illegal alien?

Bidders to supply goods and services to the state will be prohibited for one year from entering into a contract with the state if they have knowingly employed illegal immigrants.

TN.19 How do state agencies ensure compliance?

Each agency must require its contractors and subcontractors to submit attestations on compliance semiannually during the term of the contract.

TEXAS

On December 3, 2014, Governor Rick Perry of Texas signed Executive Order RP 80 requiring all agencies under the direction of the governor to use E-Verify to verify the employment eligibility of all *current* and prospective employees. The same order applies to all contractors and subcontractors that have contracts for services with any agency under the direction of the governor.

Under H.B. No. 1196 passed in 2007 in Texas, employers receiving public subsidies must sign a written statement certifying the employer has not hired unauthorized immigrants.

TX.1 Isn't the Executive Order contrary to federal law concerning the use of E-Verify?

Yes. An employer in Texas should follow federal law.

TX.2 What does H.B. No. 1196 do?

All government agencies in Texas that provide a "public subsidy" to businesses must require that the businesses submit a statement with their application certifying that each business does not and will not knowingly employ an "undocumented worker."

TX.3 Does the law apply to companies related to the company receiving the subsidy?

Yes, it applies to branches, divisions, or departments of the business.

TX.4 How is "public subsidy" defined?

A "public subsidy" is a public program, benefit, or assistance designed to stimulate the economic development of a corporation, industry, or sector of the state's economy to create or retain jobs in the state. Subsidies can include grants, loans, loan guarantees, benefits relating to an enterprise or empowerment zone, fee waivers, land price subsidies, infrastructure development, and improvements designed to benefit a single business, matching funds, tax refunds, tax rebates, or tax abatements.

TX.5 How is "undocumented worker" defined?

Anyone who is not a green-card holder or otherwise authorized to be employed in the United States is considered an "undocumented worker."

TX.6 What happens if a business violates its certification?

If a business is convicted of violating the Immigration Reform and Control Act (IRCA), the business must repay the amount of the public subsidy with interest at a rate provided in the agreement between the state agency and the business. The agency providing the subsidy is entitled to sue to recover the owing amount and will be entitled to recover attorney's fees.

UTAH

In 2010, Utah enacted S.B. 251 requiring all private employers in Utah with 15 or more employees to enroll in and use E-Verify or the Social Security Number Verification Service (SSNVS). Previously, in 2008, Utah's governor signed legislation imposing new employment verification requirements on public and private employers.

UT.1 Are there any exclusions to S.B. 251 for private employers?

Yes, employers with fewer than 15 employees are excluded, as are employers employing H-2A and H-2B workers.

UT.2 What is the verification requirement for state agency employers in Utah?

All public employers are required to register with and use a "status verification system" to verify the federal employment authorization status of any new employee. Although most individuals assume this means E-Verify, the status states that "status verification system" includes:

- E-Verify.
- An equivalent federal program designated by the U.S. Department of Homeland Security (DHS) as verifying work eligibility of newly hired employees.
- The Social Security Number Verification Service (SSNVS).
- An independent third-party system with an equal or higher degree of reliability as E-Verify or the SSNVS.

UT.3 What are the penalties for failing to register and use a status verification system?

None.

UT.4 Is the contractor responsible for the work of other contractors or subcontractors?

The contractor is responsible only if the contractor's or subcontractor's employees work under the contractor's supervision or direction.

UT.5 How are U.S. citizen workers affected by the law?

Employers may not discharge U.S. citizen or permanent resident employees and replace them with employees not authorized to work. Employers using a status verification system are protected from liability. Employees who can demonstrate they were unlawfully terminated have the right to sue an employer for damages.

UT.6 What are the Utah law's transporting and harboring provisions?

The Utah law makes it unlawful for any person to transport more than 100 miles, conceal, harbor, or shelter from detection in any place, including any building or means of transportation, any alien (a) knowing or in reckless disregard of the fact that the alien is in the United States illegally and (b) when the act is done for "commercial advantage or private financial gain." This provision could be used against employers knowingly employing unauthorized immigrants.

UT.7 What are the penalties for violating the transporting and harboring provisions?

Violating these provisions constitutes a class A misdemeanor.

UT.8 Are there exceptions to the transporting and harboring prohibitions?

Yes. Persons providing charitable or humanitarian assistance are excepted as are certain religious organizations receiving volunteer services from a minister or missionary.

VIRGINIA

Effective December 1, 2013, Virginia expanded its E-Verify law so that all contractors and their subcontractors with more than 50 employees that enter into state contracts of more than $50,000 must enroll in and use E-Verify. Contractors and subcontractors are required to verify the employment status of their employees and independent contractors, and are prohibited from employing or contracting with an individual who is not determined to be legally eligible for employment in the United States. Another E-Verify provision covers new hires of state and local agencies.

Previously, in March 2008, Virginia enacted S.B. 782, an employer sanctions bill that calls for the revocation of a corporation's right to exist in Virginia. At the same time, the legislature passed S.B. 517, which affects contractors.

VA.1 Are all contractors and subcontractors that contract with the state required to enroll in and use E-Verify?

No, they must have 50 or more employees, and the contract must be valued at more than $50,000.

VA.2 What does S.B. 517 say with respect to contractors?

The law mandates that public agencies must require contractors to certify in their contracts that the contractor may not, during the performance of the contract, knowingly employ an unauthorized alien.

VA.3 What are the penalties for a contractor violating the law?

A contractor will be denied prequalification to enter into contracts with the Commonwealth of Virginia and will be debarred from contracting with the Commonwealth for one year.

VA.4 May the debarment be removed before one year?

Yes, it ceases upon the employer's enrollment and participation in E-Verify.

VA. 5 What kinds of violations will trigger a termination of the right to do business in the state?

Corporations engaged in serious immigration law violations are subject to having their corporate existence terminated involuntarily by Virginia. Under the statute, employers must have a conviction for violating U.S. Code, Title 8, section 1324a(f), which imposes criminal penalties for people or entities engaged in a "pattern or practice of violations" of the Immigration Reform and Control Act (IRCA).

WEST VIRGINIA

In April 2007, West Virginia enacted S.B. 70, making it unlawful for employers to knowingly employ an unauthorized worker. Additionally, West Virginia requires new employees working on the grounds of the Capitol Complex to submit to an employment eligibility check through E-Verify.

WV.1 What does S.B. 70 do?

The law establishes criminal penalties separate from the Immigration Reform and Control Act (IRCA) for employers found to have knowingly hired unauthorized workers.

S.B. 70 makes it unlawful for any employer to knowingly employ, hire, recruit, or refer an unauthorized worker for private or public employment in West Virginia.

Employers are required to verify a prospective employee's legal status or authorization to work before employing the individual or contracting with the individual for employment services.

S.B. 70 also removes the ability of employers to deduct as a business expense from state income taxes any wages paid to unauthorized workers.

WV.2 What penalties do employers face if they violate the law?

An employer violating the law is guilty of a misdemeanor and, upon conviction, can be subject to the following penalties:

1. First Offense: a fine of $100 to $1,000.
2. Second offense: a fine of $500 to $5,000.
3. Third offense: a fine of $1,000 to $10,000, or jail time of 30 days to one year, or both; revocation of the business license.

Employers found knowingly providing false records regarding the employment authorization of employees to West Virginia's labor commission will be guilty of a misdemeanor and subject to imprisonment of up to one year and a fine of up to $2,500.

Employers found knowingly and with fraudulent intent to have sold, transferred, or disposed of the employer's assets to evade recordkeeping requirements will be guilty of a misdemeanor and confined to up to one year in jail and up to a $10,000 fine.

WV.3 How does S.B. 70 affect business deductions for unauthorized employees' salaries?

Employers normally can deduct wages paid to employees on the employers' state income tax returns. However, wages in excess of $600 paid to unauthorized employees may not be deducted by employers under the law. This provision went into effect on January 1, 2008, and only affects wages paid after that date.

WV.4 Can a business license be revoked under S.B. 70?

Yes. If an employer is convicted under S.B. 70 for knowingly employing an undocumented employee a third time, the state's labor commissioner may issue an order imposing the following:

- Permanent revocation of any license held by the employer.
- Suspension of a license held by the employer for a specified period.

17

NONIMMIGRANT VISAS

17.1   What are the five major immigration status/visa categories?

The major categories of immigration status and visas are the following:

- Nonimmigrant visas are for temporary visitors (for example, workers, students, visitors).
- Immigrant visas are for lawful permanent residents (green-card holders) (see Chapter 18).
- Asylees and other special groups are asylum-seekers, refugees, and temporary protected status (TPS) holders (see Chapter 19).
- Citizens.
- Undocumented immigrants.

17.2   What are the various types of nonimmigrant visas and to whom are they available?

The following are the types of nonimmigrant visas:

- H-1B visas: Available to people in "specialty occupations."

- B-1 and B-2 visas: Available to short-term visitors for pleasure or business.

- F-1 visas: Available to students.

- J-1 visas: Available to exchange visitors (for example, trainees, interns, professors or research scholars, short-term scholars, foreign doctors, camp counselors, au pairs, and students in work/travel programs in the U.S.).

- O-1 visas: Available to people with extraordinary ability in the sciences, arts, crafts, education, business, athletics, or any field of "creative endeavor."

- L visas: Available to intracompany transfers.

- E visas: Available to E-2 treaty investors and E-1 treaty traders.

- R visas: Available to religious employees.

- TN visas: Available to Canadian and Mexican professionals working pursuant to the North American Free Trade Agreement (NAFTA).

- E-3 visas: Available to Australians.

17.3 What kinds of issues are relevant for H-1B visa applicants?

In determining whether an applicant is eligible for an H-1B visa, the following are relevant issues:

- Do you have a university degree?

- Do most people in your field in the United States have university degrees?

- If you lack a degree, do you have several years of work experience in your field?

- Do you have an employer in the United States willing to hire you?

- Does the job pay as much as similarly employed U.S. employees earn?

- Does the employer typically hire only people with university degrees for the job?

- Does the employer guarantee that it will have continuous work available to you?

- If the occupation requires a license, do you have the necessary license?

17.4   How long is the H-1B visa valid?

An H-1B visa is valid for up to six years — three years initially, and then it may be extended for three years. The status can potentially be further extended if a permanent residency application has been filed.

17.5   Can an H-1B visa holder apply for a green card?

Yes, H-1B visa holders can simultaneously have green-card applications pending.

17.6   Are spouses or children of H-1B visa holders permitted to work?

Yes, under some circumstances. If an H-1B holder has been granted status under the American Competitiveness in the 21st Century Act of 2000, as amended by the 21st Century Department of Justice Appropriations Authorization Act, then a dependent spouse is eligible for work authorization. Additionally, the principal beneficiaries of an approved I-140 petition are eligible.

17.7   Are H-1B visa holders required to maintain ties to their home countries?

No.

17.8   How many H-1B visas are provided each year?

The granting of H-1B visas is limited to 65,000 people per year. But many H-1B employees are exempt from this cap, and there is an additional quota of 20,000 for people holding master's degrees or higher granted by a U.S. university.

17.9 Are H-1B visa holders permitted to change employers?

H-1B holders can change employers, but the new employer must file a petition with U.S. Citizenship and Immigration Services (USCIS) before the employee can begin work.

17.10 Are H-1B visas permitted for self-employment?

Yes, but the applicant must demonstrate all H-1B requirements, including demonstrating an ability to earn the prevailing wage. This can be extremely difficult.

17.11 What happens in the event the H-1B applicant lacks an appropriate degree?

Equivalent work experience must be demonstrated, and an evaluation from an expert must be obtained.

17.12 What kinds of issues are relevant for B-1 and B-2 visa applicants?

The following are issues B-1 and B-2 applicants will likely face in an interview at a U.S. consulate:

- Do you have a job that pays well and one you can leave for a few weeks on a vacation?
- Do you have close relatives who will be remaining in your home country when you come to the United States?
- Are you coming for a short visit?
- Do you have assets in your home country?
- Do you own property in your home country?
- Do you have a set itinerary for your trip to the United States?
- Do you have a roundtrip plane ticket?
- Do you have close community ties in your home country?

- Do you have money or proof of support from friends or relatives in the United States to show adequate financial arrangements to carry out the purpose of the trip?

- If you are coming for business, is the work you are doing work that would typically be done by a U.S. employee?

- If you are coming for business, is the main place where profits are earned outside the United States?

- If you are coming to the United States on business, will you be paid abroad rather than in the United States?

- If you are coming as a B-2 visitor for pleasure, are you coming for one of the following purposes?

  - Tourist.

  - Social visits to friends or relatives.

  - Health purposes.

  - Participant in conventions of social organizations.

  - Participant in amateur musical, sports, or similar events with no pay.

  - Spouse and children of people in the U.S. Armed Forces.

  - Accompanying B-1 business visitors.

  - Coming to marry a U.S. citizen, but the person plans on departing after the wedding.

  - Coming to marry someone on a nonimmigrant visa.

  - Nonspouse partner/spouse (regardless of gender) who accompanies an E, H, or L visa holder.

  - Parent seeking to accompany an F-1 student visa holder.

  - Language student in a course of short duration when the course of study is under 18 hours per week.

- If you are coming on a B-1 business visitor visa, are you coming for one of the following purposes?

  - Engaging in commercial transactions not involving employment (negotiating contracts, litigation, consulting with clients or business associates).

  - Participating in scientific, educational, professional, religious, or business conventions.

- Religious employees coming to do missionary work in the United States, ministers exchanging pulpits but who are paid by their own churches abroad, and ministers on evangelical tours.
- Domestic servants accompanying returning U.S. citizens who are temporarily assigned to the United States or who permanently reside in a foreign country.
- Domestic servants accompanying nonimmigrant visa holders if the applicant has worked for the employer for one year or more.
- Professional athletes receiving only tournament money.
- Foreign medical students seeking to take "elective clerkship" without pay.
- Serving on a board of directors of a U.S. company.
- Coming to the United States to set up a U.S. subsidiary and explore investment opportunities.
- Installing equipment as part of a contract.
- Participating in a volunteer service program if religious only.
- Attending an executive seminar.
- Observing the conduct of business.
- Domestic partner of a person on a nonimmigrant visa.

17.13 How long is the B-1 or B-2 visa valid?

The approved applicant may be granted an authorized stay of up to six months, but chances of obtaining the visa improve if a shorter trip is requested. A consular officer has the authority to approve a stay shorter than six months.

17.14 Are B-1 and B-2 visa holders allowed to work in the United States?

Generally speaking, no.

17.15 Nationals from which countries are eligible for the Visa Waiver Program?

Nationals from the following countries are eligible under the Visa Waiver Program (VWP) to enter the United States for up to 90 days: Andorra, Australia, Austria, Belgium, Brunei, Chile, Denmark, Finland, France, Germany, Greece,

Iceland, Ireland, Italy, Japan, Liechtenstein, Luxembourg, Monaco, the Netherlands, New Zealand, Norway, Portugal, Republic of Malta, San Marino, Singapore, Slovenia, South Korea, Spain, Sweden, Switzerland, Taiwan, and the United Kingdom. VWP entrants cannot have their status extended and cannot change to other nonimmigrant categories while in the United States.

17.16 What kinds of issues are relevant for F-1 visa applicants?

The following are issues F-1 visa applicants face in receiving approval from U.S. Citizenship and Immigration Services (USCIS):

- Do you have a residence in your home country that you do not intend to abandon?
- Have you been admitted to study full time in a degree program or in an English language program?
- Is the school where you intend to study approved for students to attend on student visas?
- Do you have proof of adequate financial resources to attend school full time without the need to work in the United States?
- If you are not going to study in an English language program in the United States, are you proficient in English?
- Will the education you obtain in the United States improve your career prospects in your home country?

17.17 What are the requirements for the F-1 visa holder?

F-1 visa holders must be enrolled full time. They have limited on-campus work eligibility. Off-campus employment is prohibited unless the student fits under limited exceptions and the employment authorization is granted by the school or U.S. Citizenship and Immigration Services (USCIS).

17.18 Can an F-1 visa holder work in the United States after completing an educational program?

Yes, F-1 visa holders can receive up to one year of work authorization upon completion of a program. Plus, if the individual has a degree in certain fields of science, technology, engineering or mathematics (STEM), he or she may receive an additional 24 months as long as the employer uses E-Verify and produces a training plan.

17.19 What limitations are there on the spouses and children of F-1 visa holders?

Spouses and children are not entitled to work unless they independently secure a work status. Children can enroll in K–12 education. A spouse cannot study unless he or she has a separate student visa.

17.20 What kinds of issues are relevant for J-1 visa applicants?

The following are relevant issues that J-1 visa applicants face in receiving approval:

- Are you coming to the United States to participate in an exchange program designed by the U.S. Department of State?
- Do you have fluency in English and sufficient funds to live here if the program does not pay J-1 visa holders?
- If you are looking at the au pair program, have you registered with one of the eight designated au pair programs in the United States?
- If you are a doctor seeking to train in the United States, are you admitted to a medical residency or fellowship program, and have you obtained sponsorship from the Educational Commission for Foreign Medical Graduates?
- If you are coming for a business trainee or intern visa, have you found an employer to provide you with a training opportunity?
- If you have found a training opportunity, have you found a program sponsor?

17.21 Is there a requirement for J-1 visa holders to return home before switching to another visa?

Yes, there is often a requirement for J-1 visa holders to return home for two years before switching to another visa.

17.22 What are the time requirements for J-1 visa holders?

Time limits vary depending on the type of program:

- Training participants: 18 months.
- Interns: 12 months.
- Scholars and professors: up to three years.
- Au pairs: 12 months, and can renew for six, nine, or 12 months.
- Medical residents: up to seven years.
- Students: no limit.

Students are eligible for up to 18 months of postgraduate work authorization (36 months, if postdoctoral work), but students must be enrolled full time.

17.23 What about employment opportunities in the United States for the spouses and children of J-1 visa holders?

Spouses and children of J-1 visa holders are entitled to work authorization.

17.24 What kinds of issues are relevant for O-1 visa applicants?

The following are relevant issues for approval of an O-1 visa:

- Are you one of the top people in your field in your country?
- Do you have an employer, manager, or agent in the United States who can sign your application?
- Is there a peer organization willing to say that it has no objection to your being granted an O-1 visa?
- Can you show that you have won a major international award or at least three of the following?
    - Documentation of the applicant's receipt of nationally or internationally recognized prizes or awards for excellence in the field of endeavor.
    - Documentation of the applicant's membership in associations in the field for which classification is sought, which requires out-

standing achievements of their members, as judged by recognized national or international experts in their disciplines or fields.

– Published material in professional or major trade publications or in major media about the applicant, relating to the applicant's work in the field for which classification is sought, which must include the title, date, and author of such published material, and any necessary translation.

– Evidence of the applicant's participation on a panel, or individually, as a judge of the work of others in the same or in an allied field of specialization for which classification is sought.

– Evidence of the applicant's original scientific, scholarly, or business-related contributions of major significance in the field.

– Evidence of the applicant's authorship of scholarly articles in the field, in professional journals, or in other major media.

– Evidence that the applicant has been employed in a critical or essential capacity for organizations and establishments that have a distinguished reputation.

– Evidence that the applicant has commanded and now commands a high salary or other remuneration for services, evidenced by contracts or other reliable documentation.

17.25 What is the time limit on the issuance of O-1 approvals?

O-1 visa holders can be admitted for up to three years at a time.

17.26 Are O-1 visa holders required to maintain a residence outside of the United States?

No.

17.27 May O-1 visa holders apply for a green card?

Yes, they can have a green-card application pending while on O-1 status without problems.

17.28 What kinds of issues are relevant for L visa applicants?

The following are questions L visa applicants will face in seeking approval of their visa application:

- Are you coming to the United States to work for a company or its subsidiary, affiliate or branch that has offices both in the United States and outside the United States?

- Have you worked for the company abroad full time for at least one year of the last three?

- Are you coming to the United States as an owner, executive, manager, or employee with specialized knowledge of the company's operations?

17.29 What are the time limits for L visa holders?

The time limits for L visa holders are seven-year stays for owners, executives, and managers and five-year stays for specialized knowledge employees. However, the longest that an initial stay can be granted is three years with a two-year extension(s) thereafter. If the matter involves the opening of a U.S. office, the initial stay is granted for only one year.

17.30 Are green cards easy for L visa holders to obtain?

Yes, L visa holders who are owners, managers, and executives can easily obtain green cards.

17.31 Are spouses of L visa holders allowed to work?

Yes, if they apply for and receive an Employment Authorization Document (EAD).

17.32 Which type of employee has a difficult time getting an L visa?

Employees working on a contract basis at other employers have a difficult time, as do employees who claim specialized knowledge but cannot document that they bring skills not readily available in the local job market. Additionally, if the U.S. location is new, there are greater difficulties receiving approval.

17.33 What kinds of questions are relevant for E-1 and E-2 visa applicants?

The following questions are asked of E-1 and E-2 visa applicants in obtaining visa approval:

- If you are seeking an E-1 Treaty Trader visa, are you currently working for a business that has a substantial volume of trading business with the United States (more than 50 percent)?

- Are you a national of a country that has a bilateral trade treaty with the United States?

- Are you coming to the United States to work as an owner, executive, manager, or essential skills employee?

- Is at least 50 percent of the business owned by foreign nationals who are not U.S. citizens or permanent residents?

- For E-2 visas, are you investing a substantial amount of money (substantial amount of money is not defined) in a commercial investment in the United States?

17.34 What are the time limits for E visa holders?

There are no limits on the total time in E visa status.

17.35 Are spouses of E visa holders allowed to work?

Yes, if they apply for and receive an Employment Authorization Document (EAD).

17.36 What is the impact of permanent residency applications on E visa holders?

Permanent residency applications do not adversely affect the granting of E visas.

17.37 What kinds of issues are relevant for R visa applicants?

The following are issues that R visa applicants will face in obtaining approval from U.S. Citizenship and Immigration Services (USCIS):

- Are you coming to the United States to work as a minister or to work in a religious vocation or occupation?
- Have you been a member of the religious denomination for at least two years?
- Is the employer a nonprofit organization (most churches, synagogues, and mosques qualify as well as institutions affiliated with them)?

17.38 What is the time limit for R visa holders?

R visas are valid for up to five years.

17.39 At what point may R visas convert to green cards?

R visas are convertible to a green card after two years of work, unless the applicant already has two years' experience in the religious occupation.

17.40 Has U.S. Citizenship and Immigration Services changed the process to acquire an R visa?

Yes, change-of-status petitions now take many months because U.S. Citizenship and Immigration Services (USCIS) conducts site visits to a petitioning religious institution.

17.41 What kinds of issues are relevant for TN visa applicants?

The following are relevant issues for TN visa applicants:

- Are you coming to the United States to work in an occupation listed within the North American Free Trade Agreement (NAFTA) occupation schedule?
- Are you a citizen or national of Canada or Mexico?

- Do you meet the minimum job requirements for that position as listed in the TN NAFTA schedule?

17.42 What is the time limit for TN visa holders?

TN visas are valid for three years and can be extended in three-year increments.

17.43 Are TN visa holders required to demonstrate intent to immigrate to the United States?

No. The TN visa is a nonimmigrant visa; therefore, the beneficiary cannot have immigrant intent.

17.44 How do Canadians apply for TN visa status?

Canadians can apply for TN status at the port of entries with "TN offer letters" or through filing a petition with U.S. Citizenship and Immigration Services (USCIS).

17.45 How do Mexicans apply for TN visa status?

Mexicans can apply directly at U.S. consulates.

17.46 Where are TN visa extensions and change-of-status applications filed?

They may be filed in the United States with U.S. Citizenship and Immigration Services (USCIS). TN visa extensions may also be filed at a port of entry for Canadians.

17.47 Are degrees in a field required?

Yes, most jobs require a degree in the field; however, for management consultants, they are not required. Note, however, that these cases are closely scrutinized.

17.48 How would TN visa holders be impacted if NAFTA was revoked by President Trump?

TN visa holders would lose their work authorization status, as TN visas are directly tied to NAFTA.

17.49 What kinds of issues are relevant for E-3 visa applicants?

The following are relevant issues for E-3 visa applicants:

- Are you Australian?
- Do you have a university degree?
- Do most people in your field in the United States have university degrees?
- If you lack a degree, do you have several years of work experience in your field?
- Do you have an employer in the United States willing to hire you?
- Does the job pay as much as similarly employed U.S. workers earn?
- Does the employer typically hire only people with university degrees for the job?
- Does the employer guarantee that it will have continuous work available to you?
- If the occupation requires a license, do you have the necessary license?

17.50 Do E-3 applicants require advanced U.S. Citizenship and Immigration Services approval?

No. Like the E-1 and E-2, E-3 applications can be filed directly at a U.S. consulate abroad.

17.51 May spouses of E-3 visa holders be eligible for an Employment Authorization Document?

Yes, spouses of E-3 visa holders may be eligible for an Employment Authorization Document (EAD) when they accompany the E-3 visa holder to the United States.

17.52 Is a Labor Condition Application required of the E-3 visa holder?

Yes, and the prevailing wage must be paid.

17.53 What is the time limit for E-3 visa holders?

Unlike the H-1B (yet similar to the E-1 and E-2), there is no limit on the number of years an E-3 visa holder can hold E-3 status.

17.54 Are the nonimmigrant visas listed in this chapter a complete listing?

No. Currently, there are more than 25 major nonimmigrant visa classifications. The discussion in this chapter covers only the most common ones.

18

IMMIGRANT VISAS

18.1   What are the four basic categories of immigrant visas?

The four basic categories of immigrant visas are the following:

1. Family-sponsored immigrants.
2. Employment-based immigrants.
3. Diversity immigrants.
4. Refugees and asylees (see Chapter 19).

18.2   What kinds of issues and waiting periods are relevant for family-sponsored immigrants?

For immediate relatives

Faster processing exists and there are no quotas. The types of questions relevant for family-sponsored immigrants include:

- Are you a spouse of a U.S. citizen?
- Are you a child of a U.S. citizen and under the age of 21?

- Are you the parent of a U.S. citizen over the age of 21?

For preference categories

The types of questions and waiting periods relevant for family-sponsored immigrants include:

- First Preference: Are you the adult, unmarried child of a U.S. citizen? If so, then the wait is approximately 6½ years (or more for nationals of Mexico and the Philippines).

- Second Preference A: Are you under the age of 18 and a child of a green-card holder or the spouse of a green-card holder? If so, then the wait is approximately two years.

- Second Preference B: Are you the adult, unmarried child of a green-card holder? If so, then the wait is approximately 6½ years (or more for nationals of Mexico and the Philippines).

- Third Preference: Are you a married child of a U.S. citizen? If so, then the wait is approximately 12 years (or more for nationals of Mexico and Philippines).

- Fourth Preference: Are you a brother or sister of a U.S. citizen? If so, then the wait is 13 years (or more for nationals of India, Mexico, and the Philippines).

18.3   How are these waiting periods determined?

The waiting periods are based on the U.S. Department of State's *Visa Bulletin* published in April 2017. These bulletins (found at www.travel.state.gov) are published monthly and announce the current waiting periods. The periods listed above should be considered as estimates; for accurate waiting periods, the current *Visa Bulletin* must be checked.

18.4   What is the implication of marriage to a U.S. citizen?

Marriage to a U.S. citizen is a common and expeditious way to acquire permanent residency status. U.S. Citizenship and Immigration Services (USCIS) must still evaluate the marriage and determine whether it was entered into with the primary purpose of acquiring a green card.

18.5   Can a person convert from one immigrant-preference or immediate-relative category to another?

Cases may convert automatically from one category to another when a person's age and marital status change; certain rights and priority dates may be retained for children when they turn age 21.

18.6   What kinds of issues are relevant for Diversity Visa applicants?

The following kinds of issues are relevant to the U.S. Citizenship and Immigration Services (USCIS) for Diversity Visa applicants:

- Are you a high school graduate?
- Do you work in a field typically requiring two years of work experience, and do you have at least two years of work experience in the field?
- Were you born in an eligible lottery country?

18.7   What kinds of issues are relevant to the Diversity Visa green-card lottery?

The following kinds of issues are relevant to the U.S. Citizenship and Immigration Services (USCIS) to the Diversity Visa green card lottery:

- The U.S. government allocates 50,000 visas per year for people to receive through a random computer drawing.
- Fewer than 1 in 40 applicants will succeed.
- It is easy to enter the lottery.
- The entry period is limited and is usually in the last quarter of the calendar year (October to December).

18.8   What kinds of issues are relevant for the EB-1-1 green card?

The following are relevant issues in U.S. Citizenship and Immigration Services' (USCIS) determination of whether to approve an EB-1-1:

- Are you a person of extraordinary ability in the sciences, arts, education, business, or athletics?

- Are you one of the top people in your field?

- Can you show that you have won a major international award or at least three of the following?

  - Documentation of your receipt of nationally or internationally recognized prizes or awards for excellence in the field of endeavor.

  - Documentation of your membership in associations in the field for which classification is sought, which requires outstanding achievements of association members, as judged by recognized national or international experts in their disciplines or fields.

  - Published material in professional or major trade publications or in major media about you, relating to your work in the field for which classification is sought, which must include the title, date, and author of such published material, and any necessary translation.

  - Evidence of your participation on a panel, or individually, as a judge of the work of others in the same or in an allied field of specialization for which classification is sought.

  - Evidence of your original scientific, scholarly, or business-related contributions of major significance in the field.

  - Evidence of your authorship of scholarly articles in the field, in professional journals, or in other major media.

  - Evidence that you have been employed in a critical or essential capacity for organizations and establishments that have a distinguished reputation.

  - Evidence that you have commanded and now command a high salary or other remuneration for services, evidenced by contracts or other reliable documentation.

18.9   Is employment necessary to obtain the EB-1-1 green card?

No, but the applicant must demonstrate an intention to secure employment.

18.10 What kinds of issues are relevant for the EB-1-2 green card?

The following kinds of issues are relevant to the U.S. Citizenship and Immigration Services (USCIS) EB-1-2 green card:

- Are you recognized internationally as outstanding in a specific academic area?

- Do you have three years' experience in teaching or research in your area?

- Are you coming to the United States to work in a tenured or tenure-track teaching position or in a long-term research position?

- Can you present evidence that you are recognized internationally in your academic field by presenting evidence of at least two of the following?

  - Receipt of major prizes or awards of outstanding achievement.

  - Membership in an association that requires outstanding achievement.

  - Published material in the professional publications written by others about your work.

  - Participation as a judge of the work of others.

  - Original scientific research.

  - Authorship of scholarly books or articles in the field.

See also 18.8, except substitute EB-1-2 for EB-1-1.

18.11 Is the EB-1-3 green card identical to the L-1 visa?

Yes, it is virtually identical to the L-1 intracompany transfer nonimmigrant visa. However, it is not available to specialized knowledge employees, and the U.S. branch must be operating for at least one year (see Chapter 17).

18.12 What kinds of issues are relevant for the EB-2 green card?

The following kinds of issues are relevant to the U.S. Citizenship and Immigration Services (USCIS) EB-2 green card:

- Do you have a degree beyond a bachelor's degree, or do you have a bachelor's degree plus five years of work experience in your field?

- Do you meet the definition of exceptional ability by showing three of the following?

  - Degree relating to the area of exceptional ability.

  - Letter from a current or former employer showing at least 10 years of experience.

  - License to practice the profession.

  - A salary or remuneration demonstrating exceptional ability.

  - Membership in a professional association.

  - Recognition for achievements and significant contributions to the industry or field by peers, governmental entities, or a professional or business organization.

- Do you have a job offer and labor certification, or are you basing your green-card application on benefiting the nation's interest?

- If you are planning on basing your green-card application on a labor certification, do you work in a field that has a shortage of U.S. employees in the local area where you intend to work?

- If your claim is based on a labor certification, are you going to be paid the prevailing wage for similarly employed employees in the city where you are going to work?

- If your claim is based on a labor certification, has your employer attempted to recruit U.S. citizens or permanent residents to fill the position?

- If your claim is based on a national interest waiver, do you meet the following tests?

  - The person seeks employment in an area of substantial intrinsic merit.

  - The benefit will be national in scope.

  - The national interest would be adversely affected if a labor certification were required.

See also 18.8 and 18.10.

18.13 What is the processing time for the EB-2 green card?

Processing times vary, but labor certification cases typically take six months to one year, and national interest cases take six to 18 months.

18.14 Is employment a requirement for the EB-2 application?

Employment is not required in national interest waiver cases.

18.15 Who is eligible for the EB-3 green card?

The EB-3 is available to university graduates; people working in jobs requiring an employee with at least two years' experience can file under this category if the employer secures a labor certification.

18.16 What is the subcategory of the EB-3 green card?

It is for unskilled employees who do not have work experience or an education requirement, but who still require a labor certification.

18.17 Is the EB-4 green card the same as the R-1 visa?

Yes, they basically have the same requirements except that an EB-4 applicant must have been working in the field for at least a two-year period (see Chapter 17).

18.18 What kinds of issues are relevant for the EB-5 green card?

- Are you investing in a business in the United States?
- Is the business new, or are you buying into a restructured business?
- Are you investing at least $500,000 if the business is in a rural, high-unemployment area or in a designated target employment area (TEA), or $1 million if located elsewhere? (As of the date of this publication,

USCIS had proposed increasing amounts to $1.35 million for TEAs and $1.8 million for non-TEAs).

- Is your investment in the form of cash, equipment, inventory, other tangible property, cash equivalents, and indebtedness secured by assets owned by the entrepreneur?

- Is the investment "at risk"?

- Can you document that the source of the funds is legitimate?

- Will the investment result in the creation of at least 10 full-time jobs for U.S. employees?

See also 18.12.

18.19 What does U.S. Citizenship and Immigration Services consider when granting the EB-5 green card?

U.S. Citizenship and Immigration Services (USCIS) scrutinizes these cases carefully. Although, technically, the investment and job creation need not take place until after granting the green card, in practice, USCIS will deny an EB-5 unless the investment and job creation take place before the application is submitted. Applicants can avoid having to show direct job creation by investing in a preapproved regional investment center. Applicants applying through regional centers also do not need to show they are involved in management.

19

ASYLEES AND REFUGEES

RELEVANT APPENDIX:

APPENDIX B: U.S. DEPARTMENT OF HOMELAND
SECURITY'S HANDBOOK FOR EMPLOYERS: GUIDANCE FOR
COMPLETING FORM I-9, M-274

19.1   What are asylees and refugees?

There are certain protected groups of foreign nationals in the United States. Most common are the asylees and refugees. Under the 1980 Refugee Act, a refugee is defined as "any person who is outside of any country of such person's nationality ... who is unable or unwilling to return to, and is unable or unwilling to avail himself or herself of the protection of that country because of persecution or a well-founded fear of persecution on account of race, religion, nationality, membership in a particular social group, or political opinion."

Asylees demonstrate the same well-founded fear of persecution, except that they are in the United States when they apply for such status.

Asylees and refugees are eligible for employment authorization and have special paths to permanent residency.

19.2   What is the difference between asylee and refugee status?

In almost every way, the requirements for refugee status and asylum are the same. The most important difference is that an asylee makes his or her application while in the United States, whereas the refugee applies *outside* of his or her home country, but also *outside* of the United States.

19.3   Are there other protected statuses?

Yes, temporary protected status (TPS) exists, which is available to nationals of designated countries facing armed conflict, environmental disaster, and other extraordinary and temporary conditions.

19.4   If someone arrives in the United States as a refugee, how does that person obtain work authorization?

When a person enters as a refugee, he or she will receive a Form I-94 (Arrival/Departure Record) stamped to indicate "Employment Authorized." One may use this Form I-94 to prove eligibility to work for up to 90 days of employment. However, the Form I-94 will not have an expiration date; thus, the employee should write "N/A" for the expiration date in Section 1 of the Form I-9.

19.5   How does a refugee get an Employment Authorization Document (EAD) beyond the 90 days associated with Form I-94?

An application for an EAD (I-766) will be prepared as part of the refugee's travel packet, and the application will be sent from the port of entry to U.S. Citizenship and Immigration Services (USCIS) for expeditious processing. Thereafter, the EAD will be delivered to the refugee's resettlement agency.

19.6   If the employer originally accepts Form I-94 for proof of work authorization for a refugee, what list should it be recorded in?

The Form I-94 is a List A document.

19.7   After 90 days of employment, what should an employer do regarding the refugee's work authorization?

The employer should request the refugee-employee to present documentation that he or she is still eligible for employment. More than likely, the employee will present an Employment Authorization Document (EAD), which is a List A document; the employer should cross-out the Form I-94 information and add the EAD in the List A column. However, the employee is entitled to present other valid documentation, such as an unexpired List B document and an unrestricted Social Security Card, which is a List C document. The employer should record these and cross-out the Form I-94 information.

> **19.7: As always, when crossing out information and/or adding information on the Form I-9, one should initial and date the addition or deletion.**

19.8   How does an asylee establish work authorization?

1. An asylee may receive a Form I-94 stamped to indicate asylee status. Unlike the refugee's Form I-94, an asylee's Form I-94 is a List C document. Thus, the asylee must present a valid List B document with the Form I-94.

    or

2. The asylee may present a valid List B document plus an unrestricted Social Security card, which is a List C document.

19.9   How does an asylee-employee properly record status in Section 1 of the Form I-9?

An asylee-employee must check the fourth box—"An alien authorized to work"—and write "N/A" for the expiration date.

19.10 Must an employer re-verify an asylee-employee who presents a valid List B document and a Form I-94 for List C?

No, the Form I-94 for an asylee does not have an expiration date so it does not require re-verification.

19.11 How does an asylee receive an Employment Authorization Document (EAD)?

It depends. If asylum is granted by the Asylum Office of U.S. Citizenship and Immigration Services (USCIS), USCIS will take the necessary action to provide work authorization documentation. If an immigration judge or the Board of Immigration Appeals (BIA) grants asylum, the asylee will be provided instructions to visit the local USCIS office through an InfoPass appointment, or file an I-765, Application for Employment Authorization. In these cases, the asylee should provide to USCIS the decision of the immigration judge or BIA.

19.12 If an asylee or refugee provides an Employment Authorization Document (EAD) with an expiration date, must the employer re-verify work authorization before the card expires?

Yes, the EAD in this case is just like other EADs, which must be re-verified with a new EAD or some other document showing work authorization.

19.13 May an employer accept a copy of the decision of the immigration judge or BIA as proof of work authorization and record it on the Form I-9?

No.

APPENDIX A

SAMPLE FORM I-9, I-9 SUPPLEMENT, AND I-9 INSTRUCTIONS

SAMPLE FORM I-9

SAMPLE FORM I-9 SUPPLEMENT: SECTION 1 PREPARER
AND/OR TRANSLATOR CERTIFICATION

FORM I-9 INSTRUCTIONS

Sample Form I-9

Employment Eligibility Verification

Department of Homeland Security

U.S. Citizenship and Immigration Services

USCIS
Form I-9
OMB No. 1615-0047
Expires 08/31/2019

▶ **START HERE:** Read instructions carefully before completing this form. The instructions must be available, either in paper or electronically, during completion of this form. Employers are liable for errors in the completion of this form.

ANTI-DISCRIMINATION NOTICE: It is illegal to discriminate against work-authorized individuals. Employers **CANNOT** specify which document(s) an employee may present to establish employment authorization and identity. The refusal to hire or continue to employ an individual because the documentation presented has a future expiration date may also constitute illegal discrimination.

Section 1. Employee Information and Attestation *(Employees must complete and sign Section 1 of Form I-9 no later than the first day of employment, but not before accepting a job offer.)*

Last Name *(Family Name)*	First Name *(Given Name)*	Middle Initial	Other Last Names Used *(if any)*

Address *(Street Number and Name)*	Apt. Number	City or Town	State	ZIP Code

Date of Birth *(mm/dd/yyyy)*	U.S. Social Security Number	Employee's E-mail Address	Employee's Telephone Number
	☐☐☐ - ☐☐ - ☐☐☐☐		

I am aware that federal law provides for imprisonment and/or fines for false statements or use of false documents in connection with the completion of this form.

I attest, under penalty of perjury, that I am (check one of the following boxes):

☐ 1. A citizen of the United States

☐ 2. A noncitizen national of the United States *(See instructions)*

☐ 3. A lawful permanent resident   (Alien Registration Number/USCIS Number): _____

☐ 4. An alien authorized to work   until (expiration date, if applicable, mm/dd/yyyy): _____
Some aliens may write "N/A" in the expiration date field. *(See instructions)*

Aliens authorized to work must provide only one of the following document numbers to complete Form I-9:
An Alien Registration Number/USCIS Number OR Form I-94 Admission Number OR Foreign Passport Number.

1. Alien Registration Number/USCIS Number: _____
OR
2. Form I-94 Admission Number: _____
OR
3. Foreign Passport Number: _____
Country of Issuance: _____

QR Code - Section 1
Do Not Write In This Space

Signature of Employee	Today's Date *(mm/dd/yyyy)*

Preparer and/or Translator Certification (check one):
☐ I did not use a preparer or translator.   ☐ A preparer(s) and/or translator(s) assisted the employee in completing Section 1.
(Fields below must be completed and signed when preparers and/or translators assist an employee in completing Section 1.)

I attest, under penalty of perjury, that I have assisted in the completion of Section 1 of this form and that to the best of my knowledge the information is true and correct.

Signature of Preparer or Translator	Today's Date *(mm/dd/yyyy)*

Last Name *(Family Name)*	First Name *(Given Name)*

Address *(Street Number and Name)*	City or Town	State	ZIP Code

🛑 *Employer Completes Next Page* 🛑

Form I-9 07/17/17 N   Page 1 of 3

Employment Eligibility Verification

Department of Homeland Security

U.S. Citizenship and Immigration Services

US
Form
OMB No. 1615-
Expires 08/31/20

Section 2. Employer or Authorized Representative Review and Verification

(Employers or their authorized representative must complete and sign Section 2 within 3 business days of the employee's first day of employment. You must physically examine one document from List A OR a combination of one document from List B and one document from List C as listed on the "Lists of Acceptable Documents.")

Employee Info from Section 1	Last Name *(Family Name)*	First Name *(Given Name)*	M.I.	Citizenship/Immigration Status

List A Identity and Employment Authorization	OR	List B Identity	AND	List C Employment Authorization
Document Title		Document Title		Document Title
Issuing Authority		Issuing Authority		Issuing Authority
Document Number		Document Number		Document Number
Expiration Date *(if any)(mm/dd/yyyy)*		Expiration Date *(if any)(mm/dd/yyyy)*		Expiration Date *(if any)(mm/dd/yyyy)*
Document Title				
Issuing Authority		Additional Information		QR Code - Sections 2 & 3 Do Not Write In This Space
Document Number				
Expiration Date *(if any)(mm/dd/yyyy)*				
Document Title				
Issuing Authority				
Document Number				
Expiration Date *(if any)(mm/dd/yyyy)*				

Certification: I attest, under penalty of perjury, that (1) I have examined the document(s) presented by the above-named employee, (2) the above-listed document(s) appear to be genuine and to relate to the employee named, and (3) to the best of my knowledge the employee is authorized to work in the United States.

The employee's first day of employment *(mm/dd/yyyy)*: _____   *(See instructions for exemptions)*

Signature of Employer or Authorized Representative	Today's Date *(mm/dd/yyyy)*	Title of Employer or Authorized Representative
Last Name of Employer or Authorized Representative	First Name of Employer or Authorized Representative	Employer's Business or Organization Name

Employer's Business or Organization Address (Street Number and Name)	City or Town	State	ZIP Code

Section 3. Reverification and Rehires *(To be completed and signed by employer or authorized representative.)*

A. New Name *(if applicable)*			B. Date of Rehire *(if applicable)*
Last Name *(Family Name)*	First Name *(Given Name)*	Middle Initial	Date *(mm/dd/yyyy)*

C. If the employee's previous grant of employment authorization has expired, provide the information for the document or receipt that establishes continuing employment authorization in the space provided below.

Document Title	Document Number	Expiration Date *(if any) (mm/dd/yyyy)*

I attest, under penalty of perjury, that to the best of my knowledge, this employee is authorized to work in the United States, and if the employee presented document(s), the document(s) I have examined appear to be genuine and to relate to the individual.

Signature of Employer or Authorized Representative	Today's Date *(mm/dd/yyyy)*	Name of Employer or Authorized Representative

Form I-9 07/17/17 N

Page 2 of 3

249

OF ACCEPTABLE DOCUMENTS

ments must be UNEXPIRED

ay present one selection from List A
ection from List B and one selection from List C.

...ish ...ty and ...ment Authorization	OR	LIST B Documents that Establish Identity	AND	LIST C Documents that Establish Employment Authorization
1. U.S. Passport or U.S. Passport Card		1. Driver's license or ID card issued by a State or outlying possession of the United States provided it contains a photograph or information such as name, date of birth, gender, height, eye color, and address		1. A Social Security Account Number card, unless the card includes one of the following restrictions: (1) NOT VALID FOR EMPLOYMENT (2) VALID FOR WORK ONLY WITH INS AUTHORIZATION (3) VALID FOR WORK ONLY WITH DHS AUTHORIZATION
2. Permanent Resident Card or Alien Registration Receipt Card (Form I-551)				
3. Foreign passport that contains a temporary I-551 stamp or temporary I-551 printed notation on a machine-readable immigrant visa		2. ID card issued by federal, state or local government agencies or entities, provided it contains a photograph or information such as name, date of birth, gender, height, eye color, and address		2. Certification of report of birth issued by the Department of State (Forms DS-1350, FS-545, FS-240)
4. Employment Authorization Document that contains a photograph (Form I-766)		3. School ID card with a photograph		3. Original or certified copy of birth certificate issued by a State, county, municipal authority, or territory of the United States bearing an official seal
5. For a nonimmigrant alien authorized to work for a specific employer because of his or her status: a. Foreign passport; and b. Form I-94 or Form I-94A that has the following: (1) The same name as the passport; and (2) An endorsement of the alien's nonimmigrant status as long as that period of endorsement has not yet expired and the proposed employment is not in conflict with any restrictions or limitations identified on the form.		4. Voter's registration card		
		5. U.S. Military card or draft record		
		6. Military dependent's ID card		4. Native American tribal document
		7. U.S. Coast Guard Merchant Mariner Card		5. U.S. Citizen ID Card (Form I-197)
		8. Native American tribal document		6. Identification Card for Use of Resident Citizen in the United States (Form I-179)
		9. Driver's license issued by a Canadian government authority		
		For persons under age 18 who are unable to present a document listed above:		7. Employment authorization document issued by the Department of Homeland Security
6. Passport from the Federated States of Micronesia (FSM) or the Republic of the Marshall Islands (RMI) with Form I-94 or Form I-94A indicating nonimmigrant admission under the Compact of Free Association Between the United States and the FSM or RMI		10. School record or report card		
		11. Clinic, doctor, or hospital record		
		12. Day-care or nursery school record		

Examples of many of these documents appear in Part 13 of the Handbook for Employers (M-274).

Refer to the instructions for more information about acceptable receipts.

Sample Form I-9 Supplement

Form I-9 Supplement,
Section 1 Preparer and/or Translator Certification

Department of Homeland Security
U.S. Citizenship and Immigration Services

USCIS
Form I-9
Supplement
OMB No. 1615-0047
Expires 08/31/2019

Employee Name:	Last Name *(Family Name)*	First Name *(Given Name)*	Middle Initial

Instructions: This supplement may be used if extra spaces are required to document more than one preparer and/or translator assisting an employee in completing Section 1 of Form I-9. The preparer and/or translator must enter the employee's name in the spaces provided. Each preparer or translator must complete, sign and date a separate certification area. Employers must retain completed supplement sheets with the employee's completed Form I-9.

I attest, under penalty of perjury, that I have assisted in the completion of Section 1 of this form and that to the best of my knowledge the information is true and correct.

Signature of Preparer or Translator		Today's Date *(mm/dd/yyyy)*	
Last Name *(Family Name)*	First Name *(Given Name)*		
Address *(Street Number and Name)*	City or Town	State	ZIP Code

I attest, under penalty of perjury, that I have assisted in the completion of Section 1 of this form and that to the best of my knowledge the information is true and correct.

Signature of Preparer or Translator		Today's Date *(mm/dd/yyyy)*	
Last Name *(Family Name)*	First Name *(Given Name)*		
Address *(Street Number and Name)*	City or Town	State	ZIP Code

I attest, under penalty of perjury, that I have assisted in the completion of Section 1 of this form and that to the best of my knowledge the information is true and correct.

Signature of Preparer or Translator		Today's Date *(mm/dd/yyyy)*	
Last Name *(Family Name)*	First Name *(Given Name)*		
Address *(Street Number and Name)*	City or Town	State	ZIP Code

I attest, under penalty of perjury, that I have assisted in the completion of Section 1 of this form and that to the best of my knowledge the information is true and correct.

Signature of Preparer or Translator		Today's Date *(mm/dd/yyyy)*	
Last Name *(Family Name)*	First Name *(Given Name)*		
Address *(Street Number and Name)*	City or Town	State	ZIP Code

Form I-9 Supplement 07/17/17 N

Page 1 of 1

Form I-9 Instructions

Instructions for Form I-9,
Employment Eligibility Verification

Department of Homeland Security
U.S. Citizenship and Immigration Services

USCIS
Form I-9
OMB No. 1615-0047
Expires 08/31/2019

Anti-Discrimination Notice. It is illegal to discriminate against work-authorized individuals in hiring, firing, recruitment or referral for a fee, or in the employment eligibility verification (Form I-9 and E-Verify) process based on that individual's citizenship status, immigration status or national origin. Employers **CANNOT** specify which document(s) the employee may present to establish employment authorization and identity. The employer must allow the employee to choose the documents to be presented from the Lists of Acceptable Documents, found on the last page of Form I-9. The refusal to hire or continue to employ an individual because the documentation presented has a future expiration date may also constitute illegal discrimination. For more information, call the Immigrant and Employee Rights Section (IER) in the Department of Justice's Civil Rights Division at 1-800-255-7688 (employees), 1-800-255-8155 (employers), or 1-800-237-2515 (TTY), or visit https://www.justice.gov/crt/immigrant-and-employee-rights-section.

What is the Purpose of This Form?

Employers must complete Form I-9 to document verification of the identity and employment authorization of each new employee (both citizen and noncitizen) hired after November 6, 1986, to work in the United States. In the Commonwealth of the Northern Mariana Islands (CNMI), employers must complete Form I-9 to document verification of the identity and employment authorization of each new employee (both citizen and noncitizen) hired after November 27, 2011.

General Instructions

Both employers and employees are responsible for completing their respective sections of Form I-9. For the purpose of completing this form, the term "employer" means all employers, including those recruiters and referrers for a fee who are agricultural associations, agricultural employers, or farm labor contractors, as defined in section 3 of the Migrant and Seasonal Agricultural Worker Protection Act, Public Law 97-470 (29 U.S.C. 1802). An "employee" is a person who performs labor or services in the United States for an employer in return for wages or other remuneration. The term "Employee" does not include those who do not receive any form of remuneration (volunteers), independent contractors or those engaged in certain casual domestic employment. Form I-9 has three sections. Employees complete Section 1. Employers complete Section 2 and, when applicable, Section 3. Employers may be fined if the form is not properly completed. See 8 USC § 1324a and 8 CFR § 274a.10. Individuals may be prosecuted for knowingly and willfully entering false information on the form. Employers are responsible for retaining completed forms. **Do not mail completed forms to U.S. Citizenship and Immigration Services (USCIS) or Immigration and Customs Enforcement (ICE).**

These instructions will assist you in properly completing Form I-9. The employer must ensure that all pages of the instructions and Lists of Acceptable Documents are available, either in print or electronically, to all employees completing this form. When completing the form on a computer, the English version of the form includes specific instructions for each field and drop-down lists for universally used abbreviations and acceptable documents. To access these instructions, move the cursor over each field or click on the question mark symbol (⍰) within the field. Employers and employees can also access this full set of instructions at any time by clicking the Instructions button at the top of each page when completing the form on a computer that is connected to the Internet.

Employers and employees may choose to complete any or all sections of the form on paper or using a computer, or a combination of both. Forms I-9 obtained from the USCIS website are not considered electronic Forms I-9 under DHS regulations and, therefore, cannot be electronically signed. Therefore, regardless of the method you used to enter information into each field, you must print a hard copy of the form, then sign and date the hard copy by hand where required.

Employers can obtain a blank copy of Form I-9 from the USCIS website at https://www.uscis.gov/sites/default/files/files/form/i-9.pdf. This form is in portable document format (.pdf) that is fillable and savable. That means that you may download it, or simply print out a blank copy to enter information by hand. You may also request paper Forms I-9 from USCIS.

Certain features of Form I-9 that allow for data entry on personal computers may make the form appear to be more than two pages. When using a computer, Form I-9 has been designed to print as two pages. Using more than one preparer and/or translator will add an additional page to the form, regardless of your method of completion. You are not required to print, retain or store the page containing the Lists of Acceptable Documents.

The form will also populate certain fields with N/A when certain user choices ensure that particular fields will not be completed. The Print button located at the top of each page that will print any number of pages the user selects. Also, the Start Over button located at the top of each page will clear all the fields on the form.

The Spanish version of Form I-9 does not include the additional instructions and drop-down lists described above. Employers in Puerto Rico may use either the Spanish or English version of the form. Employers outside of Puerto Rico must retain the English version of the form for their records, but may use the Spanish form as a translation tool. Additional guidance to complete the form may be found in the Handbook for Employers: Guidance for Completing Form I-9 (M-274) and on USCIS' Form I-9 website, I-9 Central.

Completing Section I: Employee Information and Attestation

You, the employee, must complete each field in Section 1 as described below. Newly hired employees must complete and sign Section 1 no later than the first day of employment. Section 1 should never be completed before you have accepted a job offer.

Entering Your Employee Information

Last Name *(Family Name)*: Enter your full legal last name. Your last name is your family name or surname. If you have two last names or a hyphenated last name, include both names in the Last Name field. *Examples of correctly entered last names include De La Cruz, O'Neill, Garcia Lopez, Smith-Johnson, Nguyen.* If you only have one name, enter it in this field, then enter "Unknown" in the First Name field. You may not enter "Unknown" in both the Last Name field and the First Name field.

First Name *(Given Name)*: Enter your full legal first name. Your first name is your given name. *Some examples of correctly entered first names include Jessica, John-Paul, Tae Young, D'Shaun, Mai.* If you only have one name, enter it in the Last Name field, then enter "Unknown" in this field. You may not enter "Unknown" in both the First Name field and the Last Name field.

Middle Initial: Your middle initial is the first letter of your second given name, or the first letter of your middle name, if any. If you have more than one middle name, enter the first letter of your first middle name. If you do not have a middle name, enter N/A in this field.

Other Last Names Used: Provide all other last names used, if any (e.g., maiden name). Enter N/A if you have not used other last names. For example, if you legally changed your last name from Smith to Jones, you should enter the name Smith in this field.

Address (Street Name and Number): Enter the street name and number of the current address of your residence. If you are a border commuter from Canada or Mexico, you may enter your Canada or Mexico address in this field. If your residence does not have a physical address, enter a description of the location of your residence, such as "3 miles southwest of Anytown post office near water tower."

Apartment: Enter the number(s) or letter(s) that identify(ies) your apartment. If you do not live in an apartment, enter N/A.

City or Town: Enter your city, town or village in this field. If your residence is not located in a city, town or village, enter your county, township, reservation, etc., in this field. If you are a border commuter from Canada, enter your city and province in this field. If you are a border commuter from Mexico, enter your city and state in this field.

State: Enter the abbreviation of your state or territory in this field. If you are a border commuter from Canada or Mexico, enter your country abbreviation in this field.

ZIP Code: Enter your 5-digit ZIP code. If you are a border commuter from Canada or Mexico, enter your 5- or 6-digit postal code in this field.

Date of Birth: Enter your date of birth as a 2-digit month, 2-digit day, and 4-digit year (mm/dd/yyyy). For example, enter January 8, 1980 as 01/08/1980.

U.S. Social Security Number: Providing your 9-digit Social Security number is voluntary on Form I-9 unless your employer participates in E-Verify. If your employer participates in E-Verify and:

    1. You have been issued a Social Security number, you must provide it in this field; or

    2. You have applied for, but have not yet received a Social Security number, leave this field blank until you receive a Social Security number.

Employee's E-mail Address (Optional): Providing your e-mail address is optional on Form I-9, but the field cannot be left blank. To enter your e-mail address, use this format: name@site .domain. One reason Department of Homeland Security (DHS) may e-mail you is if your employer uses E-Verify and DHS learns of a potential mismatch between the information provided and the information in government records. This e-mail would contain information on how to begin to resolve the potential mismatch. You may use either your personal or work e-mail address in this field. Enter N/A if you do not enter your e-mail address.

Employee's Telephone Number (Optional): Providing your telephone number is optional on Form I-9, but the field cannot be left blank. If you enter your area code and telephone number, use this format: 000-000-0000. Enter N/A if you do not enter your telephone number.

Attesting to Your Citizenship or Immigration Status

You must select one box to attest to your citizenship or immigration status.

1. **A citizen of the United States.**

2. **A noncitizen national of the United States:** An individual born in American Samoa, certain former citizens of the former Trust Territory of the Pacific Islands, and certain children of noncitizen nationals born abroad.

3. **A lawful permanent resident:** An individual who is not a U.S. citizen and who resides in the United States under legally recognized and lawfully recorded permanent residence as an immigrant. This term includes conditional residents. Asylees and refugees should not select this status, but should instead select "An Alien authorized to work" below.

   If you select "lawful permanent resident," enter your 7- to 9-digit Alien Registration Number (A-Number), including the "A," or USCIS Number in the space provided. When completing this field using a computer, use the dropdown provided to indicate whether you have entered an Alien Number or a USCIS Number. At this time, the USCIS Number is the same as the A-Number without the "A" prefix.

4. **An alien authorized to work:** An individual who is not a citizen or national of the United States, or a lawful permanent resident, but is authorized to work in the United States.

   If you select this box, enter the date that your employment authorization expires, if any, in the space provided. In most cases, your employment authorization expiration date is found on the document(s) evidencing your employment authorization. Refugees, asylees and certain citizens of the Federated States of Micronesia, the Republic of the Marshall Islands, or Palau, and other aliens whose employment authorization does not have an expiration date should enter N/A in the Expiration Date field. In some cases, such as if you have Temporary Protected Status, your employment authorization may have been automatically extended; in these cases, you should enter the expiration date of the automatic extension in this space.

   Aliens authorized to work must enter one of the following to complete Section1:
   1. Alien Registration Number (A-Number)/USCIS Number; or
   2. Form I-94 Admission Number; or
   3. Foreign Passport Number and the Country of Issuance

   Your employer may not ask you to present the document from which you supplied this information.

   Alien Registration Number/USCIS Number: Enter your 7- to 9-digit Alien Registration Number (A-Number), including the "A," or your USCIS Number in this field. At this time, the USCIS Number is the same as your A-Number without the "A" prefix. When completing this field using a computer, use the dropdown provided to indicate whether you have entered an Alien Number or a USCIS Number. If you do not provide an A-Number or USCIS Number, enter N/A in this field then enter either a Form I-94 Admission Number, or a Foreign Passport and Country of Issuance in the fields provided.

   Form I-94 Admission Number: Enter your 11-digit I-94 Admission Number in this field. If you do not provide an I-94 Admission Number, enter N/A in this field, then enter either an Alien Registration Number/USCIS Number or a Foreign Passport Number and Country of Issuance in the fields provided.

   Foreign Passport Number: Enter your Foreign Passport Number in this field. If you do not provide a Foreign Passport Number, enter N/A in this field, then enter either an Alien Number/USCIS Number or a I-94 Admission Number in the fields provided.

   Country of Issuance: If you entered your Foreign Passport Number, enter your Foreign Passport's Country of Issuance. If you did not enter your Foreign Passport Number, enter N/A.

Signature of Employee: After completing Section 1, sign your name in this field. If you used a form obtained from the USCIS website, you must print the form to sign your name in this field. By signing this form, you attest under penalty of perjury (28 U.S.C. § 1746) that the information you provided, along with the citizenship or immigration status you selected, and all information and documentation you provide to your employer, is complete, true and correct, and you are aware that you may face severe penalties provided by law and may be subject to criminal prosecution for knowingly and willfully making false statements or using false documentation when completing this form. Further, falsely attesting to U.S. citizenship may subject employees to penalties, removal proceedings and may adversely affect an employee's ability to seek future immigration benefits. If you cannot sign your name, you may place a mark in this field to indicate your signature. Employees who use a preparer or translator to help them complete the form must still sign or place a mark in the Signature of Employee field on the printed form.

If you used a preparer, translator, and other individual to assist you in completing Form I-9:

- Both you and your preparer(s) and/or translator(s) must complete the appropriate areas of Section 1, and then sign Section 1. If Section 1 was completed on a form obtained from the USCIS website, the form must be printed to sign these fields. You and your preparer(s) and/or translator(s) also should review the instructions for **Completing the Preparer and/or Translator Certification** below.

- If the employee is a minor (individual under 18) who cannot present an identity document, the employee's parent or legal guardian can complete Section 1 for the employee and enter "minor under age 18" in the signature field. If Section 1 was completed on a form obtained from the USCIS website, the form must be printed to enter this information. The minor's parent or legal guardian should review the instructions for Completing the Preparer and/or Translator Certification below. Refer to the Handbook for Employers: Guidance for Completing Form I-9 (M-274) for more guidance on completion of Form I-9 for minors. If the minor's employer participates in E-Verify, the employee must present a list B identity document with a photograph to complete Form I-9.

- If the employee is a person with a disability (who is placed in employment by a nonprofit organization, association or as part of a rehabilitation program) who cannot present an identity document, the employee's parent, legal guardian or a representative of the nonprofit organization, association or rehabilitation program can complete Section 1 for the employee and enter "Special Placement" in this field. If Section 1 was completed on a form obtained from the USCIS website, the form must be printed to enter this information. The parent, legal guardian or representative of the nonprofit organization, association or rehabilitation program completing Section 1 for the employee should review the instructions for Completing the Preparer and/or Translator Certification below. Refer to the Handbook for Employers: Guidance for Completing Form I-9 (M-274) for more guidance on completion of Form I-9 for certain employees with disabilities.

Today's Date: Enter the date you signed Section 1 in this field. Do not backdate this field. Enter the date as a 2-digit month, 2-digit day and 4-digit year (mm/dd/yyyy). For example, enter January 8, 2014 as 01/08/2014. A preparer or translator who assists the employee in completing Section 1 may enter the date the employee signed or made a mark to sign Section 1 in this field. Parents or legal guardians assisting minors (individuals under age 18) and parents, legal guardians or representatives of a nonprofit organization, association or rehabilitation program assisting certain employees with disabilities must enter the date they completed Section 1 for the employee.

Completing the Preparer and/or Translator Certification

If you did not use a preparer or translator to assist you in completing Section 1, you, the employee, must check the box marked **I did not use a Preparer or Translator**. If you check this box, leave the rest of the fields in this area blank.

If one or more preparers and/or translators assist the employee in completing the form using a computer, the preparer and/or translator must check the box marked **"A preparer(s) and/or translator(s) assisted the employee in completing Section 1"**, then select the number of Certification areas needed from the dropdown provided. Any additional Certification areas generated will result in an additional page. Form I-9 Supplement, Section 1 Preparer and/or Translator Certification can be separately downloaded from the USCIS Form I-9 webpage, which provides additional Certification areas for those completing Form I-9 using a computer who need more Certification areas than the 5 provided or those who are completing Form I-9 on paper. The first preparer and/or translator must complete all the fields in the Certification area on the same page the employee has signed. There is no limit to the number of preparers and/or translators an employee can use, but each additional preparer and/or translator must complete and sign a separate Certification area. Ensure the employee's last name, first name and middle initial are entered at the top of any additional pages. The employer must ensure that any additional pages are retained with the employee's completed Form I-9.

Signature of Preparer or Translator: Any person who helped to prepare or translate Section 1 of Form I-9 must sign his or her name in this field. If you used a form obtained from the USCIS website, you must print the form to sign your name in this field. The Preparer and/or Translator Certification must also be completed if "Individual under Age 18" or "Special Placement" is entered in lieu of the employee's signature in Section 1.

Today's Date: The person who signs the Preparer and/or Translator Certification must enter the date he or she signs in this field on the printed form. Do not backdate this field. Enter the date as a 2-digit month, 2-digit day, and 4-digit year (mm/dd/yyyy). For example, enter January 8, 2014 as 01/08/2014.

Last Name *(Family Name):* Enter the full legal last name of the person who helped the employee in preparing or translating Section 1 in this field. The last name is also the family name or surname. If the preparer or translator has two last names or a hyphenated last name, include both names in this field.

First Name *(Given Name):* Enter the full legal first name of the person who helped the employee in preparing or translating Section 1 in this field. The first name is also the given name.

Address (Street Name and Number): Enter the street name and number of the current address of the residence of the person who helped the employee in preparing or translating Section 1 in this field. Addresses for residences in Canada or Mexico may be entered in this field. If the residence does not have a physical address, enter a description of the location of the residence, such as "3 miles southwest of Anytown post office near water tower." If the residence is an apartment, enter the apartment number in this field.

City or Town: Enter the city, town or village of the residence of the person who helped the employee in preparing or translating Section 1 in this field. If the residence is not located in a city, town or village, enter the name of the county, township, reservation, etc., in this field. If the residence is in Canada, enter the city and province in this field. If the residence is in Mexico, enter the city and state in this field.

State: Enter the abbreviation of the state, territory or country of the preparer or translator's residence in this field.

ZIP Code: Enter the 5-digit ZIP code of the residence of the person who helped the employee in preparing or translating Section 1 in this field. If the preparer or translator's residence is in Canada or Mexico, enter the 5- or 6-digit postal code.

Presenting Form I-9 Documents

Within 3 business days of starting work for pay, you must present to your employer documentation that establishes your identity and employment authorization. For example, if you begin employment on Monday, you must present documentation on or before Thursday of that week. However, if you were hired to work for less than 3 business days, you must present documentation no later than the first day of employment.

Choose which unexpired document(s) to present to your employer from the Lists of Acceptable Documents. An employer cannot specify which document(s) you may present from the Lists of Acceptable Documents. You may present either one selection from List A or a combination of one selection from List B and one selection from List C. Some List A documents, which show both identity and employment authorization, are combination documents that must be presented together to be considered a List A document: for example, the foreign passport together with a Form I-94 containing an endorsement of the alien's nonimmigrant status and employment authorization with a specific employer incident to such status. List B documents show identity only and List C documents show employment authorization only. If your employer participates in E-Verify and you present a List B document, the document must contain a photograph. If you present acceptable List A documentation, you should not be asked to present, nor should you provide, List B and List C documentation. If you present acceptable List B and List C documentation, you should not be asked to present, nor should you provide, List A documentation. If you are unable to present a document(s) from these lists, you may be able to present an acceptable receipt. Refer to the Receipts section below.

Your employer must review the document(s) you present to complete Form I-9. If your document(s) reasonably appears to be genuine and to relate to you, your employer must accept the documents. If your document(s) does not reasonably appear to be genuine or to relate to you, your employer must reject it and provide you with an opportunity to present other documents from the Lists of Acceptable Documents. Your employer may choose to make copies of your document(s), but must return the original(s) to you. Your employer must review your documents in your physical presence.

Your employer will complete the other parts of this form, as well as review your entries in Section 1. Your employer may ask you to correct any errors found. Your employer is responsible for ensuring all parts of Form I-9 are properly completed and is subject to penalties under federal law if the form is not completed correctly.

Minors (individuals under age 18) and certain employees with disabilities whose parent, legal guardian or representative completed Section 1 for the employee are only required to present an employment authorization document from List C. Refer to the Handbook for Employers: Guidance for Completing Form I-9 (M-274) for more guidance on minors and certain individuals with disabilities.

Receipts

If you do not have unexpired documentation from the Lists of Acceptable Documents, you may be able to present a receipt(s) in lieu of an acceptable document(s). New employees who choose to present a receipt(s) must do so within three business days of their first day of employment. If your employer is reverifying your employment authorization, and you choose to present a receipt for reverification, you must present the receipt by the date your employment authorization expires. Receipts are not acceptable if employment lasts fewer than three business days.

There are three types of acceptable receipts:

1. A receipt showing that you have applied to replace a document that was lost, stolen or damaged. You must present the actual document within 90 days from the date of hire or, in the case of reverification, within 90 days from the date your original employment authorization expires.

2. The arrival portion of Form I-94/I-94A containing a temporary I-551 stamp and a photograph of the individual. You must present the actual Permanent Resident Card (Form I-551) by the expiration date of the temporary I-551 stamp, or, if there is no expiration date, within 1 year from the date of admission.

3. The departure portion of Form I-94/I-94A with a refugee admission stamp. You must present an unexpired Employment Authorization Document (Form I-766) or a combination of a List B document and an unrestricted Social Security Card within 90 days from the date of hire or, in the case of reverification, within 90 days from the date your original employment authorization expires.

Receipts showing that you have applied for an initial grant of employment authorization, or for renewal of your expiring or expired employment authorization, are not acceptable.

Completing Section 2: Employer or Authorized Representative Review and Verification

You, the employer, must ensure that all parts of Form I-9 are properly completed and may be subject to penalties under federal law if the form is not completed correctly. Section 1 must be completed no later than the employee's first day of employment. You may not ask an individual to complete Section 1 before he or she has accepted a job offer. Before completing Section 2, you should review Section 1 to ensure the employee completed it properly. If you find any errors in Section 1, have the employee make corrections, as necessary and initial and date any corrections made.

You or your authorized representative must complete Section 2 by examining evidence of identity and employment authorization within 3 business days of the employee's first day of employment. For example, if an employee begins employment on Monday, you must review the employee's documentation and complete Section 2 on or before Thursday of that week. However, if you hire an individual for less than 3 business days, Section 2 must be completed no later than the first day of employment.

Entering Employee Information from Section 1

This area, titled, "Employee Info from Section 1" contains fields to enter the employee's last name, first name, middle initial exactly as he or she entered them in Section 1. This area also includes a Citizenship/Immigration Status field to enter the number of the citizenship or immigration status checkbox the employee selected in Section 1. These fields help to ensure that the two pages of an employee's Form I-9 remain together. When completing Section 2 using a computer, the number entered in the Citizenship/Immigration Status field provides drop-downs that directly relate to the employee's selected citizenship or immigration status.

Entering Documents the Employee Presents

You, the employer or authorized representative, must physically examine, in the employee's physical presence, the unexpired document(s) the employee presents from the Lists of Acceptable Documents to complete the Document fields in Section 2.

You cannot specify which document(s) an employee may present from these lists. If you discriminate in the Form I-9 process based on an individual's citizenship status, immigration status, or national origin, you may be in violation of the law and subject to sanctions such as civil penalties and be required to pay back pay to discrimination victims. A document is acceptable as long as it reasonably appears to be genuine and to relate to the person presenting it. Employees must present one selection from List A or a combination of one selection from List B and one selection from List C.

List A documents show both identity and employment authorization. Some List A documents are combination documents that must be presented together to be considered a List A document, such as a foreign passport together with a Form I-94 containing an endorsement of the alien's nonimmigrant status.

List B documents show identity only, and List C documents show employment authorization only. If an employee presents a List A document, do not ask or require the employee to present List B and List C documents, and vice versa. If an employer participates in E-Verify and the employee presents a List B document, the List B document must include a photograph.

If an employee presents a receipt for the application to replace a lost, stolen or damaged document, the employee must present the replacement document to you within 90 days of the first day of work for pay, or in the case of reverification, within 90 days of the date the employee's employment authorization expired. Enter the word "Receipt" followed by the title of the receipt in Section 2 under the list that relates to the receipt.

When your employee presents the replacement document, draw a line through the receipt, then enter the information from the new document into Section 2. Other receipts may be valid for longer or shorter periods, such as the arrival portion of Form I-94/ I-94A containing a temporary I-551 stamp and a photograph of the individual, which is valid until the expiration date of the temporary I-551 stamp or, if there is no expiration date, valid for one year from the date of admission.

Ensure that each document is an unexpired, original (no photocopies, except for certified copies of birth certificates) document. Certain employees may present an expired employment authorization document, which may be considered unexpired, if the employee's employment authorization has been extended by regulation or a Federal Register Notice. Refer to the Handbook for Employers: Guidance for Completing Form I-9 (M-274) or I-9 Central for more guidance on these special situations.

Refer to the M-274 for guidance on how to handle special situations, such as students (who may present additional documents not specified on the Lists) and H-1B and H-2A nonimmigrants changing employers.

Minors (individuals under age 18) and certain employees with disabilities whose parent, legal guardian or representative completed Section 1 for the employee are only required to present an employment authorization document from List C. Refer to the M-274 for more guidance on minors and certain persons with disabilities. If the minor's employer participates in E-Verify, the minor employee also must present a List B identity document with a photograph to complete Form I-9.

You must return original document(s) to the employee, but may make photocopies of the document(s) reviewed. Photocopying documents is voluntary unless you participate in E-Verify. E-Verify employers are only required to photocopy certain documents. If you are an E-Verify employer who chooses to photocopy documents other than those you are required to photocopy, you should apply this policy consistently with respect to Form I-9 completion for all employees. For more information on the types of documents that an employer must photocopy if the employer uses E-Verify, visit E-Verify's website at www.dhs.gov/e-verify. For non-E-Verify employers, if photocopies are made, they should be made consistently for ALL new hires and reverified employees.

Photocopies must be retained and presented with Form I-9 in case of an inspection by DHS or another federal government agency. You must always complete Section 2 by reviewing original documentation, even if you photocopy an employee's document(s) after reviewing the documentation. Making photocopies of an employee's document(s) cannot take the place of completing Form I-9. You are still responsible for completing and retaining Form I-9.

List A - Identity and Employment Authorization: If the employee presented an acceptable document(s) from List A or an acceptable receipt for a List A document, enter the document(s) information in this column. If the employee presented a List A document that consists of a combination of documents, enter information from each document in that combination in a separate area under List A as described below. All documents must be unexpired. If you enter document information in the List A column, you should not enter document information in the List B or List C columns. If you complete Section 2 using a computer, a selection in List A will fill all the fields in the Lists B and C columns with N/A.

Document Title: If the employee presented a document from List A, enter the title of the List A document or receipt in this field. The abbreviations provided are available in the dropdown when the form is completed on a computer. When completing the form on paper, you may choose to use these abbreviations or any other common abbreviation to enter the document title or issuing authority. If the employee presented a combination of documents, use the second and third Document Title fields as necessary.

Full name of List A Document	Abbreviations
U.S. Passport	U.S. Passport
U.S. Passport Card	U.S. Passport Card
Permanent Resident Card (Form I-551)	Perm. Resident Card (Form I-551)
Alien Registration Receipt Card (Form I-551)	Alien Reg. Receipt Card (Form I-551)
Foreign passport containing a temporary I-551 stamp	1. Foreign Passport 2. Temporary I-551 Stamp
Foreign passport containing a temporary I-551 printed notation on a machine-readable immigrant visa (MRIV)	1. Foreign Passport 2. Machine-readable immigrant visa (MRIV)
Employment Authorization Document (Form I-766)	Employment Auth. Document (Form I-766)
For a nonimmigrant alien authorized to work for a specific employer because of his or her status, a foreign passport with Form I/94/I-94A that contains an endorsement of the alien's nonimmigrant status	1. Foreign Passport, work-authorized non-immigrant 2. Form I-94/I94A 3. "Form I-20" or "Form DS-2019" Note: In limited circumstances, certain J-1 students may be required to present a letter from their Responsible Officer in order to work. Enter the document title, issuing authority, document number and expiration date from this document in the Additional Information field.
Passport from the Federated States of Micronesia (FSM) with Form I-94/I-94A	1. FSM Passport with Form I-94 2. Form I-94/I94A
Passport from the Republic of the Marshall Islands (RMI) with Form I-94/I94A	1. RMI Passport with Form I-94 2. Form I-94/I94A
Receipt: The arrival portion of Form I-94/I-94A containing a temporary I-551 stamp and photograph	Receipt: Form I-94/I-94A w/I-551 stamp, photo
Receipt: The departure portion of Form I-94/I-94A with an unexpired refugee admission stamp	Receipt: Form I-94/I-94A w/refugee stamp
Receipt for an application to replace a lost, stolen or damaged Permanent Resident Card (Form I-551)	Receipt replacement Perm. Res. Card (Form I-551)
Receipt for an application to replace a lost, stolen or damaged Employment Authorization Document (Form I-766)	Receipt replacement EAD (Form I-766)
Receipt for an application to replace a lost, stolen or damaged foreign passport with Form I-94/I-94A that contains an endorsement of the alien's nonimmigrant status	1. Receipt: Replacement Foreign Passport, work-authorized nonimmigrant 2. Receipt: Replacement Form I-94/I-94A 3. Form I-20 or Form DS-2019 (if presented)
Receipt for an application to replace a lost, stolen or damaged passport from the Federated States of Micronesia with Form I-94/I-94A	1. Receipt: Replacement FSM Passport with Form I-94 2. Receipt: Replacement Form I-94/I-94A
Receipt for an application to replace a lost, stolen or damaged passport from the Republic of the Marshall Islands with Form I-94/I-94A	1. Receipt: Replacement RMI Passport with Form I-94 2. Receipt: Replacement Form I-94/I-94A

Issuing Authority: Enter the issuing authority of the List A document or receipt. The issuing authority is the specific entity that issued the document. If the employee presented a combination of documents, use the second and third Issuing Authority fields as necessary.

Document Number: Enter the document number, if any, of the List A document or receipt presented. If the document does not contain a number, enter N/A in this field. If the employee presented a combination of documents, use the second and third Document Number fields as necessary. If the document presented was a Form I-20 or DS-2019, enter the Student and Exchange Visitor Information System (SEVIS) number in the third Document Number field exactly as it appears on the Form I-20 or the DS-2019.

Expiration Date (if any) (mm/dd/yyyy): Enter the expiration date, if any, of the List A document. The document is not acceptable if it has already expired. If the document does not contain an expiration date, enter N/A in this field. If the document uses text rather than a date to indicate when it expires, enter the text as shown on the document, such as "D/S"(which means, "duration of status"). For a receipt, enter the expiration date of the receipt validity period as described above. If the employee presented a combination of documents, use the second and third Expiration Date fields as necessary. If the document presented was a Form I-20 or DS-2019, enter the program end date here.

List B - Identity: If the employee presented an acceptable document from List B or an acceptable receipt for the application to replace a lost, stolen, or destroyed List B document, enter the document information in this column. If a parent or legal guardian attested to the identity of an employee who is an individual under age 18 or certain employees with disabilities in Section 1, enter either "Individual under age 18" or "Special Placement" in this field. Refer to the Handbook for Employers: Guidance for Completing Form I-9 (M-274) for more guidance on individuals under age 18 and certain person with disabilities.

If you enter document information in the List B column, you must also enter document information in the List C column. If an employee presents acceptable List B and List C documents, do not ask the employees to present a List A document. No entries should be made in the List A column. If you complete Section 2 using a computer, a selection in List B will fill all the fields in the List A column with N/A.

Document Title: If the employee presented a document from List B, enter the title of the List B document or receipt in this field. The abbreviations provided are available in the dropdown when the form is completed on a computer. When completing the form on paper, you may choose to use these abbreviations or any other common abbreviations to document the document title or issuing authority.

Full name of List B Document	Abbreviations
Driver's license issued by a State or outlying possession of the United States	Driver's license issued by state/territory
ID card issued by a State or outlying possession of the United States	ID card issued by state/territory
ID card issued by federal, state, or local government agencies or entities	Government ID
School ID card with photograph	School ID
Voter's registration card	Voter registration card
U.S. Military card	U.S. Military card
U.S. Military draft record	U.S. Military draft record
Military dependent's ID card	Military dependent's ID card
U.S. Coast Guard Merchant Mariner Card	USCG Merchant Mariner card
Native American tribal document	Native American tribal document
Driver's license issued by a Canadian government authority	Canadian driver's license
School record (for persons under age 18 who are unable to present a document listed above)	School record (under age 18)
Report card (for persons under age 18 who are unable to present a document listed above)	Report card (under age 18)
Clinic record (for persons under age 18 who are unable to present a document listed above)	Clinic record (under age 18)
Doctor record (for persons under age 18 who are unable to present a document listed above)	Doctor record (under age 18)
Hospital record (for persons under age 18 who are unable to present a document listed above)	Hospital record (under age 18)
Day-care record (for persons under age 18 who are unable to present a document listed above)	Day-care record (under age 18)
Nursery school record (for persons under age 18 who are unable to present a document listed above)	Nursery school record (under age 18)

Full name of List B Document	Abbreviations
Individual under age 18 endorsement by parent or guardian	Individual under Age 18
Special placement endorsement for persons with disabilities	Special Placement
Receipt for the application to replace a lost, stolen or damaged Driver's License issued by a State or outlying possession of the United States	Receipt: Replacement driver's license
Receipt for the application to replace a lost, stolen or damaged ID card issued by a State or outlying possession of the United States	Receipt: Replacement ID card
Receipt for the application to replace a lost, stolen or damaged ID card issued by federal, state, or local government agencies or entities	Receipt: Replacement Gov't ID
Receipt for the application to replace a lost, stolen or damaged School ID card with photograph	Receipt: Replacement School ID
Receipt for the application to replace a lost, stolen or damaged Voter's registration card	Receipt: Replacement Voter reg. card
Receipt for the application to replace a lost, stolen or damaged U.S. Military card	Receipt: Replacement U.S. Military card
Receipt for the application to replace a lost, stolen or damaged Military dependent's ID card	Receipt: Replacement U.S. Military dep. card
Receipt for the application to replace a lost, stolen or damaged U.S. Military draft record	Receipt: Replacement Military draft record
Receipt for the application to replace a lost, stolen or damaged U.S. Coast Guard Merchant Mariner Card	Receipt: Replacement Merchant Mariner card
Receipt for the application to replace a lost, stolen or damaged Driver's license issued by a Canadian government authority	Receipt: Replacement Canadian DL
Receipt for the application to replace a lost, stolen or damaged Native American tribal document	Receipt: Replacement Native American tribal doc
Receipt for the application to replace a lost, stolen or damaged School record (for persons under age 18 who are unable to present a document listed above)	Receipt: Replacement School record (under age 18)
Receipt for the application to replace a lost, stolen or damaged Report card (for persons under age 18 who are unable to present a document listed above)	Receipt: Replacement Report card (under age 18)
Receipt for the application to replace a lost, stolen or damaged Clinic record (for persons under age 18 who are unable to present a document listed above)	Receipt: Replacement Clinic record (under age 18)
Receipt for the application to replace a lost, stolen or damaged Doctor record (for persons under age 18 who are unable to present a document listed above)	Receipt: Replacement Doctor record (under age 18)
Receipt for the application to replace a lost, stolen or damaged Hospital record (for persons under age 18 who are unable to present a document listed above)	Receipt: Replacement Hospital record (under age 18)
Receipt for the application to replace a lost, stolen or damaged Day-care record (for persons under age 18 who are unable to present a document listed above)	Receipt: Replacement Day-care record (under age 18)
Receipt for the application to replace a lost, stolen or damaged Nursery school record (for persons under age 18 who are unable to present a document listed above)	Receipt: Replacement Nursery school record (under age 18)

Issuing Authority: Enter the issuing authority of the List B document or receipt. The issuing authority is the entity that issued the document. If the employee presented a document that is issued by a state agency, include the state as part of the issuing authority.

Document Number: Enter the document number, if any, of the List B document or receipt exactly as it appears on the document. If the document does not contain a number, enter N/A in this field.

Expiration Date (if any) (mm/dd/yyyy): Enter the expiration date, if any, of the List B document. The document is not acceptable if it has already expired. If the document does not contain an expiration date, enter N/A in this field. For a receipt, enter the expiration date of the receipt validity period as described in the Receipt section above.

List C - Employment Authorization: If the employee presented an acceptable document from List C, or an acceptable receipt for the application to replace a lost, stolen, or destroyed List C document, enter the document information in this column. If you enter document information in the List C column, you must also enter document information in the List B column. If an employee presents acceptable List B and List C documents, do not ask the employee to present a list A document. No entries should be made in the List A column.

> **Document Title:** If the employee presented a document from List C, enter the title of the List C document or receipt in this field. The abbreviations provided are available in the dropdown when the form is completed on a computer. When completing the form on paper, you may choose to use these abbreviations or any other common abbreviations to document the document title or issuing authority. If you are completing the form on a computer, and you select an Employment authorization document issued by DHS, the field will populate with List C #7 and provide a space for you to enter a description of the documentation the employee presented. Refer to the M-274 for guidance on entering List C #7 documentation.

Full name of List C Document	Abbreviations
Social Security Account Number card without restrictions	(Unrestricted) Social Security Card
Certification of Birth Abroad (Form FS-545)	Form FS-545
Certification of Report of Birth (Form DS-1350)	Form DS-1350
Consular Report of Birth Abroad (Form FS-240)	Form FS-240
Original or certified copy of a U.S. birth certificate bearing an official seal	Birth Certificate
Native American tribal document	Native American tribal document
U.S. Citizen ID Card (Form I-197)	Form I-197
Identification Card for use of Resident Citizen in the United States (Form I-179)	Form I-179
Employment authorization document issued by DHS (List C #7)	Employment Auth. document (DHS) List C #7
Receipt for the application to replace a lost, stolen or damaged Social Security Account Number Card without restrictions	Receipt: Replacement Unrestricted SS Card
Receipt for the application to replace a lost, stolen or damaged Original or certified copy of a U.S. birth certificate bearing an official seal	Receipt: Replacement Birth Certificate
Receipt for the application to replace a lost, stolen or damaged Native American Tribal Document	Receipt: Replacement Native American Tribal Doc.
Receipt for the application to replace a lost, stolen or damaged Employment Authorization Document issued by DHS	Receipt: Replacement Employment Auth. Doc. (DHS)

Issuing Authority: Enter the issuing authority of the List C document or receipt. The issuing authority is the entity that issued the document.

Document Number: Enter the document number, if any, of the List C document or receipt exactly as it appears on the document. If the document does not contain a number, enter N/A in this field.

Expiration Date (if any) (mm/dd/yyyy): Enter the expiration date, if any, of the List C document. The document is not acceptable if it has already expired, unless USCIS has extended the expiration date on the document. For instance, if a conditional resident presents a Form I-797 extending his or her conditional resident status with the employee's expired Form I-551, enter the future expiration date as indicated on the Form I-797. If the document has no expiration date, enter N/A in this field. For a receipt, enter the expiration date of the receipt validity period as described in the Receipt section above.

Additional Information: Use this space to notate any additional information required for Form I-9 such as:

- Employment authorization extensions for Temporary Protected Status beneficiaries, F-1 OPT STEM students, CAP-GAP, H-1B and H-2A employees continuing employment with the same employer or changing employers, and other nonimmigrant categories that may receive extensions of stay
- Additional document(s) that certain nonimmigrant employees may present
- Discrepancies that E-Verify employers must notate when participating in the IMAGE program
- Employee termination dates and form retention dates
- E-Verify case number, which may also be entered in the margin or attached as a separate sheet per E-Verify requirements and your chosen business process.
- Any other comments or notations necessary for the employer's business process

You may leave this field blank if the employee's circumstances do not require additional notations.

Entering Information in the Employer Certification

Employee's First Day of Employment: Enter the employee's first day of employment as a 2-digit month, 2-digit day and 4-digit year (mm/dd/yyyy).

Signature of Employer or Authorized Representative: Review the form for accuracy and completeness. The person who physically examines the employee's original document(s) and completes Section 2 must sign his or her name in this field. If you used a form obtained from the USCIS website, you must print the form to sign your name in this field. By signing Section 2, you attest under penalty of perjury (28 U.S.C. § 1746) that you have physically examined the documents presented by the employee, the document(s) reasonably appear to be genuine and to relate to the employee named, that to the best of your knowledge the employee is authorized to work in the United States, that the information you entered in Section 2 is complete, true and correct to the best of your knowledge, and that you are aware that you may face severe penalties provided by law and may be subject to criminal prosecution for knowingly and willfully making false statements or knowingly accepting false documentation when completing this form.

Today's Date: The person who signs Section 2 must enter the date he or she signed Section 2 in this field. Do not backdate this field. If you used a form obtained from the USCIS website, you must print the form to write the date in this field. Enter the date as a 2-digit month, 2-digit day and 4-digit year (mm/dd/yyyy). For example, enter January 8, 2014 as 01/08/2014.

Title of Employer or Authorized Representative: Enter the title, position or role of the person who physically examines the employee's original document(s), completes and signs Section 2.

Last Name of the Employer or Authorized Representative: Enter the full legal last name of the person who physically examines the employee's original documents, completes and signs Section 2. Last name refers to family name or surname. If the person has two last names or a hyphenated last name, include both names in this field.

First Name of the Employer or Authorized Representative: Enter the full legal first name of the person who physically examines the employee's original documents, completes, and signs Section 2. First name refers to the given name.

Employer's Business or Organization Name: Enter the name of the employer's business or organization in this field.

Employer's Business or Organization Address (Street Name and Number): Enter an actual, physical address of the employer. If your company has multiple locations, use the most appropriate address that identifies the location of the employer. Do not provide a P.O. Box address.

City or Town: Enter the city or town for the employer's business or organization address. If the location is not a city or town, you may enter the name of the village, county, township, reservation, etc. that applies.

State: Enter the two-character abbreviation of the state for the employer's business or organization address.

ZIP Code: Enter the 5-digit ZIP code for the employer's business or organization address.

Completing Section 3: Reverification and Rehires

Section 3 applies to both reverification and rehires. When completing this section, you must also complete the Last Name, First Name and Middle Initial fields in the Employee Info from Section 1 area at the top of Section 2, leaving the Citizenship/Immigration Status field blank. When completing Section 3 in either a reverification or rehire situation, if the employee's name has changed, record the new name in Block A.

Reverification

Reverification in Section 3 must be completed prior to the earlier of:

- The expiration date, if any, of the employment authorization stated in Section 1, or
- The expiration date, if any, of the List A or List C employment authorization document recorded in Section 2 (with some exceptions listed below).

Some employees may have entered "N/A" in the expiration date field in Section 1 if they are aliens whose employment authorization does not expire, e.g. asylees, refugees, certain citizens of the Federated States of Micronesia, the Republic of the Marshall Islands, or Palau. Reverification does not apply for such employees unless they choose to present evidence of employment authorization in Section 2 that contains an expiration date and requires reverification, such as Form I-766, Employment Authorization Document.

You should not reverify U.S. citizens and noncitizen nationals, or lawful permanent residents (including conditional residents) who presented a Permanent Resident Card (Form I-551). Reverification does not apply to List B documents.

For reverification, an employee must present an unexpired document(s) (or a receipt) from either List A or List C showing he or she is still authorized to work. You CANNOT require the employee to present a particular document from List A or List C. The employee is also not required to show the same type of document that he or she presented previously. See specific instructions on how to complete Section 3 below.

Rehires

If you rehire an employee within three years from the date that the Form I-9 was previously executed, you may either rely on the employee's previously executed Form I-9 or complete a new Form I-9.

If you choose to rely on a previously completed Form I-9, follow these guidelines.

- If the employee remains employment authorized as indicated on the previously executed Form I-9, the employee does not need to provide any additional documentation. Provide in Section 3 the employee's rehire date, any name changes if applicable, and sign and date the form.

- If the previously executed Form I-9 indicates that the employee's employment authorization from Section 1 or employment authorization documentation from Section 2 that is subject to reverification has expired, then reverification of employment authorization is required in Section 3 in addition to providing the rehire date. If the previously executed Form I-9 is not the current version of the form, you must complete Section 3 on the current version of the form.

- If you already used Section 3 of the employee's previously executed Form I-9, but are rehiring the employee within three years of the original execution of Form I-9, you may complete Section 3 on a new Form I-9 and attach it to the previously executed form.

Employees rehired after three years of original execution of the Form I-9 must complete a new Form I-9.

Complete each block in Section 3 as follows:

Block A - New Name: If an employee who is being reverified or rehired has also changed his or her name since originally completing Section 1 of this form, complete this block with the employee's new name. Enter only the part of the name that has changed, for example: if the employee changed only his or her last name, enter the last name in the Last Name field in this Block, then enter N/A in the First Name and Middle Initial fields. If the employee has not changed his or her name, enter N/A in each field of Block A.

Block B - Date of Rehire: Complete this block if you are rehiring an employee within three years of the date Form I-9 was originally executed. Enter the date of rehire in this field. Enter N/A in this field if the employee is not being rehired.

Block C - Complete this block if you are reverifying expiring or expired employment authorization or employment authorization documentation of a current or rehired employee. Enter the information from the List A or List C document(s) (or receipt) that the employee presented to reverify his or her employment authorization. All documents must be unexpired.

> **Document Title**: Enter the title of the List A or C document (or receipt) the employee has presented to show continuing employment authorization in this field.

> **Document Number**: Enter the document number, if any, of the document you entered in the Document Title field exactly as it appears on the document. Enter N/A if the document does not have a number.

> **Expiration Date (if any) (mm/dd/yyyy)**: Enter the expiration date, if any, of the document you entered in the Document Title field as a 2-digit month, 2-digit day, and 4-digit year (mm/dd/yyyy). If the document does not contain an expiration date, enter N/A in this field.

Signature of Employer or Authorized Representative: The person who completes Section 3 must sign in this field. If you used a form obtained from the USCIS website, you must print Section 3 of the form to sign your name in this field. By signing Section 3, you attest under penalty of perjury (28 U.S.C. §1746) that you have examined the documents presented by the employee, that the document(s) reasonably appear to be genuine and to relate to the employee named, that to the best of your knowledge the employee is authorized to work in the United States, that the information you entered in Section 3 is complete, true and correct to the best of your knowledge, and that you are aware that you may face severe penalties provided by law and may be subject to criminal prosecution for knowingly and willfully making false statements or knowingly accepting false documentation when completing this form.

Today's Date: The person who completes Section 3 must enter the date Section 3 was completed and signed in this field. Do not backdate this field. If you used a form obtained from the USCIS website, you must print Section 3 of the form to enter the date in this field. Enter the date as a 2-digit month, 2-digit day, and 4-digit year (mm/dd/yyyy). For example, enter January 8, 2014 as 01/08/2014.

Name of Employer or Authorized Representative: The person who completed, signed and dated Section 3 must enter his or her name in this field.

What is the Filing Fee?

There is no fee for completing Form I-9. This form is not filed with USCIS or any government agency. Form I-9 must be retained by the employer and made available for inspection by U.S. Government officials as specified in the "USCIS Privacy Act Statement" below.

USCIS Forms and Information

For additional guidance about Form I-9, employers and employees should refer to the *Handbook for Employers: Guidance for Completing Form I-9 (M-274)* or USCIS' Form I-9 website at https://www.uscis.gov/i-9-central.

You can also obtain information about Form I-9 by e-mailing USCIS at I-9Central@dhs.gov, or by calling 1-888-464-4218 or 1-877-875-6028 (TTY).

You may download and obtain the English and Spanish versions of Form I-9, the *Handbook for Employers,* or the instructions to Form I-9 from the USCIS website at https://www.uscis.gov/i-9. To complete Form I-9 on a computer, you will need the latest version of Adobe Reader, which can be downloaded for free at http://get.adobe.com/reader/. You may order USCIS forms by calling our toll-free number at 1-800-870-3676. You may also obtain forms and information by contacting the USCIS National Customer Service Center at 1-800-375-5283 or 1-800-767-1833 (TTY).

Information about E-Verify, a fast, free, internet-based system that allows businesses to determine the eligibility of their employees to work in the United States, can be obtained from the USCIS website at http://www.uscis.gov/e-verify, by e-mailing USCIS at E-Verify@dhs.gov or by calling 1-888-464-4218 or 1-877-875-6028 (TTY).

Employees with questions about Form I-9 and/or E-Verify can reach the USCIS employee hotline by calling 1-888-897-7781 or 1-877-875-6028 (TTY).

Photocopying Blank and Completed Forms I-9 and Retaining Completed Forms I-9

Employers may photocopy or print blank Forms I-9 for future use. All pages of the instructions and Lists of Acceptable Documents must be available, either in print or electronically, to all employees completing this form. Employers must retain each employee's completed Form I-9 for as long as the individual works for the employer and for a specified period after employment has ended. Employers are required to retain the pages of the form on which the employee and employer entered data. If copies of documentation presented by the employee are made, those copies must also be retained. Once the individual's employment ends, the employer must retain this form and attachments for either 3 years after the date of hire (i.e., first day of work for pay) or 1 year after the date employment ended, whichever is later. In the case of recruiters or referrers for a fee (only applicable to those that are agricultural associations, agricultural employers, or farm labor contractors), the retention period is 3 years after the date of hire (i.e., first day of work for pay).

Forms I-9 obtained from the USCIS website that are not printed and signed manually (by hand) are not considered complete. In the event of an inspection, retaining incomplete forms may make you subject to fines and penalties associated with incomplete forms.

Employers should ensure that information employees provide on Form I-9 is used only for Form I-9 purposes. Completed Forms I-9 and all accompanying documents should be stored in a safe, secure location.

Form I-9 may be generated, signed, and retained electronically, in compliance with Department of Homeland Security regulations at 8 CFR 274a.2.

USCIS Privacy Act Statement

AUTHORITIES: The authority for collecting this information is the Immigration Reform and Control Act of 1986, Public Law 99-603 (8 USC § 1324a).

PURPOSE: This information is collected by employers to comply with the requirements of the Immigration Reform and Control Act of 1986. This law requires that employers verify the identity and employment authorization of individuals they hire for employment to preclude the unlawful hiring, or recruiting or referring for a fee, of aliens who are not authorized to work in the United States.

DISCLOSURE: Providing the information collected by this form is voluntary. However an employer should not continue to employ an individual without a completed form. Failure of the employer to prepare and/or ensure proper completion of this form for each employee hired in the United States after November 6, 1986 or in the Commonwealth of the Mariana Islands after November 27, 2011, may subject the employer to civil and/or criminal penalties. In addition, employing individuals knowing that they are unauthorized to work in the United States may subject the employer to civil and/or criminal penalties.

ROUTINE USES: This information will be used by employers as a record of their basis for determining eligibility of an employee to work in the United States. The employer must retain this form for the required period and make it available for inspection by authorized officials of the Department of Homeland Security, Department of Labor and the Department of Justice, Civil Rights Division, Immigrant and Employee Rights Section.

Paperwork Reduction Act

An agency may not conduct or sponsor an information collection and a person is not required to respond to a collection of information unless it displays a currently valid OMB control number. The public reporting burden for this collection of information is estimated at 35 minutes per response, when completing the form manually, and 26 minutes per response when using a computer to aid in completion of the form, including the time for reviewing instructions and completing and retaining the form. Send comments regarding this burden estimate or any other aspect of this collection of information, including suggestions for reducing this burden, to: U.S. Citizenship and Immigration Services, Regulatory Coordination Division, Office of Policy and Strategy, 20 Massachusetts Avenue NW, Washington, DC 20529-2140; OMB No. 1615-0047. **Do not mail your completed Form I-9 to this address.**

APPENDIX B

M-274: U.S. Department of Homeland Security's Handbook for Employers: Guidance for Completing Form I-9

M-274: Handbook for Employers (July 14, 2017)

**U.S. Citizenship and
Immigration Services**

Handbook for Employers M-274

Guidance for Completing Form I-9 (Employment Eligibility Verification Form) | Current as of July 2017

U.S. Citizenship
and Immigration
Services

Last Reviewed/Updated: 07/14/2017

Table of Contents

1.0 Why Employers Must Verify Employment Authorization and Identity of New Employees

In 1986, Congress reformed U.S. immigration laws. These reforms, the result of a bipartisan effort, preserved the tradition of legal immigration while seeking to close the door to illegal entry. The employer sanctions provisions, found in section 274A of the Immigration and Nationality Act (INA), were added by the Immigration Reform and Control Act of 1986 (IRCA). These provisions further changed with the passage of the Immigration Act of 1990 and the Illegal Immigration Reform and Immigrant Responsibility Act (IIRIRA) of 1996.

Employment is often the magnet that attracts individuals to reside in the United States illegally. The purpose of the employer sanctions law is to remove this magnet by requiring employers to hire only individuals who may legally work here: U.S. citizens, noncitizen nationals, lawful permanent residents, and aliens authorized to work. To comply with the law, employers must verify the identity and employment authorization of each person they hire, complete and retain a Form I-9, Employment Eligibility Verification (PDF), for each employee, and refrain from discriminating against individuals on the basis of national origin or citizenship. At the same time that it created employer sanctions, Congress also prohibited employment discrimination based on citizenship, immigration status, and national origin. This part of the law is referred to as the anti-discrimination provisions. See Section 11.0 Unlawful Discrimination and Penalties for Prohibited Practices for more information on unlawful discrimination.

This handbook provides guidance on how to properly complete Form I-9, which helps employers verify that individuals are authorized to work in the United States. Every employer must complete a Form I-9 for every new employee you hire after Nov. 6, 1986. This includes U. S. citizens and noncitizen nationals who are automatically eligible for employment in the United States.

Form I-9 (PDF) and instructions for Form I-9 (PDF) are available for download from the USCIS website at uscis.gov/i-9-central. Employers may also call the USCIS Forms Request Line toll-free at 800-870-3676 to get print versions of Form I-9 and instructions.

Employers must use the current version of Form I-9. A revision date with an "N" next to it indicates that all previous versions with earlier revision dates are no longer valid. You may also use subsequent versions that have a "Y" next to the revision date.

Form I-9 is available in English and Spanish. Employers in the United States and U.S. territories may use the Spanish version of Form I-9 as a translation guide for Spanish-speaking employees, but must complete and retain the English version. Employers in Puerto Rico may use either the Spanish or the English version of Form I-9 to verify new employees.

1.1 The Homeland Security Act

The Homeland Security Act of 2002 created an executive department combining numerous federal agencies with a mission dedicated to homeland security. On March 1, 2003, the authorities of the former Immigration and Naturalization Service (INS) were transferred to three new agencies in the U.S. Department of Homeland Security (DHS): U.S. Citizenship and Immigration Services (USCIS), U.S. Customs and Border Protection (CBP), and U.S. Immigration and Customs Enforcement (ICE). The two DHS immigration components most involved with the matters discussed in this handbook are USCIS and ICE. USCIS is responsible for most documentation of alien employment authorization, for Form I-9, and for the E-Verify employment eligibility verification program. ICE is responsible for enforcement of the penalty provisions of section 274A of the INA and for other immigration enforcement within the United States.

Under the Homeland Security Act, the U. S. Department of Justice (DOJ) retained certain important responsibilities related to Form I-9 as well. In particular, the Immigrant and Employee Rights Section (IER) in the Department of Justice's Civil Rights Division is responsible for enforcement of the anti-discrimination provision in section 274B of the INA, while the Executive Office for Immigration Review (EOIR) is responsible for the administrative adjudication of cases under sections 274A, 274B, and 274C (civil document fraud) of the INA.

1.2 E-Verify: The Web-Based Verification Companion to Form I-9

Since verification of the employment authorization and identity of new hires became law in 1986, Form I-9 has been the foundation of the verification process. To improve the accuracy and integrity of this process, USCIS operates an electronic employment confirmation system called E-Verify.

E-Verify is a system that provides access to federal databases to help employers confirm the employment authorization of new hires. E-Verify is free and can be used by employers in all 50 states, as well as the District of Columbia, Puerto Rico, Guam, the U.S. Virgin Islands, and the Commonwealth of the Northern Mariana Islands.

Employers who participate in E-Verify must complete Form I-9 for each newly hired employee in the United States. E-Verify employers may accept any document or combination of documents on Form I-9, but if the employee chooses to present a List B and C combination, the List B (identity only) document must have a photograph.

After completing a Form I-9 for your new employee, create a case in E-Verify that includes information from Sections 1 and 2 of Form I-9. After creating the case, you will receive a response from E-Verify regarding the employment authorization of the employee. In some cases, E-Verify will provide a response indicating a tentative nonconfirmation of the employee's employment authorization. This does not necessarily mean that the employee is unauthorized to work in the United States. Rather, it means that E-Verify is unable to immediately confirm the employee's authorization to work. In the case of a tentative nonconfirmation, you must notify the employee, and an employee who wishes to contest a tentative nonconfirmation result should contact the appropriate agency (DHS or the Social Security Administration) within the prescribed time periods.

You must also follow certain procedures when using E-Verify that were designed to protect employees from unfair employment actions. You must use E-Verify for all new hires, both U .S. citizens and noncitizens, and may not use the system selectively. You may not use E-Verify to prescreen applicants for employment, check employees hired before the company became a participant in E-Verify (except contractors with a federal contract that requires use of E-Verify), or reverify employees who have temporary employment authorization. You may not terminate or take other adverse action against an employee based on a tentative nonconfirmation.

E-Verify strengthens the Form I-9 employment eligibility verification process that all employers, by law, must follow. By adding E-Verify to the existing Form I-9 process, employers can benefit from knowing that it has taken an additional constructive step toward maintaining a legal workforce.

You can enroll in E-Verify at uscis.gov/e-verify, which provides instructions for completing the enrollment process. For more information, contact E-Verify at 888-464-4218, or visit the website listed above.

Federal Contractors

On Nov. 14, 2008, the Civilian Agency Acquisition Council and the Defense Acquisition Regulations Council issued a final rule amending the Federal Acquisition Regulation (FAR) (FAR case 2007-013, Employment Eligibility Verification). This regulation was originally scheduled to be effective on Jan. 15, 2009, but the effective date was delayed until Sept. 8, 2009. The regulation requires contractors with a federal contract that contains a FAR E-Verify clause to use E-Verify for their new hires and all employees (existing and new) assigned to the contract. Federal contracts issued on or after Sept. 8, 2009, as well as older contracts that have been modified may contain the FAR E-Verify clause.

Federal contractors who have a federal contract that contains the FAR E-Verify clause must follow special rules when completing and updating Form I-9. For more in- formation, please see the E-Verify Supplemental Guide for Federal Contractors available at uscis.gov/e-verify.

2.0 Who Must Complete Form I-9

You must complete Form I-9 each time you hire any person to perform labor or services in the United States in return for wages or other remuneration. Remuneration is anything of value given in exchange for labor or services, including food and lodging. The requirement to complete Form I-9 applies to new employees hired after Nov. 6, 1986. This requirement does not apply to employees hired on or before Nov. 6, 1986, who are continuing in their employment and have a reasonable expectation of employment at all times.

Ensure that the employee completes Section 1 of Form I-9 at the time of hire. "Hire" means the beginning of employment in exchange for wages or other remuneration. The time of hire is noted on the form as the first day of employment. Employees may complete Section 1 before the time of hire, but no earlier than acceptance of the job offer. Review the employee's document(s) and fully complete Section 2 within three business days of the hire. For example, if the employee begins employment on Monday, you must complete Section 2 by Thursday.

If you hire a person for fewer than three business days, Sections 1 and 2 must be fully completed at the time of hire – in other words, by the first day of employment.

Do not complete a Form I-9 for employees who are:

- Hired on or before Nov. 6, 1986, (or on or before Nov. 27, 2007 if employment is in the Commonwealth of the Northern Mariana Islands (CNMI)) who are continuing in their employment and have a reasonable expectation of employment at all times;

- Employed for casual domestic work in a private home on a sporadic, irregular or intermittent basis;

- Independent contractors;

- Employed by a contractor providing contract services (such as employee leasing or temporary agencies) and are providing labor to you; or

- Not physically working on U.S. soil.

Note: *You cannot hire an individual who you know is not authorized to work in the United States.*

3.0 Completing Section 1 of Form I-9

Have the employee complete Section 1 at the time of hire (by the first day of their employment for pay) by filling in the correct information and signing and dating the form. If the employee enters the information by hand, ensure that the employee prints the information clearly.

A preparer and/or translator may help an employee complete Form I-9. The preparer and/or translator must read the form to the employee, assist them in completing Section 1, and have the employee sign or mark the form where appropriate. The preparer and/or translator must then complete the Preparer and/or Translator Certification block. If the employee used multiple preparers or translator, each subsequent preparer and/or translator must complete a separate Preparer/Translator Certification block on a Form I-9 Supplement and attach the Supplement to the employee's form.

You are responsible for reviewing and ensuring that your employee fully and properly completes Section 1.

Note: *Employees may voluntarily provide their Social Security numbers on Form I-9 unless you participate in the E-Verify program. Employees must provide E-Verify employers with their Social Security numbers. Employees who can satisfy Form I-9 requirements may work while awaiting their Social Security numbers.*
You may not ask an employee to provide you a specific document with their Social Security number on it. To do so may constitute unlawful discrimination. For more information on E-Verify, see Section 1.2 E-Verify: The Web-Based Verification Companion to Form I-9. For more information on unlawful discrimination, see Section 11.0 Unlawful Discrimination and Penalties for Prohibited Practices
Providing an e-mail address or telephone number in Section 1 is voluntary.

Figure 1: Completing Section 1: Employee Information and Attestation

Section 1. Employee Information and Attestation (*Employees must complete and sign Section 1 of Form I-9 no later than the first day of employment, but not before accepting a job offer.*)

Last Name (Family Name)	First Name (Given Name)	Middle Initial	Other Last Names Used (if any)
Washington	George	A	N/A

Address (Street Number and Name)	Apt. Number	City or Town	State	ZIP Code
123 Star Spangled Way	1	Westmoreland	VA	20002

Date of Birth (mm/dd/yyyy)	U.S. Social Security Number	Employee's E-mail Address	Employee's Telephone Number
02/02/1982	123-45-6789	gwashington@email.com	202-123-4567

I am aware that federal law provides for imprisonment and/or fines for false statements or use of false documents in connection with the completion of this form.

I attest, under penalty of perjury, that I am (check one of the following boxes):

[X] 1. A citizen of the United States

[ ] 2. A noncitizen national of the United States (See instructions)

[ ] 3. A lawful permanent resident   (Alien Registration Number/USCIS Number):

[ ] 4. An alien authorized to work   until (expiration date, if applicable, mm/dd/yyyy):
Some aliens may write "N/A" in the expiration date field. (See instructions)

Aliens authorized to work must provide only one of the following document numbers to complete Form I-9:
An Alien Registration Number/USCIS Number OR Form I-94 Admission Number OR Foreign Passport Number.

1. Alien Registration Number/USCIS Number:
OR
2. Form I-94 Admission Number:
OR
3. Foreign Passport Number:
Country of Issuance:

QR Code - Section 1 / Do Not Write In This Space

Signature of Employee	Today's Date (mm/dd/yyyy)
George Washington	01/22/2017

Preparer and/or Translator Certification (check one):
[ ] I did not use a preparer or translator.   [X] A preparer(s) and/or translator(s) assisted the employee in completing Section 1.
(*Fields below must be completed and signed when preparers and/or translators assist an employee in completing Section 1.*)

I attest, under penalty of perjury, that I have assisted in the completion of Section 1 of this form and that to the best of my knowledge the information is true and correct.

Signature of Preparer or Translator	Today's Date (mm/dd/yyyy)
Abigail Adams	01/22/2017

Last Name (Family Name)	First Name (Given Name)
Adams	Abigail

Address (Street Number and Name)	City or Town	State	ZIP Code
123 American Way	Weymouth	MA	20001

(1) Have the employee enter their full legal name and other last names that they have used in the past or present (such as a maiden name) if any.

- Have employees with two last names (family names) include both in the Last Name field. Employees who hyphenate their last names should include the hyphen (-) between the names. Employees with only one name should enter it in the Last Name field and enter "Unknown" in the First Name field. "Unknown" may not be entered in both the Last Name and the First Name fields.

- Employees with two first names (given names) should include both in the First Name field. Employees who hyphenate their first name should include the hyphen (-) between the names.

- Have the employee enter their middle initial in the Middle Initial field. Enter "N/A" if the employee does not have a middle initial.

- Have the employee enter their maiden name or any other legal last name they may have used in the Other Last Names Used field. Enter "N/A" if the employee has not used other last names.

(2) The employee should enter their home address, apt. number, city or town, state and ZIP Code. Employees who have no Apt. Number should enter "N/A" in that field. Employees who do not have a street address should enter a description of the location of their residence, such as "Two miles south of I-81, near the water tower."

(3) Employees should enter their date of birth as a two-digit month, two-digit day, and four-digit year: (mm/dd/yyyy) in this field. For example January 8, 1980 should be entered as 01/08/1980. Employees may voluntarily provide a Social Security number unless the employer participates in E-Verify. If the employer participates in E-Verify and:

- The employee has been issued a Social Security number, they must provide it on Form I-9; or

- The employee has applied for, but has not yet received the Social Security number, have the employee leave this field blank. Employees who can satisfy Form I-9 requirements may work while awaiting their Social Security numbers.

It is optional for the employee to provide an email address and telephone number in Section 1. If the employee chooses to provide an email address, it should be entered in the name@site.domain format. Employees who do not wish to enter an e-mail address or telephone number should enter "N/A" in these fields.

(4) Have the employee read the warning and attest to their citizenship or immigration status by checking one of the following boxes provided on the form:

- A citizen of the United States

- **A noncitizen national of the United States**: An individual born in American Samoa, certain former citizens of the former Trust Territory of the Pacific Islands, and certain children of noncitizen nationals born abroad.

- **A lawful permanent resident**: An individual who is not a U.S. citizen and who resides in the United States under legally recognized and lawfully recorded permanent residence as an immigrant. This term includes conditional residents. Asylees and refugees should not select this status, but should instead select "An alien authorized to work" below. Employees who select this box should enter their seven to nine-digit Alien Registration Number (A-Number) or USCIS Number in the space provided. The USCIS Number is the same as the A-Number without the "A" prefix.

- **An alien authorized to work**: An individual who is not a citizen or national of the United States, or a lawful permanent resident, but is authorized to work in the United States. For example, asylees, refugees, and certain citizens of the Federated States of Micronesia, the Republic of the Marshall Islands, or Palau should select this status.

(5) Have the employee sign and date the form, entering the date in Section 1 as a two-digit month, two-digit day, and four-digit year (mm/dd/yyyy).

(6) If the employee used a preparer and/or translator to complete the form, that person must certify that they assisted the employee by completing the Preparer and/or Translator Certification block. If the employee did not use a preparer and/or translator, have the employee check the box marked "I did not use a preparer or translator." If the employee used one or multiple preparers or translators and is completing the paper Form I-9, print out the Form I-9 Supplement, Section 1 Preparer and/or Translator Certification. If the employee used one or multiple preparers and/or translators and is completing Form I-9 using a computer, check the second box marked "A preparer(s) and/or translator(s) assisted the employee in completing Section 1" and select the number of preparers or translators the employee used in the drop down box next to "How Many?"

3.1 Failure to Complete Section 1

You must ensure that all parts of Form I-9 are properly completed; otherwise, you may be subject to penalties under federal law. Section 1 must be completed no later than the employee's first day of employment. You may not ask an individual who has not accepted a job offer to complete Section 1. Before completing Section 2, you should review Section 1 to ensure the employee completed it properly. If you find any errors in Section 1, have the employee make any necessary corrections and initial and date them.

4.0 Completing Section 2 of Form I-9

Within three business days of the date employment begins, the employee must present to you an original document or documents that show their identity and employment authorization. For example, if an employee begins employment on Monday, you must review the employee's documentation and complete Section 2 on or before Thursday of that week. However, if you hire an individual for less than three business days, you must complete Section 2 no later than the first day of employment. The employee must be allowed to choose which document(s) they will present from the Form I-9 Lists of Acceptable Documents. You cannot specify which document(s) an employee will present from the list.

Physically examine each original document the employee presents to determine if the document reasonably appears to be genuine and relates to the person presenting it. Make sure the person who examines the documents is the same person who attests and signs Section 2.

The employee must be physically present with the document examiner. Examine one selection from List A or a combination of one selection from List B and one selection from List C. If an employee presents a List A document, do not ask or require the employee to present List B or List C documents. If an employee presents List B and List C documents, do not ask or require the employee to present a List A document.

You must accept any document(s) from the Lists of Acceptable Documents that reasonably appear on their face to be genuine and relate to the person presenting them. You may not specify which document(s) the employee must present. Enter the document title, issuing authority, number, and expiration date (if any) in Section 2 from original documents supplied by the employee. If you choose to make copies of the documents, do so for all employees, regardless of national origin or citizenship status, or you may be in violation of anti-discrimination laws. Return the original documents to your employee.

Fill in the date employment begins and information in the certification block. Sign and date Form I-9.

Note: If you participate in E-Verify, and the employee presents a combination of List B and List C documents, then the List B document must contain a photograph. For more information, visit uscis.gov/e-verify.

You may designate or contract with someone such as a personnel officer, foreman, agent, or anyone else acting on your behalf, including a notary public, to complete Section 2. Note that anyone else who completes Form I-9 on your behalf must carry out full Form I-9 responsibilities. It is not acceptable for the designated person to physically examine the employee's employment authorization and identity documents, and leave Section 2 for you to complete. You are liable for any violations in connection with the form or the verification process, including any violations of the employer sanctions laws committed by the person designated to act on your behalf.

Figure 2: Section 2: Employer or Authorized Representative Review and Verification

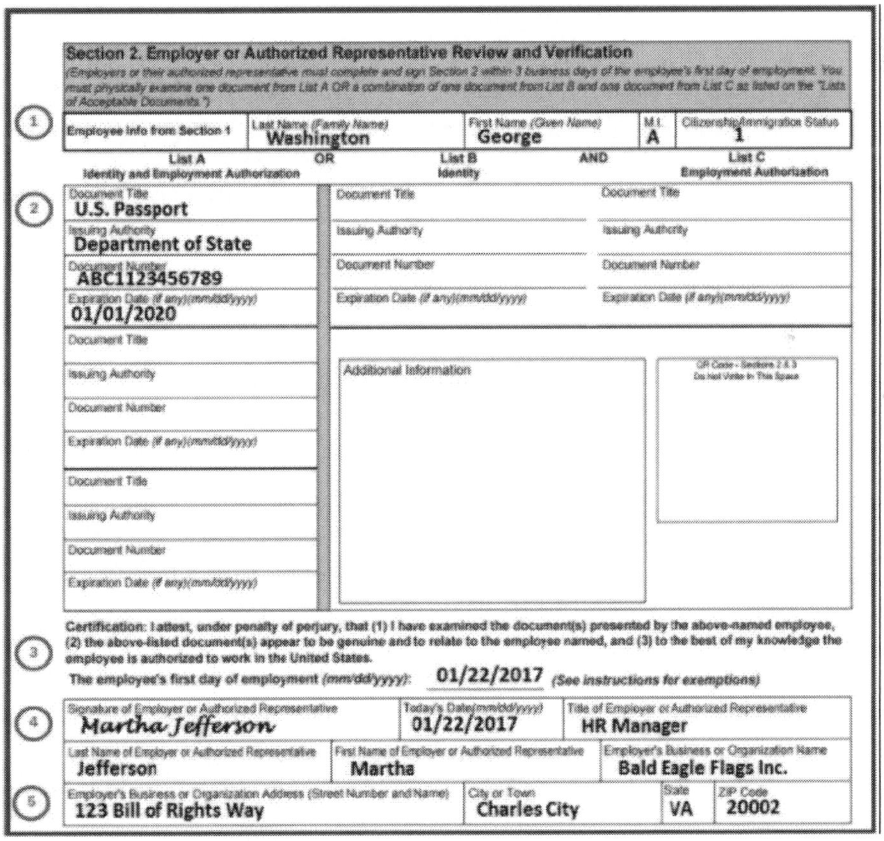

Section 2. Employer or Authorized Representative Review and Verification

(1) Employee Info from Section 1 — Last Name (Family Name): Washington — First Name (Given Name): George — M.I.: A — Citizenship/Immigration Status: 1

List A (Identity and Employment Authorization) OR List B (Identity) AND List C (Employment Authorization)

(2) Document Title: U.S. Passport
Issuing Authority: Department of State
Document Number: ABC1123456789
Expiration Date (if any)(mm/dd/yyyy): 01/01/2020

Additional Information

(3) Certification: I attest, under penalty of perjury, that (1) I have examined the document(s) presented by the above-named employee, (2) the above-listed document(s) appear to be genuine and to relate to the employee named, and (3) to the best of my knowledge the employee is authorized to work in the United States.

The employee's first day of employment (mm/dd/yyyy): 01/22/2017 (See instructions for exemptions)

(4) Signature of Employer or Authorized Representative: *Martha Jefferson* — Today's Date (mm/dd/yyyy): 01/22/2017 — Title of Employer or Authorized Representative: HR Manager

Last Name of Employer or Authorized Representative: Jefferson — First Name of Employer or Authorized Representative: Martha — Employer's Business or Organization Name: Bald Eagle Flags Inc.

(5) Employer's Business or Organization Address (Street Number and Name): 123 Bill of Rights Way — City or Town: Charles City — State: VA — ZIP Code: 20002

(1) At the top of Section 2, enter the employee's last name, first name, and middle initial exactly as this information was entered in Section 1. Enter the number that correlates with the citizenship or immigration status box the employee selected in Section 1.

(2) Enter the document title(s), issuing authority, document number, and the expiration date from original documents supplied by the employee. You may use either common abbreviations for the document title or issuing authority, for example, "DL" for driver's license and "SSA" for Social Security Administration, or the suggestions in the form instructions.

The "Additional Information" space is for Form I-9 notes, such as:

- Notations that describe special circumstances such as employment authorization extensions for F-1 STEM OPT students, CAP-GAP, H-1B and H-2A employees continuing employment with the same employer or changing employers, and TPS, AC-21, 240-day, 180-day, and120-day work authorization extensions, as required

- Information from additional documents that F-1 or J-1 nonimmigrant employees may present including the Student and Exchange Visitor (SEVIS) number and the program end date from Forms I-20, Certificate of Eligibility for Nonimmigrant Student Status, or DS-2019, Certificate of Eligibility for Exchange Visitor (J-1) Status, as required

- Employee termination dates and form retention dates

- E-Verify case verification number, which may also be entered in the margin or attached as a separate sheet per E-Verify requirements and your chosen business process

- Discrepancies that E-Verify employers must notate when participating in the IMAGE program

- Any other comments or notations necessary for the employer's business process

(3) Enter the first day of employment for wages or other remuneration (such as date of hire) in the space for "The employee's first day of employment (mm/dd/yyyy)." Recruiters and referrers for a fee do not enter the employee's first day of employment.

Staffing agencies may choose to use either the date an employee is assigned to their first job or the date the new employee is entered into the assignment pool as the first day of employment.

(4) Employer or authorized representative attests to physically examining the documents provided by completing the Last Name, First Name, Employer's Business or Organization Name fields and signing and dating the signature and date fields.

(5) Enter the business's street address, city or town, state and ZIP Code.

Sometimes, you must accept a receipt in lieu of a List A, List B, or a List C document if the employee presents one. New employees who choose to present a receipt(s) must do so within three business days of their first day of employment. Employees who choose to present a receipt for reverification must present it by the date their employment authorization expires. Receipts are not acceptable if employment lasts less than three business days.

Table 1 shown below provides a list of acceptable receipts an employee can present. If an employee presents a receipt for the application to replace a lost, stolen or damaged document, the employee must present the replacement document to you within 90 days from the first day of work for pay, or in the case of reverification, within 90 days from the date the employee's employment authorization expired. Enter the word "Receipt" followed by the title of the document in Section 2 under the list that relates to the receipt. When completing the form using a computer, scroll down in the appropriate list to select the receipt presented. See Table 1 below for more information.

When your employee presents the original replacement document, cross out the word "Receipt," then enter the information from the new document into Section 2. Other receipts may be valid for longer or shorter periods. This includes the arrival portion of Form I-94/I-94A, Arrival Departure Record, containing a temporary I-551 stamp and a photograph of the individual. This receipt is valid until the expiration date of the temporary I-551 stamp or one year from the date of admission, if there is no expiration date.

Table 1: Receipts

Receipt	Who may present this receipt?	Is this receipt proof of employment authorization and/ or identity?	How long is this receipt valid?	What must the employee present at the end of the receipt validity period?
A receipt for a replacement of a lost, stolen, or damaged document	All employees	A receipt fulfills the verification requirements of the document for which the receipt was issued (can be List A, List B, or List C).	90 days from date of hire or, for reverification, 90 days from the date employment authorization expires.	The actual document for which the receipt was issued.
The arrival portion of the Form I-94 or I-94A containing a Temporary I-551 stamp and photograph	Lawful permanent residents	Employment authorization and identity (List A).	Until the expiration date of the Temporary I-551 stamp, or if no expiration date, one year from date of admission.	The actual Form I-551 (Permanent Resident Card, or "Green Card").
The departure portion of Form I-94 or I-94A with an unexpired refugee admission stamp	Refugees	Employment authorization and identity (List A).	90 days from date of hire or, for reverification, 90 days from the date employment authorization expires.	An unexpired EAD (Form I-766) or a combination of a valid List B document and an unrestricted Social Security card.

4.1 Future Expiration Dates

Future expiration dates may appear on the employment authorization documents of individuals, including, among others, lawful permanent residents, asylees and refugees. USCIS includes expiration dates on some documents issued to individuals with permanent employment authorization. The existence of a future expiration date:

- Does not preclude continuous employment authorization;

- Does not mean that subsequent employment authorization will not be granted; and

- Should not be considered in determining whether the individual is qualified for a particular position.

Considering a future employment authorization expiration date in determining whether an individual is qualified for a particular job may constitute employment discrimination. For more information on unlawful discrimination, see Section 11.0 *Unlawful Discrimination and Penalties for Prohibited Practices*. However, you may need to reverify the employee's authorization to work when certain List A or List C documents expire. For example, the Employment Authorization Document (Form I-766) must be reverified on or before the expiration date. See Section 5.0 *Form I-9 Completing Section 3* for more information on reverification.

4.2 Automatic Extensions of Employment Authorization Documents (EADs) in Certain Circumstances

Automatic Extensions Based on Timely Employment Authorization Document (Form I-766) Renewal Application

Foreign nationals in certain employment eligibility categories who file an EAD renewal application may receive automatic extensions of their expiring EAD for up to 180 days. The extension begins on the date the EAD expires and continues for up to 180 days unless the renewal application is denied. An automatic EAD extension depends on these requirements:

- The employee must have timely filed an application to renew their EAD before it expires (except certain employees granted Temporary Protected Status (TPS)), and the application remains pending;

- The eligibility category on the face of the EAD is the same eligibility category code on the Form I-797C Notice of Action, the employee received from USCIS indicating USCIS's receipt of their renewal application (except employees with TPS who may have a C19/A12 combination); and

- The eligibility category is listed on uscis.gov as eligible for EAD automatic extensions. As of the date of publication of this M-274, Handbook for Employers, eligibility categories codes for a 180-day automatic extension are A03, A05, A07, A08, A10, C08, C09, C10, C16, C20, C22, C24, C31 and A12 or C19.

The employee's expired EAD in combination with the Form I-797C Notice of Action showing that the EAD renewal application was timely filed and showing the same qualifying eligibility category as that on the expired EAD is an acceptable document for Form I-9. This document combination is considered an unexpired Employment Authorization Document (Form I-766) under List A.

To find the eligibility category code on your employee's employment authorization document, see Figure 3 below:

Figure 3: Auto-Extended Employment Authorization Documents

Finding the Category Notation and Expiration Date on an EAD

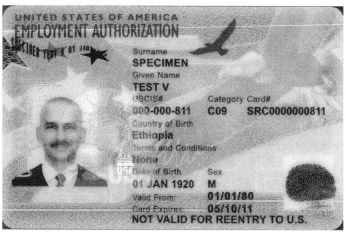

The category notation appears on the face of the Employment Authorization Document (Form I-766) under "Category."

The expiration date appears on the face of the Employment Authorization Document (I-766) to the right of "Card Expires."

Finding the Auto-Extended EAD Expiration Date on the I-797C: Sample 1

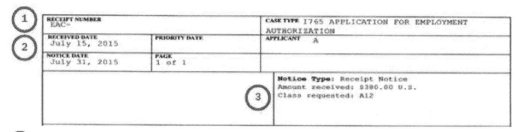

①The receipt number appears on the face of the I-797C Notice of Action in the "Receipt Number" field.

②The filing date is the date USCIS received the application and appears in the "Received Date" field. This date should be on or before the expiration date on the face of the Employment Authorization Document.

③The category code may appear on the face of the I-797C Notice of Action in the "Class Requested" field. If you do not see this field, see Sample 2 below.

Finding the Auto-Extended EAD Expiration Date on the I-797C: Sample 2

NOTICE TYPE		NOTICE DATE
Receipt		November 25, 2016
CASE TYPE		USCIS ALIEN NUMBER
I-765, Application for Employment Authorization		A
RECEIPT NUMBER	RECEIVED DATE	PAGE
	November 25, 2016	1 of 1
		DATE OF BIRTH

PAYMENT INFORMATION:

Application/Petition Fee: $410.00
Biometrics Fee: $0.00
Total Amount Received: $410.00
Total Balance Due: $0.00

ı,ıllıılllıqıılıllıllıqlı,lı-llı-llllllllllllıqlllıllı-llı-llıllıllıllıqlı,

NAME AND MAILING ADDRESS

③ Eligibility Category: C31

① The receipt number appears on the face of the I-797C Notice of Action in the "Receipt Number" field.

② The filing date is the date USCIS received the application and appears in the "Received Date" field. This date should be on or before the expiration date on the face of the Employment Authorization Document.

③ The category code may appear on the face of the I-797C Notice of Action in the "Eligible Category" field. If you do not see this field, see Sample 1 above.

Automatic EAD Extensions for TPS Beneficiaries

Beneficiaries of TPS may present an Employment Authorization Document (Form I-766) that is expired on its face with a C19 eligibility code but a Form I-797C Notice of Action indicating the eligibility category code A12. Therefore, just for TPS beneficiaries, the eligibility category codes do not need to be the same, but can be either C19 or A12.

TPS beneficiaries may receive an automatic extension of their Employment Authorization Document (Form I-766) if they file their renewal application in accordance with the applicable Federal Register notice regarding procedures for renewing TPS-related employment documentation, which may or may not require that the application be filed prior to the expiration of the Employment Authorization Document (Form I-766).

TPS beneficiaries have other ways to receive an automatic extension of their EAD. In many circumstances, their EAD may be automatically extended under a notice published in the Federal Register based on an extension of the TPS country designation. In these instances, DHS will inform the public in the Federal Register notice that TPS status and employment authorization for TPS beneficiaries are being extended. You may not require employees to prove they are a national of a country that has been designated for TPS.

Guidance on Completing Form I-9

For a current employee, update Section 2 of Form I-9 with the new expiration date as follows:

- Draw a line through the old expiration date and write the new expiration date in the margin of Section 2;
- Write EAD EXT in Section 2;
- Initial and date the correction.

The new expiration date to enter is the date 180 days from the date the card expires, which is the date on the face of the expired EAD. Employees whose employment authorization was automatically extended along with their EAD (such as adjustment of status applicants, but not asylees who are employment authorized incident to status) may cross out the "employment authorized until" date in Section 1, write the date that is 180 days from the date their current EAD expires, and initial and date the change.

New employees may present the expired EAD and Form I-797C Notice of Action indicating USCIS's receipt of the employee's timely filed renewal application. When completing Section 1, the employee should enter the date that is 180 days from the "card expires" date of their expired EAD in the "employment authorized until mm/dd/yyyy" field.

When completing Section 2, the employer should enter into the Expiration Date field the date the automatic extension period expires, not the expiration date on the face of the expired EAD. The automatic extension expiration date is the date 180 days from the "card expires" date on the EAD. Note that this expiration date may be cut short if the employee's renewal application is denied before the 180-day period expires. The employer should enter the receipt number from the I-797C Notice of Action as the document number on Form I-9.

Reverification

Reverification is required when the employee's automatic extension ends, no later than 180-days after the expiration date of the Employment Authorization Document (Form I-766). Reverification can also be done before the end of the180-day extended time period, upon receipt of any document that shows current employment authorization, such as any document from List A or List C.

4.3 Failure of an Employee to Present Acceptable Documents

You may terminate an employee who fails to produce an acceptable document or documents, or an acceptable receipt for a document within three business days of the date employment begins. Employers that fail to properly complete Form I-9 risk violating section 274A of the INA and are subject to civil money penalties.

5.0 Completing Section 3 of Form I-9

5.1 Reverifying Employment Authorization for Current Employees

When an employee's employment authorization or, in most cases, employment authorization documentation expires, you must reverify their employment authorization no later than the date employment authorization expires. You may use Section 3 of Form I-9, or if Section 3 has already been used for a previous reverification or update, then use Section 3 of a new Form I-9. If you complete Form I-9 on paper, you must:

- Enter the last name, first name and middle initial from the original Form I-9 at the top of Section 2 leaving the Citizenship/Immigration Status field blank (only for those using Section 3 of a new form);

- Complete Section 3;

- Keep only the second page of the new Form I-9 with the original.

When completing the Form I-9 using a computer, you must enter the last name, first name and middle initial from the original Form I-9 at the top of Section 3.

When you complete Section 3 on a computer and print, Sections 2 and 3 will appear on the same page. The employee must present a document that shows current employment authorization such as any document from List A or List C, including an unrestricted Social Security card. You cannot continue to employ an employee who cannot provide you with proof of current employment authorization.

Note: Reverification is never required for U.S. citizens and noncitizen nationals. Do not reverify the following documents after they expire: U.S. passports, U.S. passport cards, Alien Registration Receipt Cards/Permanent Resident Cards (Form I-551), and List B documents.

Employees whose immigration status, employment authorization or employment authorization documents expire should file the necessary application or petition well in advance to ensure they maintain continuous employment authorization and valid employment authorization documents. Certain employees, such as H-1B or L-1 nonimmigrants who are authorized to work for a specific employer and on whose behalf an application for an extension of stay has been filed may continue working for the same employer for up to 240 days from the date the authorized period of stay expires. See *Section 7.0 Evidence of Status for Certain Categories*.

Employees in certain categories may be eligible for a 180-day automatic extension of their expired EAD. See Section 4.2 *Automatic Extensions of Employment Authorization Documents in Certain Circumstances* for more information, including eligible categories.

Note: You must reverify an employee's employment authorization on Form I-9 no later than the date that the employee's employment authorization or EAD expires, whichever is sooner.

5.2 Reverifying or Updating Employment Authorization for Rehired Employees

If you rehire an employee within three years from the date their Form I-9 was previously completed, you may either rely on the employee's previously executed Form I-9 or complete a new one. If you choose to rely on a previously completed Form I-9, follow these guidelines:

- If the employee remains employment authorized as indicated on the previous Form I-9, the employee does not need to provide any additional documentation. In Section 3, provide the employee's rehire date, any name changes, and sign and date the form.

- If the previous Form I-9 indicates that the employee's employment authorization has expired, you must reverify employment authorization in Section 3 in addition to providing the rehire date. If the previously executed Form I-9 is not the current version of the form, you must complete Section 3 on the current version of the form.

- If you already used Section 3 of the employee's previously completed Form I-9, but are rehiring the employee within three years of the original execution of Form I-9, you may complete Section 3 on a new Form I-9 and attach it to the previously completed form.

Employees rehired after three years of the original completion of the Form I-9 must complete a new Form I-9.

To reverify:

1. Enter the date of rehire in Block B of Section 3.

2. Enter the document title, number and expiration date (if any) of the document(s) the employee presents in Block C of Section 3.

3. Sign and date Section 3.

4. If you choose to use a new Form I-9, enter the employee's name at the top of page 2 of a new Form I-9 and complete Section 3 of the new Form I-9, retaining the new form with the previously completed one.

5. You must reverify the employee on a new Form I-9 if the version of the form you used for the previous verification is no longer valid. Please check uscis.gov/i-9 for the current Form I-9.

Updating an employee's name is optional. To update:

1. Enter the date of rehire in Block B and the employee's new name, if applicable, in Block A of Section 3.

2. Sign and date Section 3.

3. If you are updating on a new Form I-9, enter the employee's name at the top of page 2 and use Section 3 of the new Form I-9 to update. Keep the new Form I-9 with the previously completed one.

Figure 4: Completing Section 3: Reverification and Rehires

① Enter the employee's new name, if applicable, in block A.

② Enter the employee's date of rehire, if applicable, in block B.

③ Enter the document title, number, and expiration date (if any) of document(s) presented in block C.

④ Sign and date Section 3.

Note: If you need to reverify the employment authorization of an existing employee who completed an earlier version of Form I-9, the employee must provide any List A or C document(s) they choose from the Lists of Acceptable Documents for the most current version of the Form I-9. Enter the new document(s) information in Section 3 of the current version of Form I-9 and keep it with the previously completed Form I-9. Visit I-9 Central at uscis.gov/i-9-central for the most current version of the Form I-9.

5.3 Recording Changes of Name and Other Identity Information for Current Employees

In the case of a rehire or reverification, if an employee has had a legal change of name, such as following marriage, record the employee's legal change of name in the space provided in Section 3. If you learn of a legal change of name at a time other than during a rehire or reverification, USCIS recommends that you update Form I-9 with the new name in the space provided in Section 3 of Form I-9 so that you maintain correct information on the form. In either situation, you should take steps to be reasonably assured of the employee's identity and the veracity of the employee's claim of a legal name change. These steps may include asking the employee for the reason for the legal change of name and to provide documentation of a legal change of name to keep with Form I-9, so that your actions are well-documented in the event of a Form I-9 inspection.

You may encounter situations other than a legal change of name where an employee informs you (or you have reason to believe) that their identity is different from that previously used to complete the Form I-9. For example, an employee may have been working under a false identity, has subsequently obtained work authorization in their true identity, and wishes to regularize their employment records. In that case you should complete a new Form I-9. Write the original hire date in Section 2 and attach the new Form I-9 to the previously completed Form I-9 and include a written explanation.

In cases where an employee has worked for you using a false identity but is currently authorized to work, the Form I-9 rules do not require termination of employment.

In addition, there may be other laws, contractual obligations, or company policies that you should consider before taking action. For example, the INA prohibits discrimination based on citizenship status and national origin. See Section 11.0 *Unlawful Discrimination and Penalties for Prohibited Practices* for more information.

For E-Verify employers:

- USCIS recommends that you encourage your employees to record their legal name change with the Social Security Administration to avoid mismatches in E-Verify.

- If you complete a new Form I-9 in a new identity situation as described above, e.g., where a name change to Form I-9 information is not a legal name change, you should confirm the new Form I-9 information through E-Verify. If you do not complete a new Form I-9, you should not create a new E-Verify case.

- Federal contractors who are subject to the Federal Acquisition Regulation (FAR) E-Verify clause and who choose to verify existing employees by updating an already-completed Form I-9 are subject to special rules regarding when they must complete a new Form I-9. Employers who choose to update Form I-9 for existing employees must complete a new Form I-9 when an employee changes their name. For more information, see the E-Verify Supplemental Guide for Federal Contractors, at uscis.gov/e-verify.

6.0 Guidance for Minors and Employees with Disabilities

6.1 Minors (Individuals under Age 18)

Figure 5: Completing Section 1 of Form I-9 for minors without List B documents

Section 1. Employee Information and Attestation *(Employees must complete and sign Section 1 of Form I-9 no later than the first day of employment, but not before accepting a job offer.)*				
Last Name *(Family Name)* **Adams**	First Name *(Given Name)* **John**	Middle Initial **A**	Other Last Names Used *(if any)* **N/A**	

Address *(Street Number and Name)* **123 2nd Street**	Apt. Number **1**	City or Town **Braintree**	State **MA**	ZIP Code **20002**

Date of Birth *(mm/dd/yyyy)* **10/30/2007**	U.S. Social Security Number **1 2 3 - 4 5 - 6 7 8 9**	Employee's E-mail Address **jadams@email.com**	Employee's Telephone Number **202-111-2222**

I am aware that federal law provides for imprisonment and/or fines for false statements or use of false documents in connection with the completion of this form.

I attest, under penalty of perjury, that I am (check one of the following boxes):

[X] 1. A citizen of the United States

[ ] 2. A noncitizen national of the United States *(See instructions)*

[ ] 3. A lawful permanent resident   (Alien Registration Number/USCIS Number): _____

[ ] 4. An alien authorized to work   until (expiration date, if applicable, mm/dd/yyyy): _____
Some aliens may write "N/A" in the expiration date field. *(See instructions)*

Aliens authorized to work must provide only one of the following document numbers to complete Form I-9:
An Alien Registration Number/USCIS Number OR Form I-94 Admission Number OR Foreign Passport Number.

1. Alien Registration Number/USCIS Number: _____
OR
2. Form I-94 Admission Number: _____
OR
3. Foreign Passport Number: _____
Country of Issuance: _____

QR Code - Section 1
Do Not Write In This Space

(1) | Signature of Employee *Individual Under Age 18* | Today's Date *(mm/dd/yyyy)* **01/22/2017**

Preparer and/or Translator Certification (check one):
[ ] I did not use a preparer or translator.   [X] A preparer(s) and/or translator(s) assisted the employee in completing Section 1.
(Fields below must be completed and signed when preparers and/or translators assist an employee in completing Section 1.)

I attest, under penalty of perjury, that I have assisted in the completion of Section 1 of this form and that to the best of my knowledge the information is true and correct.

(2) | Signature of Preparer or Translator *Martha Washington* | Today's Date *(mm/dd/yyyy)* **01/22/2017**

Last Name *(Family Name)* **Washington**	First Name *(Given Name)* **Martha**		

Address *(Street Number and Name)* **123 1st Street**	City or Town **Charles City**	State **VA**	ZIP Code **20001**

(1) The minor's parent or legal guardian completes Section 1 and enters "Individual under age 18" in the signature block.

(2) The parent or legal guardian completes the Preparer and/or Translator Certification block.

Figure 6: Completing Section 2 of Form I-9 for minors without List B documents

Section 2. Employer or Authorized Representative Review and Verification
(Employers or their authorized representative must complete and sign Section 2 within 3 business days of the employee's first day of employment. You must physically examine one document from List A OR a combination of one document from List B and one document from List C as listed on the "Lists of Acceptable Documents.")

(1) Employee Info from Section 1 | Last Name *(Family Name)* **Adams** | First Name *(Given Name)* **John** | M.I. **A** | Citizenship/Immigration Status **1**

List A	OR	List B	AND	List C
Identity and Employment Authorization		Identity		Employment Authorization

(2)

Document Title	Document Title **Individual Under Age 18**	Document Title **Social Security Card**
Issuing Authority	Issuing Authority	Issuing Authority **Social Security Administartion**
Document Number	Document Number	Document Number **123-45-6789**
Expiration Date *(if any)(mm/dd/yyyy)*	Expiration Date *(if any)(mm/dd/yyyy)*	Expiration Date *(if any)(mm/dd/yyyy)* **N/A**
Document Title		
Issuing Authority	Additional Information	QR Code - Sections 2 & 3 Do Not Write In This Space
Document Number		
Expiration Date *(if any)(mm/dd/yyyy)*		
Document Title		
Issuing Authority		
Document Number		
Expiration Date *(if any)(mm/dd/yyyy)*		

(3) Certification: I attest, under penalty of perjury, that (1) I have examined the document(s) presented by the above-named employee, (2) the above-listed document(s) appear to be genuine and to relate to the employee named, and (3) to the best of my knowledge the employee is authorized to work in the United States.

The employee's first day of employment *(mm/dd/yyyy)*: **01/22/17** *(See instructions for exemptions)*

(4) Signature of Employer or Authorized Representative *Susan Anthony* | Today's Date*(mm/dd/yyyy)* **01/22/2017** | Title of Employer or Authorized Representative **HR Supervisor**

Last Name of Employer or Authorized Representative **Anthony** | First Name of Employer or Authorized Representative **Susan** | Employer's Business or Organization Name **Bald Eagle Flags Inc.**

(5) Employer's Business or Organization Address (Street Number and Name) **50 States Road** | City or Town **Braintree** | State **MA** | ZIP Code **20001**

(1) At the top of Section 2, enter the employee's last name, first name, and middle initial exactly as this information was entered in Section 1. Enter the number that correlates with the citizenship or immigration status box selected for the employee in Section 1.

(2) Enter "Individual under age 18" under List B and enter the List C document the minor presents. Enter the document title, issuing authority, document number, and the expiration date from the original List C document.

(3) Enter the date employment began.

(4) The employer or authorized representative attests to physically examining the documents provided by completing the Last Name, First Name, their Employer's Business or Organization Name fields and signing and dating the signature and date fields.

(5) Enter the business's street address, city or town, state and ZIP Code.

6.2 Employees with Disabilities (Special Placement)

Individuals who have a physical or mental impairment which substantially limits one or more of their major life activities and who are placed in jobs by a nonprofit organization, association or as part of a rehabilitation program may establish identity under List B by using procedures similar to those used by individuals under 18 years of age who are unable to produce a List B identity document and otherwise qualify to use these procedures. The individual will still be required to present an employment authorization document from List C. If the employer participates in E-Verify, the individual's List B identity document must contain a photograph. Complete Form I-9 as shown below.

Figure 7: Completing Section 1 of Form I-9 for employees with disabilities (special placement)

Section 1. Employee Information and Attestation *(Employees must complete and sign Section 1 of Form I-9 no later than the first day of employment, but not before accepting a job offer.)*

Last Name *(Family Name)*	First Name *(Given Name)*	Middle Initial	Other Last Names Used *(if any)*
Jefferson	Thomas	A	N/A

Address *(Street Number and Name)*	Apt. Number	City or Town	State	ZIP Code
123 Bald Eagle Circle	2	Shadwell	VA	20001

Date of Birth *(mm/dd/yyyy)*	U.S. Social Security Number	Employee's E-mail Address	Employee's Telephone Number
04/13/1983	1 2 3 - 4 5 - 6 7 8 9	tjefferson@email.com	202-222-1111

I am aware that federal law provides for imprisonment and/or fines for false statements or use of false documents in connection with the completion of this form.

I attest, under penalty of perjury, that I am (check one of the following boxes):

[X] 1. A citizen of the United States

[ ] 2. A noncitizen national of the United States *(See instructions)*

[ ] 3. A lawful permanent resident   (Alien Registration Number/USCIS Number):

[ ] 4. An alien authorized to work   until (expiration date, if applicable, mm/dd/yyyy):
Some aliens may write "N/A" in the expiration date field. *(See instructions)*

Aliens authorized to work must provide only one of the following document numbers to complete Form I-9:
An Alien Registration Number/USCIS Number OR Form I-94 Admission Number OR Foreign Passport Number.

1. Alien Registration Number/USCIS Number:
                    OR
2. Form I-94 Admission Number:
                    OR
3. Foreign Passport Number:

Country of Issuance:

QR Code - Section 1
Do Not Write In This Space

Signature of Employee *Special Placement*	Today's Date *(mm/dd/yyyy)* 01/22/2017

Preparer and/or Translator Certification (check one):
[ ] I did not use a preparer or translator.   [X] A preparer(s) and/or translator(s) assisted the employee in completing Section 1.
(Fields below must be completed and signed when preparers and/or translators assist an employee in completing Section 1.)

I attest, under penalty of perjury, that I have assisted in the completion of Section 1 of this form and that to the best of my knowledge the information is true and correct.

Signature of Preparer or Translator *Martha Washington*	Today's Date *(mm/dd/yyyy)* 01/22/2017

Last Name *(Family Name)* Washington	First Name *(Given Name)* Martha

Address *(Street Number and Name)*	City or Town	State	ZIP Code
123 American Flag Blvd	Chestnut Grove	VA	20002

(1) The representative of the nonprofit organization, association, rehabilitation program, parent or legal guardian of an individual with a disability completes Section 1 and enters, "Special Placement" in the Signature of Employee field and dates the form.

(2) The representative, parent or legal guardian completes the Preparer and/or Translator Certification block.

Figure 8: Completing Section 2 of Form I-9 for employees with disabilities (special placement)

Section 2. Employer or Authorized Representative Review and Verification

(Employers or their authorized representative must complete and sign Section 2 within 3 business days of the employee's first day of employment. You must physically examine one document from List A OR a combination of one document from List B and one document from List C as listed on the "Lists of Acceptable Documents.")

① Employee Info from Section 1

Last Name *(Family Name)*	First Name *(Given Name)*	M.I.	Citizenship/Immigration Status
Jefferson	Thomas	A	1

List A	OR	List B	AND	List C
Identity and Employment Authorization		Identity		Employment Authorization

②

List A	List B	List C
Document Title	Document Title **Special Placement**	Document Title **Social Security Card**
Issuing Authority	Issuing Authority	Issuing Authority **Social Security Administration**
Document Number	Document Number	Document Number **123-45-6789**
Expiration Date *(if any)(mm/dd/yyyy)*	Expiration Date *(if any)(mm/dd/yyyy)*	Expiration Date *(if any)(mm/dd/yyyy)* **N/A**
Document Title		
Issuing Authority		
Document Number		
Expiration Date *(if any)(mm/dd/yyyy)*		
Document Title		
Issuing Authority		
Document Number		
Expiration Date *(if any)(mm/dd/yyyy)*		

Additional Information

QR Code - Sections 2 & 3
Do Not Write In This Space

Certification: I attest, under penalty of perjury, that (1) I have examined the document(s) presented by the above-named employee, (2) the above-listed document(s) appear to be genuine and to relate to the employee named, and (3) to the best of my knowledge the employee is authorized to work in the United States.

③ The employee's first day of employment *(mm/dd/yyyy)*:   **01/22/2017**   *(See instructions for exemptions)*

④

Signature of Employer or Authorized Representative *Abigail Adams*	Today's Date*(mm/dd/yyyy)* **01/22/2017**	Title of Employer or Authorized Representative **HR Chief**
Last Name of Employer or Authorized Representative **Adams**	First Name of Employer or Authorized Representative **Abigail**	Employer's Business or Organization Name **Bald Eagle Flags Inc.**

⑤

Employer's Business or Organization Address (Street Number and Name) **1 We The People Way**	City or Town **Weymouth**	State **MA**	ZIP Code **20001**

① At the top of Section 2, enter the employee's last name, first name and middle initial exactly as this information was entered in Section 1. Enter the number that correlates with the citizenship or immigration status box selected for the employee in Section 1.

② Enter "Special Placement" under List B and enter information about the List C document that the employee with a disability presents.

③ Enter the date employment began.

④ The employer or authorized representative attests to physically examining the documents provided by completing the Last Name, First Name, Employer's Business or Organization Name fields and signing and dating the signature and date fields.

⑤ Enter the business's street address, city or town, state and ZIP Code.

7.0 Evidence of Status for Certain Categories

7.1 Lawful Permanent Residents (LPR)

Employees must be allowed to choose which document(s) they will present from the Lists of Acceptable Documents. You cannot specify which document(s) an employee must present. Employees who attest to being an LPR in Section 1 may choose to present a List A document (such as a Permanent Resident Card, Form I-551) or a List B and List C document combination (such as a state-issued driver's license and unrestricted Social Security card). If the employee presents a List A document, do not ask or require the employee to present List B and List C documents. If an employee presents List B and List C documents, do not ask or require the employee to present a List A document.

There are different versions of Form I-551, Permanent Resident Card. Some Permanent Resident Cards may contain no expiration date, a 10-year expiration date, or a two-year expiration date. Cards that expire in 10 years or have no expiration date are issued to LPRs with no conditions on their status. All Permanent Resident Cards, whether they have an expiration date or no expiration date, are List A documents that should not be reverified.

LPRs and conditional residents may be issued temporary I-551 documents. These documents are acceptable for Form I-9 as follows:

- The combination of an expired Permanent Resident Card and a Form I-797, Notice of Action, that indicates that the card is valid for an additional year, is an acceptable List C evidence of employment authorization for one year as indicated on Form I-797. At the end of the one-year period, you must reverify.

- Reverification is necessary if an employee presents a foreign passport with either a temporary I-551 stamp or I-551 printed notation on a machine-readable immigrant visa (MRIV) when the stamp or MRIV expires, or one year after the admission date if the stamp or MRIV does not contain an expiration date.

  MRIVs are usually issued with the following language on the visa: "UPON ENDORSEMENT SERVES AS TEMPORARY I-551 EVIDENCING PERMANENT RESIDENCE FOR 1 YEAR." The one year time period begins on the date of admission. If, in the rare instance, an immigrant visa is issued without the statement "FOR 1 YEAR," employers should treat the MRIV as evidence of permanent residence status for one year from the date of admission.

  If the stamp in the passport is endorsed "CR-1" and is near but not on the immigrant visa, it is still a valid endorsement.

- If an employee presents the arrival portion of Form I-94/Form I-94A Arrival Departure Record, containing an unexpired temporary I-551 stamp and a photograph of the individual, this combination of documents is an acceptable List A receipt for the Permanent Resident Card. The employee must present their Permanent Resident Card to the employer no later than when the stamp expires, or one year after the issuance date of the Form I-94 if the stamp does not contain an expiration date.

7.2 Native Americans

A Native American tribal document establishes both identity and employment authorization on Form I-9. If an employee presents a Native American tribal document, you do not need any other documents from the employee to complete Section 2. To be acceptable for Form I-9 purposes, a Native American tribal document must be issued by a tribe recognized by the U.S. federal government. Members of federally recognized tribes who are LPRs, aliens authorized to work, and noncitizen nationals may have a Native American tribal document issued by such tribes. Because federal recognition of tribes can change over time, you may check the Bureau of Indian Affairs website at bia.gov to determine if the tribe is federally recognized.

The following documents are not considered Native American tribal documents for Form I-9 purposes and cannot be used for either List B or List C:

- A tribal membership document issued by a Canadian First Nation such as a Canadian Indian tribe, rather than a U.S. Indian tribe, including a U.S. Indian tribe that grants membership and issues tribal membership documents to Canadian nationals

- A Certificate of Indian Status (commonly referred to as an "INAC card") issued by Aboriginal Affairs and Northern Development Canada (formerly known as Indian and Northern Affairs Canada, or "INAC")

While individuals who possess such documents might possibly qualify for employment authorization under INA § 289 (and, if applicable, 8 CFR § 289.2), their tribal membership cards issued by a Canadian First Nation, or INAC cards issued by the Government of Canada, cannot, by themselves, establish work authorization.

Note for E-Verify Employers: *Section 403 of the E-Verify authorizing statute requires that all List B documents must contain a photograph. This includes Native American tribal documents presented as a List B document. If the employee's Native American tribal document does not contain a photograph, you should request the employee provide a List B document with a photograph. The Native American tribal document is acceptable as the employee's List C document. Your employee may also choose to provide a List A document in place of a List B and List C document.*

7.3 Refugees and Asylees

Refugees and asylees are authorized to work because of their immigration status. When completing Form I-9, the refugee or asylee should indicate "alien authorized to work" in Section 1 of Form I-9. Since refugees and asylees are authorized to work indefinitely because of their immigration status, a refugee or asylee should enter "N/A" on the expiration date line in Section 1.

Many refugees and asylees may choose to present an unexpired EAD (Employment Authorization Document, Form I-766). However, neither refugees nor asylees are required to present an EAD to meet Form I-9 requirements. They may present other acceptable documents for Form I-9, such as Form I-94/Form I-94A indicating refugee or asylee status. They may also present List B and List C combinations, such as a state-issued driver's license and an unrestricted Social Security card.

In addition, refugees and asylees may present an expired EAD with Form I-797C Notice of Action from USCIS for Form I-765, Application for Employment Authorization if Form I-797C lists the same employment authorization category as the expired EAD. This combination is considered an unexpired employment authorization and identity document (List A) and is valid for up to 180 days after the "card expires" date on the face of the EAD.

See Section 4.2 *Automatic Extensions of Employment Authorization Documents in Certain Circumstances* for more information about eligible categories and Form I-9 completion instructions for an employee who is a beneficiary of an employment authorization document auto-extension.

Note: *The Social Security Administration issues unrestricted Social Security cards to refugees and asylees. These are List C documents for Form I-9 purposes and are not subject to reverification. Application procedures for Social Security cards can be found on the Social Security Administration's site at ssa.gov.*

Refugees

Upon admission to the United States, DHS provides refugees with electronic or paper Forms I-94 Arrival-Departure Record) that proves their status and employment authorization. The departure portion of a Form I-94 containing an unexpired refugee admission stamp or a Form I-94 computer-generated printout with an admission class of "RE" is an acceptable receipt establishing both employment authorization and identity for 90 days. During this time USCIS should be processing an EAD for the refugee.

At the end of the 90-day receipt period, the refugee must present either an EAD or a document from List B, such as a state-issued driver's license, with a document from List C, such as an unrestricted Social Security card.

Refugees may also present an expired EAD in combination with an I-797C Notice of Action from USCIS indicating timely filing of the renewal application for an EAD (provided the I-797C indicates the same employment authorization category as the expired employment authorization document). This combination is considered an unexpired employment authorization and identity document (List A) and is valid for up to 180 days after the "card expires" date on the face of the EAD.

See Section 4.2 *Automatic Extensions of Employment Authorization Documents in Certain Circumstances* for more information about eligible categories and Form I-9 completion instructions for an employee who is a beneficiary of a 180-day employment authorization document auto-extension.

Asylees

After being granted asylum in the United States, DHS issues asylees paper Forms I-94 that evidence their status and employment authorization with a stamp or notation indicating asylee status, such as "asylum granted indefinitely" or the appropriate provision of law (8 CFR 274a.12(a)(5) or INA 208). A computer-generated print out of Form I-94 with an admission class of "AY" is also acceptable from the asylee. The Form I-94 is considered a List C document that demonstrates employment authorization in the United States and does not expire. Asylees who choose to present this document will need to present a List B identity document, such as a state-issued driver's license or identification card.

USCIS also issues asylees EADs which are acceptable as List A documents. Decisions from immigration judges or the Board of Immigration Appeals (BIA) granting asylum are not acceptable List C documents because they are not issued by DHS.

Asylees may also present an expired Employment Authorization Document (Form I-766) in combination with an I-797C Notice of Action from USCIS indicating timely filing of the renewal application for an EAD (provided the I-797C lists the same employment authorization category as the expired EAD). This combination is considered an unexpired employment authorization and identity document (List A) and is valid for up to 180 days after the 'card expires' date on the face of the EAD.

See Section 4.2 *Automatic Extensions of Employment Authorization Documents in Certain Circumstances* for more information about eligible categories and Form I-9 completion instructions for employees who are beneficiaries of an employment authorization document auto-extension.

7.4 Exchange Visitors and Students

Each year, thousands of exchange visitors, international students, and their dependents come to the United States to study and work.

7.4.1 Exchange Visitors (J-1s)

The Department of State (DOS) administers the exchange visitor program and designates the sponsors. Responsible officers within the program issue Form DS-2019, Certificate of Eligibility for Exchange Visitor (J-1) Status. Exchange visitors come to the United States for a specific period of time to participate in a particular program or activity, as described on their Form DS-2019. Only J-1 exchange visitors may use Form DS-2019 for employment when such employment is part of their program. Currently, DOS designates public and private entities to act as exchange sponsors for the following programs.

Exchange Visitor Programs

- SECONDARY STUDENT
- ASSOCIATE DEGREE STUDENT
- BACHELOR'S DEGREE STUDENT
- MASTER'S DEGREE STUDENT
- DOCTORAL STUDENT
- NON-DEGREE STUDENT
- STUDENT INTERN
- TRAINEE (SPECIALTY)
- TRAINEE (NON-SPECIALTY)
- TEACHER
- PROFESSOR
- INTERNATIONAL VISITOR
- PHYSICIAN
- GOVERNMENT VISITOR
- RESEARCH SCHOLAR
- SHORT-TERM SCHOLAR
- SPECIALIST
- CAMP COUNSELOR
- SUMMER WORK/TRAVEL
- AU PAIR AND EDUCARE
- TRAINEE
- INTERN

Pilot Programs

- Summer Work/Travel: Australia
- Summer Work/Travel: New Zealand
- Intern Work/Travel: Ireland
- WEST (Work/English Study/Travel): South Korea

High school or secondary school students and international visitors are not authorized to work.

Other J-1 students may be authorized by their responsible officer for part-time on-campus employment according to the terms of a scholarship, fellowship or assistantship, or off-campus employment based on serious, urgent, unforeseen economic circumstances. J-1 students may also be authorized for a maximum of 18 months (or, for Ph.D. students, a maximum of 36 months) of practical training during or immediately after their studies. J-1 practical training includes paid off-campus employment and/or unpaid internships that are part of the student's program of study. Their responsible officer must authorize employment in writing for practical training. Special rules apply to student interns.

Employment for other J-1 exchange visitors is sometimes job- and site-specific or limited to a few months.

For more information about these categories and their employment authorization, contact the responsible officer whose name and telephone number are on Form DS-2019 or the DOS website at exchanges.state.gov.

USCIS does not issue EADs (Employment Authorization Documents, Forms I-766) to J-1 exchange visitors. However, they are issued several other documents that, in combination are List A documents and are evidence of employment authorization for J-1 exchange visitors who are not students:

- Unexpired foreign passport;
- Form I-94/Form I-94A Arrival Departure Record indicating J-1 non-immigrant status; and
- Form DS-2019 with the responsible officer's endorsement.

J-1 students may present the documents above if they also have a letter from the responsible officer authorizing employment.

Or

List B and List C documents.

For example, the J-1student could present a List B document (such as a state driver's license) and under List C #7, a Form I-94 in combination with Form DS-2019 and a letter from a responsible officer. The documents by themselves do not qualify. Some exchange visitors may extend their status. If you have questions about any exchange visitor's continued employment authorization, contact the responsible officer whose name and telephone number are on Form DS-019.

Dependents of a J-1 exchange visitor are classified as J-2 nonimmigrants and are only authorized to work if USCIS has issued them an EAD. A J-2 nonimmigrant's foreign passport and Form I-94/Form I-94A are not evidence of identity and employment authorization for purposes of Form I-9.

7.4.2 F-1 and M-1 Nonimmigrant Students

Foreign students pursuing academic studies and/ or language training programs are classified as F-1 nonimmigrants, while foreign students pursuing nonacademic or vocational studies are classified as M-1 nonimmigrants. Designated school officials (DSO) at certified schools issue Form I-20, Certificate of Eligibility for Nonimmigrant (F-1)/(M-1) Students.

F-1 nonimmigrant foreign students may be eligible to work under certain conditions. There are several types of employment authorization for students, including:

- On-campus employment,
- Curricular practical training,
- Off-campus employment based on severe economic hardship,
- Employment sponsored by an international organization, and
- Optional practical training.

Foreign students in F-1 nonimmigrant status may work on campus without the approval of a DSO or USCIS.

On-campus employment is authorized until the student completes their course of study. The F-1 nonimmigrant admission notation on Form I-94/I-94A Arrival Departure Record usually states "D/S" indicating duration of status. The F-1 student's Form

I-20 bears the latest date they can complete their studies. Enter this date in Section 1 as the date employment authorization expires.

To complete Section 2, the combination of the F-1 student's unexpired foreign passport and Form I-94/94A Arrival Departure Record indicating F-1 nonimmigrant status is a List A document for on-campus employment. Employers are not required to record information from the student's Form I-20 in Section 2.

Foreign students in F-1 nonimmigrant status may work:

- On the school's premises, including on-location commercial firms that provide services for students on campus, such as the school bookstore or cafeteria
- At an off-campus location that is educationally affiliated with the school.

Employment that does not provide direct services to students is not on-campus employment. For example, an on-campus commercial firm, such as a construction company that builds a school building, does not provide direct student services. Guidelines for on-campus employment are available at ice.gov/sevis/employment.

On-campus employment is limited to 20 hours a week when school is in session. An exception to this limitation applies in cases of emergent circumstances announced by DHS in a notice published in the Federal Register.

Curricular practical training (CPT) allows students to accept paid alternative work/study, internship, cooperative education, or any other type of required internship or practicum that is offered by sponsoring employers through cooperative agreements with the school. The curricular practical training program must be an integral part of the curriculum of the student's degree program. The DSO must authorize CPT on the student's Form I-20. The employment end date shown in the employment authorization section of the Form I-20 should be entered in Section 1 as the date employment authorization expires.

The following documents establish the student's identity and employment authorization for Form I-9 purposes and should be entered in Section 2:

List A documents include the combination of:

- Unexpired foreign passport;
- Form I-20 with the DSO endorsement for employment; and
- Form I-94/Form I-94A indicating F-1 nonimmigrant status.

Or

List B and List C documents. The F-1 student could present a List B document (such as a state driver's license) and under List C #7, Form I-94 indicating F-1 nonimmigrant status with a properly endorsed Form I-20. The documents by themselves do not qualify.

An acceptable Form I-20 for CPT must have all employment authorization fields completed. These fields include employment status, employment type, start and end date of employment, and the employer's name and location.

For the other types of employment available to certain foreign students, such as optional practical training (OPT) employment authorization, STEM (Science, Technology, Engineering, and Mathematics), OPT extension, or off-campus employment based on severe economic hardship, employment authorization must be granted by USCIS and will be evidenced by an EAD issued by USCIS.

Border commuter students who enter the United States as an F-1 nonimmigrant may only work as part of their curricular practical training or post-completion optional practical training (OPT).

M-1 students may only accept employment if it is part of a practical training program after completion of their course of study. USCIS will issue the EAD with authorization granted for a maximum period of six months of full-time practical training, depending on the length of the students' full-time study.

Dependents of F-1 and M-1 foreign students have an F-2 or M-2 status and are not eligible for employment authorization.

7.4.3 Optional Practical Training (OPT) for F-1 Students – EAD Required

OPT provides practical training experience that directly relates to an F-1 student's major area of study. An F-1 student authorized for OPT may work up to 20 hours per week while school is in session and full-time (20 or more hours per week) when school is not in session. After completing their course of study, students also may participate in OPT for work experience. USCIS may authorize an F-1 student to have up to 12 months of OPT upon completion of their degree program. Certain F-1 students may be eligible for an extension of their OPT, see Section 7.4.4 F-1 STEM OPT Extension.

The designated school official must update Form I-20 to indicate OPT recommendation or approval. OPT employment must be directly related to the student's field of study noted on Form I-20. The student must obtain an EAD from USCIS before they are authorized to work. The student may not begin employment until the date indicated on the EAD.

The EAD establishes the student's identity and employment authorization for Form I-9 purposes and the employer should record the card number and expiration date under List A in Section 2. When the student's EAD expires, the employer must reverify the student's employment authorization in Section 3.

7.4.4 F-1 STEM OPT Extension

An F-1 student who received a bachelor's, master's, or doctoral degree in science, technology, engineering, or mathematics (STEM) from an accredited and SEVP- certified school may apply for a 24-month extension of their optional practical training (OPT). Employment must be directly related to the student's major area of study. The employer must be enrolled in and be in good standing with E-Verify. The E-Verify company identification number is required for the student to apply to USCIS for the STEM extension using Form I-765, Application for Employment Authorization. A STEM student may change employers or work at a different hiring site for the same employer, but the new employer or new hiring site must be enrolled in and be in good standing with E-Verify before the student begins their STEM OPT with the new employer or hiring site.

The EAD issued to the F-1 STEM OPT student states "STU: STEM OPT ONLY." The following documents establish a student's identity and employment authorization for Form I-9:

- Unexpired EAD or
- For certain instances where students have timely- filed Forms I-765 pending, an expired EAD presented with Form I-20 endorsed by the student's designated school official recommending a STEM extension.

If the student presents an expired EAD and an endorsed Form I-20 recommending a STEM extension, the employer should enter the following information under List A in Section 2:

- EAD document title;
- EAD document number;
- Date the EAD expired in the expiration date space; and
- "180-day ext." in the Additional Information field.

The expired EAD with an endorsed Form I-20 is acceptable until USCIS makes a decision on the student's application, but for not more than180 days from the date the student's initial OPT EAD expires. Employment authorization must be reverified after 180 days from the date the EAD expires to continue employment.

Acceptable Forms I-20 for STEM OPT students must have all Employment Authorization fields completed. These fields include: employment status, employment type, start and end date of employment, and the employer's name and location.

- Employers have specific responsibilities when providing practical training opportunities to STEM OPT students. Some employer responsibilities include:
- Enrolling in E-Verify and remaining in good standing before employing an F-1 STEM OPT student.
- Implementing a formal training plan to augment the student's academic learning through practical experience.
- Completing the employer's portion and certifying Form I-983, Training Plan for STEM OPT Students.
- Reporting to the DSO and updating Form I-983 if there are any changes to or material deviations from the student's formal training plan.
- Reporting to the DSO when a student's employment is terminated for any reason before the end of the authorized extension period.

Additional employer requirements and information on an employer's responsibilities are available at studyinthestates.dhs.gov.

7.4.5 Cap-Gap

F-1 students who seek to change to H-1B status may be eligible for a cap-gap extension of status and employment authorization through September 30 of the calendar year for which the H-1B petition is being filed, but only if the H-1B status will begin on October 1. The term cap-gap refers to the period between the time a nonimmigrant's F-1 student status would ordinarily end and their H-1B status begins. If you employ an F-1 nonimmigrant student in OPT and you timely filed an H-1B petition for that student, they may be able to continue working beyond the expiration date on their OPT EAD (Employment Authorization Document, FormI-766) while waiting for the start date of an approved or pending H-1B petition.

There are two types of cap-gap extensions:

1.   Extensions of F-1 status only (without OPT).

If a student is in F-1 status when you file an H-1B petition with an October 1 start date, but the student is not currently participating in OPT, the student will receive a cap-gap extension of their F-1 status, but will not be authorized to work until USCIS approves the H-1B petition and the H-1B status begins on October 1.

2.   Extensions of F-1 status and OPT.

If a student is in F-1 status when you file an H-1B petition with an October 1 start date and is currently participating in post-completion OPT, they will receive an automatic cap-gap extension of both their F-1 student status and their authorized period of post-completion OPT. If the H-1B petition is selected and remains pending or is approved, the student will remain authorized to work as an F-1 student with OPT through September 30.

The following documents establish identity and employment authorization for Form I-9 purposes for students who have had their status and employment authorization extended through cap-gap:

- Expired EAD; and,

- Form I-20 endorsed by the student's DSO recommending the cap-gap extension.

- These documents are acceptable through September 30 of the year in which the employer filed the H-1B petition unless the H-1B petition is rejected, not selected, denied, revoked or withdrawn before October 1.

- To verify employment authorization in Section 2 or conduct reverification in Section 3 during the cap-gap period, the employer should record:

- EAD document title;

- EAD document number;

- Date the EAD expired in the expiration date space; and,

- "CAP-GAP" in the Additional Information field.

7.5 H-1B Specialty Occupations

U.S. businesses use the H-1B program to temporarily employ foreign workers in a specialty occupation that requires theoretical or technical expertise in a certain field, such as science, engineering or computer programming. As a U.S. employer, you may submit a Form I-129, Petition for a Nonimmigrant Worker, to USCIS for nonimmigrants who have certain skills, provided they meet established requirements. You must also include an approved Form ETA 9035, *Labor Condition Application*, with Form I-129 and other documentation.

(a) A Newly Hired Employee With H-1B Classification

If USCIS approves your petition, you will receive Form I-797, Notice of Approval, from USCIS, which indicates that the foreign worker has been approved for H-1B classification. Once your employee begins working for you, **you must both complete Form I-9**.

(b) H-1B Extensions

H-1B petitions can be approved for an initial period of up to three years, after which USCIS may grant extensions for up to an additional three years. Certain H-1B workers may be extended beyond the six-year ceiling.

For more information about H-1B extensions, please visit uscis.gov.

(c) H-1B Continuing Employment With the Same Employer

For an H-1B worker to continue working for you beyond the expiration of their current H-1B status as indicated by the expiration date on their Form I-797 Notice of Action approval notice, you must request an extension of stay before their H-1B petition expires. Upon submitting a timely filed Form I-129 petition seeking an extension of the employee's status, the employee is authorized to continue to work while the petition is being processed for a period not to exceed 240 days, or until USCIS denies your petition, whichever comes first. When your employee's work authorization expires, you should write "240-Day Ext." and enter the date you submitted Form I-129 to USCIS in the Additional Information field in Section 2. Also your employee may update Section 1 by crossing out the expiration date of their employment authorization noted in the attestation. The employee may write in the new date that the automatic extension of employment authorization ends and initial and date this update in the margin of Section 1. You must reverify the employee's employment authorization in Section 3 once you receive a decision on the H-1B petition or by the end of the 240-day period, whichever comes first.

See Section 7.7.1 *Completing Form I-9 for Nonimmigrant Categories When Requesting Extensions of Stay*.

(d) H-1B Employees Changing Employers (Porting)

An H-1B employee who is changing H-1B employers may begin working for the new employer as soon as the employer files a Form I-129 petition on behalf of the employee. The new petition must not be frivolous and must have been filed prior to the expiration of the individual's period of authorized stay. The new employer must complete a new Form I-9 for this newly hired employee. An H-1B employee's unexpired Form I-94/Form I-94A issued for employment with the previous employer, along with their foreign passport, would qualify as a List A document. The new employer should write "AC-21" and enter the date Form I-129 was submitted to USCIS in the Additional Information field in Section 2.

See Section 7.7.1 *Completing Form I-9 for Nonimmigrant Categories When Requesting Extensions of Stay*.

For more information about employing H-1B workers, please visit uscis.gov.

Please go to uscis.gov/files/form/i-129instr.pdf (PDF, 347 KB)for further instructions on filing extensions of stay.

7.6 H-2A Temporary Agricultural Worker Program

The H-2A program allows U.S. employers to bring foreign workers to the United States to fill temporary or seasonal agricultural jobs usually lasting no longer than one year, for which U.S. workers are not available. Before filing a petition with USCIS, you must first obtain a valid temporary labor certification for H-2A workers from the U.S. Department of Labor (DOL). Once certified, you can include multiple workers when filing a Form I-129, Petition for a Nonimmigrant Worker, to request H-2A classification from USCIS. If USCIS approves your petition, you can hire the foreign workers for which you petitioned to fill the temporary job.

(a) Newly Hired Employee in H-2A Classification

Complete a new Form I-9 for this employee as you would for any employee. An H-2A worker's unexpired Form I-94/Form I-94A Arrival Departure Record indicating their H-2A status, along with their foreign passport, would qualify as a List A document. Enter these documents in Section 2 under List A, along with the expiration date of your employee's H-2A status found on their Form I-94/ Form I-94A.

(b) H-2A Continuing Employment With the Same Employer

You may extend your worker's H-2A status in increments of no longer than one year by timely filing with USCIS a new Form I-129 petition on behalf of the worker. In most cases, a new temporary labor certification from DOL is required before you can file Form I-129. To avoid disruption of employment, you should file a petition to extend the employee's employment authorization status well before it expires. When your H-2A employee's work authorization expires, you must update their Form I-9 by writing "240-Day Ext." and entering the date you submitted Form I-129 to USCIS in the Additional Information box in Section 2. USCIS may extend a single H-2A petition for up to two weeks without an additional approved labor certification under certain circumstances. In such a case, write "two-week extension" and enter the date you submitted Form I-129 to USCIS in the Additional Information box in Section 2.

Upon submitting a new Form I-129 petition to USCIS, the H-2A worker is authorized to continue to work while the petition is being processed for a period not to exceed 240 days, or until USCIS denies your petition, whichever comes first. You must reverify the employee's employment authorization in Section 3 once you receive a decision on the H-2A petition or by the end of the 240-day period, whichever comes first.

See Section 7.7.1 *Completing Form I-9 for Nonimmigrant Categories When Requesting Extensions of Stay*.

(c) H-2A Extension With a New Employer

In most cases, an H-2A worker may not begin working for a new employer until USCIS approves the petition requesting a change of employer. However, if you have enrolled in E-Verify, you may employ an H-2A worker as soon as you submit a new Form I-129 petition on their behalf. The H-2A worker is authorized to work while USCIS processes the petition for a period not to exceed 120 days, or until USCIS denies your petition, whichever comes first. You and your newly hired employee must complete Form I-9. The H-2A employee's unexpired Form I-94/Form I-94A indicating their H-2A status, along with their foreign passport, would qualify as a List A document. You should write "120-Day Ext." and enter the date you submitted Form I-129 to USCIS in the Additional Information box in Section 2.

If USCIS denies the new petition before the 120-day period expires, USCIS will automatically terminate the H-2A worker's employment authorization within 15 calendar days of its denial decision. USCIS may also terminate employment authorization if you fail to remain an E-Verify employer in good standing. You must reverify the employee's employment authorization in Section 3 either by the end of the 120-day period or once you receive a decision on the H-2A petition, whichever comes first. If your petition is denied, count 15 days from the date of the denial for the date the employee's employment authorization expires.

See Section 7.7.1 Completing Form I-9 for Nonimmigrant Categories When Requesting Extensions of Stay.

For more information about employing H-2A workers, please visit uscis.gov.

7.7 Extensions of Stay for Other Nonimmigrant Categories

Other nonimmigrants also may receive extensions of stay if their employers file Form I-129, Petition for a Nonimmigrant Worker (or Form I-129CW, Petition for a CNMI-Only Nonimmigrant Transitional Worker for CW-nonimmigrants) with USCIS on their behalf, before their status expires. These employees are authorized to continue working while their petitions are being processed for a period not to exceed 240 days, or until USCIS denies the petition, whichever comes first. On these employees' Form I-9, write "240-day Ext." and the date Form I-129 was submitted to USCIS in the Additional Information box in Section 2. Also your employee may update Section 1 by crossing out the expiration date of their employment authorization noted in the attestation. The employee may write in the new date that the automatic extension of employment authorization ends and initial and date this update in the margin of Section 1.

Other categories include: CW-1 H-1B, H-1B1, H-2A, H-2B, H-3, L-1, O-1, O-2, P-1, P-2, P-3, R-1, TN, A3, E-1, E-2, E-3, G-5, and I. Note that individuals in the E-1 and E-2 categories are employers.

Go to uscis.gov/sites/default/files/files/form/i-129instr.pdf (PDF, 347 KB) for further instructions on filing extensions of stay.

See Section 7.7.1 Completing Form I-9 for Nonimmigrant Categories when Requesting Extensions of Stay.

For more information about employing other types of nonimmigrant workers, please visit uscis.gov.

7.7.1 Completing Form I-9 for Nonimmigrant Categories When Requesting Extensions of Stay

You must submit a timely filed Form I-129 (or I-129CW) petition to USCIS to request an extension of stay on behalf of an employee in one of the above categories. While the petition is pending, your existing employee is authorized to continue to work for you for 120 days, 240 days, or longer, depending on the category petitioned for, or until USCIS denies your petition, whichever comes first.

Keep the following documents with the employee's existing Form I-9 to show that you filed for an extension of stay on their behalf:

- A copy of the new Form I-129 or Form I-129CW;

- Proof of payment for filing a new Form I-129 or Form I-129CW

- Evidence that you mailed the new Form I-129 or Form I-129CW to USCIS.

After submitting Form I-129 or Form I-129CW to USCIS, you will receive a notice from USCIS acknowledging that your petition is pending; you should keep it with the employee's Form I-9. After you receive the I-797C, Notice of Action, which bears the amount of the filing fee submitted and acknowledges USCIS' receipt of the new Form I-129 petition, it is not necessary to maintain a copy of the Form I-129 application, proof of payment, and mailing receipt for Form I-9 purposes. You should retain the I-797C, Notice of Action to show that you filed for an extension of stay on the employee's behalf.

If USCIS approves the application/petition for an extension of stay, you will receive a Form I-797A, Notice of Action which includes an expiration date and an attached Form I-94A, Arrival/Departure Record. Enter the document title, number and expiration date listed on the notice in Section 3 of Form I-9. You must give your employee the Form I-94A, which is evidence of their employment-authorized nonimmigrant status.

7.7.2 Automatic Extensions of EADs in Certain Circumstances

DHS regulations provide for up to180-day automatic extension of employment authorization of certain Form I-766, Employment Authorization Documents (EADs) for some individuals who have timely filed a renewal of their EADs. For qualifying individuals except TPS beneficiaries, timely filed means prior to the expiration of their most recent EAD. For TPS beneficiaries, timely filed means filing as instructed by the Federal Register notice announcing the TPS registration procedures. The TPS automatic extension will terminate early if USCIS denies the renewal application before the 180th day is reached. DHS has determined that 15 employment eligible categories can receive automatic renewal of their EADs. The following are the eligible category codes which can be found on the face of the expired EAD: A03, A05, A07, A08, A10, A12 or C19, C08, C09, C10, C16, C20, C22, C24, C31. For an updated list, visit uscis.gov. See Section 4.2 *Automatic Extensions of Employment Authorization Documents in Certain Circumstances.*

7.7.3 Documentation for Form I-9

The combination of an expired EAD noting a qualifying eligibility code, in combination with a Form I-797C, Notice of Action acknowledging receipt of an EAD renewal application and noting an eligibility category code that matches the expired EAD constitutes an unexpired EAD (Form I-766) under List A of Form I-9, so long as Form I-797C indicates that the renewal application was filed before the previous EAD expired. However, for TPS beneficiaries, the codes will be A-12 or C-19, but do not have to match, and the employer can consider the renewal application as timely filed if it was filed by the dates stated in the current TPS Federal Register notice applicable for the individual's country.

Therefore, when the expiration date on the automatically extended EAD is reached, the employer and the employee should update the employment authorization/EAD expiration dates stated on the previously completed Form I-9 (Sections 1 and 2 or 3) to reflect the extended expiration date while the renewal application is pending. Cross out the dates and write the last date of the automatic extension period and initial the correction. Note that the employee must make and initial the correction if one is necessary in Section 1, while the employer must make and initial the correction in Section 2 or 3. If the automatically extended EAD is being presented by the individual to a new employer, then the expiration dates to be entered on Form I-9 should be the last date of the automatic extension. If the employer is retaining copies of documents with Form I-9, then both the expired EAD and the Form I-797 should be retained. At the end of the expiration date, you must reverify by updating Section 3. See Section 4.2, Figure 3 for more information.

8.0 Leaves of Absence, Layoffs, Corporate Mergers and Other Interruptions of Employment

You must complete a new Form I-9 when a hire takes place, unless you are rehiring an employee within three years of the date of their previous Form I-9. However, in certain situations, a hire is not considered to have taken place despite an interruption in employment. In case of an interruption in employment, you should determine whether the employee is continuing in their employment and has a reasonable expectation of employment at all times.

These situations constitute continuing employment:

- Approved paid or unpaid leave on account of study, illness or disability of a family member, illness or pregnancy, maternity or paternity leave, vacation, union business, or other temporary leave approved by the employer.

- Promotions, demotions or pay raises.

- Temporary layoff for lack of work.

- Strikes or labor disputes.

- Reinstatement after disciplinary suspension for wrongful termination found unjustified by any court, arbitrator or administrative body, or other- wise resolved through reinstatement or settlement.

- Transfer from one distinct unit of an employer to another distinct unit of the same employer; the employer may transfer the employee's Form I-9 to the receiving unit.

- Seasonal employment.

- Continuing employment with a related, successor, or reorganized employer, provided that the employer obtains and maintains, from the previous employer, records and Form I-9 where applicable. A related, successor or reorganized employer includes:

- The same employer at another location;

- An employer who continues to employ any employee of another employer's workforce, where both employers belong to the same multi-employer association and the employee continues to work in the same bargaining unit under the same collective bargaining agreement. For these purposes, any agent designated to complete and maintain Form I-9 must enter the employee's date of hire and/or termination each time the employee is hired and/or terminated by an employer of the multi-employer association.

- Employers who have acquired or merged with another company have two options:

Option A: Treat all acquired employees as new hires and complete a new Form I-9 for every individual. Enter the effective date of acquisition or merger as the employee's first day of employment in Section 2 of the new Form I-9.

If you choose Option A, avoid engaging in discrimination by completing a new Form I-9 for all of your acquired employees, without regard to actual or perceived citizenship status or national origin.

Option B: Treat all acquired individuals as employees who are continuing in their uninterrupted employment status and retain the previous owner's Form I-9 for each acquired employee. Note that you are liable for any errors or omissions on the previously completed Form I-9.

Employees hired on or before Nov. 6, 1986, who are continuing in their employment and have a reasonable expectation of employment at all times are exempt from completing Form I-9 and cannot be verified in E-Verify. For help with making this determination, see 8 CFR 274a.2(b)(1)(viii) and 8 CFR 274a.7. If you determine that an employee hired on or before Nov. 6, 1986 is not continuing in their employment or does not have a reasonable expectation of employment at all times, the employee may be required to complete a Form I-9.

Federal contractors with the FAR E-Verify clause are subject to special rules regarding the verification of existing employees. For more information, see the E-Verify Supplemental Guide for Federal Contractors at uscis.gov/e-verify.

To determine whether an employee continuing in his or employment had a reasonable expectation of employment at all times, consider several factors, including, but not limited to:

- The individual was employed on a regular and substantial basis. A determination of a regular and substantial basis is established by a comparison of other workers similarly employed by the employer.

- The individual complied with the employer's established and published policy regarding their absence.

- The employer's past history of recalling absent employees for employment indicates the likelihood that the individual in question will resume employment with the employer within a reasonable time in the future.

- The former position held by the individual has not been taken permanently by another worker.

- The individual has not sought or obtained benefits during their absence from employment with the employer that are inconsistent with an expectation of resuming employment within a reasonable time in the future.

- The financial condition of the employer indicates the ability of the employer to permit the individual in question to resume employment within a reasonable time in the future.

- The oral and/or written communication between employer, the employer's supervisory employees and the individual indicates that it is reasonably likely that the individual will resume employment within a reasonable time in the future.

Continue to maintain and store the previously completed Form I-9 as if there was no interruption in employment. Inspect the previously completed Form I-9 and, if necessary, update the form or conduct reverification.

If you determine that your employee was terminated and is now rehired, and the rehire occurs within three years from the date the original Form I-9 was completed, you have an option to complete a new form or rely on the original one.

8.1 Special Rules for Members of Employer Associations

Special rules apply for employers who are members of an association of two or more employers that have entered into a collective bargaining agreement with one or more employee organizations. An employer who is a member of the employer association will be deemed to have complied with the employment eligibility verification requirements for its employee if:

- The employee is a member of a collective-bargaining unit and is employed under a collective bargaining agreement between one or more employee organizations and an association of two or more employers by an employer that is a member of such association, and

- Another employer that is a member of the same employer association (or an agent of the employer association on behalf of the employer), has previously complied with the employment eligibility verification requirements for this individual within three years (or, if less, the period of time that the individual is authorized to be employed in the United States)

Penalties for employing aliens knowing they are unauthorized to work in the United States still apply.

8.2 Special Rules for State Employment Agencies

A state employment agency, sometimes known as a state workforce agency, may choose to verify the employment authorization and identity of an individual it refers for employment on Form I-9. In such a case, the agency must issue a certification to you so that you receive it within 21 business days of the date the referred individual is hired. If an agency refers a potential employee to you with a job order, other appropriate referral form or telephonically authorized referral, and the agency sends you a certification within 21 business days of the referral, you do not have to check documents or complete a Form I-9 if you hire that person. Before receiving the certification, you should retain the job order, referral form or annotation reflecting the telephonically authorized referral as you would Form I-9. When you receive the certification, you must review it to ensure that it relates to the person hired and observe the person sign the certification. You must also retain the certification as you would a Form I-9 and make it available for inspection, if requested. Check with your state employment agency to see if it provides this service and become familiar with its certification document.

9.0 Correcting Form I-9

If the employer, recruiter, or referrer for a fee ("employer") discovers an error in Section 1 of an employee's Form I-9, the employer should bring itself into compliance immediately and ask the employee to correct the error. Employers and/or their authorized representative may only correct errors made in Section 2 or Section 3 of Form I-9.

To correct the form:

- Draw a line through the incorrect information;
- Enter the correct information;
- Initial and date the correction.

Correcting Section 1

If the employer and/or their authorized representative discover information has been omitted in Section 1, the employer should ask the employee to enter the missing information. If the employee is remotely located, the employer should develop the appropriate business process to allow the employee to enter the missing information in Section 1.

When correcting Section 1, the employee should:

- Enter the omitted information;
- Initial and date near the newly entered information.

The employer should attach a written explanation of what happened.

If the employee's employment has terminated, the employer should attach a written explanation to the Form I-9 explaining the error and place in the employee's file.

Corrections by a Preparer/Translator Assisting with Section 1

Upon discovering an error, the preparer and/or translator should:

- Make the correction or help the employee make the correction by drawing a line through the incorrect information and entering the correct information;
- Have the employee initial and date the correction;
- Initial and date the correction if the preparer/translator makes the correction.

If the preparer and/or translator who helps with the correction completed the Preparer and/or Translator Certification block when the employee initially completed Form I-9, they should not complete the certification block again. If the preparer and/or translator did not previously complete the preparer and/or

Correcting Section 2 and Section 3

If the employer and/or their authorized representative discover information has been omitted in Section 2 or 3, the employer should enter the omitted information to the extent possible and initial and date in the same area. Also, it would be helpful to attach a written explanation of what happened to the Form I-9. If an employer failed to enter the date Section 2 and/or 3 was completed, the form should not be back dated. The employer should enter the current date and initial by the date field.

To correct multiple recording errors on the form, you may redo the section on a new Form I-9 and attach it to the old form. A new Form I-9 can be completed if major errors (such as entire sections were left blank or Section 2 was completed based on unacceptable documents) need to be corrected. A note should be attached to the employee's Form I-9 regarding the reason changes were made to an existing Form I-9 or a new Form I-9 was completed.

Do NOT conceal any changes made on the form. Doing so may lead to increased liability under federal immigration law.

If you have made changes on a Form I-9 using correction fluid, we recommend you attach a signed and dated note to the corrected Form I-9 explaining what happened. You can find guidance on making corrections to Form I-9 at uscis.gov/i-9-central.

10.0 Photocopying and Retaining Form I-9

Employers must retain a Form I-9 for each person hired. This requirement applies from the date of hire, even if the employment ends shortly after hired, the hired employee never completes work for pay, or never finishes the Form I-9. Once the individual's employment has terminated, the employer must determine how long after termination the Form I-9 must be retained, either three years after the date of hire, or one year after the date employment is terminated, whichever is later. Form I-9 can be retained on paper, microform or electronically.

To store Form I-9 electronically, you may use any electronic recordkeeping, attestation, or retention system that complies with DHS standards, including most commercially available off-the-shelf computer programs and commercial automated data processing systems. However, the system must not be subject to any agreement that would restrict access to and use of it by an agency of the United States. See *Section 10.3, Electronic Retention of Form I-9* for additional requirements.

Note: *Insufficient or incomplete documentation is a violation of section 274A (a)(1)(B) of the INA (8 CFR Part 274a .2(f)(2)).*

1.   Enter date employee began work for pay: _____

                    Add three years to Line 1   A. _____

2.   Termination date: _____

                    Add one year to Line 2   B. _____

        Which date is later: A or B?

        Enter the later date here.   C. _____ Store Form I-9 until this date.

Figure 11: Form I-9 Retention Calculator

10.1 Paper Retention of Form I-9

Form I-9 can be signed and stored in paper format with original handwritten signatures. Simply photocopy or print a blank Form I-9. Ensure the employee receives the instructions for completing the form. When copying or printing the paper Form I-9, you may photocopy the two-sided form by making either double-sided or single-sided copies.

Only the pages of the Form I-9 on which you or the employee enter data must be retained. You may retain completed paper forms on-site or at an off-site storage facility for the required retention period, as long as you are able to present the Form I-9 within three days of an inspection request from DHS, the Department of Justice's Civil Rights Division, Immigrant and Employee Rights Section (IER), or U.S. Department of Labor (DOL) officers.

10.2 Microform Retention of Form I-9

You may retain copies of an original signed Form I-9 on microfilm or microfiche. Only the pages of the Form I-9 on which you or the employees enter data must be retained. To do so, you should:

- Select film stock that will preserve the image and allow its access and use for the entire retention period, which could be upward of 20 years, depending on the employee and your business.

- Use well-maintained equipment to create and view microfilms and microfiche that provides clear viewing, and can reproduce legible paper copies. DHS officers must have access to clear, readable documents should they need to inspect your forms.

- Place indexes either in the first frames of the first roll of film or in the last frames of the last roll of film of a series. For microfiche, place them in the last frames of the last microfiche or microfilm jacket of a series.

10.3 Electronic Retention of Form I-9

USCIS provides a Portable Document Format (.pdf) fillable-printable Form I-9 from its website, uscis.gov. In addition, you may generate and retain Form I-9 electronically as long as the employee receives instructions for completing the form and:

- The resulting form is legible;

- No change is made to the name, content, or sequence of the data elements and instructions;

- No additional data elements or language are inserted; and

- The standards specified in the regulations are met. (8 CFR Part 274a.2(e), (f), (g), (h) and (i) as applicable.)

You may use paper, electronic systems, or a combination of paper and electronic systems. You may complete or retain Form I-9 in an electronic generation or storage system that includes:

- Reasonable controls to ensure the integrity, accuracy and reliability of the electronic generation or storage system;

- Reasonable controls designed to prevent and detect the unauthorized or accidental creation of, addition to, alteration of, deletion of, or deterioration of an electronically completed or stored Form I-9, including the electronic signature, if used;

- An inspection and quality assurance program that regularly evaluates the electronic generation or storage system, and includes periodic checks of electronically stored Form I-9, including the electronic signature, if used;

- An indexing system that allows the identification and retrieval for viewing or reproducing of relevant documents and records maintained in an electronic storage system; and

- The ability to reproduce legible and readable paper copies.

If you choose to complete or retain Form I-9 electronically, you may use one or more electronic generation or storage systems, as long as any Form

I-9 retained in the system remains fully accessible and meets the regulations. You may change electronic storage systems as long as the systems meet the performance requirement of the regulations. For each electronic generation or storage system used, you must maintain and make available upon request complete descriptions of:

- The electronic generation and storage system, including all procedures relating to its use.

- The indexing system that allows the identification and retrieval of relevant documents and records maintained in an electronic storage system. You are not required to maintain separate indexing data- bases for each system if comparable results can be achieved without separate indexing databases.

Only the pages of the Form I-9 on which you or the employee enter data must be retained.

10.3.1 Documentation of Electronic Storage Systems

If you choose to complete or retain Form I-9 electronically, you must maintain and make available upon request documentation of the business processes that:

- Created the retained Form I-9,

- Modify and maintain the retained Form I-9, and

- Establish the authenticity and integrity of the forms, such as audit trails.

10.3.2 Electronic Signature of Form I-9

You may choose to complete a paper Form I-9 and scan and upload the original signed form to retain it electronically. Once you have securely stored Form I-9 in electronic format, you may destroy the original paper Form I-9.

If you complete Form I-9 electronically using an electronic signature, your system for capturing electronic signatures must allow signatories to acknowledge that they read the attestation and attach the electronic signature to an electronically completed Form I-9. The system must also:

- Affix the electronic signature at the time of the transaction;

- Create and preserve a record verifying the identity of the person producing the signature; and

- Upon request of the employee, provide a printed confirmation of the transaction to the person providing the signature.

Employers who complete Form I-9 electronically must attest to the required information in Section 2 of Form I-9. The system used to capture the electronic signature should include a method to acknowledge that the attestation to be signed has been read by the signatory.

Note: *If you choose to use an electronic signature to complete Form I-9, but do not comply with these standards, DHS will determine that you have not properly completed Form I-9, in violation of section 274A(a)(1) B) of the INA (8 CFR Part 274a .2(b)(2)) .*

10.4 Security

If you retain Form I-9 electronically, you must implement an effective records security program that:

- Ensures that only authorized personnel have access to electronic records;

- Provides for backup and recovery of records to protect against information loss;

- Ensures that employees are trained to minimize the risk of unauthorized or accidental alteration or erasure of electronic records; and

- Ensures that whenever an individual creates, completes, updates, modifies, alters, or corrects an electronic record, the system creates a secure and permanent record that establishes the date of access, the identity of the individual who accessed the electronic record, and the particular action taken.

Note: *If your action or inaction results in the alteration, loss or erasure of electronic records, and you knew, or reasonably should have known, that the action or inaction could have that effect, then you are in violation of section 274A(b)(3) of the INA (8 CFR Part 274a.2(g)(2)).*

10.5 Retaining Copies of Form I-9 Documentation

You may choose to copy or scan documents an employee presents when completing Form I-9, which you may retain with their Form I-9. Making photocopies of an employee's document(s) does not take the place of completing Form I-9. Even if you retain copies of documentation, you are still required to fully complete and retain Form I-9. If you choose to retain copies of an employee's documents, you must do so for all employees, regardless of actual or perceived national origin or citizenship status, or you may be in violation of anti- discrimination laws.

Copies or electronic images of presented documents must be retrievable consistent with DHS's standards on electronic retention, documentation, security, and electronic signatures for employers and employees, as specified in 8 CFR Part 274a.2(b)(3).

If you make copies or electronic images of the employee's documents, they must be either retained with the corresponding Form I-9 or stored with the employee's records in accordance with the standards for electronic records retention as specified in 8 CFR 274a.2(b)(3). However, if copies or electronic images of the employee's documents are made, they must be made available at the time of a Form I-9 inspection by DHS or another federal government agency.

10.6 Inspection

The INA specifically authorizes DHS, IER and DOL to inspect Forms I-9, including any copies of employees' documents retained with the corresponding Form I-9. DHS, IER, and DOL provide employers a minimum of three days' notice before inspecting a retained Form I-9. The employer must make Forms I-9 available upon request at the location where DHS, IER or DOL requests to see them. Forms I-9 and supporting documentation may also be sent to the agency in electronic format or hard copy if requested.

If you store Form I-9 records at an off-site location, inform the inspecting officer of the location where you store them and make arrangements for the inspection. The inspecting officers may perform an inspection at an office of an authorized agency of the United States if previous arrangements are made. Recruiters or referrers for a fee who designate an employer to complete employment verification procedures may present photocopies or printed electronic images of Forms I-9 at an inspection. If you refuse or delay an inspection, you will be in violation of DHS retention requirements.

At the time of an inspection, you must:

- Retrieve and reproduce only the Forms I-9 electronically retained in the electronic storage system and supporting documentation specifically requested by the inspecting officer. Supporting documentation includes photocopies of Form I-9 documents stored with Form I-9 and associated audit trails that show the actions performed within or on the system during a given period of time.

- Provide the inspecting officer with appropriate hardware and software, personnel, and documentation necessary to locate, retrieve, read, and reproduce any electronically stored Form I-9, any supporting documents, and their associated audit trails, reports, and other data used to maintain the authenticity, integrity, and reliability of the records.

- Provide the inspecting officer, if requested, any reasonably available or obtainable electronic summary file(s), such as spreadsheets, containing all of the information fields on any electronically stored Form I-9.

Note: *E-Verify employers who receive a request for inspection should provide Form I-9 with the E-Verify case verification number record on the Form I-9 or, if the E-Verify case number is not recorded on the Form I-9, the E-Verify Case Detail Pages in addition to Form I-9.*

11.0 Unlawful Discrimination and Penalties for Prohibited Practices

11.1 Unlawful Discrimination

Discriminating in the Form I-9 and E-Verify verification processes can violate federal law. This section describes prohibited discrimination and how to prevent prohibited discrimination in verifying an individual's employment authorization.

11.1.1 Overview of Discrimination Laws

The anti-discrimination provision of the Immigration and Nationality Act (INA), as amended, prohibits four types of unlawful conduct:

- Unfair documentary practices during the Form I-9 and E-Verify process;

- Citizenship or immigration status discrimination;

- National origin discrimination;

- Retaliation or intimidation

The Department of Justice's Civil Rights Division, Immigrant and Employee Rights Section (IER), enforces this law.

Title VII of the Civil Rights Act of 1964 (Title VII) and other federal laws prohibit employment discrimination based on race, color, national origin, religion, sex, age, disability and genetic information. The U.S. Equal Employment Opportunity Commission (EEOC) enforces these laws.

11.2. Types of Employment Discrimination Prohibited Under the INA

11.2.1 Unfair Documentary Practices

The INA prohibits discriminatory documentary practices related to verifying the employment authorization and identity of employees during the employment eligibility verification process (generally, the Form I-9 and E-Verify processes). Unfair documentary practices generally occur when employers treat individuals differently on the basis of national origin or citizenship or immigration status in the Form I-9 or E-Verify processes, or any other process an employer may use that verifies employment eligibility. Unfair documentary practices can be broadly categorized into four types of conduct:

1. Requesting that an individual produce more or different documents than are required by Form I-9 to establish the individual's identity and employment authorization;

2. Requesting that individuals present a particular document, such as a "Green Card," to establish identity and/or employment authorization;

3. Rejecting documents that reasonably appear to be genuine and to relate to the individuals presenting them; and

4. Treating groups of individuals differently when verifying employment eligibility, such as requiring certain groups of individuals who look or sound "foreign" to present particular documents the employer does not require other individuals to present.

These practices may constitute unfair documentary practices if they are committed based on citizenship or immigration status, or national origin, and should be avoided when verifying employment authorization. The INA's prohibition against unfair documentary practices covers employers with four or more employees.

11.2.2 Citizenship Status Discrimination

Citizenship or immigration status discrimination occurs when an employer treats individuals differently based on their real or perceived citizenship or immigration status with respect to hiring, firing, recruitment, or referral for a fee. U.S. citizens, U.S. nationals, recent permanent residents, asylees, and refugees are protected from this type of discrimination. The INA's provision against citizenship or immigration status discrimination covers employers with four or more employees.

11.2.3 National Origin Discrimination

National origin discrimination under the INA occurs when an employer treats individuals differently based on their national origin with respect to hiring, firing, recruitment, or referral for a fee. An individual's national origin relates to the individual's place of birth, country of origin, ethnicity, ancestry, native language, accent, or the perception that they look or sound "foreign." The INA's national origin discrimination prohibition generally covers employers with more than three and less than 15 employees and covers all employment-authorized individuals. EEOC has jurisdiction over national origin claims involving employers with 15 or more employees, regardless of the work authorization status of the discrimination victims.

11.2.4 Retaliation

An employer or other covered entity cannot intimidate, threaten, coerce, or otherwise retaliate against an individual because the individual has filed an immigration-related employment discrimination charge or complaint; has testified or participated in any IER investigation, proceeding, or hearing; or otherwise asserts his, her, or other's rights under the INA's anti-discrimination provision.

11.3 Types of Discrimination Prohibited by Title VII and Other Federal Anti-discrimination Laws

As noted in Section 11.1.1, Title VII and other federal laws also prohibit employment discrimination on the basis of national origin, as well as race, color, religion, sex, age, disability and genetic information. These laws also protect workers from retaliation. EEOC has jurisdiction over employers that employ 15 or more employees for 20 or more weeks in the preceding or current calendar year, and prohibits discrimination in any aspect of employment, including: hiring and firing; compensation, assignment, or classification of employees; transfer, promotion, layoff, or recall; job advertisements; recruitment; testing; use of company facilities; training and apprenticeship programs; fringe benefits; pay, retirement plans, and leave; or other terms and conditions of employment.

IER and EEOC share jurisdiction over national origin discrimination charges. EEOC investigates national origin discrimination claims against employers with 15 or more employees, and IER investigates national origin discrimination claims against smaller employers with more than three and less than 15 employees.

11.4 Avoiding Discrimination in Recruiting, Hiring, and the Form I-9 Process

In practice, you should treat individuals equally when recruiting and hiring, and when verifying employment authorization and identity during the Form I-9 process.

You should not:

- Have different rules or requirements for individuals because of their national origin, citizenship, or immigration status. For example, you cannot demand that non-U.S. citizens present DHS issued documents. Each individual must be allowed to choose the documents that they will present from the lists of acceptable Form I-9 documents. For example, both citizens and other employment authorized individuals may present a driver's license (List B) and an unrestricted Social Security card (List C) to establish identity and employment authorization. However, you must reject documents that do not reasonably appear to be genuine or to relate to the individual presenting them.

- Request to see employment eligibility verification documents before hire and completion of Form I-9 because an individual looks or sounds "foreign," or because the individual states that they are not a U.S. citizen.

- Refuse to accept a document, or refuse to hire an individual, because a document has a future expiration date.

- Request specific documents from individuals to run an E-Verify case or based on an E-Verify tentative nonconfirmation.

- Request that an individual run a Self Check case and/or present documents showing the individual cleared Self Check.

- Request that an employee who presented an unexpired Permanent Resident Card present a new document when the Permanent Resident Card expires.

- Request specific documents for reverification. For Example, an employee who presented an unexpired Employment Authorization Document (Form I-766) during initial verification should be requested to present any document of their choosing from either from List A or from List C during reverification.

- Limit jobs to U.S. citizens unless U.S. citizenship is required for the specific position by law; regulation; executive order; or federal, state, or local government contract.

11.5 Employers Prohibited From Retaliating Against Employees

You cannot take retaliatory action against a person who has filed a charge of discrimination with IER or the EEOC, participates in the investigation or prosecution of a discrimination complaint, such as by serving as a witness, or otherwise asserts rights under the INA's anti-discrimination provision and/or Title VII. Such retaliatory action may constitute a violation of the INA's anti-discrimination provision, Title VII, and other federal anti-discrimination law.

11.6 Procedures for Filing Charges of Employment Discrimination

IER

Discrimination charges may be filed by an individual, a person acting on behalf of such an individual, or a DHS officer who has reason to believe that discrimination has occurred. Discrimination charges must be filed with IER within 180 days of the alleged discriminatory act.

Upon receipt of a complete discrimination charge, IER will notify you within 10 days that a charge has been filed against you and start its investigation. If you refuse to cooperate with IER's investigation, IER can obtain a subpoena to compel you to produce the information and documents requested or to appear for an investigative interview.

If IER has not filed a complaint with an administrative law judge within 120 days of receiving a charge of discrimination, it will notify the charging party (other than a DHS officer) of their right to file a complaint with an administrative law judge within 90 days after receiving the notice.

Additionally, IER may also file a complaint. If a complaint is filed, the administrative law judge will conduct a hearing and issue a decision. IER may also attempt to settle a charge, or the parties may enter into a settlement agreement resolving the charge.

EEOC

A charge must be filed with the EEOC within 180 days from the date of the alleged violation to protect the charging party's rights. This 180-day filing deadline is extended to 300 days if the charge also is covered by a state or local anti-discrimination law.

11.7 Penalties for Prohibited Practices

11.7.1 Unlawful Employment

Civil Penalties

DHS or an administrative law judge may impose penal- ties if an investigation reveals that you knowingly hired or knowingly continued to employ an unauthorized alien, or failed to comply with the employment eligibility verification requirements with respect to employees hired after Nov. 6, 1986.

DHS will issue a Notice of Intent to Fine (NIF) when it intends to impose penalties. If you receive NIF, you may request a hearing before an administrative law judge. If your request for a hearing is not received within 30 days, DHS will impose the penalty and issue a Final Order, which cannot be appealed.

Hiring or Continuing to Employ Unauthorized Aliens

If DHS or an administrative law judge determines that you have knowingly hired unauthorized aliens (or are continuing to employ aliens knowing that they are or have become unauthorized to work in the United States), you may be ordered to cease and desist from such activity and pay a civil money penalty for each offense.

You will be considered to have knowingly hired an unauthorized alien if, after Nov. 6, 1986, you use a contract, subcontract or exchange, entered into, renegotiated or extended, to obtain the labor of an alien and know the alien is not authorized to work in the United States. You will be subject to the penalties above.

Failing to Comply With Form I-9 Requirements

If you fail to properly complete, retain, and/or make Form I-9 available for inspection as required by law, you may face civil money penalties for each violation. In determining the amount of the penalty, DHS considers:

- The size of the business of the employer being charged;
- The good faith of the employer;
- The seriousness of the violation;
- Whether or not the individual was an unauthorized alien; and
- The history of previous violations of the employer.

Enjoining Pattern or Practice Violations

If the Attorney General has reasonable cause to believe that a person or entity is engaged in a pattern or practice of employment, recruitment or referral in violation of section 274A (a)(1)(A) or (2) of the INA (found at 8 U .S .C. 1324a (a)(1)(A) or (2)), the Attorney General may bring civil action in the appropriate U .S. District Court requesting relief, including a permanent or temporary injunction, restraining order or other order against the person or entity, as the Attorney General deems necessary.

Requiring Indemnification

Employers found to have required a bond or indemnity from an employee against liability under the employer sanctions laws may be ordered to pay a civil money penalty for each violation and to make restitution, either to the person who was required to pay the indemnity, or, if that person cannot be located, to the U.S. Treasury.

Good Faith Defense

If you can show that you have, in good faith, complied with Form I-9 requirements, then you may have established a "good faith" defense with respect to a charge of knowingly hiring an unauthorized alien, unless the government can show that you had actual knowledge of the unauthorized status of the employee.

A good faith attempt to comply with the paperwork requirements of section 274A(b) of the INA may be ad- equate notwithstanding a technical or procedural failure to comply, unless you fail to correct a violation within 10 days after notice from DHS.

Criminal Penalties

Engaging in a Pattern or Practice of Knowingly Hiring or Continuing to Employ Unauthorized Aliens

Persons or entities who are convicted of having engaged in a pattern or practice of knowingly hiring unauthorized aliens (or continuing to employ aliens knowing that they are or have become unauthorized to work in the United States) after Nov. 6, 1986, may face fines and/or six months imprisonment.

Engaging in Fraud or False Statements, or Otherwise Misusing Visas, Immigration Permits, and Identity Documents

Persons who use fraudulent identification or employment authorization documents or documents that were lawfully issued to another person, or who make a false statement or attestation to satisfy the employment eligibility verification requirements, may be fined, or imprisoned for up to five years, or both. Other federal criminal statutes may provide higher penalties in certain fraud cases.

11.7.2 Unlawful Discrimination

If an investigation reveals that you engaged in unfair immigration-related employment practices under the INA, IER may file a lawsuit. Settlements or lawsuits may result in one or more corrective steps, including:

- Hiring or reinstating, with or without back pay, individuals directly injured by the discrimination;
- Posting notices to employees about their rights and about employers' obligations; and/or

- Educating all personnel involved in the hiring process, about the proper procedures for verifying an individual's employment eligibility, and complying with anti-discrimination laws.

The court may award attorneys' fees to prevailing parties, other than the United States, if it determines that the losing parties' argument is without foundation in law and fact.

Employers that violate the anti-discrimination provision of the INA may also be ordered to pay a civil money penalty. For more information on civil penalties, contact IER.

If you are found to have committed national origin or other prohibited discrimination under Title VII or other federal law, you may be ordered to stop the prohibited practice and to take one or more corrective steps, including:

- Hiring, reinstating or promoting with back pay, benefits, and retroactive seniority;

- Posting notices to employees about their rights and about the employer's obligations; and/or

- Removing incorrect information, such as a false warning, from an employee's personnel file.

Under Title VII, compensatory damages may also be avail- able where intentional discrimination is found. Damages may be available to compensate for actual monetary losses, for future monetary losses, and for mental anguish and inconvenience. Punitive damages may be available if you acted with malice or reckless indifference.

You may also be required to pay attorneys' fees, expert witness fees, and court costs.

11.7.3 Civil Document Fraud

If a DHS investigation reveals that an individual has knowingly committed or participated in acts relating to document fraud, DHS may take action. DHS will issue an NIF when it intends to impose penalties. Persons who receive an NIF may request a hearing before an administrative law judge. If DHS does not receive a request for a hearing within 30 days, it will impose the penalty and issue a Final Order, which is final and cannot be appealed.

Individuals found by DHS or an administrative law judge to have violated section 274C of the INA may be ordered to cease and desist from such behavior and to pay a civil money penalty.

11.8 Additional Information

For more information relating to discrimination based upon national origin and citizenship or immigration status, and discrimination during the Form I-9 and E-Verify processes, contact IER at 1-800-255-8155 (employer hotline) or 1-800-237-2515 (TTY for the deaf or hard of hearing); or visit their website at justice.gov/ ier.

For more information on Title VII and EEOC policies and procedures, call 1-800-669-4000, or 1-800-669-6820 (TTY for the deaf or hard of hearing), or visit EEOC's website at eeoc.gov.

12.0 Instructions for Recruiters and Referrers for a Fee

Under the INA, it is unlawful for an agricultural association, agricultural employer, or farm labor contractor to hire, recruit, or refer for a fee an individual for employment in the United States without complying with employment eligibility verification requirements. This provision applies to those agricultural associations, agricultural employers, and farm labor contractors who recruit persons for a fee, and those who refer persons or provide documents or information about persons to employers in return for a fee.

Note: *"Recruiter or Referrer for a Fee" is limited to agricultural associations, agricultural employers, or farm labor contractors as defined in section 3 of the Migrant and Seasonal Agricultural Worker Protection Act, Public Law 97-470 (29 U.S.C. 1802).*

This limited class of recruiters and referrers for a fee must complete Form I-9 when a person they refer is hired. Form I-9 must be fully completed within three business days of the date employment begins, or, in the case of an individual hired for fewer than three business days, at the time employment begins.

Recruiters and referrers for a fee may designate agents, such as national associations or employers, to complete the verification procedures on their behalf. If the employer is designated as the agent, the employer should provide the recruiter or referrer with a photocopy of Form I-9. However, recruiters and referrers for a fee are still responsible for compliance with the law and may be found liable for violations of the law.

Recruiters and referrers for a fee must retain Form I-9 for three years after the date the referred individual was hired by the employer. They must also make Form I-9 available for inspection by a DHS, DOL, or IER officer.

Note: *This does not preclude DHS or DOL from obtaining warrants based on probable cause for entry onto the premises of suspected violators without advance notice.*

The penalties for failing to comply with Form I-9 requirements and for requiring indemnification apply to this limited class of recruiters and referrers for a fee.

Note: *All recruiters and referrers for a fee are still liable for knowingly recruiting or referring for a fee aliens not authorized to work in the United States.*

13.0 Acceptable Documents for Verifying Employment Authorization and Identity

The following documents are acceptable for Form I-9 to establish an employee's employment authorization and identity. The comprehensive Lists of Acceptable Documents can be found here and on the last page of Form I-9. Samples of many of the acceptable documents appear in Sections 13.1 – 13.3.

To establish both identity and employment authorization, a person must present to their employer a document or combination of documents from List A, which shows both identity and employment authorization; or one document from List B, which shows identity and one document from List C, which shows employment authorization.

If a person is unable to present an acceptable document from the List of Acceptable Documents within three business days of the date work for pay begins, the employer must accept an acceptable "receipt" within that time. The employee must indicate by checking an appropriate box in Section 1 that they are authorized to be employed in the United States. The employee must also present the actual document when the receipt validity period ends.

Receipts showing that a person has applied for an initial grant of employment authorization are not acceptable. Receipts are also not acceptable if employment is for fewer than three business days. For a list of acceptable receipts for Form I-9, see Table 1 in Section 4.0. For examples of acceptable employment authorization documents issued by the Department of Homeland Security (List C #7), please visit uscis.gov/i-9-central.

Note that a USCIS-issued Notice on Form I-797C acknowledging receipt of an EAD renewal application presented in combination with an expired EAD is considered an unexpired EAD under List A in certain limited circumstances. See Section 4.2 *Automatic Extensions of Employment Authorization Documents in Certain Circumstances* for more information. This document combination is a List A document and is NOT considered a "receipt" that may be presented in lieu of an acceptable List document.

Sections 13.1-13.3 show the most recent versions and representative images of some of the various acceptable documents on the list. These images can assist you in your review of the document presented to you. These pages are not, however, comprehensive. In some cases, many variations of a particular document exist and new versions may be published subsequent to the publication date of this handbook. Keep in mind that USCIS does not expect you to be a document expert. You are expected to accept documents that reasonably appear to be genuine and to relate to the person presenting them.

LIST A: Documents That Establish Both Identity and Employment Authorization

All documents must be unexpired.

1. U.S. Passport or U.S. Passport Card

2. Permanent Resident Card or Alien Registration Receipt Card (Form I-551)

3. Foreign passport that contains a temporary I-551 stamp or temporary I-551 printed notation on a machine-readable immigrant visa (MRIV)

4. Employment Authorization Document (EAD) that contains a photograph (Form I-766).Form I-766 expired on its face combined with Form I-797 based on an automatic EAD extension in certain circumstances qualifies as unexpired Form I-766; see Section 4.2 *Automatic Extensions of Employment Authorization Documents in Certain Circumstances.*

5. For a nonimmigrant alien authorized to work for a specific employer incident to status, a foreign passport with Form I-94 or Form I-94A bearing the same name as the passport and an endorsement of the alien's nonimmigrant status, as long as the period of endorsement has not yet expired and the proposed employment is not in conflict with any restrictions or limitations identified on the form

6. Passport from the Federated States of Micronesia (FSM) or the Republic of the Marshall Islands (RMI) with Form I-94 or Form I-94A indicating nonimmigrant admission under the Compact of Free Association Between the United States and the FSM or RMI.

LIST B: Documents That Establish Identity

All documents must be unexpired.

For individuals 18 years of age or older:

1. Driver's license or ID card issued by a state or outlying possession of the United States, provided it contains a photograph or information such as name, date of birth, gender, height, eye color, and address

2. ID card issued by federal, state, or local government agencies or entities, provided it contains a photograph or information such as name, date of birth, gender, height, eye color, and address

3. School ID card with a photograph

4. Voter's registration card

5. U.S. military card or draft record

6. Military dependent's ID card

7. U.S. Coast Guard Merchant Mariner Card

8. Native American tribal document

9. Driver's license issued by a Canadian government authority

For persons under age 18 who are unable to present a document listed above:

1. School record or report card

2. Clinic, doctor, or hospital record

3. Day-care or nursery

LIST C: Documents That Establish Employment Authorization

All documents must be unexpired

1. A Social Security Account Number card unless the card includes one of the follwing restrictions:

2. NOT VALID FOR EMPLOYMENT

3. VALID FOR WORK ONLY WITH INS AUTHORIZATION

4. VALID FOR WORK ONLY WITH DHS AUTHORIZATION

5. Certification of report of birth issued by the U.S. Department of State (Forms DS-1350, FS-545, FS-240)

6. Original or certified copy of a birth certificate issued by a state, county, municipal authority or outlying territry of the United States bearing an official seal

7. Native American tribal document

8. U.S. Citizen Identification Card (Form I-197)

9. Identification Card for Use of Resident Citizen in the United States (Form I-179)

10. Employment authorization document issued by the Department of Homeland Security. For examples, please visit uscis.gov/i-9-central

13.1 List A Documents That Establish Identity and Employment Authorization
The illustrations provided do not necessarily reflect the actual size of the documents.

U.S. Passport
The U.S. Department of State issues the U.S. passport to U.S. citizens and noncitizen nationals. There are a small number of versions still in circulation that may differ from the main versions shown here.

Current U.S. Passport cover and open

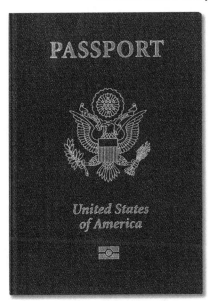 

Older U.S. Passport cover and open

 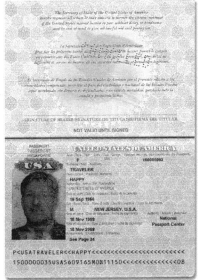

U.S. Passport Card

The U.S. Department of State began producing the passport card in July 2008. The passport card is a wallet- size card that can only be used for land and sea travel between the United States and Canada, Mexico, the Caribbean, and Bermuda.

Passport Card front and back

Permanent Resident Card (Form I-551)

On May 1, 2017 USCIS began issuing a redesigned Permanent Resident Card, Form I-551 (also known as the "Green Card"). The card contains the bearer's photo on the front and back, name, USCIS number, date of birth, card expiration date and laser engraved fingerprint. The new card does not have a signature or an optical stripe on the back. Some Permanent Resident Cards issued after May, 1 2017 may display the previous design format. Both the new and previous versions of the Permanent Resident Card remain valid until the expiration date shown on the card.

Current Permanent Resident Card (Form I-551) front and back

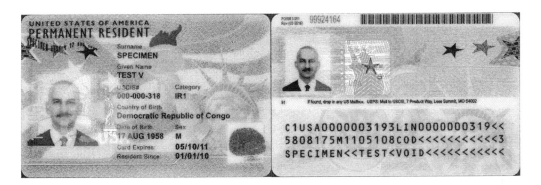

The previous version of the Permanent Resident Card was issued after April 30, 2010.This redesign changed the card color to green. The card is personalized with the bearer's photo, name, USCIS number, alien registration number, date of birth, and laser-engraved fingerprint, as well as the card expiration date. Note that on the card, shown below, the lawful permanent resident's alien registration number, commonly known as the A number, is found under the USCIS # heading. The A number is also located on the back of the card.

These cards may or may not contain a signature. A signature is not required for the card to be acceptable for Form I-9 purposes.

Previous version Permanent Resident Card (Form I-551) front and back

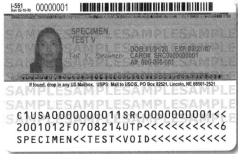

Another older version of the Permanent Resident Card shows the DHS seal and contains a detailed hologram on the front of the card. Each card is personalized with an etching showing the bearer's photo, name, fingerprint, date of birth, alien registration number, card expiration date, and card number.

Also in circulation are older Resident Alien cards, issued by the U.S. Department of Justice, Immigration and Naturalization Service, which do not have expiration dates and are valid indefinitely. These cards are peach in color and contain the bearer's fingerprint and photograph.

Older version Permanent Resident Card (Form I-551) front and back

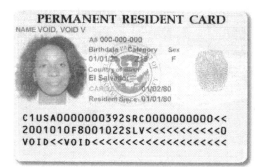

Foreign Passport with I-551 Stamp or MRIV

USCIS uses either an I-551 stamp or a temporary I-551 printed notation on a machine-readable immigrant visa (MRIV) to denote temporary evidence of lawful permanent residence. Sometimes, if no foreign passport is available, USCIS will place the I-551 stamp on a Form I-94 and affix a photograph of the bearer to the form. This document is considered a receipt.

Unexpired Foreign Passport with I-551 Stamp

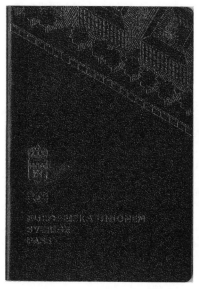

The temporary Form I-551 MRIV is evidence of permanent resident status for one year from the date of admission.

Temporary I-551 printed notation on a machine-readable immigrant visa (MRIV)

Employment Authorization Document (Form I-766)

On May 1, 2017 USCIS began issuing a redesigned Employment Authorization Document (Form I-766) EAD to certain individuals with temporary employment authorization to work in the United States. The card contains the bearer's photograph on the front and back, name, USCIS number, card number, date of birth, laser-engraved fingerprint, and the card expiration date. Cards may contain one of the following notations above the expiration date: "Not Valid for Reentry to U.S.", "Valid for Reentry to U.S." or "Serves as I-512 Parole."

Some EADs issued after May 1, 2017, may still display the previous design format. Both the existing and new EADs will remain valid until the expiration date shown on the card.

Current Employment Authorization Document (Form I-766) with notation "NOT VALID FOR REENTRY TO U.S." front and back

The older version of the Employment Authorization Document (Form I-766) contains the bearer's photograph, fingerprint, card number, Alien number, birth date, and signature, along with a holographic film and the DHS seal. The expiration date is located at the bottom of the card. Cards may contain one of the following notations above the expiration date: "Not Valid for Reentry to U.S.", "Valid for Reentry to U.S." or "Serves as I-512 Advance Parole."

Previous version Employment Authorization Document (Form I-766)

Form I-20 Accompanied by Form I-94 or Form I-94A

Form I-94 or Form I-94A for F-1 nonimmigrant students must be accompanied by a Form I-20, Certificate of Eligibility for Nonimmigrant Students, endorsed with employment authorization by the designated school official for curricular practical training. USCIS will issue an Employment Authorization Document (Form I-766) to all students (F-1 and M-1) authorized for optional practical training (OPT).

Form I-20 Accompanied by Form I-94 or Form I-94A

See Form I-94 below.

Form DS-2019 Accompanied by Form I-94 or Form I-94A

Nonimmigrant exchange visitors (J-1) must have a Form I-94 or Form I-94A accompanied by an unexpired Form DS-2019, Certificate of Eligibility for Exchange Visitor (J-1) Status, issued by the U .S. Department of State, that specifies the sponsor. J-1 exchange students also need a letter from their responsible officer authorizing their employment.

DS-2019 Accompanied by Form I-94 or Form I-94A

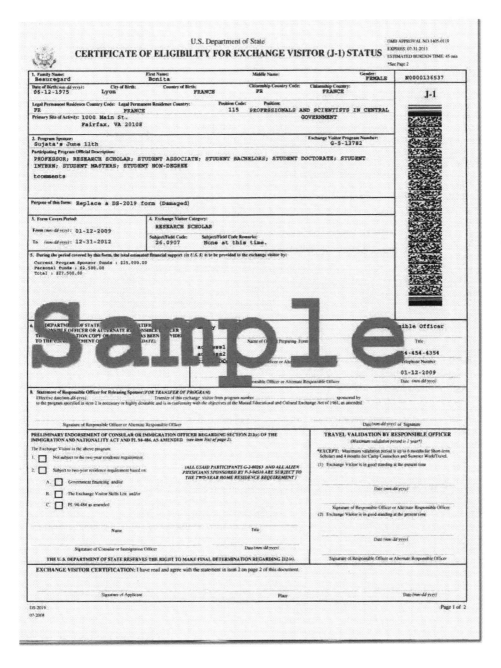

See Form I-94 below.

Form I-94 or Form I-94A Arrival/Departure Record

CBP and sometimes USCIS issue arrival-departure records to nonimmigrants. This document indicates the bearer's immigration status, the date that the status was granted, and when the status expires. The immigration status notation within the stamp on the card varies according to the status granted, for example, L-1, F-1, J-1. Form I-94 can contain a handwritten date and status or be computer-generated. Form I-94A has a computer- generated date and status. Both may be presented with documents that Form I-9 specifies are valid only when Form I-94 or Form I-94A also is presented, such as the foreign passport, Form DS-2019, or Form I-20.

Form I-9 provides space for you to record the document number and expiration date for both the passport and Form I-94 or Form I-94A.

Electronic Form I-94 Arrival/Departure Record

Form I-94 Arrival/Departure Record

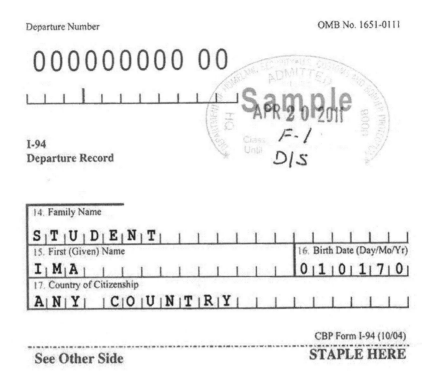

Form I-94A Arrival/Departure Record

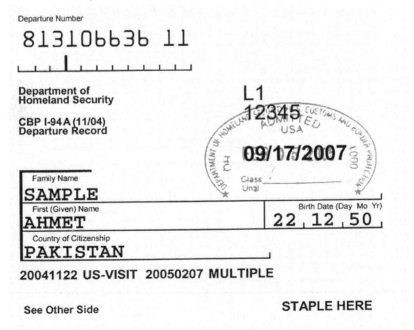

Passport of the Federated States of Micronesia and the Republic of the Marshall Islands

2003, Compacts of Free Association (CFA) between the United States and the Federated States of Micronesia (FSM) and Republic of the Marshall Islands (RMI) were amended to allow citizens of these countries to work in the United States without obtaining an Employment Authorization Document (Form I-766).

For Form I-9 purposes, citizens of these countries may present FSM or RMI passports accompanied by a Form I-94 or Form I-94A indicating nonimmigrant admission under the CFA, which are acceptable documents under List A. The exact notation on Form I-94 or Form I-94A may vary and is subject to change. The notation on Form I-94 or Form I-94A typically states "CFA/FSM" for an FSM citizen and "CFA/MIS" for an RMI citizen.

Passports of the Federated States of Micronesia and the Republic of the Marshall Islands

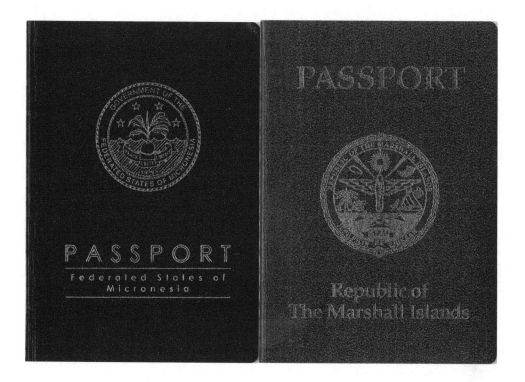

13.2 List B Documents That Establish Identity

The illustrations provided do not necessarily reflect the actual size of the documents.

State-issued Driver's License

A driver's license can be issued by any state or territory of the United States (including the District of Columbia, Puerto Rico, the U .S. Virgin Islands, Guam, American Samoa, and the Commonwealth of the Northern Mariana Islands) or by a Canadian government authority, and is acceptable if it contains a photograph or other identifying information such as name, date of birth, gender, height, eye color, and address.

Some states may place restrictive notations on their drivers' licenses. For Form I-9 purposes, these drivers' licenses may be acceptable.

Driver's License from Mississippi

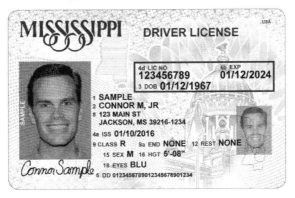

State-issued ID Card

A driver's license can be issued by any state or territory of the United States (including the District of Columbia, Puerto Rico, the U.S. Virgin Islands, Guam, American Samoa, and the Commonwealth of the Northern Mariana Islands) or by a Canadian government authority, and is acceptable if it contains a photograph or other identifying information such as name, date of birth, gender, height, eye color, and address.

Some states may place restrictive notations on their drivers' licenses. For Form I-9 purposes, these drivers' licenses may be acceptable.

Identification card from Mississippi

13.3 List C Documents That Establish Employment Authorization

The illustrations provided do not necessarily reflect the actual size of the documents.

U.S. Social Security Account Number Card

The U.S. Social Security account number card is issued by the Social Security Administration (older versions were issued by the U.S. Department of Health and Human Services), and can be presented as a List C document unless the card specifies that it does not authorize employment in the United States. Metal or plastic reproductions are not acceptable.

U.S. Social Security Card

Certifications of Birth Issued by the U.S. Department of State

These documents may vary in color and paper used. All will include a raised seal of the office that issued the document, and may contain a watermark and raised printing.

Certification of Birth Abroad Issued by the U.S. Department of State (FS-545)

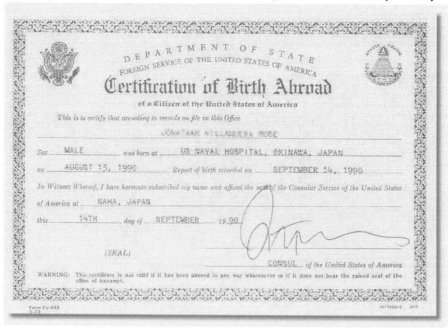

Certification of Report of Birth Issued by the U.S. Department of State (DS-1350)

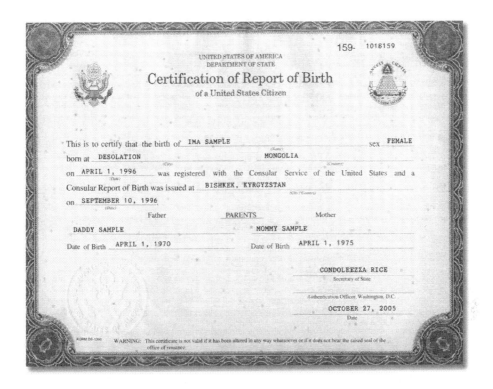

Consular Report of Birth Abroad Issued by the U.S. Department of State (FS-240)

Birth Certificate

Only an original or certified copy of a birth certificate issued by a state, county, municipal authority, or outlying possession of the United States that bears an official seal is acceptable. Versions will vary by state and year of birth.

Beginning October 31, 2010, only Puerto Rico birth certificates issued on or after July 1, 2010 are valid. Please check uscis.gov for guidance on the validity of Puerto Rico birth certificates for Form I-9 purposes.

Birth Certificate

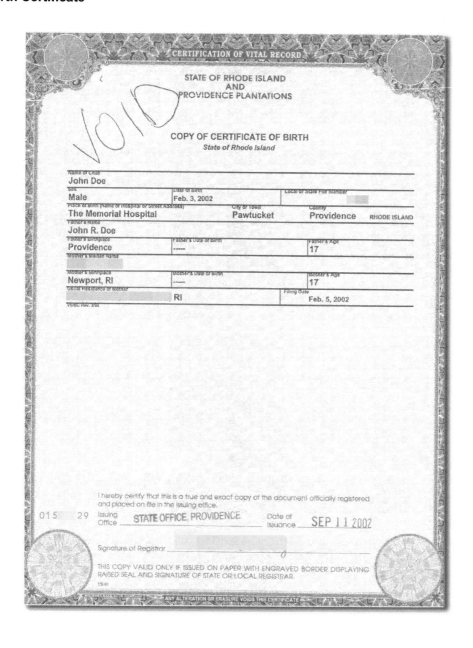

U.S. Citizen Identification Card (Form I-197)

Form I-197 was issued by the former Immigration and Naturalization Service (INS) to naturalized U.S. citizens. Although this card is no longer issued, it is valid indefinitely.

U.S. Citizen Identification Card (Form I-197)

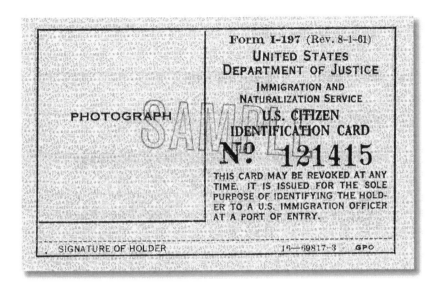

Identification Card for Use of Resident Citizen in the United States (I-179)

Form I-179 was issued by INS to U.S. citizens who are residents of the United States. Although this card is no longer issued, it is valid indefinitely.

Identification Card for Use of Resident Citizen in the United States (I-179)

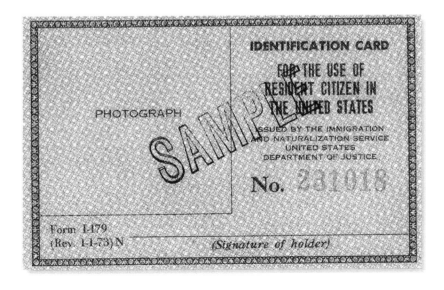

14.0 Some Questions You May Have About Form I-9

Employers should read these questions and answers carefully. They contain valuable information that, in some cases, is not found elsewhere in this handbook.

Employers and employees can find more Form I-9 information on I-9 Central at uscis.gov/i-9-central.

Questions about the Verification Process

1. Q. Do citizens and noncitizen nationals of the United States need to complete Form I-9?

A. Yes. While citizens and noncitizen nationals of the United States are automatically eligible for employment, they too must present the required documents and complete a Form I-9. U.S. citizens include persons born in the United States, Puerto Rico, Guam, the U.S. Virgin Islands, and the Commonwealth of the Northern Mariana Islands. U.S. noncitizen nationals are persons who owe permanent allegiance to the United States, which include those born in American Samoa, including Swains Island.

Note: Citizens of the Federated States of Micronesia (FSM) and the Republic of the Marshall Islands (RMI) are not noncitizen nationals, however they are eligible to work in the U.S.

2. Q. Do I need to complete Form I-9 for employees working in the CNMI?

A. Yes. You need to complete Form I-9 for employees hired for employment in the CNMI on or after Nov. 27, 2011. Employers in CNMI should have used Form I-9 CNMI between Nov. 28, 2009 and Nov. 27, 2011. If the employer did not complete Form I-9 CNMI as required during this period the employer should complete a new Form I-9 as soon as the employer discovers the omission. You should not complete Form I-9 for any employees already working for you on Nov. 27, 2009, even if you assign them new job responsibilities within your company. For more information on federal immigration law in the CNMI, go to uscis.gov/CNMI.

3. Q. Do I need to complete Form I-9 for independent contractors or their employees?

A. No. For example, if you contract with a construction company to perform renovations on your building, you do not have to complete Form I-9 for that company's employees. The construction company is responsible for completing Form I-9 for its own employees. However, you may not use a contract, subcontract or exchange to obtain the labor or services of an employee knowing that the employee is unauthorized to work.

4. Q. May I fire an employee who fails to produce the required documents within three business days of their start date?

A. Yes. You may terminate an employee who fails to produce the required document or documents, or an acceptable receipt for a document, within three business days of the date employment begins.

5. Q. What happens if I properly complete and retain a Form I-9 and DHS discovers that my employee is not actually authorized to work?

A. You cannot be charged with a verification violation. You will also have a good faith defense against the imposition of employer sanctions penalties for knowingly hiring an unauthorized individual, unless the government can show you had knowledge of the unauthorized status of the employee.

Questions about Documents

6. Q. May I specify which documents I will accept for verification?

A. No. The employee may choose which document(s) they want to present from the Lists of Acceptable Documents. You must accept any document (from List A) or combination of documents (one from List B and one from List C) listed on Form I-9 and found in Section 13.0 that reasonably appear on their face to be genuine and to relate to the person presenting them. To do otherwise could be an unfair immigration-related employment practice in violation of the anti-discrimination provision in the INA. Individuals who look and/or sound foreign must not be treated differently in the recruiting, hiring, or verification process. Please see Section 13.0 of this handbook for more information on acceptable documents.

For more information relating to discrimination during the Form I-9 process, contact IER at 1-800-255-8155 (employers) or 1-800-237-2515 (TDD) or visit IER's website at justice.gov/ier.

Note: An employer participating in E-Verify can only accept a List B document with a photograph.

7. Q. What is my responsibility concerning the authenticity of document(s) presented to me?

A. You must physically examine the document(s), and if they reasonably appear on their face to be genuine and to relate to the person presenting them, you must accept them. To do otherwise could be an unfair immigration-related employment practice. If the document(s) do not reasonably appear on their face to be genuine or to relate to the person presenting them, you must not accept them.

However, you must provide the employee with an opportunity to present other documents from the Lists of Acceptable Documents.

8. Q. My employee has presented a U.S. passport card. Is this an acceptable document?

A. Yes. The passport card is a wallet-size document issued by the U.S. Department of State. While its permissible uses for international travel are more limited than the U.S. passport book, the passport card is a fully valid passport that attests to the U.S. citizenship and identity of the bearer. As such, the passport card is considered a "passport" for purposes of Form I-9 and has been included on List A of the Lists of Acceptable Documents on Form I-9.

9. Q. Why was documentation for citizens of the Federated States of Micronesia (FSM) and the Republic of the Marshall Islands (RMI) added to the Lists of Acceptable Documents on Form I-9?

A. Under the Compacts of Free Association between the United States and FSM and RMI, most citizens of FSM and RMI are eligible to reside and work in the United States as nonimmigrants. An amendment to the Compacts eliminated the need for citizens of these two countries to obtain Employment Authorization Documents (Forms I-766) to work in the United States. However, FSM and RMI citizens may also apply for Employment Authorization Documents (Forms I-766) if they wish, or present a combination of List B and List C documents. The List A document specific to FSM and RMI citizens is a valid FSM or RMI passport with a Form I-94/Form I-94A indicating nonimmigrant admission under one of the Compacts.

10. Q. How do I know whether a Native American tribal document issued by a U.S. tribe presented by my employee is acceptable for Form I-9 purposes?

A. In order to be acceptable, a Native American tribal document should be issued by a tribe recognized by the U.S. federal government. Because federal recognition of tribes can change over time, to determine if the tribe is federally recognized, please check the Bureau of Indian Affairs website at bia.gov.

11. Q. Can the Certificate of Indian Status, commonly referred to as the status card or INAC card, be used as a Native American tribal document for Form I-9 purposes?

A. No. This card is not a Native American tribal document. It is issued by Indian and Northern Affairs Canada (INAC), which is a part of the Canadian government.

12. Q. May I accept an expired document?

A. No. Expired documents are no longer acceptable for Form I-9. However, you may accept Employment Authorization Documents (Forms I-766) and Permanent Resident Cards (Forms I-551) that appear to be expired on their face, but have been extended by USCIS.

For example, Temporary Protected Status (TPS) beneficiaries whose Employment Authorization Documents (Forms I-766) appear to be expired may be automatically extended in a Federal Register notice or, if the employee timely filed for a new Employment Authorization Document (Form I-766) the corresponding I-797C from USCIS indicating timely filing may be presented with the expired EAD to the employer as a List A document. These individuals may continue to work based on their expired Employment Authorization Documents (Forms I-766) during the automatic extension period. When the automatic extension of the Employment Authorization Document (Form I-766) expires, you must reverify the employee's employment authorization.

Please see Section 4.2 *Automatic Extensions of Employment Authorization Documents in Certain Circumstances* for more information.

Note: *Some documents, such as birth certificates and Social Security cards, do not contain an expiration date and should be treated as unexpired.*

13. Q. How can I tell if a DHS-issued document has expired? If it has expired, should I reverify the employee?

A. Some INS-issued documents, such as older versions of the Alien Registration Receipt Card (Form I-551), do not have expiration dates, and are still acceptable for Form I-9 purposes. However, all subsequent DHS-issued Permanent Resident Cards (Forms I-551) contain two-year or 10-year expiration dates. You should not reverify an expired Alien Registration Receipt Card/Permanent Resident Card (Form I-551). Other DHS-issued documents, such as the Employment Authorization Document (Form I-766) also have expiration dates. These dates can be found on the face of the document. Generally, Employment Authorization Documents (Forms I-766) must be reverified upon expiration.

14. Q. May I accept a photocopy of a document presented by an employee?

A. No. Employees must present original documents. The only exception is that an employee may present a certified copy of a birth certificate.

15. Q. I noticed on Form I-9 that under List A there are three spaces for document numbers and expiration dates. Does this mean I have to see three List A documents?

A. No. Form I-9 (Rev. 11/14/16 N) includes an expanded document entry area in Section 2. The additional spaces are provided in case an employee presents a List A document that is really a combination of more than one document. For example, an F-1 student in curricular practical training may present, under List A, a foreign passport, Form I-94/Form I-94A and Form I-20 that specifies that you are their approved employer. Form I-9 provides space for you to enter the document number and expiration date for all three documents. Another instance where an employer may need to enter document information for three documents is for J-1 exchange visitors. If an employee provides you with one document from List A (such as a U.S. passport), or a combination of two documents (such as a foreign passport and Form I-94/94A), you do not need to fill out any unused space(s) under List A.

16. Q. When I review an employee's identity and employment authorization documents, should I make copies of them?

A. If you participate in E-Verify and the employee presents a document used as part of Photo Matching, currently the U.S. passport and passport card, Permanent Resident Card (Form I-551) and the Employment Authorization Document (Form I-766), you must retain a photocopy of the document they present. Other documents may be added to Photo Matching in the future. If you do not participate in E-Verify, you are not required to make photocopies of documents. However, if you wish to make photocopies of documents other than those used in E-Verify, you must do so for all employees. Photocopies must not be used for any other purpose. Photocopying documents does not relieve you of your obligation to fully complete Section 2 of Form I-9, nor is it an acceptable substitute for proper completion of Form I-9 in general.

17. Q. When can employees present receipts for documents in lieu of actual documents from the Lists of Acceptable Documents?

A. The "receipt rule" is designed to cover situations in which an employee is authorized to work at the time of initial hire or reverification, but they are not in possession of a document listed on the Lists of Acceptable Documents accompanying Form I-9. Receipts showing that a person has applied for an initial grant of employment authorization are not acceptable.

An individual may present a receipt in lieu of a document listed on Form I-9 to complete Section 2 or Section 3 of Form I-9. The receipt is valid for a temporary period. There are three different documents that qualify as receipts under the rule:

1. A receipt for a replacement document when the document has been lost, stolen, or damaged. The receipt is valid for 90 days, after which the individual must present the replacement document to complete Form I-9.

2. Form I-94/I-94A containing a temporary I-551 stamp and a photograph. The individual must present the actual Form I-551 by the expiration date of the temporary I-551 stamp or within one year from the date of issuance of Form I-94/Form I-94A if the I-551 stamp does not contain an expiration date.

3. A Form I-94/Form I-94A containing an unexpired refugee admission stamp. This is considered a receipt for either an Employment Authorization Document (Form I-766) or a combination of an unrestricted Social Security card and List B document. The employee must present an Employment Authorization Document (Form I-766) or an unrestricted Social Security card in combination with a List B document to complete Form I-9 within 90 days after the date of hire or, in the case of reverification, the date employment authorization expires. For more information on receipts, see Table 1 in <u>Section 4.0</u>.

18. Q. My nonimmigrant employee has presented a foreign passport with a Form I-94/Form I-94A (List A, Item 5). How do I know if this employee is authorized to work?

A. You, as the employer, likely have submitted a petition to USCIS on the nonimmigrant employee's behalf. However, there are some exceptions to this rule:

1. You made an offer of employment to a Canadian passport holder who entered the United States under the North American Free Trade Agreement (NAFTA) with an offer letter from your company. This nonimmigrant worker will have a Form I-94/Form I-94A indicating a TN immigration status, and may choose to present it with their passport under List A. The employee may also present Form I-94/ Form I-94A indicating a TN immigration status as a List C document, in which case your employee will need to present a List B document (such as a Canadian driver's license) to satisfy Section 2 of Form I-9.

2. A student working in on-campus employment or participating in curricular practical training. See Section 7.4.2.

3. A J-1 exchange visitor. See Section 7.4.1.

Most employees who present a foreign passport in combination with a Form I-94 or I-94A (List A, Item 5) are restricted to work only for the employer who petitioned on their behalf. If you did not submit a petition for an employee who presents such documentation, then that non- immigrant worker is not usually authorized to work for you. See Section 7.0 for more information on nonimmigrant employees.

19. Q. My new employee presented two documents to complete Form I-9, each containing a different last name. One document matches the name she entered in Section 1. The employee explained that she had just gotten married and changed her last name, but had not yet changed the name on the other document. Can I accept the document with the different name?

A. You may accept a document with a different name than the name entered in Section 1 provided that you resolve the question of whether the document reasonably relates to the employee. You also may wish to attach a brief memo to Form I-9 stating the reason for the name discrepancy, along with any supporting documentation the employee provides. An employee may provide documentation to support their name change, but is not required to do so. If, however, you determine that the document with a different name does not reasonably appear to be genuine and to relate to her, you may ask her to provide other documents from the Lists of Acceptable Documents on Form I-9.

20. Q. My employee entered a compound last name in Section 1 of Form I-9. The documents she presented contain only one of these names. Can I accept this document?

A. DHS does not require employees to use any specific naming standard for Form I-9. If a new employee enters more than one last name in Section 1, but presents a document that contains only one of those last names, the document they present for Section 2 is acceptable as long as you are satisfied that the document reasonably appears to be genuine and to relate to the employee. It is helpful for individuals attesting to lawful permanent resident status who have more than one name to enter their name on Form I-9 as it appears on their Permanent Resident Card (Form I-551).

21. Q. The name on the document my employee presented to me is spelled slightly differently than the name they entered in Section 1 of Form I-9. Can I accept this document?

A. If the document contains a slight spelling variation, and the employee has a reasonable explanation for the variation, the document is acceptable as long as you are satisfied that the document otherwise reasonably appears to be genuine and to relate to the employee.

22. Q. My employee's Employment Authorization Document (Form I-766) expired and the employee now wants to show me a Social Security card. Do I need to see a current DHS document?

A. No. During reverification, an employee must be allowed to choose what documentation to present from either List A or List C. If an employee presents an unrestricted Social Security card upon reverification, the employee does not also need to present a current DHS document. However, if an employee presents a restricted Social Security card upon reverification, you must reject the restricted Social Security card, since it is not an acceptable Form I-9 document, and ask the employee to choose different documentation from List A or List C of Form I-9.

23. Q. My employee presented me with a document issued by INS rather than DHS. Can I accept it?

A. Yes, you can accept a document issued by INS if the document is unexpired and reasonably appears to be genuine and to relate to the individual presenting it. Effective March 1, 2003, the functions of the former INS were transferred to three agencies within the new DHS: USCIS, CBP, and ICE. Most immigration documents acceptable for Form I-9 use are issued by USCIS. Some documents issued by the former INS before March 1, 2003, such as Permanent Resident Cards or Forms I-94 noting asylee status, may still be within their period of validity. If otherwise acceptable, a document should not be rejected because it was issued by INS rather than DHS. It should also be noted that INS documents may bear dates of issuance after March 1, 2003, as it took some time in 2003 to modify document forms to reflect the new USCIS identity.

Questions about Completing and Retaining Form I-9

24. Q. Can an employee leave any part of Section 1 on Form I-9 blank?

A. Employees must complete every applicable field in Section 1 of Form I-9 with the exception of the Social Security number field. However, employees must enter their Social Security number in this field if you participate in E-Verify. The e-mail address and telephone number fields are optional but if an employee chooses not to provide this information, they must enter "N/A." Do not leave these fields blank.

Note: *Not all employees who attest to being an Alien Authorized to Work will have an expiration date for their employment authorization. However, refugees and asylees who present an Em-*

ployment Authorization Document (Form I-766) EAD have employment authorization that does not expire. These individuals should put "N/A" where Section 1 asks for an expiration date.

25. Q. How do I correct a mistake on an employee's Form I-9?

A. If you find a mistake on an employee's Form I-9, you must have the employee correct errors in Section 1. Employers must make corrections in Section 2. To correct Form I-9 draw a line through the portions of the form that contain incorrect information and then enter the correct information. Initial and date your correction. If you have previously made changes on Form I-9 using correction fluid, USCIS recommends that you attach a note to the corrected Form I-9 explaining what happened. Be sure to sign and date the note.

26. Q. What should I do if I need to reverify an employee who filled out an earlier version of Form I-9?

A. If you used a version of Form I-9 when you originally verified the employee that is no longer valid, and you are now reverifying the employment authorization of that employee, the employee must provide any document(s) they choose from the current Lists of Acceptable Documents. Enter this new document(s) in Section 3 of the current version of Form I-9 and retain it with the previously completed Form I-9. To see if your form is an acceptable version of Form I-9, go to uscis.gov/i-9.

For more information on reverification, please see Section 5.0.

27. Q. Do I need to complete a new Form I-9 when one of my employees is promoted within my company or transfers to another company office at a different location?

A. No. You do not need to complete a new Form I-9 for employees who have been promoted or transferred.

28. Q. What do I do when an employee's employment authorization expires?

A. To continue to employ an individual whose employment authorization has expired, you will need to reverify the employee in Section 3 of Form I-9. Reverification must occur no later than the date that employment authorization expires. The employee must present a document from either List A or List C that shows either an extension of their initial employment authorization or new employment authorization. You must review this document and, if it reasonably appears on its face to be genuine and to relate to the person presenting it, enter the document title, number, and expiration date (if any), in the Reverification and Rehires section (Section 3), and sign in the appropriate space.

If the version of Form I-9 that you used for the employee's original verification is no longer valid, you must complete Section 3 of the current Form I-9 upon reverification and attach it to the original Form I-9.

You may want to establish a calendar notification system for employees whose employment authorization will expire and provide the employee with at least 90 days' notice prior to the expiration date of the employment authorization.

You may not reverify an expired U.S. passport or passport card, an Alien Registration Receipt Card/Permanent Resident Card (Form I-551), or a List B document that has expired.

Some workers are eligible for an automatic extension of their Employment Authorization Document for 180 days, in certain circumstances. If your employee presents an expired Employment Authorization Document (Form I-766) in combination with an I-797C Notice of Action from USCIS indicating both timely filing for a renewal of their Employment Authorization document and eligibility for a 180-day automatic extension of their Employment Authorization Document (Form I-766), you should not reverify the employee based on the expiration date on the face of the Employment Authorization Document (FormI-766); instead, update Section 2 of Form I-9 at that time. When the automatic extension of the Employment Authorization Document (Form I-766) expires (180 days after the expiration date on the face of the Employment Authorization Document (Form I-766)), you must reverify the employee's employment authorization. Please see Section 4.2 Automatic Extensions of Employment Authorization Documents in Certain Circumstances for eligible categories and additional information.

Note: *You cannot refuse to accept a document because it has a future expiration date. You must accept any document (from List A or List C) listed on Form I-9 that on its face reasonably appears to be genuine and to relate to the person presenting it. To do otherwise could be an unfair immigration-related employment practice in violation of the anti-discrimination provision of the INA.*

29. Q. Can I avoid reverifying an employee on Form I-9 by not hiring persons whose employment authorization has an expiration date?

A. No. You cannot refuse to hire persons solely because their employment authorization is temporary. The existence of a future expiration date does not preclude continuous employment authorization for an employee and does not mean that subsequent employment authorization will not be granted. In addition, consideration of a future employment authorization expiration date in determining whether an individual is qualified for a particular job may be an unfair immigration- related employment practice in violation of the anti-discrimination provision of the INA.

30. Q. Can I contract with someone to complete Form I-9 for my business?

A. Yes. You can contract with another person or business to verify employees' identities and employment authorization and to complete Form I-9 for you. However, you are still responsible for the contractor's actions and are liable for any violations of the employer sanctions laws.

31. Q. How does the Immigrant and Employee Rights Section in the Department of Justice's Civil Rights Division (IER) obtain the necessary information to determine whether an employer has committed an unfair immigration-related employment practice under the anti-discrimination provision of the INA?

A. IER will notify you in writing to initiate an investigation, request information and documents, and interview your employees. If you refuse to cooperate, IER can obtain a subpoena to compel you to produce the information requested or to appear for an investigative interview.

32. Q. Do I have to complete Form I-9 for Canadians or Mexicans who entered the United States under the North American Free Trade Agreement (NAFTA)?

A. Yes. You must complete Form I-9 for all employees. NAFTA entrants must show identity and employment authorization documents just like all other employees.

33. Q. If I am a recruiter or referrer for a fee, do I have to fill out Form I-9 on individuals that I recruit or refer?

A. No, with three exceptions: Agricultural associations, agricultural employers, and farm labor contractors must complete Form I-9 on all individuals who are recruited or referred for a fee. However, all recruiters and referrers for a fee must complete Form I-9 for their own employees hired after Nov. 6, 1986. Also, all recruiters and referrers for a fee are liable for knowingly recruiting or referring for a fee individuals not authorized to work in the United States and must comply with federal anti-discrimination laws.

34. Q. If I am self-employed, do I have to fill out a Form I-9 on myself?

A. A self-employed person does not need to complete a Form I-9 on their own behalf unless the person is an employee of a separate business entity, such as a corporation or partnership. If the person is an employee of a separate business entity, he or she, and any other employees, will have to complete Form I-9.

35. Q. I have heard that some state employment agencies, commonly known as state workforce agencies, can certify that people they refer are authorized to work. Is that true?

A. Yes. A state employment agency may choose to verify the employment authorization and identity of an individual it refers for employment on Form I-9. In such a case, the agency must issue a certification to you so that you receive it within 21 business days from the date the referred individual is hired. If an agency refers a potential employee to you with a job order, other appropriate referral form or telephonically authorized referral, and the agency sends you a certification within 21 business days of the referral, you do not have to check documents or complete a Form I-9 if you hire that person. Before receiving the certification, you must retain the job order, referral form, or annotation reflecting the telephonically authorized referral as you would Form I-9. When you receive the certification, you must review the certification to ensure that it relates to the person hired and observe the person sign the certification. You must also retain the certification as you would a Form I-9 and make it available for inspection, if requested. You should check with your state employment agency to see if it provides this service and become familiar with its certification document.

Questions about Avoiding Discrimination

36. Q. What is the INA's Anti-Discrimination Provision?

A. The Immigration and Nationality Act's (INA) anti-discrimination provision, codified at 8 U.S.C. § 1324b, is a law that prohibits certain discriminatory employment practices against workers who are eligible to work in the United States:

- Citizenship or immigration status discrimination with respect to hiring, firing, and recruitment or referral for a fee, by employers with four or more workers, subject to certain exceptions. Employers may not treat individuals differently because they are or are not U.S. citizens or because of their work-authorized immigration status. U.S. citizens, U.S. nationals, recent lawful permanent residents, asylees, and refugees are protected from this type of discrimination under the INA. An employer may restrict hiring to U.S. citizens only when required to do so by law, regulation, executive order, or government contract.

- National origin discrimination with respect to hiring, firing, and recruitment or referral for a fee, by employers with four to 14 workers. Employers may not treat individuals differently because of their place of birth, country of origin, ancestry, native language, accent or because they are perceived as looking or sounding "foreign." The Equal Employment Opportunity Commission has jurisdiction over national origin discrimination claims against employers with 15 or more workers, regardless of the work authorization status of the discrimination victims.

- Unfair documentary practices related to verifying the employment eligibility of employees during the Form I-9 or E-Verify processes. Employers may not, on the basis of citizenship, immigration status, or national origin, request more or different documents than are required to verify employment eligibility and identity, reject reasonably genuine-looking documents, or specify certain documents over others.

- Intimidation or Retaliation. Employers may not intimidate, threaten, coerce, or retaliate against individuals who file charges with IER, who cooperate with an IER investigation, who contest an action that may constitute unfair documentary practices or discrimination based upon citizenship, immigration status, or national origin, or who otherwise assert their rights under the INA's anti-discrimination provision.

37. Q. Can I limit hiring only to U.S. citizens?

A. Employers cannot limit positions to U.S. citizens only unless they are required to do so by a law, executive order, regulation, or government contract that requires specific positions to be filled only by U.S. citizens. If a job applicant is discouraged or rejected from employment based on citizenship status, the employer may be committing citizenship status discrimination in violation of the anti-discrimination provision of the INA.

38. Q. Can I refuse to hire someone based on national origin?

A. Failure to hire an individual based on the person's national origin may violate the anti- discrimination provision of the INA if the employer employs four to 14 employees, or may violate Title VII of the Civil Rights Act (enforced by the Equal Employment Opportunity Commission (EEOC)) if the employer has 15 or more employees. If a small employer has rejected your employment application based on your national origin, contact IER to determine whether IER or the EEOC has jurisdiction to assist you.

39. Q. Can I ask an employee to show a specific document for the Form I-9?

A. No. For employment eligibility verification, an employee must be allowed to choose which documents to show from the Form I-9 Lists of Acceptable Documents. If the documentation reasonably appears to be genuine and to relate to the employee, the employer must accept it. An employer may be violating the anti-discrimination provision of the INA if the employer requires an employee to show specific documents or more documents than required based on the employee's citizenship, immigration status or national origin.

40. Q. Can I refuse to accept an employee's documentation if I would prefer to see another type of documentation?

A. No. For employment eligibility verification, an employee must be allowed to choose which documents to show from the Form I-9 Lists of Acceptable Documents. If the documentation reasonably appears to be genuine and to relate to the employee, the employer must accept it. An employer may be violating the anti-discrimination provision of the INA if the employer rejects the valid documentation an employee presents based on the employee's citizenship, immigration status or national origin.

41. Q. Can I ask my employee to show the same type of document for reverification as the employee showed to complete Section 2?

A. No. For reverification, an employee may choose which unexpired List A or List C document to present. An employer may be violating the anti-discrimination provision of the INA if the employer requires an employee to show specific documents for reverification based on the employee's citizenship, immigration status or national origin.

For more information on these or any other discrimination-related questions, call IER's employer hotline at 1-800-255-8155 or 1-800-237-2515 (TTY). You can also visit IER's website at justice.gov/ier.

For more information on avoiding discrimination in the Form I-9 and E-Verify processes, visit justice.gov/ier.

Questions about Different Versions of Form I-9

42. Q. Is Form I-9 available in different languages?

A. Form I-9 is available in English and Spanish. However, only employers in Puerto Rico may use the Spanish version to meet the verification and retention requirements of the law. Employers in the United States and other U.S. territories may use the Spanish version as a translation guide for Spanish-speaking employees, but the English version must be completed and retained in the employer's records. Employees may also use or ask for a preparer and/or translator to assist them in completing the form.

43. Q. Are employers in Puerto Rico required to use the Spanish version of Form I-9?

A. No. Employers in Puerto Rico may use either the Spanish or the English version of Form I-9 to verify new employees.

44. Q. May I continue to use earlier versions of Form I-9?

A. No, employers must use the current version of Form I-9. A revision date with an "N" next to it indicates that all previous versions with earlier revision dates, in English or Spanish, are no longer valid . You may also use subsequent versions that have a "Y" next to the revision date. If in doubt, go to uscis.gov/i-9-central to view or download the most current form.

45. Q. Where do I get the Spanish version of Form I-9?

A. You may download the Spanish version of this form from the USCIS website at uscis.gov/i-9-central. For employers without internet access, you may call the USCIS Forms Request Line toll-free at 800-870-3676.

For more questions and answers on Form I-9 topics, go to uscis.gov/i-9-central and select I-9 Central Questions & Answers.

REMEMBER:

1. Hiring employees without complying with the employment eligibility verification requirements is a violation of the employer sanctions laws.

2. This law requires employees hired after Nov. 6,1986, to present documentation that establishes identity and employment authorization. Employers must record this information on Form I-9.

3. Employers may not discriminate against employees on the basis of national origin or citizenship status.

U.S. Citizenship and Immigration Services

www.uscis.gov ✦ 1 800 375 5283

APPENDIX C

EXAMPLES OF CORRECT FORMS I-9

Form I-9: Alien Employment Authorization Document, with No Preparer

Employment Eligibility Verification
Department of Homeland Security
U.S. Citizenship and Immigration Services

USCIS
Form I-9
OMB No. 1615-0047
Expires 08/31/2019

▶ **START HERE:** Read instructions carefully before completing this form. The instructions must be available, either in paper or electronically, during completion of this form. Employers are liable for errors in the completion of this form.

ANTI-DISCRIMINATION NOTICE: It is illegal to discriminate against work-authorized individuals. Employers **CANNOT** specify which document(s) an employee may present to establish employment authorization and identity. The refusal to hire or continue to employ an individual because the documentation presented has a future expiration date may also constitute illegal discrimination.

Section 1. Employee Information and Attestation *(Employees must complete and sign Section 1 of Form I-9 no later than the **first day of employment**, but not before accepting a job offer.)*

Last Name *(Family Name)*	First Name *(Given Name)*		Middle Initial	Other Last Names Used *(if any)*		
Diaz	Jose		N/A	Diaz-Lopez		

Address *(Street Number and Name)*		Apt. Number	City or Town		State	ZIP Code
975 Scenic Drive		N/A	Anytown		TN	33321

Date of Birth *(mm/dd/yyyy)*	U.S. Social Security Number	Employee's E-mail Address	Employee's Telephone Number
01/16/1990	9 5 1 - 5 9 - 5 1 3 5	N/A	N/A

I am aware that federal law provides for imprisonment and/or fines for false statements or use of false documents in connection with the completion of this form.

I attest, under penalty of perjury, that I am (check one of the following boxes):

☐ 1. A citizen of the United States

☐ 2. A noncitizen national of the United States *(See instructions)*

☐ 3. A lawful permanent resident (Alien Registration Number/USCIS Number): _____

☒ 4. An alien authorized to work until (expiration date, if applicable, mm/dd/yyyy):   04/01/2017 _____
   Some aliens may write "N/A" in the expiration date field. *(See instructions)*

Aliens authorized to work must provide only one of the following document numbers to complete Form I-9:
An Alien Registration Number/USCIS Number OR Form I-94 Admission Number OR Foreign Passport Number.

1. Alien Registration Number/USCIS Number: 195135796 _____

   OR

2. Form I-94 Admission Number: _____

   OR

3. Foreign Passport Number: _____

   Country of Issuance: _____

QR Code - Section 1
Do Not Write In This Space

Signature of Employee */ Signature /*	Today's Date *(mm/dd/yyyy)* 08/31/2015

Preparer and/or Translator Certification (check one):

☒ I did not use a preparer or translator.   ☐ A preparer(s) and/or translator(s) assisted the employee in completing Section 1.
(Fields below must be completed and signed when preparers and/or translators assist an employee in completing Section 1.)

I attest, under penalty of perjury, that I have assisted in the completion of Section 1 of this form and that to the best of my knowledge the information is true and correct.

Signature of Preparer or Translator	Today's Date *(mm/dd/yyyy)*
Last Name *(Family Name)*	First Name *(Given Name)*

Address *(Street Number and Name)*	City or Town	State	ZIP Code

STOP   *Employer Completes Next Page*   **STOP**

Employment Eligibility Verification
Department of Homeland Security
U.S. Citizenship and Immigration Services

USCIS
Form I-9
OMB No. 1615-0047
Expires 08/31/2019

Section 2. Employer or Authorized Representative Review and Verification

(Employers or their authorized representative must complete and sign Section 2 within 3 business days of the employee's first day of employment. You must physically examine one document from List A OR a combination of one document from List B and one document from List C as listed on the "Lists of Acceptable Documents.")

Employee Info from Section 1	Last Name (Family Name) Diaz	First Name (Given Name) Jose	M.I. N/A	Citizenship/Immigration Status 4

List A Identity and Employment Authorization	OR	List B Identity	AND	List C Employment Authorization
Document Title EAD		Document Title		Document Title
Issuing Authority USCIS		Issuing Authority		Issuing Authority
Document Number 195135796		Document Number		Document Number
Expiration Date (if any)(mm/dd/yyyy) 04/01/2017		Expiration Date (if any)(mm/dd/yyyy)		Expiration Date (if any)(mm/dd/yyyy)
Document Title				
Issuing Authority		Additional Information		QR Code - Sections 2 & 3 Do Not Write In This Space
Document Number				
Expiration Date (if any)(mm/dd/yyyy)				
Document Title				
Issuing Authority				
Document Number				
Expiration Date (if any)(mm/dd/yyyy)				

Certification: I attest, under penalty of perjury, that (1) I have examined the document(s) presented by the above-named employee, (2) the above-listed document(s) appear to be genuine and to relate to the employee named, and (3) to the best of my knowledge the employee is authorized to work in the United States.

The employee's first day of employment *(mm/dd/yyyy):*   08/31/2015   *(See instructions for exemptions)*

Signature of Employer or Authorized Representative *| Signature |*	Today's Date (mm/dd/yyyy) 08/31/2015	Title of Employer or Authorized Representative HR Manager
Last Name of Employer or Authorized Representative Employer	First Name of Employer or Authorized Representative Emily	Employer's Business or Organization Name ABC Widgets

Employer's Business or Organization Address (Street Number and Name) 555 Jackson Lane	City or Town Anytown	State TN	ZIP Code 33322

Section 3. Reverification and Rehires *(To be completed and signed by employer or authorized representative.)*

A. New Name (if applicable)			B. Date of Rehire (if applicable)
Last Name (Family Name)	First Name (Given Name)	Middle Initial	Date (mm/dd/yyyy)

C. If the employee's previous grant of employment authorization has expired, provide the information for the document or receipt that establishes continuing employment authorization in the space provided below.

Document Title EAD	Document Number 195135796	Expiration Date (if any)(mm/dd/yyyy) 03/31/2019

I attest, under penalty of perjury, that to the best of my knowledge, this employee is authorized to work in the United States, and if the employee presented document(s), the document(s) I have examined appear to be genuine and to relate to the individual.

Signature of Employer or Authorized Representative *| Signature |*	Today's Date (mm/dd/yyyy) 03/15/2017	Name of Employer or Authorized Representative Employer, Emily

Form I-9: Alien Employment Authorization Document, with Preparer

Employment Eligibility Verification **Department of Homeland Security** U.S. Citizenship and Immigration Services		**USCIS** **Form I-9** OMB No. 1615-0047 Expires 08/31/2019

▶ **START HERE:** Read instructions carefully before completing this form. The instructions must be available, either in paper or electronically, during completion of this form. Employers are liable for errors in the completion of this form.

ANTI-DISCRIMINATION NOTICE: It is illegal to discriminate against work-authorized individuals. Employers **CANNOT** specify which document(s) an employee may present to establish employment authorization and identity. The refusal to hire or continue to employ an individual because the documentation presented has a future expiration date may also constitute illegal discrimination.

Section 1. Employee Information and Attestation *(Employees must complete and sign Section 1 of Form I-9 no later than the* ***first day of employment,*** *but not before accepting a job offer.)*

Last Name *(Family Name)*	First Name *(Given Name)*	Middle Initial	Other Last Names Used *(if any)*
Wilson	Sam	R	N/A

Address *(Street Number and Name)*	Apt. Number	City or Town	State	ZIP Code
246 Adams Ave	N/A	Anytown	TN	33321

Date of Birth *(mm/dd/yyyy)*	U.S. Social Security Number	Employee's E-mail Address	Employee's Telephone Number
05/19/1968	8 6 4 - 2 0 - 2 4 6 8	sam.wilson@abcwidgets.com	N/A

I am aware that federal law provides for imprisonment and/or fines for false statements or use of false documents in connection with the completion of this form.

I attest, under penalty of perjury, that I am (check one of the following boxes):

☐ 1. A citizen of the United States

☐ 2. A noncitizen national of the United States *(See instructions)*

☐ 3. A lawful permanent resident (Alien Registration Number/USCIS Number): _____

☒ 4. An alien authorized to work until (expiration date, if applicable, mm/dd/yyyy):   12/01/2017
    Some aliens may write "N/A" in the expiration date field. *(See instructions)*

Aliens authorized to work must provide only one of the following document numbers to complete Form I-9:
An Alien Registration Number/USCIS Number OR Form I-94 Admission Number OR Foreign Passport Number.

	QR Code - Section 1 Do Not Write In This Space

1. Alien Registration Number/USCIS Number: 579135678
                OR
2. Form I-94 Admission Number: _____
                OR
3. Foreign Passport Number: _____
    Country of Issuance: _____	

Signature of Employee */ Signature /*	Today's Date *(mm/dd/yyyy)*

Preparer and/or Translator Certification (check one):

☐ I did not use a preparer or translator.   ☒ A preparer(s) and/or translator(s) assisted the employee in completing Section 1.
(Fields below must be completed and signed when preparers and/or translators assist an employee in completing Section 1.)

I attest, under penalty of perjury, that I have assisted in the completion of Section 1 of this form and that to the best of my knowledge the information is true and correct.

Signature of Preparer or Translator */ Signature /*	Today's Date *(mm/dd/yyyy)* 08/31/2017

Last Name *(Family Name)*	First Name *(Given Name)*		
Employer	Emily		

Address *(Street Number and Name)*	City or Town	State	ZIP Code
555 Jackson Lane	Anytown	TN	33322

STOP   *Employer Completes Next Page*   **STOP**

Employment Eligibility Verification
Department of Homeland Security
U.S. Citizenship and Immigration Services

USCIS
Form I-9
OMB No. 1615-0047
Expires 08/31/2019

Section 2. Employer or Authorized Representative Review and Verification

(Employers or their authorized representative must complete and sign Section 2 within 3 business days of the employee's first day of employment. You must physically examine one document from List A OR a combination of one document from List B and one document from List C as listed on the "Lists of Acceptable Documents.")

Employee Info from Section 1	Last Name (Family Name) Wilson	First Name (Given Name) Sam	M.I. R	Citizenship/Immigration Status 4

List A Identity and Employment Authorization	OR	List B Identity	AND	List C Employment Authorization

List A	List B	List C
Document Title **EAD**	Document Title	Document Title
Issuing Authority **USCIS**	Issuing Authority	Issuing Authority
Document Number **579135678**	Document Number	Document Number
Expiration Date (if any)(mm/dd/yyyy) **12/01/2017**	Expiration Date (if any)(mm/dd/yyyy)	Expiration Date (if any)(mm/dd/yyyy)
Document Title		
Issuing Authority	Additional Information	QR Code - Sections 2 & 3 Do Not Write In This Space
Document Number		
Expiration Date (if any)(mm/dd/yyyy)		
Document Title		
Issuing Authority		
Document Number		
Expiration Date (if any)(mm/dd/yyyy)		

Certification: I attest, under penalty of perjury, that (1) I have examined the document(s) presented by the above-named employee, (2) the above-listed document(s) appear to be genuine and to relate to the employee named, and (3) to the best of my knowledge the employee is authorized to work in the United States.

The employee's first day of employment (mm/dd/yyyy): 09/01/2017 (See instructions for exemptions)

Signature of Employer or Authorized Representative / Signature /	Today's Date (mm/dd/yyyy) 09/02/2017	Title of Employer or Authorized Representative HR Manager
Last Name of Employer or Authorized Representative Employer	First Name of Employer or Authorized Representative Emily	Employer's Business or Organization Name ABC Widgets
Employer's Business or Organization Address (Street Number and Name) 555 Jackson Lane	City or Town Anytown	State TN	ZIP Code 33322

Section 3. Reverification and Rehires (To be completed and signed by employer or authorized representative.)

A. New Name (if applicable)			B. Date of Rehire (if applicable)
Last Name (Family Name)	First Name (Given Name)	Middle Initial	Date (mm/dd/yyyy)

C. If the employee's previous grant of employment authorization has expired, provide the information for the document or receipt that establishes continuing employment authorization in the space provided below.

Document Title	Document Number	Expiration Date (if any)(mm/dd/yyyy)

I attest, under penalty of perjury, that to the best of my knowledge, this employee is authorized to work in the United States, and if the employee presented document(s), the document(s) I have examined appear to be genuine and to relate to the individual.

Signature of Employer or Authorized Representative	Today's Date (mm/dd/yyyy)	Name of Employer or Authorized Representative

Form I-9: Lawful Permanent Resident with Green Card, with No Preparer

Employment Eligibility Verification	**USCIS**
Department of Homeland Security	**Form I-9**
U.S. Citizenship and Immigration Services	OMB No. 1615-0047
	Expires 08/31/2019

▶ **START HERE:** Read instructions carefully before completing this form. The instructions must be available, either in paper or electronically, during completion of this form. Employers are liable for errors in the completion of this form.

ANTI-DISCRIMINATION NOTICE: It is illegal to discriminate against work-authorized individuals. Employers **CANNOT** specify which document(s) an employee may present to establish employment authorization and identity. The refusal to hire or continue to employ an individual because the documentation presented has a future expiration date may also constitute illegal discrimination.

Section 1. Employee Information and Attestation *(Employees must complete and sign Section 1 of Form I-9 no later than the **first day of employment**, but not before accepting a job offer.)*

Last Name *(Family Name)*	First Name *(Given Name)*	Middle Initial	Other Last Names Used *(if any)*		
Paul	Christy	E	Smith		

Address *(Street Number and Name)*	Apt. Number	City or Town	State	ZIP Code
642 Madison St.	N/A	Anytown	TN	33321

Date of Birth *(mm/dd/yyyy)*	U.S. Social Security Number	Employee's E-mail Address	Employee's Telephone Number
12/12/1985	4 2 0 - 9 7 - 5 3 1 0	N/A	(615) 516-4202

I am aware that federal law provides for imprisonment and/or fines for false statements or use of false documents in connection with the completion of this form.

I attest, under penalty of perjury, that I am (check one of the following boxes):

☐ 1. A citizen of the United States

☐ 2. A noncitizen national of the United States *(See instructions)*

☒ 3. A lawful permanent resident (Alien Registration Number/USCIS Number):   A789123579

☐ 4. An alien authorized to work until (expiration date, if applicable, mm/dd/yyyy): _____
Some aliens may write "N/A" in the expiration date field. *(See instructions)*

Aliens authorized to work must provide only one of the following document numbers to complete Form I-9:
An Alien Registration Number/USCIS Number OR Form I-94 Admission Number OR Foreign Passport Number.

	QR Code - Section 1
1. Alien Registration Number/USCIS Number: _____	Do Not Write In This Space
OR	
2. Form I-94 Admission Number: _____	
OR	
3. Foreign Passport Number: _____	
Country of Issuance: _____	

Signature of Employee	*| Signature |*	Today's Date *(mm/dd/yyyy)*	08/31/2017

Preparer and/or Translator Certification (check one):
☒ I did not use a preparer or translator.   ☐ A preparer(s) and/or translator(s) assisted the employee in completing Section 1.
(Fields below must be completed and signed when preparers and/or translators assist an employee in completing Section 1.)

I attest, under penalty of perjury, that I have assisted in the completion of Section 1 of this form and that to the best of my knowledge the information is true and correct.

Signature of Preparer or Translator		Today's Date *(mm/dd/yyyy)*
Last Name *(Family Name)*	First Name *(Given Name)*	
Address *(Street Number and Name)*	City or Town	State	ZIP Code

STOP *Employer Completes Next Page* **STOP**

<table>
<tr><td colspan="2">Employment Eligibility Verification
Department of Homeland Security
U.S. Citizenship and Immigration Services</td><td>USCIS
Form I-9
OMB No. 1615-0047
Expires 08/31/2019</td></tr>
</table>

Section 2. Employer or Authorized Representative Review and Verification

(Employers or their authorized representative must complete and sign Section 2 within 3 business days of the employee's first day of employment. You must physically examine one document from List A OR a combination of one document from List B and one document from List C as listed on the "Lists of Acceptable Documents.")

Employee Info from Section 1	Last Name *(Family Name)* Paul	First Name *(Given Name)* Christy	M.I. E	Citizenship/Immigration Status 3

List A Identity and Employment Authorization	OR	List B Identity	AND	List C Employment Authorization
Document Title Permanent Resident Card		**Document Title**		**Document Title**
Issuing Authority USCIS		**Issuing Authority**		**Issuing Authority**
Document Number A789123579		**Document Number**		**Document Number**
Expiration Date *(if any)(mm/dd/yyyy)* 11/30/2022		**Expiration Date** *(if any)(mm/dd/yyyy)*		**Expiration Date** *(if any)(mm/dd/yyyy)*
Document Title				
Issuing Authority		**Additional Information**		QR Code - Sections 2 & 3 Do Not Write In This Space
Document Number				
Expiration Date *(if any)(mm/dd/yyyy)*				
Document Title				
Issuing Authority				
Document Number				
Expiration Date *(if any)(mm/dd/yyyy)*				

Certification: I attest, under penalty of perjury, that (1) I have examined the document(s) presented by the above-named employee, (2) the above-listed document(s) appear to be genuine and to relate to the employee named, and (3) to the best of my knowledge the employee is authorized to work in the United States.

The employee's first day of employment *(mm/dd/yyyy)*:   09/01/2017   *(See instructions for exemptions)*

Signature of Employer or Authorized Representative */ Signature /*	Today's Date *(mm/dd/yyyy)* 09/02/2017	Title of Employer or Authorized Representative HR Manager
Last Name of Employer or Authorized Representative Employer	First Name of Employer or Authorized Representative Emily	Employer's Business or Organization Name ABC Widgets

Employer's Business or Organization Address (Street Number and Name) 555 Jackson Lane	City or Town Anytown	State TN	ZIP Code 33322

Section 3. Reverification and Rehires *(To be completed and signed by employer or authorized representative.)*

A. New Name *(if applicable)*			B. Date of Rehire *(if applicable)*
Last Name *(Family Name)*	First Name *(Given Name)*	Middle Initial	Date *(mm/dd/yyyy)*

C. If the employee's previous grant of employment authorization has expired, provide the information for the document or receipt that establishes continuing employment authorization in the space provided below.

Document Title	Document Number	Expiration Date *(if any)(mm/dd/yyyy)*

I attest, under penalty of perjury, that to the best of my knowledge, this employee is authorized to work in the United States, and if the employee presented document(s), the document(s) I have examined appear to be genuine and to relate to the individual.

Signature of Employer or Authorized Representative	Today's Date *(mm/dd/yyyy)*	Name of Employer or Authorized Representative

Form I-9: U.S. Citizen with Driver's License

Employment Eligibility Verification		**USCIS**
Department of Homeland Security		**Form I-9**
U.S. Citizenship and Immigration Services		OMB No. 1615-0047
		Expires 08/31/2019

▶ **START HERE:** Read instructions carefully before completing this form. The instructions must be available, either in paper or electronically, during completion of this form. Employers are liable for errors in the completion of this form.

ANTI-DISCRIMINATION NOTICE: It is illegal to discriminate against work-authorized individuals. Employers **CANNOT** specify which document(s) an employee may present to establish employment authorization and identity. The refusal to hire or continue to employ an individual because the documentation presented has a future expiration date may also constitute illegal discrimination.

Section 1. Employee Information and Attestation *(Employees must complete and sign Section 1 of Form I-9 no later than the **first day of employment**, but not before accepting a job offer.)*

Last Name *(Family Name)*	First Name *(Given Name)*	Middle Initial	Other Last Names Used *(if any)*
Wilson	Roberta	W	Crosby

Address *(Street Number and Name)*	Apt. Number	City or Town	State	ZIP Code
543 Washington Dr.	19	Anytown	TN	33321

Date of Birth *(mm/dd/yyyy)*	U.S. Social Security Number	Employee's E-mail Address	Employee's Telephone Number
09/14/1987	7 5 3 - 1 3 - 5 7 9 1	N/A	N/A

I am aware that federal law provides for imprisonment and/or fines for false statements or use of false documents in connection with the completion of this form.

I attest, under penalty of perjury, that I am (check one of the following boxes):

☒ 1. A citizen of the United States

☐ 2. A noncitizen national of the United States *(See instructions)*

☐ 3. A lawful permanent resident (Alien Registration Number/USCIS Number): _____

☐ 4. An alien authorized to work until (expiration date, if applicable, mm/dd/yyyy): _____
Some aliens may write "N/A" in the expiration date field. *(See instructions)*

Aliens authorized to work must provide only one of the following document numbers to complete Form I-9:
An Alien Registration Number/USCIS Number OR Form I-94 Admission Number OR Foreign Passport Number.

QR Code - Section 1
Do Not Write In This Space

1. Alien Registration Number/USCIS Number: _____
OR
2. Form I-94 Admission Number: _____
OR
3. Foreign Passport Number: _____
Country of Issuance: _____

Signature of Employee *| Signature |*	Today's Date *(mm/dd/yyyy)* 08/31/2017

Preparer and/or Translator Certification (check one):
☒ I did not use a preparer or translator.   ☐ A preparer(s) and/or translator(s) assisted the employee in completing Section 1.
(Fields below must be completed and signed when preparers and/or translators assist an employee in completing Section 1.)

I attest, under penalty of perjury, that I have assisted in the completion of Section 1 of this form and that to the best of my knowledge the information is true and correct.

Signature of Preparer or Translator		Today's Date *(mm/dd/yyyy)*
Last Name *(Family Name)*		First Name *(Given Name)*

Address *(Street Number and Name)*	City or Town	State	ZIP Code

🛑   *Employer Completes Next Page*   🛑

Employment Eligibility Verification
Department of Homeland Security
U.S. Citizenship and Immigration Services

USCIS
Form I-9
OMB No. 1615-0047
Expires 08/31/2019

Section 2. Employer or Authorized Representative Review and Verification

(Employers or their authorized representative must complete and sign Section 2 within 3 business days of the employee's first day of employment. You must physically examine one document from List A OR a combination of one document from List B and one document from List C as listed on the "Lists of Acceptable Documents.")

Employee Info from Section 1	Last Name *(Family Name)* Wilson	First Name *(Given Name)* Roberta	M.I. W	Citizenship/Immigration Status 1

List A — Identity and Employment Authorization	OR	List B — Identity	AND	List C — Employment Authorization
Document Title		Document Title Driver's License		Document Title SS Card
Issuing Authority		Issuing Authority State of TN		Issuing Authority SSA
Document Number		Document Number 86420246		Document Number 753-13-5791
Expiration Date *(if any)(mm/dd/yyyy)*		Expiration Date *(if any)(mm/dd/yyyy)* 09/30/2019		Expiration Date *(if any)(mm/dd/yyyy)*
Document Title				
Issuing Authority		Additional Information		QR Code - Sections 2 & 3 Do Not Write In This Space
Document Number				
Expiration Date *(if any)(mm/dd/yyyy)*				
Document Title				
Issuing Authority				
Document Number				
Expiration Date *(if any)(mm/dd/yyyy)*				

Certification: I attest, under penalty of perjury, that (1) I have examined the document(s) presented by the above-named employee, (2) the above-listed document(s) appear to be genuine and to relate to the employee named, and (3) to the best of my knowledge the employee is authorized to work in the United States.

The employee's first day of employment *(mm/dd/yyyy)*: 09/01/2017   *(See instructions for exemptions)*

Signature of Employer or Authorized Representative */ Signature /*	Today's Date *(mm/dd/yyyy)* 09/03/2017	Title of Employer or Authorized Representative HR Manager
Last Name of Employer or Authorized Representative Employer	First Name of Employer or Authorized Representative Emily	Employer's Business or Organization Name ABC Widgets

Employer's Business or Organization Address (Street Number and Name) 555 Jackson Lane	City or Town Anytown	State TN	ZIP Code 33322

Section 3. Reverification and Rehires *(To be completed and signed by employer or authorized representative.)*

A. New Name *(if applicable)*			B. Date of Rehire *(if applicable)*
Last Name *(Family Name)*	First Name *(Given Name)*	Middle Initial	Date *(mm/dd/yyyy)*

C. If the employee's previous grant of employment authorization has expired, provide the information for the document or receipt that establishes continuing employment authorization in the space provided below.

Document Title	Document Number	Expiration Date *(if any)(mm/dd/yyyy)*

I attest, under penalty of perjury, that to the best of my knowledge, this employee is authorized to work in the United States, and if the employee presented document(s), the document(s) I have examined appear to be genuine and to relate to the individual.

Signature of Employer or Authorized Representative	Today's Date *(mm/dd/yyyy)*	Name of Employer or Authorized Representative

Form I-9: U.S. Citizen with Passport

Employment Eligibility Verification
Department of Homeland Security
U.S. Citizenship and Immigration Services

USCIS
Form I-9
OMB No. 1615-0047
Expires 08/31/2019

▶ **START HERE:** Read instructions carefully before completing this form. The instructions must be available, either in paper or electronically, during completion of this form. Employers are liable for errors in the completion of this form.

ANTI-DISCRIMINATION NOTICE: It is illegal to discriminate against work-authorized individuals. Employers **CANNOT** specify which document(s) an employee may present to establish employment authorization and identity. The refusal to hire or continue to employ an individual because the documentation presented has a future expiration date may also constitute illegal discrimination.

Section 1. Employee Information and Attestation *(Employees must complete and sign Section 1 of Form I-9 no later than the first day of employment, but not before accepting a job offer.)*

Last Name *(Family Name)*	First Name *(Given Name)*	Middle Initial	Other Last Names Used *(if any)*
James	Jesse	J	N/A

Address *(Street Number and Name)*	Apt. Number	City or Town	State	ZIP Code
543 Mud Lane		Anytown	TN	33321

Date of Birth *(mm/dd/yyyy)*	U.S. Social Security Number	Employee's E-mail Address	Employee's Telephone Number
12/12/1970	4 2 0 - 2 4 - 6 8 0 1	jesse.james@aol.com	N/A

I am aware that federal law provides for imprisonment and/or fines for false statements or use of false documents in connection with the completion of this form.

I attest, under penalty of perjury, that I am (check one of the following boxes):

☒ 1. A citizen of the United States

☐ 2. A noncitizen national of the United States *(See instructions)*

☐ 3. A lawful permanent resident *(Alien Registration Number/USCIS Number):* _____

☐ 4. An alien authorized to work until (expiration date, if applicable, mm/dd/yyyy): _____
Some aliens may write "N/A" in the expiration date field. *(See instructions)*

Aliens authorized to work must provide only one of the following document numbers to complete Form I-9:
An Alien Registration Number/USCIS Number OR Form I-94 Admission Number OR Foreign Passport Number.

1. Alien Registration Number/USCIS Number: _____
OR
2. Form I-94 Admission Number: _____
OR
3. Foreign Passport Number: _____
Country of Issuance: _____

QR Code - Section 1
Do Not Write In This Space

Signature of Employee	*| Signature |*	Today's Date *(mm/dd/yyyy)*

Preparer and/or Translator Certification (check one):
☒ I did not use a preparer or translator. ☐ A preparer(s) and/or translator(s) assisted the employee in completing Section 1.
(Fields below must be completed and signed when preparers and/or translators assist an employee in completing Section 1.)

I attest, under penalty of perjury, that I have assisted in the completion of Section 1 of this form and that to the best of my knowledge the information is true and correct.

Signature of Preparer or Translator	Today's Date *(mm/dd/yyyy)*

Last Name *(Family Name)*	First Name *(Given Name)*

Address *(Street Number and Name)*	City or Town	State	ZIP Code

🛑 *Employer Completes Next Page* 🛑

| | | **Employment Eligibility Verification**
Department of Homeland Security
U.S. Citizenship and Immigration Services | **USCIS**
Form I-9
OMB No. 1615-0047
Expires 08/31/2019 |

Section 2. Employer or Authorized Representative Review and Verification

(Employers or their authorized representative must complete and sign Section 2 within 3 business days of the employee's first day of employment. You must physically examine one document from List A OR a combination of one document from List B and one document from List C as listed on the "Lists of Acceptable Documents.")

Employee Info from Section 1	Last Name *(Family Name)* James	First Name *(Given Name)* Jesse	M.I. J	Citizenship/Immigration Status 1

List A Identity and Employment Authorization	OR	List B Identity	AND	List C Employment Authorization

List A	List B	List C
Document Title Passport	Document Title	Document Title
Issuing Authority U.S. Gov't	Issuing Authority	Issuing Authority
Document Number 15951484	Document Number	Document Number
Expiration Date *(if any)(mm/dd/yyyy)* 12/15/2022	Expiration Date *(if any)(mm/dd/yyyy)*	Expiration Date *(if any)(mm/dd/yyyy)*
Document Title		
Issuing Authority	Additional Information	QR Code - Sections 2 & 3 Do Not Write In This Space
Document Number		
Expiration Date *(if any)(mm/dd/yyyy)*		
Document Title		
Issuing Authority		
Document Number		
Expiration Date *(if any)(mm/dd/yyyy)*		

Certification: I attest, under penalty of perjury, that (1) I have examined the document(s) presented by the above-named employee, (2) the above-listed document(s) appear to be genuine and to relate to the employee named, and (3) to the best of my knowledge the employee is authorized to work in the United States.

The employee's first day of employment *(mm/dd/yyyy)*:   09/01/2017   *(See instructions for exemptions)*

Signature of Employer or Authorized Representative */ Signature /*	Today's Date *(mm/dd/yyyy)* 09/01/2017	Title of Employer or Authorized Representative HR Manager
Last Name of Employer or Authorized Representative Employer	First Name of Employer or Authorized Representative Emily	Employer's Business or Organization Name ABC Widgets

Employer's Business or Organization Address (Street Number and Name) 555 Jackson Lane	City or Town Anytown	State TN	ZIP Code 33322

Section 3. Reverification and Rehires *(To be completed and signed by employer or authorized representative.)*

A. New Name *(if applicable)*			B. Date of Rehire *(if applicable)*
Last Name *(Family Name)*	First Name *(Given Name)*	Middle Initial	Date *(mm/dd/yyyy)*

C. If the employee's previous grant of employment authorization has expired, provide the information for the document or receipt that establishes continuing employment authorization in the space provided below.

Document Title	Document Number	Expiration Date *(if any)(mm/dd/yyyy)*

I attest, under penalty of perjury, that to the best of my knowledge, this employee is authorized to work in the United States, and if the employee presented document(s), the document(s) I have examined appear to be genuine and to relate to the individual.

Signature of Employer or Authorized Representative	Today's Date *(mm/dd/yyyy)*	Name of Employer or Authorized Representative

APPENDIX D

EXAMPLES OF INCORRECT FORMS I-9

Form I-9: U.S. Citizen with Expired Driver's License, Missing Document

Employment Eligibility Verification

Department of Homeland Security
U.S. Citizenship and Immigration Services

USCIS
Form I-9
OMB No. 1615-0047
Expires 08/31/2019

▶ **START HERE:**   Read instructions carefully before completing this form. The instructions must be available, either in paper or electronically, during completion of this form. Employers are liable for errors in the completion of this form.

ANTI-DISCRIMINATION NOTICE: It is illegal to discriminate against work-authorized individuals. Employers **CANNOT** specify which document(s) an employee may present to establish employment authorization and identity. The refusal to hire or continue to employ an individual because the documentation presented has a future expiration date may also constitute illegal discrimination.

Section 1. Employee Information and Attestation *(Employees must complete and sign Section 1 of Form I-9 no later than the* **first day of employment***, but not before accepting a job offer.)*

Last Name *(Family Name)*	First Name *(Given Name)*	Middle Initial	Other Last Names Used *(if any)*
Smith	Jane	A	N/A

Address *(Street Number and Name)*	Apt. Number	City or Town	State	ZIP Code
123 Main Street	N/A	Anytown	TN	33321

Date of Birth *(mm/dd/yyyy)*	U.S. Social Security Number	Employee's E-mail Address	Employee's Telephone Number
12/20/1967	9 8 7 - 6 5 - 4 3 2 1	N/A	555-555-5421

I am aware that federal law provides for imprisonment and/or fines for false statements or use of false documents in connection with the completion of this form.

I attest, under penalty of perjury, that I am (check one of the following boxes):

- ☒ 1. A citizen of the United States
- ☐ 2. A noncitizen national of the United States *(See instructions)*
- ☐ 3. A lawful permanent resident (Alien Registration Number/USCIS Number): _____
- ☐ 4. An alien authorized to work until (expiration date, if applicable, mm/dd/yyyy): _____
  Some aliens may write "N/A" in the expiration date field. *(See instructions)*

Aliens authorized to work must provide only one of the following document numbers to complete Form I-9:
An Alien Registration Number/USCIS Number OR Form I-94 Admission Number OR Foreign Passport Number.

1. Alien Registration Number/USCIS Number: _____

   OR

2. Form I-94 Admission Number: _____

   OR

3. Foreign Passport Number: _____

   Country of Issuance: _____

QR Code - Section 1
Do Not Write In This Space

Signature of Employee */ Signature /*	Today's Date *(mm/dd/yyyy)* 09/02/2017

Preparer and/or Translator Certification (check one):
☒ I did not use a preparer or translator.   ☐ A preparer(s) and/or translator(s) assisted the employee in completing Section 1.
(Fields below must be completed and signed when preparers and/or translators assist an employee in completing Section 1.)

I attest, under penalty of perjury, that I have assisted in the completion of Section 1 of this form and that to the best of my knowledge the information is true and correct.

Signature of Preparer or Translator	Today's Date *(mm/dd/yyyy)*
Last Name *(Family Name)*	First Name *(Given Name)*

Address *(Street Number and Name)*	City or Town	State	ZIP Code

🛑   *Employer Completes Next Page*   🛑

Employment Eligibility Verification
Department of Homeland Security
U.S. Citizenship and Immigration Services

USCIS
Form I-9
OMB No. 1615-0047
Expires 08/31/2019

Section 2. Employer or Authorized Representative Review and Verification

(Employers or their authorized representative must complete and sign Section 2 within 3 business days of the employee's first day of employment. You must physically examine one document from List A OR a combination of one document from List B and one document from List C as listed on the "Lists of Acceptable Documents.")

Employee Info from Section 1	Last Name *(Family Name)* Smith	First Name *(Given Name)* Jane	M.I. A	Citizenship/Immigration Status 1

List A Identity and Employment Authorization	OR	List B Identity	AND	List C Employment Authorization

List A	List B	List C
Document Title	Document Title Driver's Licence	Document Title
Issuing Authority	Issuing Authority Tennessee	Issuing Authority
Document Number	Document Number 2535450	Document Number — Missing List C document
Expiration Date *(if any)(mm/dd/yyyy)*	Expiration Date *(if any)(mm/dd/yyyy)* 01/01/2014	Expiration Date *(if any)(mm/dd/yyyy)*
Document Title		
Issuing Authority	Additional Information — Expired - should not accept	QR Code - Sections 2 & 3 Do Not Write In This Space
Document Number		
Expiration Date *(if any)(mm/dd/yyyy)*		
Document Title		
Issuing Authority		
Document Number	Signature missing	
Expiration Date *(if any)(mm/dd/yyyy)*		

Certification: I attest, under penalty of perjury, that (1) I have examined the document(s) presented by the above-named employee, (2) the above-listed document(s) appear to be genuine and to relate to the employee named, and (3) to the best of my knowledge the employee is authorized to work in the United States.

The employee's first day of employment *(mm/dd/yyyy)*: 09/01/2017   *(See instructions for exemptions)*

Signature of Employer or Authorized Representative	Today's Date *(mm/dd/yyyy)* 09/01/2017	Title of Employer or Authorized Representative HR Manager
Last Name of Employer or Authorized Representative Employer	First Name of Employer or Authorized Representative Emily	Employer's Business or Organization Name ABC Widgets
Employer's Business or Organization Address (Street Number and Name) 555 Jackson Lane	City or Town Anytown	State TN	ZIP Code 33322

Section 3. Reverification and Rehires *(To be completed and signed by employer or authorized representative.)*

A. New Name *(if applicable)*			B. Date of Rehire *(if applicable)*
Last Name *(Family Name)*	First Name *(Given Name)*	Middle Initial	Date *(mm/dd/yyyy)*

C. If the employee's previous grant of employment authorization has expired, provide the information for the document or receipt that establishes continuing employment authorization in the space provided below.

Document Title	Document Number	Expiration Date *(if any)(mm/dd/yyyy)*

I attest, under penalty of perjury, that to the best of my knowledge, this employee is authorized to work in the United States, and if the employee presented document(s), the document(s) I have examined appear to be genuine and to relate to the individual.

Signature of Employer or Authorized Representative	Today's Date *(mm/dd/yyyy)*	Name of Employer or Authorized Representative

Form I-9: Alien with Employment Authorization Document, Box Not Checked, Incorrect SSN

Employment Eligibility Verification
Department of Homeland Security
U.S. Citizenship and Immigration Services

USCIS
Form I-9
OMB No. 1615-0047
Expires 08/31/2019

▶ **START HERE:** Read instructions carefully before completing this form. The instructions must be available, either in paper or electronically, during completion of this form. Employers are liable for errors in the completion of this form.

ANTI-DISCRIMINATION NOTICE: It is illegal to discriminate against work-authorized individuals. Employers **CANNOT** specify which document(s) an employee may present to establish employment authorization and identity. The refusal to hire or continue to employ an individual because the documentation presented has a future expiration date may also constitute illegal discrimination.

Section 1. Employee Information and Attestation *(Employees must complete and sign Section 1 of Form I-9 no later than the **first day of employment**, but not before accepting a job offer.)*

Last Name *(Family Name)*	First Name *(Given Name)*	Middle Initial	Other Last Names Used *(if any)*
Smith	Sam	A.	N/A

Address *(Street Number and Name)*	Apt. Number	City or Town	State	ZIP Code
437 Smith Cove	N/A	Incorrect SS#	TN	33321

Date of Birth *(mm/dd/yyyy)*	U.S. Social Security Number	Employee's E-mail Address	Employee's Telephone Number
12/20/1967	0 0 0 - 0 0 - 0 0 0 0	N/A	555-123-1234

I am aware that federal law provides for imprisonment and/or fines for false statements or use of false documents in connection with the completion of this form.

No box checked

I attest, under penalty of perjury, that I am (check one of the following boxes):

☐ 1. A citizen of the United States

☐ 2. A noncitizen national of the United States *(See instructions)*

☐ 3. A lawful permanent resident (Alien Registration Number/USCIS Number): _____

☐ 4. An alien authorized to work until (expiration date, if applicable, mm/dd/yyyy): _____
Some aliens may write "N/A" in the expiration date field. *(See instructions)*

Aliens authorized to work must provide only one of the following document numbers to complete Form I-9:
An Alien Registration Number/USCIS Number OR Form I-94 Admission Number OR Foreign Passport Number.

1. Alien Registration Number/USCIS Number: _____
OR
2. Form I-94 Admission Number: _____
OR
3. Foreign Passport Number: _____

Country of Issuance: _____

QR Code - Section 1
Do Not Write In This Space

Signature of Employee */ Signature /*	Today's Date *(mm/dd/yyyy)* 08/31/2017

Preparer and/or Translator Certification (check one):
☒ I did not use a preparer or translator.   ☐ A preparer(s) and/or translator(s) assisted the employee in completing Section 1.
(Fields below must be completed and signed when preparers and/or translators assist an employee in completing Section 1.)

I attest, under penalty of perjury, that I have assisted in the completion of Section 1 of this form and that to the best of my knowledge the information is true and correct.

Signature of Preparer or Translator	Today's Date *(mm/dd/yyyy)*

Last Name *(Family Name)*	First Name *(Given Name)*

Address *(Street Number and Name)*	City or Town	State	ZIP Code

 Employer Completes Next Page

Employment Eligibility Verification

Department of Homeland Security

U.S. Citizenship and Immigration Services

USCIS
Form I-9
OMB No. 1615-0047
Expires 08/31/2019

Section 2. Employer or Authorized Representative Review and Verification

(Employers or their authorized representative must complete and sign Section 2 within 3 business days of the employee's first day of employment. You must physically examine one document from List A OR a combination of one document from List B and one document from List C as listed on the "Lists of Acceptable Documents.")

Employee Info from Section 1	Last Name *(Family Name)* Smith	First Name *(Given Name)* Sam	M.I. A.	Citizenship/Immigration Status

List A Identity and Employment Authorization	OR	List B Identity	AND	List C Employment Authorization
Document Title EAD (Form I-766)		Document Title		Document Title *Missing 4 in box*
Issuing Authority USCIS		Issuing Authority		Issuing Authority
Document Number 07531357		Document Number		Document Number
Expiration Date *(if any)(mm/dd/yyyy)* 12/31/2017		Expiration Date *(if any)(mm/dd/yyyy)*		Expiration Date *(if any)(mm/dd/yyyy)*
Document Title				
Issuing Authority		Additional Information		QR Code - Sections 2 & 3 Do Not Write In This Space
Document Number				
Expiration Date *(if any)(mm/dd/yyyy)*				
Document Title				
Issuing Authority				
Document Number				
Expiration Date *(if any)(mm/dd/yyyy)*				

Certification: I attest, under penalty of perjury, that (1) I have examined the document(s) presented by the above-named employee, (2) the above-listed document(s) appear to be genuine and to relate to the employee named, and (3) to the best of my knowledge the employee is authorized to work in the United States.

The employee's first day of employment *(mm/dd/yyyy)*:   09/01/2017   *(See instructions for exemptions)*

Signature of Employer or Authorized Representative */ Signature /*	Today's Date *(mm/dd/yyyy)* 09/01/2017	Title of Employer or Authorized Representative HR Manager
Last Name of Employer or Authorized Representative Employer	First Name of Employer or Authorized Representative Emily	Employer's Business or Organization Name ABC Widgets

Employer's Business or Organization Address (Street Number and Name) 555 Jackson Lane	City or Town Anytown	State TN	ZIP Code 33322

Section 3. Reverification and Rehires *(To be completed and signed by employer or authorized representative.)*

A. New Name *(if applicable)*			B. Date of Rehire *(if applicable)*
Last Name *(Family Name)*	First Name *(Given Name)*	Middle Initial	Date *(mm/dd/yyyy)*

C. If the employee's previous grant of employment authorization has expired, provide the information for the document or receipt that establishes continuing employment authorization in the space provided below.

Document Title	Document Number	Expiration Date *(if any)(mm/dd/yyyy)*

I attest, under penalty of perjury, that to the best of my knowledge, this employee is authorized to work in the United States, and if the employee presented document(s), the document(s) I have examined appear to be genuine and to relate to the individual.

Signature of Employer or Authorized Representative	Today's Date *(mm/dd/yyyy)*	Name of Employer or Authorized Representative

Form I-9: Lawful Permanent Resident, Name Missing, Over-documented

Employment Eligibility Verification
Department of Homeland Security
U.S. Citizenship and Immigration Services

USCIS
Form I-9
OMB No. 1615-0047
Expires 08/31/2019

▶ **START HERE:**   Read instructions carefully before completing this form. The instructions must be available, either in paper or electronically, during completion of this form. Employers are liable for errors in the completion of this form.

ANTI-DISCRIMINATION NOTICE: It is illegal to discriminate against work-authorized individuals. Employers **CANNOT** specify which document(s) an employee may present to establish employment authorization and identity. The refusal to hire or continue to employ an individual because the documentation presented has a future expiration date may also constitute illegal discrimination.

Section 1. Employee Information and Attestation *(Employees must complete and sign Section 1 of Form I-9 no later than the* **first day of employment**, *but not before accepting a job offer.)*

Last Name *(Family Name)*	First Name *(Given Name)*	Middle Initial	Other Last Names Used *(if any)*
Rodriguez	Guadalupe	A.	Gomez

Address *(Street Number and Name)*	Apt. Number	City or Town	State	ZIP Code
123 Main Street	N/A	Anytown	TN	33321

Date of Birth *(mm/dd/yyyy)*	U.S. Social Security Number	Employee's E-mail Address	Employee's Telephone Number
12/20/1967	2 1 3 - 4 5 - 5 4 3 2	GuadalupeRodriguez487@gmail.com	555-123-9874

I am aware that federal law provides for imprisonment and/or fines for false statements or use of false documents in connection with the completion of this form.

I attest, under penalty of perjury, that I am (check one of the following boxes):

☐ 1. A citizen of the United States

☐ 2. A noncitizen national of the United States *(See instructions)*

☒ 3. A lawful permanent resident (Alien Registration Number/USCIS Number):   A975331350

☐ 4. An alien authorized to work until (expiration date, if applicable, mm/dd/yyyy): _____
Some aliens may write "N/A" in the expiration date field. *(See instructions)*

Aliens authorized to work must provide only one of the following document numbers to complete Form I-9:
An Alien Registration Number/USCIS Number OR Form I-94 Admission Number OR Foreign Passport Number.

1. Alien Registration Number/USCIS Number: _____
OR
2. Form I-94 Admission Number: _____
OR
3. Foreign Passport Number: _____
   Country of Issuance: _____

QR Code - Section 1
Do Not Write In This Space

Signature of Employee *| Signature |*	Today's Date *(mm/dd/yyyy)* 08/29/2017

Preparer and/or Translator Certification (check one):
☒ I did not use a preparer or translator.   ☐ A preparer(s) and/or translator(s) assisted the employee in completing Section 1.
(Fields below must be completed and signed when preparers and/or translators assist an employee in completing Section 1.)

I attest, under penalty of perjury, that I have assisted in the completion of Section 1 of this form and that to the best of my knowledge the information is true and correct.

Signature of Preparer or Translator	Today's Date *(mm/dd/yyyy)*

Last Name *(Family Name)*	First Name *(Given Name)*

Address *(Street Number and Name)*	City or Town	State	ZIP Code

STOP   *Employer Completes Next Page*   **STOP**

Employment Eligibility Verification
Department of Homeland Security
U.S. Citizenship and Immigration Services

USCIS
Form I-9
OMB No. 1615-0047
Expires 08/31/2019

No name

Section 2. Employer or Authorized Representative Review and Verification

(Employers or their authorized representative must complete and sign Section 2 within 3 business days of the employee's first day of employment. You must physically examine one document from List A OR a combination of one document from List B and one document from List C as listed on the "Lists of Acceptable Documents.")

Employee Info from Section 1	Last Name *(Family Name)*	First Name *(Given Name)*	M.I.	Citizenship/Immigration Status

List A — Identity and Employment Authorization	OR	List B — Identity	AND	List C — Employment Authorization

List A	List B	List C
Document Title Permanent Resident Card	Document Title Driver's License	Document Title Birth Certificate
Issuing Authority USCIS	Issuing Authority TN	Issuing Authority TN
Document Number A975331350	Document Number 1235791	Document Number 654321
Expiration Date *(if any)(mm/dd/yyyy)* 10/01/2018	Expiration Date *(if any)(mm/dd/yyyy)* 01/01/2019	Expiration Date *(if any)(mm/dd/yyyy)*
Document Title		
Issuing Authority	Additional Information	QR Code - Sections 2 & 3 Do Not Write In This Space
Document Number		
Expiration Date *(if any)(mm/dd/yyyy)*		
Document Title		
Issuing Authority		
Document Number		
Expiration Date *(if any)(mm/dd/yyyy)*		

Overdocumentation - all lists used - should only be List A or List B + C

Certification: I attest, under penalty of perjury, that (1) I have examined the document(s) presented by the above-named employee, (2) the above-listed document(s) appear to be genuine and to relate to the employee named, and (3) to the best of my knowledge the employee is authorized to work in the United States.

The employee's first day of employment *(mm/dd/yyyy)*:   09/01/2017   *(See instructions for exemptions)*

Signature of Employer or Authorized Representative */ Signature /*	Today's Date *(mm/dd/yyyy)* 08/01/2017	Title of Employer or Authorized Representative HR Manager	
Last Name of Employer or Authorized Representative Employer	First Name of Employer or Authorized Representative Emily	Employer's Business or Organization Name ABC Widgets	
Employer's Business or Organization Address (Street Number and Name) 555 Jackson Lane	City or Town Anytown	State TN	ZIP Code 33322

Section 3. Reverification and Rehires *(To be completed and signed by employer or authorized representative)*

A. New Name *(if applicable)*			B. Date of Rehire *(if applicable)*
Last Name *(Family Name)*	First Name *(Given Name)*	Middle Initial	Date *(mm/dd/yyyy)*

C. If the employee's previous grant of employment authorization has expired, provide the information for the document or receipt that establishes continuing employment authorization in the space provided below.

Document Title	Document Number	Expiration Date *(if any)(mm/dd/yyyy)*

I attest, under penalty of perjury, that to the best of my knowledge, this employee is authorized to work in the United States, and if the employee presented document(s), the document(s) I have examined appear to be genuine and to relate to the individual.

Signature of Employer or Authorized Representative	Today's Date *(mm/dd/yyyy)*	Name of Employer or Authorized Representative

Form I-9: Lawful Permanent Resident with No List B Items

Employment Eligibility Verification	**USCIS**
Department of Homeland Security	**Form I-9**
U.S. Citizenship and Immigration Services	OMB No. 1615-0047 Expires 08/31/2019

▶ **START HERE:**   Read instructions carefully before completing this form. The instructions must be available, either in paper or electronically, during completion of this form. Employers are liable for errors in the completion of this form.

ANTI-DISCRIMINATION NOTICE: It is illegal to discriminate against work-authorized individuals. Employers **CANNOT** specify which document(s) an employee may present to establish employment authorization and identity. The refusal to hire or continue to employ an individual because the documentation presented has a future expiration date may also constitute illegal discrimination.

Section 1. Employee Information and Attestation *(Employees must complete and sign Section 1 of Form I-9 no later than the first day of employment, but not before accepting a job offer.)*

Last Name *(Family Name)*	First Name *(Given Name)*	Middle Initial	Other Last Names Used *(if any)*
Cook	Cameron	C	N/A

Address *(Street Number and Name)*	Apt. Number	City or Town	State	ZIP Code
123 Mud Lane	15	Anytown	TN	33321

Date of Birth *(mm/dd/yyyy)*	U.S. Social Security Number	Employee's E-mail Address	Employee's Telephone Number
05/12/1980	8 9 8 - 7 6 - 5 4 3 2	cccook@gmail.com	615-432-1098

I am aware that federal law provides for imprisonment and/or fines for false statements or use of false documents in connection with the completion of this form.

I attest, under penalty of perjury, that I am (check one of the following boxes):

☐ 1. A citizen of the United States

☐ 2. A noncitizen national of the United States *(See instructions)*

☒ 3. A lawful permanent resident (Alien Registration Number/USCIS Number):   567898765

☐ 4. An alien authorized to work until (expiration date, if applicable, mm/dd/yyyy): _____
Some aliens may write "N/A" in the expiration date field. *(See instructions)*

Aliens authorized to work must provide only one of the following document numbers to complete Form I-9:
An Alien Registration Number/USCIS Number OR Form I-94 Admission Number OR Foreign Passport Number.

1. Alien Registration Number/USCIS Number: _____
        OR

2. Form I-94 Admission Number: _____
        OR

3. Foreign Passport Number: _____

Country of Issuance: _____

| QR Code - Section 1 |
| Do Not Write In This Space |

Signature of Employee	*/ Signature /*	Today's Date *(mm/dd/yyyy)* 09/01/2017

Preparer and/or Translator Certification (check one):

☒ I did not use a preparer or translator.   ☐ A preparer(s) and/or translator(s) assisted the employee in completing Section 1.
(Fields below must be completed and signed when preparers and/or translators assist an employee in completing Section 1.)

I attest, under penalty of perjury, that I have assisted in the completion of Section 1 of this form and that to the best of my knowledge the information is true and correct.

Signature of Preparer or Translator	Today's Date *(mm/dd/yyyy)*

Last Name *(Family Name)*	First Name *(Given Name)*

Address *(Street Number and Name)*	City or Town	State	ZIP Code

🛑   *Employer Completes Next Page*   🛑

Employment Eligibility Verification
Department of Homeland Security
U.S. Citizenship and Immigration Services

USCIS
Form I-9
OMB No. 1615-0047
Expires 08/31/2019

Section 2. Employer or Authorized Representative Review and Verification

(Employers or their authorized representative must complete and sign Section 2 within 3 business days of the employee's first day of employment. You must physically examine one document from List A OR a combination of one document from List B and one document from List C as listed on the "Lists of Acceptable Documents.")

Employee Info from Section 1	Last Name *(Family Name)* Cook	First Name *(Given Name)* Cameron	M.I. C	Citizenship/Immigration Status 3

List A Identity and Employment Authorization	OR	List B Identity	AND	List C Employment Authorization
Document Title		Document Title		Document Title Social Security Card
Issuing Authority		Issuing Authority		Issuing Authority SSA
Document Number		Document Number		Document Number 898-76-5432
Expiration Date *(if any)(mm/dd/yyyy)*		Expiration Date *(if any)(mm/dd/yyyy)*		Expiration Date *(if any)(mm/dd/yyyy)*
Document Title				
Issuing Authority		Additional Information		QR Code - Sections 2 & 3 Do Not Write In This Space
Document Number				
Expiration Date *(if any)(mm/dd/yyyy)*				
Document Title				
Issuing Authority				
Document Number				
Expiration Date *(if any)(mm/dd/yyyy)*				

Missing items from List B

Certification: I attest, under penalty of perjury, that (1) I have examined the document(s) presented by the above-named employee, (2) the above-listed document(s) appear to be genuine and to relate to the employee named, and (3) to the best of my knowledge the employee is authorized to work in the United States.

The employee's first day of employment *(mm/dd/yyyy)*:   09/01/2017   *(See instructions for exemptions)*

Signature of Employer or Authorized Representative */ Signature /*	Today's Date *(mm/dd/yyyy)* 09/01/2017	Title of Employer or Authorized Representative HR Manager
Last Name of Employer or Authorized Representative Employer	First Name of Employer or Authorized Representative Emily	Employer's Business or Organization Name ABC Widgets

Employer's Business or Organization Address (Street Number and Name) 555 Jackson Lane	City or Town Anytown	State TN	ZIP Code 33322

Section 3. Reverification and Rehires *(To be completed and signed by employer or authorized representative.)*

A. New Name *(if applicable)*			B. Date of Rehire *(if applicable)*
Last Name *(Family Name)*	First Name *(Given Name)*	Middle Initial	Date *(mm/dd/yyyy)*

C. If the employee's previous grant of employment authorization has expired, provide the information for the document or receipt that establishes continuing employment authorization in the space provided below.

Document Title	Document Number	Expiration Date *(if any)(mm/dd/yyyy)*

I attest, under penalty of perjury, that to the best of my knowledge, this employee is authorized to work in the United States, and if the employee presented document(s), the document(s) I have examined appear to be genuine and to relate to the individual.

Signature of Employer or Authorized Representative	Today's Date *(mm/dd/yyyy)*	Name of Employer or Authorized Representative

Form I-9: Alien with No Documentation

| **Employment Eligibility Verification**
Department of Homeland Security
U.S. Citizenship and Immigration Services | **USCIS**
Form I-9
OMB No. 1615-0047
Expires 08/31/2019 |

▶ **START HERE:** Read instructions carefully before completing this form. The instructions must be available, either in paper or electronically, during completion of this form. Employers are liable for errors in the completion of this form.

ANTI-DISCRIMINATION NOTICE: It is illegal to discriminate against work-authorized individuals. Employers **CANNOT** specify which document(s) an employee may present to establish employment authorization and identity. The refusal to hire or continue to employ an individual because the documentation presented has a future expiration date may also constitute illegal discrimination.

Section 1. Employee Information and Attestation *(Employees must complete and sign Section 1 of Form I-9 no later than the **first day of employment**, but not before accepting a job offer.)*

Last Name (Family Name) Herrera	First Name (Given Name) Patrick	Middle Initial B	Other Last Names Used (if any) N/A		
Address (Street Number and Name) 123 Scenic Drive	Apt. Number	City or Town Anytown		State TN	ZIP Code 33321

Date of Birth (mm/dd/yyyy) 04/24/1996	U.S. Social Security Number 7 5 3 - 2 4 - 6 8 0 0	Employee's E-mail Address N/A	Employee's Telephone Number N/A

I am aware that federal law provides for imprisonment and/or fines for false statements or use of false documents in connection with the completion of this form.

I attest, under penalty of perjury, that I am (check one of the following boxes):

☐ 1. A citizen of the United States

☐ 2. A noncitizen national of the United States *(See instructions)*

☐ 3. A lawful permanent resident (Alien Registration Number/USCIS Number):

☒ 4. An alien authorized to work until (expiration date, if applicable, mm/dd/yyyy):
Some aliens may write "N/A" in the expiration date field. *(See instructions)*   ← N/A missing

Aliens authorized to work must provide only one of the following document numbers to complete Form I-9:
An Alien Registration Number/USCIS Number OR Form I-94 Admission Number OR Foreign Passport Number.

QR Code - Section 1
Do Not Write In This Space

1. Alien Registration Number/USCIS Number: _____
       OR
2. Form I-94 Admission Number: 54321238
       OR
3. Foreign Passport Number: _____
       Country of Issuance: _____

Signature of Employee */ Signature /*	Today's Date (mm/dd/yyyy) 09/01/2017

Preparer and/or Translator Certification (check one):

☐ I did not use a preparer or translator.   ☒ A preparer(s) and/or translator(s) assisted the employee in completing Section 1.
(Fields below must be completed and signed when preparers and/or translators assist an employee in completing Section 1.)

I attest, under penalty of perjury, that I have assisted in the completion of Section 1 of this form and that to the best of my knowledge the information is true and correct.

Signature of Preparer or Translator */ Signature /*	Today's Date (mm/dd/yyyy) 09/01/2017

Last Name (Family Name) Employer	First Name (Given Name) Emily		
Address (Street Number and Name) 555 Jackson Lane	City or Town Anytown	State TN	ZIP Code 33322

🛑   *Employer Completes Next Page*   🛑

Employment Eligibility Verification
Department of Homeland Security
U.S. Citizenship and Immigration Services

USCIS
Form I-9
OMB No. 1615-0047
Expires 08/31/2019

Section 2. Employer or Authorized Representative Review and Verification

(Employers or their authorized representative must complete and sign Section 2 within 3 business days of the employee's first day of employment. You must physically examine one document from List A OR a combination of one document from List B and one document from List C as listed on the "Lists of Acceptable Documents.")

Employee Info from Section 1	Last Name (Family Name) Herrera	First Name (Given Name) Patrick	M.I. B	Citizenship/Immigration Status 4

List A Identity and Employment Authorization	OR	List B Identity	AND	List C Employment Authorization
Document Title		Document Title		Document Title
Issuing Authority		Issuing Authority		Issuing Authority
Document Number		Document Number		Document Number
Expiration Date (if any)(mm/dd/yyyy)		Expiration Date (if any)(mm/dd/yyyy)		Expiration Date (if any)(mm/dd/yyyy)
Document Title				
Issuing Authority		Additional Information		QR Code - Sections 2 & 3 Do Not Write In This Space
Document Number				
Expiration Date (if any)(mm/dd/yyyy)				
Document Title		Items missing from List A - or - B and C		
Issuing Authority				
Document Number				
Expiration Date (if any)(mm/dd/yyyy)				

Certification: I attest, under penalty of perjury, that (1) I have examined the document(s) presented by the above-named employee, (2) the above-listed document(s) appear to be genuine and to relate to the employee named, and (3) to the best of my knowledge the employee is authorized to work in the United States.

The employee's first day of employment (mm/dd/yyyy): 09/01/2017   (See instructions for exemptions)

Signature of Employer or Authorized Representative / Signature /	Today's Date (mm/dd/yyyy) 09/02/2017	Title of Employer or Authorized Representative HR Manager
Last Name of Employer or Authorized Representative Employer	First Name of Employer or Authorized Representative Emily	Employer's Business or Organization Name ABC Widgets

Employer's Business or Organization Address (Street Number and Name) 555 Jackson Lane	City or Town Anytown	State TN	ZIP Code 33322

Section 3. Reverification and Rehires (To be completed and signed by employer or authorized representative.)

A. New Name (if applicable)			B. Date of Rehire (if applicable)
Last Name (Family Name)	First Name (Given Name)	Middle Initial	Date (mm/dd/yyyy)

C. If the employee's previous grant of employment authorization has expired, provide the information for the document or receipt that establishes continuing employment authorization in the space provided below.

Document Title	Document Number	Expiration Date (if any)(mm/dd/yyyy)

I attest, under penalty of perjury, that to the best of my knowledge, this employee is authorized to work in the United States, and if the employee presented document(s), the document(s) I have examined appear to be genuine and to relate to the individual.

Signature of Employer or Authorized Representative	Today's Date (mm/dd/yyyy)	Name of Employer or Authorized Representative

Form I-9: Alien with No Signature, No Date

Employment Eligibility Verification	**USCIS**
Department of Homeland Security	**Form I-9**
U.S. Citizenship and Immigration Services	OMB No. 1615-0047 Expires 08/31/2019

▶ **START HERE:**   Read instructions carefully before completing this form. The instructions must be available, either in paper or electronically, during completion of this form. Employers are liable for errors in the completion of this form.

ANTI-DISCRIMINATION NOTICE: It is illegal to discriminate against work-authorized individuals. Employers **CANNOT** specify which document(s) an employee may present to establish employment authorization and identity. The refusal to hire or continue to employ an individual because the documentation presented has a future expiration date may also constitute illegal discrimination.

Section 1. Employee Information and Attestation *(Employees must complete and sign Section 1 of Form I-9 no later than the **first day of employment**, but not before accepting a job offer.)*

Last Name *(Family Name)*	First Name *(Given Name)*	Middle Initial	Other Last Names Used *(if any)*
Jones	Sarah	A.	Smith

Address *(Street Number and Name)*	Apt. Number	City or Town	State	ZIP Code
123 North Main Street	N/A	Anytown	TN	33321

Date of Birth *(mm/dd/yyyy)*	U.S. Social Security Number	Employee's E-mail Address	Employee's Telephone Number
12/20/1967	5 6 7 - 1 2 - 0 1 2 3	Jonesfamilymom@gmail.com	555-123-4567

I am aware that federal law provides for imprisonment and/or fines for false statements or use of false documents in connection with the completion of this form.

I attest, under penalty of perjury, that I am (check one of the following boxes):

☐ 1. A citizen of the United States

☐ 2. A noncitizen national of the United States *(See instructions)*

☐ 3. A lawful permanent resident *(Alien Registration Number/USCIS Number):*

☒ 4. An alien authorized to work until (expiration date, if applicable, mm/dd/yyyy):   05//01/2018
    Some aliens may write "N/A" in the expiration date field. *(See instructions)*

Aliens authorized to work must provide only one of the following document numbers to complete Form I-9:
An Alien Registration Number/USCIS Number OR Form I-94 Admission Number OR Foreign Passport Number.

QR Code - Section 1
Do Not Write In This Space

1. Alien Registration Number/USCIS Number: A421864680
        OR

2. Form I-94 Admission Number: _____
        OR

No Employee signature

3. Foreign Passport Number: _____

    Country of Issuance: _____

No date

Signature of Employee	Today's Date *(mm/dd/yyyy)*

Preparer and/or Translator Certification (check one):

☒ I did not use a preparer or translator.   ☐ A preparer(s) and/or translator(s) assisted the employee in completing Section 1.
(Fields below must be completed and signed when preparers and/or translators assist an employee in completing Section 1.)

I attest, under penalty of perjury, that I have assisted in the completion of Section 1 of this form and that to the best of my knowledge the information is true and correct.

Signature of Preparer or Translator	Today's Date *(mm/dd/yyyy)*

Last Name *(Family Name)*	First Name *(Given Name)*		

Address *(Street Number and Name)*	City or Town	State	ZIP Code

🛑   *Employer Completes Next Page*   🛑

Employment Eligibility Verification
Department of Homeland Security
U.S. Citizenship and Immigration Services

USCIS
Form I-9
OMB No. 1615-0047
Expires 08/31/2019

Section 2. Employer or Authorized Representative Review and Verification

(Employers or their authorized representative must complete and sign Section 2 within 3 business days of the employee's first day of employment. You must physically examine one document from List A OR a combination of one document from List B and one document from List C as listed on the "Lists of Acceptable Documents.")

Employee Info from Section 1	Last Name (Family Name) Jones	First Name (Given Name) Sarah	M.I. A.	Citizenship/Immigration Status 4

List A	OR	List B	AND	List C
Identity and Employment Authorization		Identity		Employment Authorization

List A	List B	List C
Document Title EAD (Form I-766)	Document Title	Document Title
Issuing Authority USCIS	Issuing Authority	Issuing Authority
Document Number A421864680	Document Number	Document Number
Expiration Date (if any)(mm/dd/yyyy) 05/01/2018	Expiration Date (if any)(mm/dd/yyyy)	Expiration Date (if any)(mm/dd/yyyy)
Document Title		
Issuing Authority	Additional Information	QR Code - Sections 2 & 3 Do Not Write In This Space
Document Number		
Expiration Date (if any)(mm/dd/yyyy)		
Document Title		
Issuing Authority		
Document Number		
Expiration Date (if any)(mm/dd/yyyy)		

Certification: I attest, under penalty of perjury, that (1) I have examined the document(s) presented by the above-named employee, (2) the above-listed document(s) appear to be genuine and to relate to the employee named, and (3) to the best of my knowledge the employee is authorized to work in the United States.

The employee's first day of employment (mm/dd/yyyy):   09/01/2017   (See instructions for exemptions)

Signature of Employer or Authorized Representative *| Signature |*	Today's Date (mm/dd/yyyy) 09/01/2017	Title of Employer or Authorized Representative HR Manager
Last Name of Employer or Authorized Representative Employer	First Name of Employer or Authorized Representative Emily	Employer's Business or Organization Name ABC Widgets

Employer's Business or Organization Address (Street Number and Name) 555 Jackson Lane	City or Town Anytown	State TN	ZIP Code 33322

Section 3. Reverification and Rehires (To be completed and signed by employer or authorized representative.)

A. New Name (if applicable)			B. Date of Rehire (if applicable)
Last Name (Family Name)	First Name (Given Name)	Middle Initial	Date (mm/dd/yyyy)

C. If the employee's previous grant of employment authorization has expired, provide the information for the document or receipt that establishes continuing employment authorization in the space provided below.

Document Title	Document Number	Expiration Date (if any)(mm/dd/yyyy)

I attest, under penalty of perjury, that to the best of my knowledge, this employee is authorized to work in the United States, and if the employee presented document(s), the document(s) I have examined appear to be genuine and to relate to the individual.

Signature of Employer or Authorized Representative	Today's Date (mm/dd/yyyy)	Name of Employer or Authorized Representative

Form I-9: Alien with Invalid Date and Identification

Employment Eligibility Verification	**USCIS**
Department of Homeland Security	**Form I-9**
U.S. Citizenship and Immigration Services	OMB No. 1615-0047
	Expires 08/31/2019

▶ **START HERE:**   Read instructions carefully before completing this form. The instructions must be available, either in paper or electronically, during completion of this form. Employers are liable for errors in the completion of this form.

ANTI-DISCRIMINATION NOTICE: It is illegal to discriminate against work-authorized individuals. Employers **CANNOT** specify which document(s) an employee may present to establish employment authorization and identity. The refusal to hire or continue to employ an individual because the documentation presented has a future expiration date may also constitute illegal discrimination.

Section 1. Employee Information and Attestation *(Employees must complete and sign Section 1 of Form I-9 no later than the **first day of employment**, but not before accepting a job offer.)*

Last Name (Family Name)	First Name (Given Name)	Middle Initial	Other Last Names Used (if any)	
Lopez	Alexander	N/A	Lopez-Rodriguez	

Address (Street Number and Name)	Apt. Number	City or Town	State	ZIP Code
531 Scenic Drive	N/A	Anytown	TN	33321

Date of Birth (mm/dd/yyyy)	U.S. Social Security Number	Employee's E-mail Address	Employee's Telephone Number
09/09/1975	☐☐☐-☐☐-☐☐☐☐	N/A	N/A

I am aware that federal law provides for imprisonment and/or fines for false statements or use of false documents in connection with the completion of this form.

I attest, under penalty of perjury, that I am (check one of the following boxes):

☐ 1. A citizen of the United States

☐ 2. A noncitizen national of the United States *(See instructions)*

☐ 3. A lawful permanent resident (Alien Registration Number/USCIS Number): _____

☒ 4. An alien authorized to work until (expiration date, if applicable, mm/dd/yyyy):   04/01/2017
    Some aliens may write "N/A" in the expiration date field. *(See instructions)*

Aliens authorized to work must provide only one of the following document numbers to complete Form I-9:
An Alien Registration Number/USCIS Number OR Form I-94 Admission Number OR Foreign Passport Number.

QR Code - Section 1
Do Not Write In This Space

1. Alien Registration Number/USCIS Number: 753124842
          OR
2. Form I-94 Admission Number: _____
          OR
3. Foreign Passport Number: _____

    Country of Issuance: _____

Invalid date

Signature of Employee *| Signature |*	Today's Date (mm/dd/yyyy) 09/09/1975

Preparer and/or Translator Certification (check one):
☒ I did not use a preparer or translator.   ☐ A preparer(s) and/or translator(s) assisted the employee in completing Section 1.
(Fields below must be completed and signed when preparers and/or translators assist an employee in completing Section 1.)

I attest, under penalty of perjury, that I have assisted in the completion of Section 1 of this form and that to the best of my knowledge the information is true and correct.

Signature of Preparer or Translator	Today's Date (mm/dd/yyyy)	
Last Name (Family Name)	First Name (Given Name)	
Address (Street Number and Name)	City or Town	State	ZIP Code

🛑   *Employer Completes Next Page*   🛑

Employment Eligibility Verification

Department of Homeland Security

U.S. Citizenship and Immigration Services

USCIS
Form I-9
OMB No. 1615-0047
Expires 08/31/2019

Section 2. Employer or Authorized Representative Review and Verification

(Employers or their authorized representative must complete and sign Section 2 within 3 business days of the employee's first day of employment. You must physically examine one document from List A OR a combination of one document from List B and one document from List C as listed on the "Lists of Acceptable Documents.")

Employee Info from Section 1	Last Name *(Family Name)*	First Name *(Given Name)*	M.I.	Citizenship/Immigration Status
	Lopez	Alexander	N/A	4

List A Identity and Employment Authorization	OR	List B Identity	AND	List C Employment Authorization

List A	List B	List C
Document Title Permanent Resident Card	Document Title	Document Title
Issuing Authority USCIS	Issuing Authority	Issuing Authority
Document Number 753124842	Document Number	Document Number
Expiration Date *(if any)(mm/dd/yyyy)* 04/01/2017	Expiration Date *(if any)(mm/dd/yyyy)*	Expiration Date *(if any)(mm/dd/yyyy)*
Document Title		
Issuing Authority	Additional Information	QR Code - Sections 2 & 3 Do Not Write In This Space
Document Number		
Expiration Date *(if any)(mm/dd/yyyy)*		
Document Title		
Issuing Authority		
Document Number		
Expiration Date *(if any)(mm/dd/yyyy)*		

> **Wrong type of ID used when compared to status of authorized to work**

Certification: I attest, under penalty of perjury, that (1) I have examined the document(s) presented by the above-named employee, (2) the above-listed document(s) appear to be genuine and to relate to the ~~~~ best of my knowledge the employee is authorized to work in the United States.

> **Untimely completed**

The employee's first day of employment *(mm/dd/yyyy):*   03/01/2015   *(See instructions for exemptions)*

Signature of Employer or Authorized Representative */ Signature /*	Today's Date *(mm/dd/yyyy)* 09/01/2015	Title of Employer or Authorized Representative HR Manager
Last Name of Employer or Authorized Representative Employer	First Name of Employer or Authorized Representative Emily	Employer's Business or Organization Name ABC Widgets

Employer's Business or Organization Address (Street Number and Name) 555 Jackson Lane	City or Town Anytown	State TN	ZIP Code 33322

Section 3. Reverification and Rehires *(To be completed and signed by employer or authorized representative.)*

A. New Name *(if applicable)*			B. Date of Rehire *(if applicable)*
Last Name *(Family Name)*	First Name *(Given Name)*	Middle Initial	Date *(mm/dd/yyyy)* 03/31/2019

> **Missing Document Number**

C. If the employee's previous grant of ~~~~ s expired, provide the information for the document or receipt that establishes continuing employment authorization ~~~~

Document Title EAD	Document Number	Expiration Date *(if any)(mm/dd/yyyy)* 03/31/2019

> **Needs signature**

I attest, under penalty of perjury, that to the best of my knowledge, this employee is authorized to work in the United States, and if the employee presented document(s), the document(s) I have examined appear to be genuine and to relate to the individual.

Signature of Employer or Authorized Representative	Today's Date *(mm/dd/yyyy)* 03/25/2017	Name of Employer or Authorized Representative Employer, Emily

Form I-9: Confusing Documentation, No Start Date

Employment Eligibility Verification
Department of Homeland Security
U.S. Citizenship and Immigration Services

USCIS
Form I-9
OMB No. 1615-0047
Expires 08/31/2019

▶ **START HERE:** Read instructions carefully before completing this form. The instructions must be available, either in paper or electronically, during completion of this form. Employers are liable for errors in the completion of this form.

ANTI-DISCRIMINATION NOTICE: It is illegal to discriminate against work-authorized individuals. Employers **CANNOT** specify which document(s) an employee may present to establish employment authorization and identity. The refusal to hire or continue to employ an individual because the documentation presented has a future expiration date may also constitute illegal discrimination.

Section 1. Employee Information and Attestation *(Employees must complete and sign Section 1 of Form I-9 no later than the **first day of employment**, but not before accepting a job offer.)*

Last Name *(Family Name)*	First Name *(Given Name)*	Middle Initial	Other Last Names Used *(if any)*		
Doe	John	D.	N/A		

Address *(Street Number and Name)*	Apt. Number	City or Town		State	ZIP Code
123 Main Street	N/A	Anytown		TN	33321

Date of Birth *(mm/dd/yyyy)*	U.S. Social Security Number	Employee's E-mail Address	Employee's Telephone Number
12/20/1967	9 8 7 - 6 5 - 4 3 2 1	BusterDoe487@gmail.com	555-555-1987

I am aware that federal law provides for imprisonment and/or fines for false statements or use of false documents in connection with the completion of this form.

I attest, under penalty of perjury, that I ~~am~~ [Inconsistent with use of a Permanent Resident Card]):

☒ 1. A citizen of the United States

☐ 2. A noncitizen national of the United States *(See instructions)*

☐ 3. A lawful permanent resident (Alien Registration Number/USCIS Number): _____

☐ 4. An alien authorized to work until (expiration date, if applicable, mm/dd/yyyy): _____
     Some aliens may write "N/A" in the expiration date field. *(See instructions)*

Aliens authorized to work must provide only one of the following document numbers to complete Form I-9:
An Alien Registration Number/USCIS Number OR Form I-94 Admission Number OR Foreign Passport Number.

1. Alien Registration Number/USCIS Number: _____
             OR
2. Form I-94 Admission Number: _____
             OR
3. Foreign Passport Number: _____
   Country of Issuance: _____

QR Code - Section 1
Do Not Write In This Space

Signature of Employee	Today's Date *(mm/dd/yyyy)*
/ Signature /	09/01/2017

Preparer and/or Translator Certification (check one):
☒ I did not use a preparer or translator. ☐ A preparer(s) and/or translator(s) assisted the employee in completing Section 1.
(Fields below must be completed and signed when preparers and/or translators assist an employee in completing Section 1.)

I attest, under penalty of perjury, that I have assisted in the completion of Section 1 of this form and that to the best of my knowledge the information is true and correct.

Signature of Preparer or Translator	Today's Date *(mm/dd/yyyy)*

Last Name *(Family Name)*	First Name *(Given Name)*		

Address *(Street Number and Name)*	City or Town	State	ZIP Code

🛑 *Employer Completes Next Page* 🛑

Employment Eligibility Verification

Department of Homeland Security

U.S. Citizenship and Immigration Services

USCIS
Form I-9
OMB No. 1615-0047
Expires 08/31/2019

Section 2. Employer or Authorized Representative Review and Verification

(Employers or their authorized representative must complete and sign Section 2 within 3 business days of the employee's first day of employment. You must physically examine one document from List A OR a combination of one document from List B and one document from List C as listed on the "Lists of Acceptable Documents.")

Employee Info from Section 1	Last Name *(Family Name)* Doe	First Name *(Given Name)* John	M.I. D.	Citizenship/Immigration Status 1

List A Identity and Employment Authorization	OR	List B Identity	AND	List C Employment Authorization

Document Title Permanent Resident Card	Document Title	Document Title
Issuing Authority USCIS	Issuing Authority	Issuing Authority
Document Number A1400072370	Document Number	Document Number
Expiration Date *(if any)(mm/dd/yyyy)* 01/20/2020	Expiration Date *(if any)(mm/dd/yyyy)*	Expiration Date *(if any)(mm/dd/yyyy)*

Document Title
Issuing Authority
Document Number
Expiration Date *(if any)(mm/dd/yyyy)*

Document Title
Issuing Authority
Document Number
Expiration Date *(if any)(mm/dd/yyyy)*

Additional Information

No 1st day of employment

QR Code - Sections 2 & 3
Do Not Write In This Space

Certification: I attest, under penalty of perjury, that (1) I have examined the document(s) presented by the above-named employee, (2) the above-listed document(s) appear to be genuine and to relate to the employee named, and (3) to the best of my knowledge the employee is authorized to work in the United States.

The employee's first day of employment *(mm/dd/yyyy)*: _____ *(See instructions for exemptions)*

Signature of Employer or Authorized Representative *| Signature |*	Today's Date *(mm/dd/yyyy)* 09/01/2017	Title of Employer or Authorized Representative HR Manager
Last Name of Employer or Authorized Representative Employer	First Name of Employer or Authorized Representative Emily	Employer's Business or Organization Name ABC Widgets

Employer's Business or Organization Address (Street Number and Name) 555 Jackson Lane	City or Town Anytown	State TN	ZIP Code 33322

Section 3. Reverification and Rehires *(To be completed and signed by employer or authorized representative.)*

A. New Name *(if applicable)*			B. Date of Rehire *(if applicable)*
Last Name *(Family Name)*	First Name *(Given Name)*	Middle Initial	Date *(mm/dd/yyyy)*

C. If the employee's previous grant of employment authorization has expired, provide the information for the document or receipt that establishes continuing employment authorization in the space provided below.

Document Title	Document Number	Expiration Date *(if any)(mm/dd/yyyy)*

I attest, under penalty of perjury, that to the best of my knowledge, this employee is authorized to work in the United States, and if the employee presented document(s), the document(s) I have examined appear to be genuine and to relate to the individual.

Signature of Employer or Authorized Representative	Today's Date *(mm/dd/yyyy)*	Name of Employer or Authorized Representative

Form I-9: Incorrect Boxes Checked, Wrong Column Completed

Employment Eligibility Verification
Department of Homeland Security
U.S. Citizenship and Immigration Services

USCIS
Form I-9
OMB No. 1615-0047
Expires 08/31/2019

▶ **START HERE:** Read instructions carefully before completing this form. The instructions must be available, either in paper or electronically, during completion of this form. Employers are liable for errors in the completion of this form.

ANTI-DISCRIMINATION NOTICE: It is illegal to discriminate against work-authorized individuals. Employers **CANNOT** specify which document(s) an employee may present to establish employment authorization and identity. The refusal to hire or continue to employ an individual because the documentation presented has a future expiration date may also constitute illegal discrimination.

Section 1. Employee Information and Attestation *(Employees must complete and sign Section 1 of Form I-9 no later than the first day of employment, but not before accepting a job offer.)*

Last Name *(Family Name)*	First Name *(Given Name)*	Middle Initial	Other Last Names Used *(if any)*
Doe	Jane	A.	N/A

Address *(Street Number and Name)*	Apt. Number	City or Town	State	ZIP Code
123 Main Street	N/A	Anytown	TN	33321

Date of Birth *(mm/dd/yyyy)*	U.S. Social Security Number	Employee's E-mail Address	Employee's Telephone Number
12/20/1967	1 2 3 - 4 5 - 6 7 8 9	Apple367@gmail.com	N/A

I am aware that federal law provides for imprisonment and/or fines for false statements or use of false documents in connection with the completion of this form.

I attest, under penalty of perjury, that I am (check one of the following boxes):

☒ 1. A citizen of the United States   **2 boxes are checked**

☐ 2. A noncitizen national of the United States *(See instructions)*

☒ 3. A lawful permanent resident (Alien Registration Number/USCIS Number):   A937331500

☐ 4. An alien authorized to work until (expiration date, if applicable, mm/dd/yyyy): _____
Some aliens may write "N/A" in the expiration date field. *(See instructions)*

Aliens authorized to work must provide only one of the following document numbers to complete Form I-9:
An Alien Registration Number/USCIS Number OR Form I-94 Admission Number OR Foreign Passport Number.

1. Alien Registration Number/USCIS Number: _____
     OR
2. Form I-94 Admission Number: _____
     OR
3. Foreign Passport Number: _____
     Country of Issuance: _____

QR Code - Section 1
Do Not Write In This Space

Signature of Employee	Today's Date *(mm/dd/yyyy)*
| Signature |	09/01/2017

Preparer and/or Translator Certification (check one):
☒ I did not use a preparer or translator.   ☐ A preparer(s) and/or translator(s) assisted the employee in completing Section 1.
(Fields below must be completed and signed when preparers and/or translators assist an employee in completing Section 1.)

I attest, under penalty of perjury, that I have assisted in the completion of Section 1 of this form and that to the best of my knowledge the information is true and correct.

Signature of Preparer or Translator	Today's Date *(mm/dd/yyyy)*

Last Name *(Family Name)*	First Name *(Given Name)*		

Address *(Street Number and Name)*	City or Town	State	ZIP Code

🛑   *Employer Completes Next Page*   🛑

Employment Eligibility Verification

Department of Homeland Security

U.S. Citizenship and Immigration Services

USCIS
Form I-9
OMB No. 1615-0047
Expires 08/31/2019

Section 2. Employer or Authorized Representative Review and Verification

(Employers or their authorized representative must complete and sign Section 2 within 3 business days of the employee's first day of employment. You must physically examine one document from List A OR a combination of one document from List B and one document from List C as listed on the "Lists of Acceptable Documents.")

Employee Info from Section 1	Last Name *(Family Name)* Doe	First Name *(Given Name)* Jane	M.I. A.	Citizenship/Immigration Status 3

List A Identity and Employment Authorization	OR	List B Identity	AND	List C Employment Authorization
Document Title		Document Title Permanent Resident Card		Document Title
Issuing Authority		Issuing Authority USCIS		Issuing Authority
Document Number		Document Number A937331500		Document Number
Expiration Date *(if any)(mm/dd/yyyy)*		Expiration Date *(if any)(mm/dd/yyyy)* 04/01/2019		Expiration Date *(if any)(mm/dd/yyyy)*
Document Title				
Issuing Authority		Additional Information		QR Code - Sections 2 & 3 Do Not Write In This Space
Document Number				
Expiration Date *(if any)(mm/dd/yyyy)*		Wrong list used (should be List A)		
Document Title				
Issuing Authority				
Document Number				
Expiration Date *(if any)(mm/dd/yyyy)*				

Certification: I attest, under penalty of perjury, that (1) I have examined the document(s) presented by the above-named employee, (2) the above-listed document(s) appear to be genuine and to relate to the employee named, and (3) to the best of my knowledge the employee is authorized to work in the United States.

The employee's first day of employment *(mm/dd/yyyy):*   09/01/2017   *(See instructions for exemptions)*

Signature of Employer or Authorized Representative / Signature /	Today's Date *(mm/dd/yyyy)* 09/01/2017	Title of Employer or Authorized Representative HR Manager
Last Name of Employer or Authorized Representative Employer	First Name of Employer or Authorized Representative Emily	Employer's Business or Organization Name ABC Widgets

Employer's Business or Organization Address (Street Number and Name) 555 Jackson Lane	City or Town Anytown	State TN	ZIP Code 33322

Section 3. Reverification and Rehires *(To be completed and signed by employer or authorized representative.)*

A. New Name *(if applicable)*			B. Date of Rehire *(if applicable)*
Last Name *(Family Name)*	First Name *(Given Name)*	Middle Initial	Date *(mm/dd/yyyy)*

C. If the employee's previous grant of employment authorization has expired, provide the information for the document or receipt that establishes continuing employment authorization in the space provided below.

Document Title	Document Number	Expiration Date *(if any)(mm/dd/yyyy)*

I attest, under penalty of perjury, that to the best of my knowledge, this employee is authorized to work in the United States, and if the employee presented document(s), the document(s) I have examined appear to be genuine and to relate to the individual.

Signature of Employer or Authorized Representative	Today's Date *(mm/dd/yyyy)*	Name of Employer or Authorized Representative

Form I-9: Lawful Permanent Resident Green Card Expired, Employee Name Missing

Employment Eligibility Verification		**USCIS**
Department of Homeland Security		**Form I-9**
U.S. Citizenship and Immigration Services		OMB No. 1615-0047
		Expires 08/31/2019

▶ **START HERE:**   Read instructions carefully before completing this form. The instructions must be available, either in paper or electronically, during completion of this form. Employers are liable for errors in the completion of this form.

ANTI-DISCRIMINATION NOTICE: It is illegal to discriminate against work-authorized individuals. Employers **CANNOT** specify which document(s) an employee may present to establish employment authorization and identity. The refusal to hire or continue to employ an individual because the documentation presented has a future expiration date may also constitute illegal discrimination.

Section 1. Employee Information and Attestation *(Employees must complete and sign Section 1 of Form I-9 no later than the **first day of employment**, but not before accepting a job offer.)*

Last Name *(Family Name)*	First Name *(Given Name)*	Middle Initial	Other Last Names Used *(if any)*
Al-Obama	Mohamed	N/A	N/A

Address *(Street Number and Name)*	Apt. Number	City or Town	State	ZIP Code
123 Rosa Parks	N/A	Anytown	TN	33321

Date of Birth *(mm/dd/yyyy)*	U.S. Social Security Number	Employee's E-mail Address	Employee's Telephone Number
01/01/1983	1 2 2 - 3 3 - 4 4 5 5	N/A	(615) 333-2211

I am aware that federal law provides for imprisonment and/or fines for false statements or use of false documents in connection with the completion of this form.

I attest, under penalty of perjury, that I am (check one of the following boxes):

☐ 1. A citizen of the United States

☐ 2. A noncitizen national of the United States *(See instructions)*

☒ 3. A lawful permanent resident (Alien Registration Number/USCIS Number):   554433221

☐ 4. An alien authorized to work until (expiration date, if applicable, mm/dd/yyyy): _____
   Some aliens may write "N/A" in the expiration date field. *(See instructions)*

Aliens authorized to work must provide only one of the following document numbers to complete Form I-9:
An Alien Registration Number/USCIS Number OR Form I-94 Admission Number OR Foreign Passport Number.

1. Alien Registration Number/USCIS Number: _____
           OR

2. Form I-94 Admission Number: _____
           OR

3. Foreign Passport Number: _____

   Country of Issuance: _____

QR Code - Section 1
Do Not Write In This Space

Signature of Employee */ Signature /*	Today's Date *(mm/dd/yyyy)* 09/01/2017

Preparer and/or Translator Certification (check one):
☒ I did not use a preparer or translator.   ☐ A preparer(s) and/or translator(s) assisted the employee in completing Section 1.
(Fields below must be completed and signed when preparers and/or translators assist an employee in completing Section 1.)

I attest, under penalty of perjury, that I have assisted in the completion of Section 1 of this form and that to the best of my knowledge the information is true and correct.

Signature of Preparer or Translator	Today's Date *(mm/dd/yyyy)*
Last Name *(Family Name)*	First Name *(Given Name)*

Address *(Street Number and Name)*	City or Town	State	ZIP Code

STOP   *Employer Completes Next Page*   **STOP**

Employment Eligibility Verification
Department of Homeland Security
U.S. Citizenship and Immigration Services

USCIS
Form I-9
OMB No. 1615-0047
Expires 08/31/2019

Section 2. Employer or Authorized Representative Review and Verification

(Employers or their authorized representative must complete and sign Section 2 within 3 business days of the employee's first day of employment. You must physically examine one document from List A OR a combination of one document from List B and one document from List C as listed on the "Lists of Acceptable Documents.")

Employee Info from Section 1	Last Name *(Family Name)*	First Name *(Given Name)*	M.I.	Citizenship/Immigration Status
				3

List A Identity and Employment Authorization	OR	List B Identity	AND	List C Employment Authorization
Document Title Permanent Resident Card		Document Title		Document Title
Issuing Authority USCIS		Issuing Authority		Issuing Authority
Document Number 5544332211		Document Number		Document Number
Expiration Date *(if any)(mm/dd/yyyy)* 12/01/2016		Expiration Date *(if any)(mm/dd/yyyy)*		Expiration Date *(if any)(mm/dd/yyyy)*
Document Title				
Issuing Authority		Additional Information Missing employee information		QR Code - Sections 2 & 3 Do Not Write In This Space
Document Number				
Expiration Date *(if any)(mm/dd/yyyy)*				
Document Title		Accepted an expired green card - only can accept unexpired documents		
Issuing Authority				
Document Number				
Expiration Date *(if any)(mm/dd/yyyy)*				

Certification: I attest, under penalty of perjury, that (1) I have examined the document(s) presented by the above-named employee, (2) the above-listed document(s) appear to be genuine and to relate to the employee named, and (3) to the best of my knowledge the employee is authorized to work in the United States.

The employee's first day of employment *(mm/dd/yyyy)*:   09/01/2017   *(See instructions for exemptions)*

Signature of Employer or Authorized Representative */ Signature /*	Today's Date *(mm/dd/yyyy)* 09/01/2017	Title of Employer or Authorized Representative HR Manager
Last Name of Employer or Authorized Representative Employer	First Name of Employer or Authorized Representative Emily	Employer's Business or Organization Name ABC Widgets

Employer's Business or Organization Address (Street Number and Name) 555 Jackson Lane	City or Town Anytown	State TN	ZIP Code 33322

Section 3. Reverification and Rehires *(To be completed and signed by employer or authorized representative.)*

A. New Name *(if applicable)*			B. Date of Rehire *(if applicable)*
Last Name *(Family Name)*	First Name *(Given Name)*	Middle Initial	Date *(mm/dd/yyyy)*

C. If the employee's previous grant of employment authorization has expired, provide the information for the document or receipt that establishes continuing employment authorization in the space provided below.

Document Title	Document Number	Expiration Date *(if any)(mm/dd/yyyy)*

I attest, under penalty of perjury, that to the best of my knowledge, this employee is authorized to work in the United States, and if the employee presented document(s), the document(s) I have examined appear to be genuine and to relate to the individual.

Signature of Employer or Authorized Representative	Today's Date *(mm/dd/yyyy)*	Name of Employer or Authorized Representative

Form I-9: U.S. Citizen with Missing Date, Box Not Checked for Translator Certification

Employment Eligibility Verification
Department of Homeland Security
U.S. Citizenship and Immigration Services

USCIS
Form I-9
OMB No. 1615-0047
Expires 08/31/2019

▶ **START HERE:**   Read instructions carefully before completing this form. The instructions must be available, either in paper or electronically, during completion of this form. Employers are liable for errors in the completion of this form.

ANTI-DISCRIMINATION NOTICE: It is illegal to discriminate against work-authorized individuals. Employers **CANNOT** specify which document(s) an employee may present to establish employment authorization and identity. The refusal to hire or continue to employ an individual because the documentation presented has a future expiration date may also constitute illegal discrimination.

Section 1. Employee Information and Attestation *(Employees must complete and sign Section 1 of Form I-9 no later than the first day of employment, but not before accepting a job offer.)*

Last Name *(Family Name)*	First Name *(Given Name)*	Middle Initial	Other Last Names Used *(if any)*
Walker	Fred	E	

Address *(Street Number and Name)*	Apt. Number	City or Town	State	ZIP Code
531 Rosa Parks		Anytown	TN	33321

Date of Birth *(mm/dd/yyyy)*	U.S. Social Security Number	Employee's E-mail Address	Employee's Telephone Number
12/24/1995	7 6 5 - 6 7 - 8 9 0 1	N/A	N/A

I am aware that federal law provides for imprisonment and/or fines for false statements or use of false documents in connection with the completion of this form.

I attest, under penalty of perjury, that I am (check one of the following boxes):

[X] 1. A citizen of the United States

[ ] 2. A noncitizen national of the United States *(See instructions)*

[ ] 3. A lawful permanent resident (Alien Registration Number/USCIS Number): _____

[ ] 4. An alien authorized to work until (expiration date, if applicable, mm/dd/yyyy): _____
      Some aliens may write "N/A" in the expiration date field. *(See instructions)*

Aliens authorized to work must provide only one of the following document numbers to complete Form I-9:
An Alien Registration Number/USCIS Number OR Form I-94 Admission Number OR Foreign Passport Number.

1. Alien Registration Number/USCIS Number: _____
                     OR
2. Form I-94 Admission Number: _____
                     OR
3. Foreign Passport Number: _____
      Country of Issuance: _____ | Not checked |

QR Code - Section 1
Do Not Write In This Space

Signature of Employee */ Signature /*	Today's Date *(mm/dd/yyyy)* 09/01/2017

Preparer and/or Translator Certification (check one):

[ ] I did not use a preparer or translator.   [ ] A preparer(s) and/or translator(s) assisted the employee in completing Section 1.
(Fields below must be completed and signed when preparers and/or translators assist an employee in completing Section 1.)

I attest, under penalty of perjury, that I have assisted in the completion of Section 1 of this form and that to the best of my knowledge the information is true and correct.

Signature of Preparer or Translator	Today's Date *(mm/dd/yyyy)*
Last Name *(Family Name)*	First Name *(Given Name)*

Address *(Street Number and Name)*	City or Town	State	ZIP Code

🛑   *Employer Completes Next Page*   🛑

Employment Eligibility Verification

Department of Homeland Security

U.S. Citizenship and Immigration Services

USCIS
Form I-9
OMB No. 1615-0047
Expires 08/31/2019

Section 2. Employer or Authorized Representative Review and Verification

(Employers or their authorized representative must complete and sign Section 2 within 3 business days of the employee's first day of employment. You must physically examine one document from List A OR a combination of one document from List B and one document from List C as listed on the "Lists of Acceptable Documents.")

Employee Info from Section 1	Last Name *(Family Name)* Walker	First Name *(Given Name)* Fred	M.I. E	Citizenship/Immigration Status 1

List A Identity and Employment Authorization	OR	List B Identity	AND	List C Employment Authorization

List A	List B	List C
Document Title	Document Title Driver's License	Document Title Birth Certificate
Issuing Authority	Issuing Authority State of TN	Issuing Authority TN
Document Number	Document Number 356754202	Document Number V-2585195
Expiration Date *(if any)(mm/dd/yyyy)*	Expiration Date *(if any)(mm/dd/yyyy)*	Expiration Date *(if any)(mm/dd/yyyy)*
Document Title		
Issuing Authority	**Additional Information**	QR Code - Sections 2 & 3 Do Not Write In This Space
Document Number	Missing date	
Expiration Date *(if any)(mm/dd/yyyy)*		
Document Title		
Issuing Authority		
Document Number		
Expiration Date *(if any)(mm/dd/yyyy)*		

Certification: I attest, under penalty of perjury, that (1) I have examined the document(s) presented by the above-named employee, (2) the above-listed document(s) appear to be genuine and to relate to the employee named, and (3) to the best of my knowledge the employee is authorized to work in the United States.

The employee's first day of employment *(mm/dd/yyyy)*:   09/01/2017   *(See instructions for exemptions)*

Signature of Employer or Authorized Representative */ Signature /*	Today's Date *(mm/dd/yyyy)* 09/01/2017	Title of Employer or Authorized Representative HR Manager
Last Name of Employer or Authorized Representative Employer	First Name of Employer or Authorized Representative Emily	Employer's Business or Organization Name ABC Widgets
Employer's Business or Organization Address (Street Number and Name) 555 Jackson Lane	City or Town Anytown	State TN	ZIP Code 33322

Section 3. Reverification and Rehires *(To be completed and signed by employer or authorized representative.)*

A. New Name *(if applicable)*			B. Date of Rehire *(if applicable)*
Last Name *(Family Name)*	First Name *(Given Name)*	Middle Initial	Date *(mm/dd/yyyy)*

C. If the employee's previous grant of employment authorization has expired, provide the information for the document or receipt that establishes continuing employment authorization in the space provided below.

Document Title	Document Number	Expiration Date *(if any)(mm/dd/yyyy)*

I attest, under penalty of perjury, that to the best of my knowledge, this employee is authorized to work in the United States, and if the employee presented document(s), the document(s) I have examined appear to be genuine and to relate to the individual.

Signature of Employer or Authorized Representative	Today's Date *(mm/dd/yyyy)*	Name of Employer or Authorized Representative

APPENDIX E

E-VERIFY MEMORANDA OF UNDERSTANDING

E-VERIFY MEMORANDUM OF UNDERSTANDING FOR
EMPLOYERS

E-VERIFY MEMORANDUM OF UNDERSTANDING FOR
EMPLOYER AGENTS

E-VERIFY PROGRAM FOR EMPLOYMENT VERIFICATION
MEMORANDUM OF UNDERSTANDING

THE E-VERIFY MEMORANDUM OF UNDERSTANDING
FOR EMPLOYERS

ARTICLE I PURPOSE AND AUTHORITY

The parties to this agreement are the Department of Homeland Security (DHS) and the

_____(Employer). The purpose of this agreement is to set forth terms and conditions which the Employer will follow while participating in E-Verify.

E-Verify is a program that electronically confirms an employee's eligibility to work in the United States after completion of Form I-9, Employment Eligibility Verification (Form I-9). This Memorandum of Understanding (MOU) explains certain features of the E-Verify program and describes specific responsibilities of the Employer, the Social Security Administration (SSA), and DHS.

Authority for the E-Verify program is found in Title IV, Subtitle A, of the Illegal Immigration Reform and Immigrant Responsibility Act of 1996 (IIRIRA), Pub. L. 104-208, 110 Stat. 3009, as amended (8 U.S.C. § 1324a note). The Federal Acquisition Regulation (FAR) Subpart 22.18, "Employment Eligibility Verification" and Executive Order 12989, as amended, provide authority for Federal contractors and subcontractors (Federal contractor) to use E-Verify to verify the employment eligibility of certain employees working on Federal contracts.

ARTICLE II RESPONSIBILITIES

A. RESPONSIBILITIES OF THE EMPLOYER

1. The Employer agrees to display the following notices supplied by DHS in a prominent place that is clearly visible to prospective employees and all employees who are to be verified through the system:

a. Notice of E-Verify Participation

b. Notice of Right to Work

2. The Employer agrees to provide to the SSA and DHS the names, titles, addresses, and telephone numbers of the Employer representatives to be contacted about E-Verify. The Employer also agrees to keep such information current by providing updated information to SSA and DHS whenever the representatives' contact information changes.

3. The Employer agrees to grant E-Verify access only to current employees who need E-Verify access. Employers must promptly terminate an employee's E-Verify access if the employer is separated from the company or no longer needs access to E-Verify.

4. The Employer agrees to become familiar with and comply with the most recent version of the E-Verify User Manual.

5. The Employer agrees that any Employer Representative who will create E-Verify cases will complete the E-Verify Tutorial before that individual creates any cases.

a. The Employer agrees that all Employer representatives will take the refresher tutorials when prompted by E-Verify in order to continue using E-Verify. Failure to complete a refresher tutorial will prevent the Employer Representative from continued use of E-Verify.

6. The Employer agrees to comply with current Form I-9 procedures, with two exceptions:

a. If an employee presents a "List B" identity document, the Employer agrees to only accept "List B" documents that contain a photo. (List B documents identified in 8 C.F.R. § 274a.2(b)(1)(B)) can be presented during the Form I-9 process to establish identity.) If an employee objects to the photo requirement for religious reasons, the Employer should contact E-Verify at 888-464-4218.

b. If an employee presents a DHS Form I-551 (Permanent Resident Card), Form I-766 (Employment Authorization Document), or U.S. Passport or Passport Card to complete Form I-9, the Employer agrees to make a photocopy of the document and to retain the photocopy with the employee's Form I-9. The Employer will use the photocopy to verify the photo and to assist DHS with its review of photo mismatches that employees contest. DHS may in the future designate other documents that activate the photo screening tool.

Note: Subject only to the exceptions noted previously in this paragraph, employees still retain the right to present any List A, or List B and List C, document(s) to complete the Form I-9.

7. The Employer agrees to record the case verification number on the employee's Form I-9 or to print the screen containing the case verification number and attach it to the employee's Form I-9.

8. The Employer agrees that, although it participates in E-Verify, the Employer has a responsibility to complete, retain, and make available for inspection Forms I-9 that relate to its employees, or from other requirements of applicable regulations or laws, including the obligation to comply with the antidiscrimination requirements of section 274B of the INA with respect to Form I-9 procedures.

a. The following modified requirements are the only exceptions to an Employer's obligation to not employ unauthorized workers and comply with the anti-discrimination provision of the INA: (1) List B identity documents must have photos, as described in paragraph 6 above; (2) When an Employer confirms the identity and employment eligibility of newly hired employee using E-Verify procedures, the Employer establishes a rebuttable presumption that it has not violated section 274A(a)(1)(A) of the Immigration and Nationality Act (INA) with respect to the hiring of that employee; (3) If the Employer receives a final nonconfirmation for an employee, but continues to employ that person, the Employer must notify DHS and the Employer is subject to a civil money penalty between $550 and $1,100 for each failure to notify DHS of continued employment following a final nonconfirmation; (4) If the Employer continues to employ an employee after receiving a final nonconfirmation, then the Employer is subject to a rebuttable presumption that it has knowingly employed an unauthorized alien in violation of section 274A(a)(1)(A); and (5) no E-Verify participant is civilly or criminally liable under any law for any action taken in good faith based on information provided through the E-Verify.

b.   DHS reserves the right to conduct Form I-9 compliance inspections, as well as any other enforcement or compliance activity authorized by law, including site visits, to ensure proper use of E-Verify.

9. The Employer is strictly prohibited from creating an E-Verify case before the employee has been hired, meaning that a firm offer of employment was extended and accepted and Form I-9 was completed. The Employer agrees to create an E-Verify case for new employees within three Employer business days after each employee has been hired (after both Sections 1 and 2 of Form I-9 have been completed), and to complete as many steps of the E-Verify process as are necessary according to the E-Verify User Manual. If E-Verify is temporarily unavailable, the three-day time period will be extended until it is again operational in order to accommodate the Employer's attempting, in good faith, to make inquiries during the period

of unavailability.

10. The Employer agrees not to use E-Verify for pre-employment screening of job applicants, in support of any unlawful employment practice, or for any other use that this MOU or the E-Verify User Manual does not authorize.

11. The Employer must use E-Verify for all new employees. The Employer will not verify selectively and will not verify employees hired before the effective date of this MOU. Employers who are Federal contractors may qualify for exceptions to this requirement as described in Article II.B of this MOU.

12. The Employer agrees to follow appropriate procedures (see Article III below) regarding tentative nonconfirmations. The Employer must promptly notify employees in private of the finding and provide them with the notice and letter containing information specific to the employee's E-Verify case. The Employer agrees to provide both the English and the translated notice and letter for employees with limited English proficiency to employees. The Employer agrees to provide written referral instructions to employees and instruct affected employees to bring the English copy of the letter to the SSA. The Employer must allow employees to contest the finding, and not take adverse action against employees if they choose to contest the finding, while their case is still pending. Further, when employees contest a tentative nonconfirmation based upon a photo mismatch, the Employer must take additional steps (see Article III.B. below) to contact DHS with information necessary to resolve the challenge.

13. The Employer agrees not to take any adverse action against an employee based upon the employee's perceived employment eligibility status while SSA or DHS is processing the verification request unless the Employer obtains knowledge (as defined in 8 C.F.R. § 274a.1(l)) that the employee is not work authorized. The Employer understands that an initial inability of the SSA or DHS automated verification system to verify work authorization, a tentative nonconfirmation, a case in continuance (indicating the need for additional time for the government to resolve a case), or the finding of a photo mismatch, does not establish, and should not be interpreted as, evidence that the employee is not work authorized. In any of such cases, the employee must be provided a full and fair opportunity to contest the finding, and if he or she does so, the employee may not be terminated or suffer any adverse employment consequences based upon the employee's perceived employment eligibility status (including denying, reducing, or extending work hours, delaying or preventing training, requiring an employee to work in poorer conditions, withholding pay, refusing to assign the employee to a Federal contract or other assignment, or otherwise assuming that he or she is unauthorized to work) until and unless secondary verification by SSA or DHS has been completed and a final nonconfirmation has been issued. If the employee does not choose to contest a tentative nonconfirmation or a photo mismatch or if a secondary verification is completed and a final nonconfirmation is issued, then the Employer can find the employee is not work authorized and terminate the employee's employment. Employers or employees with questions about a final nonconfirmation may call E-Verify at 1-888-464-4218 (customer service) or 1-888-897-7781 (worker hotline).

14. The Employer agrees to comply with Title VII of the Civil Rights Act of 1964 and section 274B of the INA as applicable by not discriminating unlawfully against any individual in hiring, firing, employment eligibility verification, or recruitment or referral practices because of his or her national origin or citizenship status, or by committing discriminatory documentary practices. The Employer understands that such illegal practices can include selective verification or use of E-Verify except as provided in part D below, or

discharging or refusing to hire employees because they appear or sound "foreign" or have received tentative nonconfirmations. The Employer further understands that any violation of the immigration-related unfair employment practices provisions in section 274B of the INA could subject the Employer to civil penalties, back pay awards, and other sanctions, and violations of Title VII could subject the Employer to back pay awards, compensatory and punitive damages. Violations of either section 274B of the INA or Title VII may also lead to the termination of its participation in E-Verify. If the Employer has any questions relating to the anti-discrimination provision, it should contact OSC at 1-800-255-8155 or 1-800-237-2515 (TDD).

15. The Employer agrees that it will use the information it receives from E-Verify only to confirm the employment eligibility of employees as authorized by this MOU. The Employer agrees that it will safeguard this information, and means of access to it (such as PINS and passwords), to ensure that it is not used for any other purpose and as necessary to protect its confidentiality, including ensuring that it is not disseminated to any person other than employees of the Employer who are authorized to perform the Employer's responsibilities under this MOU, except for such dissemination as may be authorized in advance by SSA or DHS for legitimate purposes.

16. The Employer agrees to notify DHS immediately in the event of a breach of personal information. Breaches are defined as loss of control or unauthorized access to E-Verify personal data. All suspected or confirmed breaches should be reported by calling 1-888-464-4218 or via email at E-Verify@dhs.gov. Please use "Privacy Incident – Password" in the subject line of your email when sending a breach report to E-Verify.

17. The Employer acknowledges that the information it receives from SSA is governed by the Privacy Act (5 U.S.C. § 552a(i)(1) and (3)) and the Social Security Act (42 U.S.C. 1306(a)). Any person who obtains this information under false pretenses or uses it for any purpose other than as provided for in this MOU may be subject to criminal penalties.

18. The Employer agrees to cooperate with DHS and SSA in their compliance monitoring and evaluation of E-Verify, which includes permitting DHS, SSA, their contractors and other agents, upon reasonable notice, to review Forms I-9 and other employment records and to interview it and its employees regarding the Employer's use of E-Verify, and to respond in a prompt and accurate manner to DHS requests for information relating to their participation in E-Verify.

19. The Employer shall not make any false or unauthorized claims or references about its participation in E-Verify on its website, in advertising materials, or other media. The Employer shall not describe its services as federally-approved, federally-certified, or federally-recognized, or use language with a similar intent on its website or other materials provided to the public. Entering into this MOU does not mean that E-Verify endorses or authorizes your E-Verify services and any claim to that effect is false.

20. The Employer shall not state in its website or other public documents that any language used therein has been provided or approved by DHS, USCIS or the Verification Division, without first obtaining the prior written consent of DHS.

21. The Employer agrees that E-Verify trademarks and logos may be used only under license by DHS/USCIS (see M-795 (Web)) and, other than pursuant to the specific terms of such license, may not be used in any manner that might imply that the Employer's services, products, websites, or

publications are sponsored by, endorsed by, licensed by, or affiliated with DHS, USCIS, or E-Verify.

22. The Employer understands that if it uses E-Verify procedures for any purpose other than as authorized by this MOU, the Employer may be subject to appropriate legal action and termination of its participation in E-Verify according to this MOU.

B. RESPONSIBILITIES OF FEDERAL CONTRACTORS

1. If the Employer is a Federal contractor with the FAR E-Verify clause subject to the employment verification terms in Subpart 22.18 of the FAR, it will become familiar with and comply with the most current version of the E-Verify User Manual for Federal Contractors as well as the E-Verify Supplemental Guide for Federal Contractors.

2. In addition to the responsibilities of every employer outlined in this MOU, the Employer understands that if it is a Federal contractor subject to the employment verification terms in Subpart 22.18 of the FAR it must verify the employment eligibility of any "employee assigned to the contract" (as defined in FAR 22.1801). Once an employee has been verified through E-Verify by the Employer, the Employer may not create a second case for the employee through E-Verify.

 a.   An Employer that is not enrolled in E-Verify as a Federal contractor at the time of a contract award must enroll as a Federal contractor in the E-Verify program within 30 calendar days of contract award and, within 90 days of enrollment, begin to verify employment eligibility of new hires using E-Verify. The Employer must verify those employees who are working in the United States, whether or not they are assigned to the contract. Once the Employer begins verifying new hires, such verification of new hires must be initiated within three business days after the hire date. Once enrolled in E-Verify as a Federal contractor, the Employer must begin verification of employees assigned to the contract within 90 calendar days after the date of enrollment or within 30 days of an employee's assignment to the contract, whichever date is later.

 b.   Employers enrolled in E-Verify as a Federal contractor for 90 days or more at the time of a contract award must use E-Verify to begin verification of employment eligibility for new hires of the Employer who are working in the United States, whether or not assigned to the contract, within three business days after the date of hire. If the Employer is enrolled in E-Verify as a Federal contractor for 90 calendar days or less at the time of contract award, the Employer must, within 90 days of enrollment, begin to use E-Verify to initiate verification of new hires of the contractor who are working in the United States, whether or not assigned to the contract. Such verification of new hires must be initiated within three business days after the date of hire. An Employer enrolled as a Federal contractor in E-Verify must begin verification of each employee assigned to the contract within 90 calendar days after date of contract award or within 30 days after assignment to the contract, whichever is later.

 c.   Federal contractors that are institutions of higher education (as defined at 20 U.S.C. 1001(a)), state or local governments, governments of Federally recognized Indian tribes, or sureties performing under a takeover agreement entered into with a Federal agency under a performance bond may choose to only verify new and existing employees assigned to the Federal contract. Such Federal contractors may, however, elect to verify all new hires, and/or all existing employees hired after November 6, 1986. Employers in this category must begin verification of employees assigned to the contract within 90 calendar days after the date of enrollment or within 30 days of an employee's assignment to the contract, whichever date is later.

d. Upon enrollment, Employers who are Federal contractors may elect to verify employment eligibility of all existing employees working in the United States who were hired after November 6, 1986, instead of verifying only those employees assigned to a covered Federal contract. After enrollment, Employers must elect to verify existing staff following DHS procedures and begin E-Verify verification of all existing employees within 180 days after the election.

e. The Employer may use a previously completed Form I-9 as the basis for creating an E-Verify case for an employee assigned to a contract as long as:

    i. That Form I-9 is complete (including the SSN) and complies with Article

       II.A.6,

    ii. The employee's work authorization has not expired, and

    iii. The Employer has reviewed the Form I-9 information either in person or in communications with the employee to ensure that the employee's Section 1, Form I-9 attestation has not changed (including, but not limited to, a lawful permanent resident alien having become a naturalized U.S. citizen).

f. The Employer shall complete a new Form I-9 consistent with Article II.A.6 or update the previous Form I-9 to provide the necessary information if:

    i. The Employer cannot determine that Form I-9 complies with Article II.A.6,

    ii. The employee's basis for work authorization as attested in Section 1 has expired or changed, or

    iii. The Form I-9 contains no SSN or is otherwise incomplete.

Note: If Section 1 of Form I-9 is otherwise valid and up-to-date and the form otherwise complies with Article II.C.5, but reflects documentation (such as a U.S. passport or Form I-551) that expired after completing Form I-9, the Employer shall not require the production of additional documentation, or use the photo screening tool described in Article II.A.5, subject to any additional or superseding instructions that may be provided on this subject in the E-Verify User Manual.

g. The Employer agrees not to require a second verification using E-Verify of any assigned employee who has previously been verified as a newly hired employee under this MOU or to authorize verification of any existing employee by any Employer that is not a Federal contractor based on this Article.

3. The Employer understands that if it is a Federal contractor, its compliance with this MOU is a performance requirement under the terms of the Federal contract or subcontract, and the Employer consents to the release of information relating to compliance with its verification responsibilities under this MOU to contracting officers or other officials authorized to review the Employer's compliance with Federal contracting requirements.

C. RESPONSIBILITIES OF SSA

1. SSA agrees to allow DHS to compare data provided by the Employer against SSA's database. SSA

sends DHS confirmation that the data sent either matches or does not match the information in SSA's database.

2. SSA agrees to safeguard the information the Employer provides through E-Verify procedures. SSA also agrees to limit access to such information, as is appropriate by law, to individuals responsible for the verification of Social Security numbers or responsible for evaluation of E-Verify or such other persons or entities who may be authorized by SSA as governed by the Privacy Act (5 U.S.C. § 552a), the Social Security Act (42 U.S.C. 1306(a)), and SSA regulations (20 CFR Part 401).

3. SSA agrees to provide case results from its database within three Federal Government work days of the initial inquiry. E-Verify provides the information to the Employer.

4. SSA agrees to update SSA records as necessary if the employee who contests the SSA tentative nonconfirmation visits an SSA field office and provides the required evidence. If the employee visits an SSA field office within the eight Federal Government work days from the date of referral to SSA, SSA agrees to update SSA records, if appropriate, within the eight-day period unless SSA determines that more than eight days may be necessary. In such cases, SSA will provide additional instructions to the employee. If the employee does not visit SSA in the time allowed, E-Verify may provide a final nonconfirmation to the employer.

Note: If an Employer experiences technical problems, or has a policy question, the employer should contact E-Verify at 1-888-464-4218.

D. RESPONSIBILITIES OF DHS

1. DHS agrees to provide the Employer with selected data from DHS databases to enable the Employer to conduct, to the extent authorized by this MOU:

   a. Automated verification checks on alien employees by electronic means, and

   b. Photo verification checks (when available) on employees.

2. DHS agrees to assist the Employer with operational problems associated with the Employer's participation in E-Verify. DHS agrees to provide the Employer names, titles, addresses, and telephone numbers of DHS representatives to be contacted during the E-Verify process.

3. DHS agrees to provide to the Employer with access to E-Verify training materials as well as an E-Verify User Manual that contain instructions on E-Verify policies, procedures, and requirements for both SSA and DHS, including restrictions on the use of E-Verify.

4. DHS agrees to train Employers on all important changes made to E-Verify through the use of mandatory refresher tutorials and updates to the E-Verify User Manual. Even without changes to E-Verify, DHS reserves the right to require employers to take mandatory refresher tutorials.

5. DHS agrees to provide to the Employer a notice, which indicates the Employer's participation in E-Verify. DHS also agrees to provide to the Employer anti-discrimination notices issued by the Office of Special Counsel for Immigration-Related Unfair Employment Practices (OSC), Civil Rights Division, U.S. Department of Justice.

6. DHS agrees to issue each of the Employer's E-Verify users a unique user identification number and password that permits them to log in to E-Verify.

7. DHS agrees to safeguard the information the Employer provides, and to limit access to such information to individuals responsible for the verification process, for evaluation of E-Verify, or to such other persons or entities as may be authorized by applicable law. Information will be used only to verify the accuracy of Social Security numbers and employment eligibility, to enforce the INA and Federal criminal laws, and to administer Federal contracting requirements.

8. DHS agrees to provide a means of automated verification that provides (in conjunction with SSA verification procedures) confirmation or tentative nonconfirmation of employees' employment eligibility within three Federal Government work days of the initial inquiry.

9. DHS agrees to provide a means of secondary verification (including updating DHS records) for employees who contest DHS tentative nonconfirmations and photo mismatch tentative nonconfirmations. This provides final confirmation or nonconfirmation of the employees' employment eligibility within 10 Federal Government work days of the date of referral to DHS, unless DHS determines that more than 10 days may be necessary. In such cases, DHS will provide additional verification instructions.

ARTICLE III
REFERRAL OF INDIVIDUALS TO SSA AND DHS

A. REFERRAL TO SSA

1. If the Employer receives a tentative nonconfirmation issued by SSA, the Employer must print the notice as directed by E-Verify. The Employer must promptly notify employees in private of the finding and provide them with the notice and letter containing information specific to the employee's E-Verify case. The Employer also agrees to provide both the English and the translated notice and letter for employees with limited English proficiency to employees. The Employer agrees to provide written referral instructions to employees and instruct affected employees to bring the English copy of the letter to the SSA. The Employer must allow employees to contest the finding, and not take adverse action against employees if they choose to contest the finding, while their case is still pending.

2. The Employer agrees to obtain the employee's response about whether he or she will contest the tentative nonconfirmation as soon as possible after the Employer receives the tentative nonconfirmation. Only the employee may determine whether he or she will contest the tentative nonconfirmation.

3. After a tentative nonconfirmation, the Employer will refer employees to SSA field offices only as directed by E-Verify. The Employer must record the case verification number, review the employee information submitted to E-Verify to identify any errors, and find out whether the employee contests the tentative nonconfirmation. The Employer will transmit the Social Security number, or any other corrected employee information that SSA requests, to SSA for verification again if this review indicates a need to do so.

4. The Employer will instruct the employee to visit an SSA office within eight Federal Government work days. SSA will electronically transmit the result of the referral to the Employer within 10 Federal Government work days of the referral unless it determines that more than 10 days is necessary.

5. While waiting for case results, the Employer agrees to check the E-Verify system regularly for case updates.

6. The Employer agrees not to ask the employee to obtain a printout from the Social Security Administration number database (the Numident) or other written verification of the SSN from the SSA.

B. REFERRAL TO DHS

1. If the Employer receives a tentative nonconfirmation issued by DHS, the Employer must promptly notify employees in private of the finding and provide them with the notice and letter containing information specific to the employee's E-Verify case. The Employer also agrees to provide both the English and the translated notice and letter for employees with limited English proficiency to employees. The Employer must allow employees to contest the finding, and not take adverse action against employees if they choose to contest the finding, while their case is still pending.

2. The Employer agrees to obtain the employee's response about whether he or she will contest the tentative nonconfirmation as soon as possible after the Employer receives the tentative nonconfirmation. Only the employee may determine whether he or she will contest the tentative nonconfirmation.

3. The Employer agrees to refer individuals to DHS only when the employee chooses to contest a tentative nonconfirmation.

4. If the employee contests a tentative nonconfirmation issued by DHS, the Employer will instruct the employee to contact DHS through its toll-free hotline (as found on the referral letter) within eight Federal Government work days.

5. If the Employer finds a photo mismatch, the Employer must provide the photo mismatch tentative nonconfirmation notice and follow the instructions outlined in paragraph 1 of this section for tentative nonconfirmations, generally.

6. The Employer agrees that if an employee contests a tentative nonconfirmation based upon a photo mismatch, the Employer will send a copy of the employee's Form I-551, Form I-766, U.S. Passport, or passport card to DHS for review by:

   a. Scanning and uploading the document, or

   b. Sending a photocopy of the document by express mail (furnished and paid for by the employer).

7. The Employer understands that if it cannot determine whether there is a photo match/mismatch, the Employer must forward the employee's documentation to DHS as described in the preceding paragraph. The Employer agrees to resolve the case as specified by the DHS representative who will determine the photo match or mismatch.

8. DHS will electronically transmit the result of the referral to the Employer within 10 Federal Government work days of the referral unless it determines that more than 10 days is necessary.

9. While waiting for case results, the Employer agrees to check the E-Verify system regularly for case updates.

ARTICLE IV SERVICE PROVISIONS

A. NO SERVICE FEES

1. SSA and DHS will not charge the Employer for verification services performed under this MOU. The Employer is responsible for providing equipment needed to make inquiries. To access E-Verify, an Employer will need a personal computer with Internet access.

ARTICLE V MODIFICATION AND TERMINATION

A. MODIFICATION

1. This MOU is effective upon the signature of all parties and shall continue in effect for as long as the SSA and DHS operates the E-Verify program unless modified in writing by the mutual consent of all parties.

2. Any and all E-Verify system enhancements by DHS or SSA, including but not limited to E-Verify checking against additional data sources and instituting new verification policies or procedures, will be covered under this MOU and will not cause the need for a supplemental MOU that outlines these changes.

B. TERMINATION

1. The Employer may terminate this MOU and its participation in E-Verify at any time upon 30 days prior written notice to the other parties.

2. Notwithstanding Article V, part A of this MOU, DHS may terminate this MOU, and thereby the Employer's participation in E-Verify, with or without notice at any time if deemed necessary because of the requirements of law or policy, or upon a determination by SSA or DHS that there has been a breach of system integrity or security by the Employer, or a failure on the part of the Employer to comply with established E-Verify procedures and/or legal requirements. The Employer understands that if it is a Federal contractor, termination of this MOU by any party for any reason may negatively affect the performance of its contractual responsibilities. Similarly, the Employer understands that if it is in a state where E-Verify is mandatory, termination of this by any party MOU may negatively affect the Employer's business.

3. An Employer that is a Federal contractor may terminate this MOU when the Federal contract that requires its participation in E-Verify is terminated or completed. In such cases, the Federal contractor must provide written notice to DHS. If an Employer that is a Federal contractor fails to provide such notice, then that Employer will remain an E-Verify participant, will remain bound by the terms of this MOU that apply to non-Federal contractor participants, and will be required to use the E-Verify procedures to verify the employment eligibility of all newly hired employees.

4. The Employer agrees that E-Verify is not liable for any losses, financial or otherwise, if the Employer is terminated from E-Verify.

ARTICLE VI PARTIES

A. Some or all SSA and DHS responsibilities under this MOU may be performed by contractor(s), and SSA and DHS may adjust verification responsibilities between each other as necessary. By separate agreement with DHS, SSA has agreed to perform its responsibilities as described in this MOU.

B. Nothing in this MOU is intended, or should be construed, to create any right or benefit, substantive or procedural, enforceable at law by any third party against the United States, its agencies, officers, or employees, or against the Employer, its agents, officers, or employees.

C. The Employer may not assign, directly or indirectly, whether by operation of law, change of control or merger, all or any part of its rights or obligations under this MOU without the prior written consent of DHS, which consent shall not be unreasonably withheld or delayed. Any attempt to sublicense, assign, or transfer any of the rights, duties, or obligations herein is void.

D. Each party shall be solely responsible for defending any claim or action against it arising out of or related to E-Verify or this MOU, whether civil or criminal, and for any liability wherefrom, including (but not limited to) any dispute between the Employer and any other person or entity regarding the applicability of Section 403(d) of IIRIRA to any action taken or allegedly taken by the Employer.

E. The Employer understands that its participation in E-Verify is not confidential information and may be disclosed as authorized or required by law and DHS or SSA policy, including but not limited to, Congressional oversight, E-Verify publicity and media inquiries, determinations of compliance with Federal contractual requirements, and responses to inquiries under the Freedom of Information Act (FOIA).

F. The individuals whose signatures appear below represent that they are authorized to enter into this MOU on behalf of the Employer and DHS respectively. The Employer understands that any inaccurate statement, representation, data or other information provided to DHS may subject the Employer, its subcontractors, its employees, or its representatives to: (1) prosecution for false statements pursuant to 18 U.S.C. 1001 and/or; (2) immediate termination of its MOU and/or; (3) possible debarment or suspension.

G. The foregoing constitutes the full agreement on this subject between DHS and the Employer.

To be accepted as an E-Verify participant, you should only sign the Employer's Section of the signature page. If you have any questions, contact E-Verify at 1-888-464-4218.

THE E-VERIFY MEMORANDUM OF UNDERSTANDING FOR E-VERIFY EMPLOYER AGENTS

ARTICLE I

PURPOSE AND AUTHORITY

The parties to this agreement are the Department of Homeland Security (DHS) and _____ (E-Verify Employer Agent). The purpose of this agreement is to set forth terms and conditions which the E-Verify Employer Agent will follow while participating in E-Verify.

E-Verify is a program that electronically confirms an employee's eligibility to work in the United States after completion of Form I-9, Employment Eligibility Verification (Form I-9). This Memorandum of Understanding (MOU) explains certain features of the E-Verify program and describes specific responsibilities of the E-Verify Employer Agent, the Employer, DHS, and the Social Security Administration (SSA).

The Employer is not a party to this MOU; however, this MOU contains a section titled Responsibilities of the Employer. This section is provided to inform E-Verify Employer Agents acting on behalf of the Employer of the responsibilities and obligations their clients are required to meet. The Employer is bound by these responsibilities through signing a separate MOU during their enrollment as a client of the E-Verify Employer Agent. The E-Verify program requires an initial agreement between DHS and the E-Verify Employer Agent as part of the enrollment process. After agreeing to the MOU as set forth herein, completing the tutorial, and obtaining access to E-Verify as an E-Verify Employer Agent, the E-Verify Employer Agent will be given an opportunity to add a client once logged into E-Verify. All parties, including the Employer, will then be required to sign and submit a separate MOU to E-Verify. The responsibilities of the parties remain the same in each MOU.

Authority for the E-Verify program is found in Title IV, Subtitle A, of the Illegal Immigration Reform and Immigrant Responsibility Act of 1996 (IIRIRA), Pub. L. 104-208, 110 Stat. 3009, as amended (8 U.S.C. § 1324a note). The Federal Acquisition Regulation (FAR) Subpart 22.18, "Employment Eligibility Verification" and Executive Order 12989, as amended, provide authority for Federal contractors and subcontractors (Federal contractor) to use E-Verify to verify the employment eligibility of certain employees working on Federal contracts.

ARTICLE II RESPONSIBILITIES

A. RESPONSIBILITIES OF E-VERIFY EMPLOYER AGENT

1. The E-Verify Employer Agent agrees to provide to the SSA and DHS the names, titles, addresses, and telephone numbers of the E-Verify Employer Agent representatives who will be accessing information under E-Verify and shall update them as needed to keep them current.

2. The E-Verify Employer Agent agrees to become familiar with and comply with the E-Verify User Manual and provide a copy of the most current version of the E-Verify User Manual to the Employer so that the Employer can become familiar with and comply with E-Verify policy and procedures. The E-Verify Employer Agent agrees to obtain a revised E-Verify User Manual as it becomes available and to provide a copy of the revised version to the Employer no later than 30 days after the manual becomes available.

3. The E-Verify Employer Agent agrees that any person accessing E-Verify on its behalf is trained on the most recent E-Verify policy and procedures.

4. The E-Verify Employer Agent agrees that any E-Verify Employer Agent Representative who will perform employment verification cases will complete the E-Verify Tutorial before that individual initiates any cases.

a.   The E-Verify Employer Agent agrees that all E-Verify Employer Agent representatives will take the refresher tutorials initiated by the E-Verify program as a condition of continued use of E-Verify, including any tutorials for Federal contractors, if any of the Employers represented by the E-Verify Employer Agent is a Federal contractor.

b.   Failure to complete a refresher tutorial will prevent the E-Verify Employer Agent and Employer from continued use of E-Verify.

5. The E-Verify Employer Agent agrees to grant E-Verify access only to current employees who need E-Verify access. The E-Verify Employer Agent must promptly terminate an employee's E-Verify access if the employee is separated from the company or no longer needs access to E-Verify.

6. The E-Verify Employer Agent agrees to obtain the necessary equipment to use E- Verify as required by the E-Verify rules and regulations as modified from time to time.

7. The E-Verify Employer Agent agrees to, consistent with applicable laws, regulations, and policies, commit sufficient personnel and resources to meet the requirements of this MOU.

8. The E-Verify Employer Agent agrees to provide its clients with training on E-Verify processes, policies, and procedures. The E-Verify Employer Agent also agrees to provide its clients with ongoing E-Verify training as needed. E-Verify is not responsible for providing training to clients of E-Verify Employer Agents.

9. The E-Verify Employer Agent agrees to provide the Employer with the notices described in Article II.B.1 below.

10. The E-Verify Employer Agent agrees to create E-Verify cases for the Employer it represents in accordance with the E-Verify Manual, the E-Verify Web-Based Tutorial and all other published E-Verify rules and procedures. The E-Verify Employer Agent will create E-Verify cases using information provided by the Employer and will immediately communicate the response back to the Employer. If E-Verify is temporarily unavailable, the three-day time period will be extended until it is again operational in order to accommodate the E-Verify Employer Agent's attempting, in good faith, to make inquiries on behalf of the Employer during the period of unavailability.

11. When the E-Verify Employer Agent receives notice from a client company that it has received a contract with the FAR clause, then the E-Verify Employer Agent must update the company's E-Verify profile within 30 days of the contract award date.

12. If data is transmitted between the E-Verify Employer Agent and its client, then the E-Verify Employer Agent agrees to protect personally identifiable information during transmission to and from the E-Verify Employer Agent.

13. The E-Verify Employer Agent agrees to notify DHS immediately in the event of a breach of personal information. Breaches are defined as loss of control or unauthorized access to E-Verify personal data. All suspected or confirmed breaches should be reported by calling 1-888-464-4218 or via email at E-Verify@dhs.gov. Please use "Privacy Incident – Password" in the subject line of your email when sending a breach report to E-Verify.

14. The E-Verify Employer Agent agrees to fully cooperate with DHS and SSA in their compliance monitoring and evaluation of E-Verify, including permitting DHS, SSA, their contractors and other agents, upon reasonable notice, to review Forms I-9, employment records, and all records pertaining to the E-Verify Employer Agent's use of E-Verify, and to interview it and its employees regarding the use of E-

Verify, and to respond in a timely and accurate manner to DHS requests for information relating to their participation in E-Verify.

15. The E-Verify Employer Agent shall not make any false or unauthorized claims or references about its participation in E-Verify on its website, in advertising materials, or other media. The E-Verify Employer Agent shall not describe its services as federally-approved, federally-certified, or federally- recognized, or use language with a similar intent on its website or other materials provided to the public. Entering into this MOU does not mean that E-Verify endorses or authorizes your E-Verify Employer Agent services and any claim to that effect is false.

16. The E-Verify Employer Agent shall not state in its website or other public documents that any language used therein has been provided or approved by DHS, USCIS or the Verification Division, without first obtaining the prior written consent of DHS.

17. The E-Verify Employer Agent agrees that E-Verify trademarks and logos may be used only under license by DHS/USCIS (see M-795 (Web)) and, other than pursuant to the specific terms of such license, may not be used in any manner that might imply that the E-Verify Employer Agent's services, products, websites, or publications are sponsored by, endorsed by, licensed by, or affiliated with DHS, USCIS, or E-Verify.

18. The E-Verify Employer Agent understands that if it uses E-Verify procedures for any purpose other than as authorized by this MOU, the E-Verify Employer Agent may be subject to appropriate legal action and termination of its participation in E-Verify according to this MOU.

B. RESPONSIBILITIES OF THE EMPLOYER

The E-Verify Employer Agent shall ensure that the E-Verify Employer Agent and the Employers represented by the E-Verify Employer Agent carry out the following responsibilities. It is the E-Verify Employer Agent's responsibility to ensure that its clients are in compliance with all E-Verify policies and procedures.

1. The Employer agrees to display the following notices supplied by DHS in a prominent place that is clearly visible to prospective employees and all employees who are to be verified through the system:

a.   Notice of E-Verify Participation

b.   Notice of Right to Work

2. The Employer agrees to provide to the SSA and DHS the names, titles, addresses, and telephone numbers of the Employer representatives to be contacted about E-Verify. The Employer also agrees to keep such information current by providing updated information to SSA and DHS whenever the representatives' contact information changes.

3. The Employer shall become familiar with and comply with the most recent version of the E-Verify User Manual. The Employer will obtain the E-Verify User Manual from the E-Verify Employer Agent.

4. The Employer agrees to comply with current Form I-9 procedures, with two exceptions:

a.   If an employee presents a "List B" identity document, the Employer agrees to only accept "List B" documents that contain a photo. (List B documents identified in 8 C.F.R. § 274a.2(b)(1)(B)) can be presented during the Form I-9 process to establish identity.) If an employee objects to the photo requirement for religious reasons, the Employer should contact E-Verify at 1-888-464-4218.

b.   If an employee presents a DHS Form I-551 (Permanent Resident Card), Form I-766 (Employment Authorization Document), or U.S. Passport or Passport Card to complete Form I-9, the Employer agrees to make a photocopy of the document and to retain the photocopy with the employee's Form I-9. The Employer will use the photocopy to verify the photo and to assist DHS with its review of photo mismatches that employees contest. DHS may in the future designate other documents that activate the photo screening tool.

Note: Subject only to the exceptions noted previously in this paragraph, employees still retain the right to present any List A, or List B and List C, document(s) to complete the Form I-9.

5. The Employer agrees to record the case verification number on the employee's Form I-9 or to print the screen containing the case verification number and attach it to the employee's Form I-9.

6. The Employer agrees that, although it participates in E-Verify, the Employer has a responsibility to complete, retain, and make available for inspection Forms I-9 that relate to its employees, or from other requirements of applicable regulations or laws, including the obligation to comply with the antidiscrimination requirements of section 274B of the INA with respect to Form I-9 procedures.

a.   The following modified requirements are the only exceptions to an Employer's obligation to not employ unauthorized workers and comply with the anti-discrimination provision of the INA: (1) List B identity documents must have photos, as described in paragraph 4 above; (2) When an Employer confirms the identity and employment eligibility of newly hired employee using E-Verify procedures, the Employer establishes a rebuttable presumption that it has not violated section 274A(a)(1)(A) of the Immigration and Nationality Act (INA) with respect to the hiring of that employee; (3) If the Employer receives a final nonconfirmation for an employee, but continues to employ that person, the Employer must notify DHS and the Employer is subject to a civil money penalty between $550 and $1,100 for each failure to notify DHS of continued employment following a final nonconfirmation; (4) If the Employer continues to employ an employee after receiving a final nonconfirmation, then the Employer is subject to a rebuttable presumption that it has knowingly employed an unauthorized alien in violation of section 274A(a)(1)(A); and (5) no E-Verify participant is civilly or criminally liable under any law for any action taken in good faith based on information provided through the E-Verify.

b.   DHS reserves the right to conduct Form I-9 compliance inspections, as well as any other enforcement or compliance activity authorized by law, including site visits, to ensure proper use of E-Verify.

7. The Employer is strictly prohibited from creating an E-Verify case before the employee has been hired, meaning that a firm offer of employment was extended and accepted and Form I-9 was completed. The Employer agrees to create an E-Verify case for new employees within three Employer business days after each employee has been hired (after both Sections 1 and 2 of Form I-9 have been completed), and to complete as many steps of the E-Verify process as are necessary according to the E-Verify User Manual. If E-Verify is temporarily unavailable, the three-day time period will be extended until it is again operational in order to accommodate the Employer's attempting, in good faith, to make inquiries during the period of unavailability.

8. The Employer agrees not to use E-Verify for pre-employment screening of job applicants, in support of

any unlawful employment practice, or for any other use that this MOU or the E-Verify User Manual does not authorize.

9. The Employer must use E-Verify (through its E-Verify Employer Agent) for all new employees. The Employer will not verify selectively and will not verify employees hired before the effective date of this MOU. Employers who are Federal contractors may qualify for exceptions to this requirement as described in Article II.B of this MOU.

10. The Employer agrees to follow appropriate procedures (see Article III below) regarding tentative non-confirmations. The Employer must promptly notify employees in private of the finding and provide them with the notice and letter containing information specific to the employee's E-Verify case. The Employer agrees to provide both the English and the translated notice and letter for employees with limited English proficiency to employees. The Employer agrees to provide written referral instructions to employees and instruct affected employees to bring the English copy of the letter to the SSA. The Employer must allow employees to contest the finding, and not take adverse action against employees if they choose to contest the finding, while their case is still pending. Further, when employees contest a tentative nonconfirmation based upon a photo mismatch, the Employer must take additional steps (see Article III.B below) to contact DHS with information necessary to resolve the challenge.

11. The Employer agrees not to take any adverse action against an employee based upon the employee's perceived employment eligibility status while SSA or DHS is processing the verification request unless the Employer obtains knowledge (as defined in 8 C.F.R. § 274a.1(l)) that the employee is not work authorized. The Employer understands that an initial inability of the SSA or DHS automated verification system to verify work authorization, a tentative nonconfirmation, a case in continuance (indicating the need for additional time for the government to resolve a case), or the finding of a photo mismatch, does not establish, and should not be interpreted as, evidence that the employee is not work authorized. In any of such cases, the employee must be provided a full and fair opportunity to contest the finding, and if he or she does so, the employee may not be terminated or suffer any adverse employment consequences based upon the employee's perceived employment eligibility status (including denying, reducing, or extending work hours, delaying or preventing training, requiring an employee to work in poorer conditions, withholding pay, refusing to assign the employee to a Federal contract or other assignment, or otherwise assuming that he or she is unauthorized to work) until and unless secondary verification by SSA or DHS has been completed and a final nonconfirmation has been issued. If the employee does not choose to contest a tentative nonconfirmation or a photo mismatch or if a secondary verification is completed and a final nonconfirmation is issued, then the Employer can find the employee is not work authorized and terminate the employee's employment. Employers or employees with questions about a final nonconfirmation may call E-Verify at 1-888-464-4218 (customer service) or 1-888-897-7781 (worker hotline).

12. The Employer agrees to comply with Title VII of the Civil Rights Act of 1964 and section 274B of the INA as applicable by not discriminating unlawfully against any individual in hiring, firing, employment eligibility verification, or recruitment or referral practices because of his or her national origin or citizenship status, or by committing discriminatory documentary practices. The Employer understands that such illegal practices can include selective verification or use of E-Verify except as provided in part D below, or discharging or refusing to hire employees because they appear or sound "foreign" or have received tentative nonconfirmations. The Employer further understands that any violation of the immigration-related unfair

employment practices provisions in section 274B of the INA could subject the Employer to civil penalties, back pay awards, and other sanctions, and violations of Title VII could subject the Employer to back pay awards, compensatory and punitive damages.

Violations of either section 274B of the INA or Title VII may also lead to the termination of its participation in E-Verify. If the Employer has any questions relating to the anti-discrimination provision, it should contact OSC at 1-800-255-8155 or 1-800-237-2515 (TDD).

13. The Employer agrees that it will use the information it receives from E-Verify (through its E-Verify Employer Agent) only to confirm the employment eligibility of employees as authorized by this MOU. The Employer agrees that it will safeguard this information, and means of access to it (such as PINS and passwords), to ensure that it is not used for any other purpose and as necessary to protect its confidentiality, including ensuring that it is not disseminated to any person other than employees of the Employer who are authorized to perform the Employer's responsibilities under this MOU, except for such dissemination as may be authorized in advance by SSA or DHS for legitimate purposes.

14. The Employer agrees to notify DHS immediately in the event of a breach of personal information. Breaches are defined as loss of control or unauthorized access to E-Verify personal data. All suspected or confirmed breaches should be reported by calling 1-888-464-4218 or via email at E-Verify@dhs.gov. Please use "Privacy Incident – Password" in the subject line of your email when sending a breach report to E-Verify.

15. The Employer acknowledges that the information it receives through the E-Verify Employer Agent from SSA is governed by the Privacy Act (5 U.S.C. § 552a(i)(1) and (3)) and the Social Security Act (42 U.S.C. 1306(a)). Any person who obtains this information under false pretenses or uses it for any purpose other than as provided for in this MOU may be subject to criminal penalties.

16. The Employer agrees to cooperate with DHS and SSA in their compliance monitoring and evaluation of E-Verify (whether directly or through their E-Verify Employer Agent), which includes permitting DHS, SSA, their contractors and other agents, upon reasonable notice, to review Forms I-9 and other employment records and to interview it and its employees regarding the Employer's use of E-Verify, and to respond in a prompt and accurate manner to DHS requests for information relating to their participation in E-Verify.

17. The Employer shall not make any false or unauthorized claims or references about its participation in E-Verify on its website, in advertising materials, or other media. The Employer shall not describe its services as federally-approved, federally-certified, or federally-recognized, or use language with a similar intent on its website or other materials provided to the public. Entering into this MOU does not mean that E-Verify endorses or authorizes your E-Verify services and any claim to that effect is false.

18. The Employer shall not state in its website or other public documents that any language used therein has been provided or approved by DHS, USCIS or the Verification Division, without first obtaining the prior written consent of DHS.

19. The Employer agrees that E-Verify trademarks and logos may be used only under license by DHS/USCIS (see M-795 (Web)) and, other than pursuant to the specific terms of such license, may not be

used in any manner that might imply that the Employer's services, products, websites, or publications are sponsored by, endorsed by, licensed by, or affiliated with DHS, USCIS, or E-Verify.

20. The Employer understands that if it uses E-Verify procedures for any purpose other than as authorized by this MOU, the Employer may be subject to appropriate legal action and termination of its participation in E-Verify according to this MOU.

C. RESPONSIBILITIES OF FEDERAL CONTRACTORS

The E-Verify Employer Agent shall ensure that the E-Verify Employer Agent and the Employers represented by the E-Verify Employer Agent carry out the following responsibilities if the Employer is a federal contractor or becomes a Federal contractor. The E-Verify Employer Agent should instruct the client to keep the E-Verify Employer Agent informed about any changes or updates related to federal contracts. It is the E-Verify Employer Agent's responsibility to ensure that its clients are in compliance with all E-Verify policies and procedures.

1. If the Employer is a Federal contractor with the FAR E-Verify clause subject to the employment verification terms in Subpart 22.18 of the FAR, it will become familiar with and comply with the most current version of the E-Verify User Manual for Federal Contractors as well as the E-Verify Supplemental Guide for Federal Contractors.

2. In addition to the responsibilities of every employer outlined in this MOU, the Employer understands that if it is a Federal contractor subject to the employment verification terms in Subpart 22.18 of the FAR it must verify the employment eligibility of any "employee assigned to the contract" (as defined in FAR 22.1801). Once an employee has been verified through E-Verify by the Employer, the Employer may not reverify the employee through E-Verify.

a.   An Employer that is not enrolled in E-Verify as a Federal contractor at the time of a contract award must enroll as a Federal contractor in the E-Verify program within 30 calendar days of contract award and, within 90 days of enrollment, begin to verify employment eligibility of new hires using E-Verify. The Employer must verify those employees who are working in the United States, whether or not they are assigned to the contract. Once the Employer begins verifying new hires, such verification of new hires must be initiated within three business days after the hire date. Once enrolled in E-Verify as a Federal contractor, the Employer must begin verification of employees assigned to the contract within 90 calendar days after the date of enrollment or within 30 days of an employee's assignment to the contract, whichever date is later.

b.   Employers enrolled in E-Verify as a Federal contractor for 90 days or more at the time of a contract award must use E-Verify to begin verification of employment eligibility for new hires of the Employer who are working in the United States, whether or not assigned to the contract, within three business days after the date of hire. If the Employer is enrolled in E-Verify as a Federal contractor for 90 calendar days or less at the time of contract award, the Employer must, within 90 days of enrollment, begin to use E-Verify to initiate verification of new hires of the contractor who are working in the United States, whether or not assigned to the contract. Such verification of new hires must be initiated within three business days after the date of hire. An Employer enrolled as a Federal contractor in E-Verify must begin verification of each employee assigned to the contract within 90 calendar days after date of contract award or within 30 days after assignment to the contract, whichever is later.

c.   Federal contractors that are institutions of higher education (as defined at 20 U.S.C. 1001(a)), state or local governments, governments of Federally recognized Indian tribes, or sureties performing under a takeover agreement entered into with a Federal agency under a performance bond may choose to only verify new and existing employees assigned to the Federal contract. Such Federal contractors may, however, elect to verify all new hires, and/or all existing employees hired after November 6, 1986. Employers in this category must begin verification of employees assigned to the contract within 90 calendar days after the date of enrollment or within 30 days of an employee's assignment to the contract, whichever date is later.

d.   Upon enrollment, Employers who are Federal contractors may elect to verify employment eligibility of all existing employees working in the United States who were hired after November 6, 1986, instead of verifying only those employees assigned to a covered Federal contract. After enrollment, Employers must elect to verify existing staff following DHS procedures and begin E-Verify verification of all existing employees within 180 days after the election.

e.   The Employer may use a previously completed Form I-9 as the basis for creating an E-Verify case for an employee assigned to a contract as long as:

i.   That Form I-9 is complete (including the SSN) and complies with Article II.B.6,

ii.   The employee's work authorization has not expired, and

iii.   The Employer has reviewed the Form I-9 information either in person or in communications with the employee to ensure that the employee's Section 1, Form I-9 attestation has not changed (including, but not limited to, a lawful permanent resident alien having become a naturalized U.S. citizen).

f.   The Employer shall complete a new Form I-9 consistent with Article II.A.6 or update the previous Form I-9 to provide the necessary information if:

i.   The Employer cannot determine that Form I-9 complies with Article II.A.6,

ii.   The employee's basis for work authorization as attested in Section 1 has expired or changed, or

iii.   The Form I-9 contains no SSN or is otherwise incomplete.

Note: If Section 1 of the Form I-9 is otherwise valid and up-to-date and the form otherwise complies with Article II.C.5, but reflects documentation (such as a U.S. passport or Form I-551) that expired after completing Form I-9, the Employer shall not require the production of additional documentation, or use the photo screening tool described in Article II.A.5, subject to any additional or superseding instructions that may be provided on this subject in the E-Verify User Manual.

g.   The Employer agrees not to require a second verification using E-Verify of any assigned employee who has previously been verified as a newly hired employee under this MOU or to authorize verification of any existing employee by any Employer that is not a Federal contractor based on this Article.

3. The Employer understands that if it is a Federal contractor, its compliance with this MOU is a performance requirement under the terms of the Federal contract or subcontract, and the Employer consents to the release of information relating to compliance with its verification responsibilities under this MOU to contracting officers or other officials authorized to review the Employer's compliance with Federal contracting

requirements.

D. RESPONSIBILITIES OF SSA

1. SSA agrees to allow DHS to compare data provided by the Employer (through the E-Verify Employer Agent) against SSA's database. SSA sends DHS confirmation that the data sent either matches or does not match the information in SSA's database.

2. SSA agrees to safeguard the information the Employer provides (through the E-Verify Employer Agent) through E-Verify procedures. SSA also agrees to limit access to such information, as is appropriate by law, to individuals responsible for the verification of Social Security numbers or responsible for evaluation of E-Verify or such other persons or entities who may be authorized by SSA as governed by the Privacy Act (5 U.S.C. § 552a), the Social Security Act (42 U.S.C. 1306(a)), and SSA regulations (20 CFR Part 401).

3. SSA agrees to provide case results from its database within three Federal Government work days of the initial inquiry. E-Verify provides the information to the E-Verify Employer Agent.

4. SSA agrees to update SSA records as necessary if the employee who contests the SSA tentative non-confirmation visits an SSA field office and provides the required evidence. If the employee visits an SSA field office within the eight Federal Government work days from the date of referral to SSA, SSA agrees to update SSA records, if appropriate, within the eight-day period unless SSA determines that more than eight days may be necessary. In such cases, SSA will provide additional instructions to the employee. If the employee does not visit SSA in the time allowed, E-Verify may provide a final nonconfirmation to the E-Verify Employer Agent.

Note: If an Employer experiences technical problems, or has a policy question, the employer should contact E-Verify at 1-888-464-4218.

E. RESPONSIBILITIES OF DHS

1. DHS agrees to provide the Employer with selected data from DHS databases to enable the Employer (through the E-Verify Employer Agent) to conduct, to the extent authorized by this MOU

a.   Automated verification checks on alien employees by electronic means, and

b.   Photo verification checks (when available) on employees.

2. DHS agrees to assist the E-Verify Employer Agent with operational problems associated with its participation in E-Verify. DHS agrees to provide the E-Verify Employer Agent names, titles, addresses, and telephone numbers of DHS representatives to be contacted during the E-Verify process.

3. DHS agrees to provide to the E-Verify Employer Agent with access to E-Verify training materials as well as an E-Verify User Manual that contain instructions on E-Verify policies, procedures, and requirements for both SSA and DHS, including restrictions on the use of E-Verify.

4. DHS agrees to train E-Verify Employer Agents on all important changes made to E-Verify through the use of mandatory refresher tutorials and updates to the E-Verify User Manual. Even without changes to E-Verify, DHS reserves the right to require E-Verify Employer Agents to take mandatory refresher tutorials.

5. DHS agrees to provide to the Employer (through the E-Verify Employer Agent) a notice, which indicates the Employer's participation in E-Verify. DHS also agrees to provide to the Employer anti- discrimination notices issued by the Office of Special Counsel for Immigration-Related Unfair Employment Practices (OSC), Civil Rights Division, U.S. Department of Justice.

6. DHS agrees to issue each of the E-Verify Employer Agent's E-Verify users a unique user identification number and password that permits them to log in to E-Verify.

7. DHS agrees to safeguard the information the Employer provides (through the E-Verify Employer Agent), and to limit access to such information to individuals responsible for the verification process, for evaluation of E-Verify, or to such other persons or entities as may be authorized by applicable law. Information will be used only to verify the accuracy of Social Security numbers and employment eligibility, to enforce the INA and Federal criminal laws, and to administer Federal contracting requirements.

8. DHS agrees to provide a means of automated verification that provides (in conjunction with SSA verification procedures) confirmation or tentative nonconfirmation of employees' employment eligibility within three Federal Government work days of the initial inquiry.

9. DHS agrees to provide a means of secondary verification (including updating DHS records) for employees who contest DHS tentative nonconfirmations and photo mismatch tentative nonconfirmations. This provides final confirmation or nonconfirmation of the employees' employment eligibility within 10 Federal Government work days of the date of referral to DHS, unless DHS determines that more than 10 days may be necessary. In such cases, DHS will provide additional verification instructions.

ARTICLE III

REFERRAL OF INDIVIDUALS TO SSA AND DHS

The E-Verify Employer Agent shall ensure that the E-Verify Employer Agent and the Employers represented by the E-Verify Employer Agent carry out the following responsibilities. It is the E-Verify Employer Agent's responsibility to ensure that its clients are in compliance with all E-Verify policies and procedures.

A. REFERRAL TO SSA

1. If the Employer receives a tentative nonconfirmation issued by SSA, the Employer must print the tentative nonconfirmation notice as directed by E-Verify. The Employer must promptly notify employees in private of the finding and provide them with the notice and letter containing information specific to the employee's E-Verify case. The Employer also agrees to provide both the English and the translated notice and letter for employees with limited English proficiency to employees. The Employer agrees to provide written referral instructions to employees and instruct affected employees to bring the English copy of the letter to the SSA. The Employer must allow employees to contest the finding, and not take adverse action against employees if they choose to contest the finding, while their case is still pending.

2. The Employer agrees to obtain the employee's response about whether he or she will contest the tentative nonconfirmation as soon as possible after the Employer receives the tentative nonconfirmation. Only the employee may determine whether he or she will contest the tentative nonconfirmation.

3. After a tentative nonconfirmation, the Employer will refer employees to SSA field offices only as directed by E-Verify. The Employer must record the case verification number, review the employee information

submitted to E-Verify to identify any errors, and find out whether the employee contests the tentative non-confirmation. The Employer will transmit the Social Security number, or any other corrected employee information that SSA requests, to SSA for verification again if this review indicates a need to do so.

4. The Employer will instruct the employee to visit an SSA office within eight Federal Government work days. SSA will electronically transmit the result of the referral to the Employer (through the E-Verify Employer Agent) within 10 Federal Government work days of the referral unless it determines that more than 10 days is necessary.

5. While waiting for case results, the Employer agrees to check the E-Verify system regularly for case updates.

6. The Employer agrees not to ask the employee to obtain a printout from the Social Security Administration number database (the Numident) or other written verification of the SSN from the SSA.

B. REFERRAL TO DHS

1. If the Employer receives a tentative nonconfirmation issued by DHS, the Employer must promptly notify employees in private of the finding and provide them with the notice and letter containing information specific to the employee's E-Verify case. The Employer also agrees to provide both the English and the translated notice and letter for employees with limited English proficiency to employees. The Employer must allow employees to contest the finding, and not take adverse action against employees if they choose to contest the finding, while their case is still pending.

2. The Employer agrees to obtain the employee's response about whether he or she will contest the tentative nonconfirmation as soon as possible after the Employer receives the tentative nonconfirmation. Only the employee may determine whether he or she will contest the tentative nonconfirmation.

3. The Employer agrees to refer individuals to DHS only when the employee chooses to contest a tentative nonconfirmation.

4. If the employee contests a tentative nonconfirmation issued by DHS, the Employer will instruct the employee to contact DHS through its toll-free hotline (as found on the referral letter) within eight Federal Government work days.

5. If the Employer finds a photo mismatch, the Employer must provide the photo mismatch tentative nonconfirmation notice and follow the instructions outlined in paragraph 1 of this section for tentative nonconfirmations, generally.

6. The Employer agrees that if an employee contests a tentative nonconfirmation based upon a photo mismatch, the Employer will send a copy of the employee's Form I-551, Form I-766, U.S. Passport, or passport card to DHS for review by:

a. Scanning and uploading the document, or

b. Sending a photocopy of the document by express mail (furnished and paid for by the employer).

7. The Employer understands that if it cannot determine whether there is a photo match/mismatch, the Employer must forward the employee's documentation to DHS as described in the preceding paragraph. The Employer agrees to resolve the case as specified by the DHS representative who will determine the photo match or mismatch.

8. DHS will electronically transmit the result of the referral to the Employer (though the E-Verify Employer Agent) within 10 Federal Government work days of the referral unless it determines that more than 10 days is necessary.

9. While waiting for case results, the Employer agrees to check the E-Verify system regularly for case updates.

ARTICLE IV SERVICE PROVISIONS

A. NO SERVICE FEES

1. SSA and DHS will not charge the Employer or the E-Verify Employer Agent for verification services performed under this MOU. The E-Verify Employer Agent is responsible for providing equipment needed to make inquiries. To access E-Verify, an E-Verify Employer Agent will need a personal computer with Internet access.

MODIFICATION AND TERMINATION

A. MODIFICATION

1. This MOU is effective upon the signature of all parties and shall continue in effect for as long as the SSA and DHS operates the E-Verify program unless modified in writing by the mutual consent of all parties.

2. Any and all E-Verify system enhancements by DHS or SSA, including but not limited to E-Verify checking against additional data sources and instituting new verification policies or procedures, will be covered under this MOU and will not cause the need for a supplemental MOU that outlines these changes.

B. TERMINATION

1. The E-Verify Employer Agent may terminate this MOU and its participation in E-Verify at any time upon 30 days prior written notice to the other parties. In addition, any Employer represented by the E-Verify Employer Agent may voluntarily terminate its MOU upon giving DHS 30 days' written notice.

2. Notwithstanding Article V, part A of this MOU, DHS may terminate this MOU, and thereby the E-Verify Employer Agent's participation in E-Verify, with or without notice, at any time if deemed necessary because of the requirements of law or policy, or upon a determination by SSA or DHS that there has been a breach of system integrity or security by the E-Verify Employer Agent or the Employer, or a failure on the part of either party to comply with established E-Verify procedures and/or legal requirements. The Employer understands that if it is a Federal contractor, termination of this MOU by any party for any reason may negatively affect the performance of its contractual responsibilities. Similarly, the Employer understands that if it is in a state where E-Verify is mandatory, termination of this by any party MOU may negatively affect the Employer's business.

3. An E-Verify Employer Agent for an Employer that is a Federal contractor may terminate this MOU for that Employer when the Federal contract that requires its participation in E-Verify is terminated or completed. In such cases, the E-Verify Employer Agent must provide written notice to DHS. If the E-Verify Employer Agent fails to provide such notice, then that Employer will remain an E-Verify participant, will remain bound by the terms of this MOU that apply to non-Federal contractor participants, and will be required to use the E-Verify procedures to verify the employment eligibility of all newly hired employees.

4. The E-Verify Employer Agent agrees that E-Verify is not liable for any losses, financial or otherwise, if the E-Verify Employer Agent or the Employer is terminated from E-Verify.

PARTIES

A. Some or all SSA and DHS responsibilities under this MOU may be performed by contractor(s), and SSA and DHS may adjust verification responsibilities between each other as necessary. By separate agreement with DHS, SSA has agreed to perform its responsibilities as described in this MOU.

B. Nothing in this MOU is intended, or should be construed, to create any right or benefit, substantive or procedural, enforceable at law by any third party against the United States, its agencies, officers, or employees, or against the E-Verify Employer Agent, its agents, officers, or employees.

C.   The E-Verify Employer Agent may not assign, directly or indirectly, whether by operation of law, change of control or merger, all or any part of its rights or obligations under this MOU without the prior written consent of DHS, which consent shall not be unreasonably withheld or delayed. Any attempt to sublicense, assign, or transfer any of the rights, duties, or obligations herein is void.

D. Each party shall be solely responsible for defending any claim or action against it arising out of or related to E-Verify or this MOU, whether civil or criminal, and for any liability wherefrom, including (but not limited to) any dispute between the Employer and any other person or entity regarding the applicability of Section 403(d) of IIRIRA to any action taken or allegedly taken by the Employer.

E. The E-Verify Employer Agent understands that its participation in E-Verify is not confidential information and may be disclosed as authorized or required by law and DHS or SSA policy, including but not limited to, Congressional oversight, E-Verify publicity and media inquiries, determinations of compliance with Federal contractual requirements, and responses to inquiries under the Freedom of Information Act (FOIA).

F. The individuals whose signatures appear below represent that they are authorized to enter into this MOU on behalf of the E-Verify Employer Agent and DHS respectively. The E-Verify Employer Agent understands that any inaccurate statement, representation, data or other information provided to DHS may subject the Employer or the E-Verify Employer Agent, as the case may be, its subcontractors, its employees, or its representatives to: (1) prosecution for false statements pursuant to 18 U.S.C. 1001 and/or; (2) immediate termination of its MOU and/or; (3) possible debarment or suspension.

G. The foregoing constitutes the full agreement on this subject between DHS and the E-Verify Employer Agent.

If you have any questions, contact E-Verify at 1-888-464-4218.

THE E-VERIFY PROGRAM FOR EMPLOYMENT VERIFICATION MEMORANDUM OF UNDERSTANDING

ARTICLE I PURPOSE AND AUTHORITY

This Memorandum of Understanding (MOU) sets forth the agreement between the Social Security Administration (SSA), the Department of Homeland Security (DHS) and _____ [the State Employment Agency] (Agency) regarding the AGENCY's participation in the E-Verify Program (E-Verify). E-Verify is a Federal program that confirms a person's employment eligibility after the Employment Eligibility Verification Form (Form I-9) has been completed.

Authority for the E-Verify program is found in Title IV, Subtitle A, of the Illegal Immigration Reform and Immigrant Responsibility Act of 1996 (IIRIRA), Pub. L. 104-208, 110 Stat. 3009, as amended (8 U.S.C. § 1324a note).

Authority for the AGENCY to verify employment authorization of individuals referred for employment, and certify eligibility to employers in lieu of the employer verifying eligibility, is found in Section 274A(a)(5) of the Immigration and Nationality Act (INA) (8 U.S.C. § 1324a(a)(5) and Section 274a.6 of Title 8, Code of Federal Regulations (C.F.R.). The AGENCY certifies that it is a State employment agency (e.g. State Workforce Agency) as defined in 8 C.F.R. § 274a.1 ("any State government unit designated to cooperate with the United States Employment Service in the operation of the public employment service system").

Authority for the AGENCY to expend funds for participation in this program is found in the Wagner-Peyser Act (29 U.S.C. §§ 49 et seq.) and the Department of Labor regulations promulgated thereunder.

The purpose of this MOU is to provide the AGENCY with the means through E-Verify to verify the information provided through the Form I-9 process by workers to be referred by the AGENCY to any employer. For the purpose of this MOU, these workers will be referred to as "referred workers." The AGENCY will verify referred workers using the procedures provided by 8 C.F.R. § 274a.6 and this MOU.

ARTICLE II FUNCTIONS TO BE PERFORMED

A.   RESPONSIBILITIES OF THE SSA

1.   Upon completion of the Form I-9, and provided the AGENCY complies with the requirements of this MOU, SSA agrees to provide the AGENCY with available information that allows the AGENCY to confirm the accuracy of Social Security Numbers provided by referred workers and the employment authorization of such workers who are U.S. citizens.

2.   The SSA agrees to provide to the AGENCY appropriate assistance with operational problems that may arise during the AGENCY's participation in the E-Verify program. The SSA agrees to provide the AGENCY with names, titles, addresses, and telephone numbers of SSA representatives to be contacted during the E-Verify process.

3.   The SSA agrees to safeguard the information provided by the AGENCY through the E- Verify program procedures, and to limit access to such information, as is appropriate by law, to individuals responsible for the verification of Social Security Numbers and for evaluation of the E- Verify program or such other persons or entities who may be authorized by the SSA as governed by the Privacy Act (5

U.S.C. § 552a), the Social Security Act (42 U.S.C. 1306(a)), and SSA regulations (20 CFR Part 401).

4.   SSA agrees to provide a means of automated verification that is designed (in conjunction with DHS's automated system if necessary) to provide confirmation or tentative nonconfirmation of U.S. citizens' employment eligibility and accuracy of SSA records for both citizens and aliens within 3 Federal Government work days of the initial inquiry.

5.   SSA agrees to provide a means of secondary verification (including updating SSA records as may be necessary) for referred workers who contest SSA tentative nonconfirmations that is designed to provide final confirmation or nonconfirmation of U.S. citizens' employment eligibility and accuracy of SSA records for both citizens and aliens within 10 Federal Government work days of the date of referral to SSA, unless SSA determines that more than 10 days may be necessary. In such cases, SSA will provide additional verification instructions.

B.   RESPONSIBILITIES OF THE DEPARTMENT OF HOMELAND SECURITY

1.   Upon completion of the Form I-9 and after SSA verifies the accuracy of SSA records through E-Verify, DHS agrees to provide the AGENCY access to selected data on aliens from DHS's database to enable the AGENCY to conduct:

x   Automated verification checks on referred workers by electronic means, and

x   Photo verification checks (when available) on alien referred workers.

2.   DHS agrees to provide to the AGENCY appropriate assistance with operational problems that may arise during the AGENCY's participation in the E-Verify program. DHS agrees to provide the AGENCY with names, titles, addresses, and telephone numbers of DHS representatives to be contacted during the E-Verify process.

3.   DHS agrees to provide to the AGENCY a manual (the E-Verify User Manual) containing instructions on E-Verify policies, procedures and requirements for both SSA and DHS, including restrictions on the use of E-Verify. DHS agrees to provide training materials on E-Verify.

4.   DHS agrees to provide the AGENCY with a notice that must be given to referred workers, which informs the referred workers that the AGENCY participates in E-Verify. DHS also will provide the AGENCY with an anti-discrimination notice that must be given to the referred worker.

5.   DHS agrees to provide the AGENCY with a notice that must be provided by the AGENCY to each employer to whom the AGENCY refers a referred worker. The notice will inform the employer that the AGENCY has completed the Form I-9 employment eligibility verification process for the referred worker; that the AGENCY's referral may serve as evidence that the employer has complied with the verification requirements of section 274A of the INA for up to 21 business days pending receipt of AGENCY certification, as provided by 8 C.F.R. § 274a.6(c); that the AGENCY is participating in the E-Verify program; that verification of employment eligibility may or may not have been completed by the AGENCY at the time of referral; that the employer is subject to anti-discrimination requirements in its employment of the referred worker and may not take any adverse action against the referred worker based on the fact that the AGENCY may not have completed the E-Verify process at the time of referral; and that the AGENCY will follow up with the employer by providing the certification described in 8 C.F.R. § 274a.6(c)(1) within 21 days and/or further information on the referred worker's verification status.

6.   DHS agrees to issue the AGENCY a user identification number and password that permits the AGENCY to verify information provided by alien referred workers with DHS's database.

7.   DHS agrees to safeguard the information provided to DHS by the AGENCY, and to limit access to such information to individuals responsible for the verification of alien employment eligibility and for evaluation of the E-Verify program, or to such other persons or entities as may be authorized by applicable law. Information will be used only to verify the accuracy of Social Security Numbers and employment eligibility.

8.   DHS agrees to provide a means of automated verification that is designed (in conjunction with SSA verification procedures) to provide confirmation or tentative nonconfirmation of referred workers' employment eligibility within 3 Federal Government work days of the initial inquiry.

9.   DHS agrees to establish a means of secondary verification (including updating DHS records as may be necessary) for referred workers who contest DHS tentative nonconfirmations and photo non-match tentative nonconfirmations that is designed to provide final confirmation or nonconfirmation of such workers' employment eligibility within 10 Federal Government work days of the date of referral to DHS, unless DHS determines that more than 10 days may be necessary. In such cases, DHS will provide additional verification instructions.

C.   RESPONSIBILITIES OF THE STATE EMPLOYMENT AGENCY

1.   The AGENCY agrees to provide to each referred worker the DHS-supplied notice concerning the AGENCY's participation in E-Verify, and the notice concerning protections from unlawful discrimination.

2.   The AGENCY agrees to provide to the SSA and DHS the names, titles, addresses, and telephone numbers of the AGENCY representatives to be contacted regarding E-Verify.

3.   The AGENCY agrees to become familiar with and comply with the terms and procedures of the E-Verify User Manual. Including but not limited to, any supplemental information pertaining to verification by an AGENCY.

4.   The AGENCY agrees that any AGENCY representative who will perform employment verification queries will complete the E-Verify tutorial before that individual initiates any queries.
      A.   The AGENCY agrees that all AGENCY representatives will take any refresher tutorials initiated by the E-Verify program as a condition of continued use of E- Verify.
      B.   Failure to complete a refresher tutorial will preclude the AGENCY from continued use of the program.

5.   The AGENCY agrees that each AGENCY representative who will perform employment verification queries must have his or her own user ID and password.

6.   For each referred worker, the AGENCY agrees to comply with established Form I-9 procedures for state employment agencies that choose to verify identity and employment eligibility for individuals referred for employment, as provided in 8 C.F.R. § 274a.6, with two exceptions:

x   If a job candidate presents a "List B" identity document, the AGENCY agrees to only accept "List B" documents that contain a photo. (List B documents identified in 8 C.F.R. § 274a.2(b)(1)(B)) can be presented during the Form I-9 process to establish identity).

x   If a job candidate presents a DHS Form I-551 (Permanent Resident Card) or Form I-766 (Employment Authorization Document) to complete the Form I-9, the AGENCY agrees to make a photocopy of the document and to retain the photocopy with the job candidate's Form I-9. The AGENCY will use the photocopy to verify the photo and to assist the Department with its review of photo non-matches that are contested by job candidates. Note that job candidates retain the right to present any List A, or List B and List C, documentation to complete the Form I-9. DHS may in the future designate other documents that activate the Photo Screening Tool.

7.   The AGENCY understands that participation in E-Verify does not exempt the AGENCY from the responsibility to complete, retain, and make available for inspection Forms I-9 that relate to referred workers, or from other requirements of applicable regulations or laws, except for the following modified requirements applicable by reason of the AGENCY's participation in E-Verify: (1) identity documents must have photos, as described in paragraph 5 above; (2) a rebuttable presumption is established that the AGENCY has not violated Sections 274A(a)(1)(A) or 101(a)(15)(H)(ii)(a) of the Immigration and Nationality Act (INA) with respect to the referral of any individual if it obtains confirmation of the identity and employment eligibility of the individual in compliance with the terms and conditions of E-Verify; (3) the AGENCY is subject to a rebuttable presumption that it has knowingly referred an unauthorized alien in violation of Section 101(a)(15)(H)(ii)(a) if the AGENCY refers any referred worker after receiving a final nonconfirmation; and (4) no person or entity participating in E-Verify is civilly or criminally liable under any law for any action taken in good faith on information provided through the confirmation system. DHS reserves the right to conduct Form I-9 compliance inspections during the course of E- Verify, as well as to conduct any other enforcement activity authorized by law.

8.   The AGENCY agrees to initiate E-Verify verification procedures prior to any referral of a referred worker (but after both Sections 1 and 2 of the Form I-9 have been completed), and to complete as many (but only as many) steps of the E-Verify process as are necessary according to the E-Verify User Manual. The AGENCY is prohibited from initiating verification procedures before the referred worker has completed the Form I-9. In all cases, the AGENCY must use the SSA verification procedures first, and use DHS verification procedures and Photo Screening Tool only after the SSA verification response has been given.

9.   The AGENCY agrees not to use E-Verify procedures for screening of non-job applicants, support for any unlawful employment practice, or any other use not authorized by this MOU.

   x   The AGENCY must use E-Verify for all referred workers and agrees that it will not verify only certain such workers selectively.
   x   The AGENCY agrees not to use E-Verify procedures for re-verification of employment eligibility.
   x   The AGENCY agrees not to use E-Verify for any individuals referred for any employment before the date this MOU is in effect.
   x   The AGENCY understands that if the AGENCY uses E-Verify procedures for any purpose other than as authorized by this MOU, the AGENCY may be subject to appropriate legal action and the immediate termination of its access to SSA and DHS information pursuant to this MOU.
   x   The AGENCY agrees that it will not delay the referral of a referred worker or take other adverse action because of the receipt of a tentative nonconfirmation that is challenged by the worker.

10.   The AGENCY understands that the obligation to verify under this MOU applies to referred workers. There is no authority or obligation to verify any individual who is not a referred worker. The AGENCY may not refer any individual unless the individual's Form I-9 process has been completed pursuant to 8 C.F.R. § 274a.6 and the E-Verify verification procedures initiated. The AGENCY agrees that it will not deny any referral to any individual because of the need to complete the verification process pursuant to this MOU.

11.   The AGENCY agrees to follow appropriate procedures (see Article III.B. below) regarding tentative nonconfirmations, including promptly notifying referred workers of the finding, providing written instructions to such workers, allowing such workers to contest the finding, and not taking adverse action against such workers if they choose to contest the finding. Further, when referred workers contest a tentative nonconfirmation based upon a photo non-match, the AGENCY is required to take affirmative steps (see Article III.B. below) to contact DHS with information necessary to resolve the challenge.

12.   The AGENCY agrees not to take any adverse action against a referred worker (including, but not limited to, declining to refer such worker or delaying the referral) based upon the job candidate's employment eligibility status while SSA or DHS is processing the verification request unless the AGENCY obtains knowledge (as defined in 8 C.F.R. § 274a.1(l)) that the referred worker is not work authorized. The AGENCY understands that an initial inability of the SSA or DHS automated verification to verify work authorization, a tentative nonconfirmation, or the finding of a photo non-match, does not mean, and should not be interpreted as, an indication that the referred worker is not work authorized. In any of the cases listed above, the referred worker must be provided the opportunity to contest the finding, and if he or she does so, may not suffer any adverse employment or potential employment consequences until and unless secondary verification by SSA or DHS has been completed and a final nonconfirmation has been issued. If the referred worker does not choose to contest a tentative nonconfirmation or a photo non-match, then the AGENCY can find that such worker is not work authorized and take the appropriate action, including but not limited to, declining to issue or revoking the certification provided under 8 C.F.R. § 274a.6(c), and notifying the worker's employer.

13.   The AGENCY agrees to comply with Section 274B of the INA by not discriminating unlawfully against any individual in hiring, firing, or recruitment or referral practices because of his or her national origin or, in the case of a protected individual as defined in Section 274B(a)(3) of the INA, because of his or her citizenship status. The AGENCY understands that such illegal practices may include, for example, use of E-Verify on some, but not all, referred workers, refusing to refer for hire referred workers because they appear or sound "foreign", delaying a referral until a tentative nonconfirmation is wholly resolved, and termination of the referral process based upon tentative nonconfirmations. Any violation of the unfair immigration-related employment practices provisions of the INA could subject the AGENCY to civil penalties pursuant to Section 274B of the INA and the termination of its participation in E-Verify. If the AGENCY has any questions relating to the anti-discrimination provision, it should contact OSC at 1-800-255-7688 or 1-800-237-2515 (TDD).

14.   The AGENCY agrees to record the case verification number on the referred worker's Form I-9 or to print the screen containing the case verification number and attach it to the worker's Form I-9.

15.   The AGENCY agrees that it will use the information it receives from the SSA or DHS pursuant to E-Verify and this MOU only to confirm the employment eligibility of referred workers, after completion of the Form I-9. The AGENCY agrees that it will safeguard this information, and means of access to it (such as PINS and passwords) to ensure that it is not used for any other purpose and as necessary to protect its confidentiality, including ensuring that it is not disseminated to any person other than employees of the AGENCY who are authorized to perform the AGENCY's responsibilities under this MOU.

16.   The AGENCY acknowledges that the information which it receives from SSA is governed by the Privacy Act (5 U.S.C. § 552a(i)(1) and (3)) and the Social Security Act (42 U.S.C. 1306(a)), and that any person who obtains this information under false pretenses or uses it for any purpose other than as provided for in this MOU may be subject to criminal penalties.

17.   The AGENCY agrees to make employment and E-Verify related records available to DHS and the

SSA, or their designated agents or designees, and allow DHS and SSA, or their authorized agents or designees, to make periodic visits to the AGENCY for the purpose of reviewing E-Verify- related records, i.e., Forms I-9, SSA Transaction Records, DHS verification records, and certification forms described in 8 C.F.R. § 274a.6(d), which were created during the AGENCY's participation in the E-Verify Program. In addition, for the purpose of evaluating E-Verify, the AGENCY agrees to allow DHS and SSA or their authorized agents or designees, to interview it regarding its experience with E-Verify, and to interview job candidates and hired employees concerning their experience with E-Verify. Failure to comply with the terms of this paragraph may lead DHS to terminate the AGENCY's access to E-Verify.

18.   The AGENCY is authorized and encouraged to seek the cooperation and assistance of the employer of any referred worker in fulfilling the obligations of this MOU, including, but not limited to, seeking the assistance of the employer in locating workers for the purpose of providing notice of a tentative nonconfirmation and information on how to resolve it; providing the employer with information on the E-Verify process and anti-discrimination obligations; and advising the employer of any final nonconfirmation. The AGENCY understands, however, that it is expressly the AGENCY's obligation to comply with this MOU regardless of any action or inaction of an employer or other third party. If a AGENCY has reason to believe that an employer is unwilling to hire a referred worker because of the AGENCY's receipt of a tentative nonconfirmation, the AGENCY may raise such concerns with the Office of Special Counsel for Immigration-Related Unfair Employment Practices in the Civil Rights Division of the U.S. Department of Justice by calling 1-800-255-7688.

19.   The AGENCY agrees to provide the DHS-supplied notice to each employer to whom the AGENCY refers a referred worker.

20.   The AGENCY agrees that it will give immediate notice in writing to the employer of a referred worker if the worker is the subject of a final nonconfirmation, and will revoke any certification described in 8 C.F.R. § 274a.6 that has been previously provided to the employer.

ARTICLE III

REFERRAL OF INDIVIDUALS TO THE SSA AND THE DEPARTMENT OF HOMELAND SECURITY

A.   REFERRAL TO THE SSA

1.   If the AGENCY receives a tentative nonconfirmation issued by SSA, the AGENCY must print the E-Verify tentative nonconfirmation notice and promptly provide it to the referred worker so that the worker may determine whether he or she will contest the tentative nonconfirmation.

2.   The AGENCY will refer referred workers to SSA field offices only as directed by the automated system based on a tentative nonconfirmation, and only after the AGENCY records the case verification number, reviews the input to detect any transaction errors, and determines that the worker wishes to contest the tentative nonconfirmation. The AGENCY will transmit the Social Security Number to SSA for verification again if this review indicates a need to do so. The AGENCY will determine whether the referred worker contests the tentative nonconfirmation as soon as possible after the AGENCY receives it.

3.   If the employee contests an SSA tentative nonconfirmation, the AGENCY will promptly provide the referred worker with the E-Verify SSA referral letter and instruct the job candidate to visit an SSA office to resolve the discrepancy within 8 Federal Government work days. SSA will electronically transmit the result of the referral to the AGENCY within 10 Federal Government work days of the referral unless it determines that more than 10 days is necessary.

4.   The AGENCY agrees not to ask the referred worker to obtain a printout from the Social Security Number database (the Numident) or other written verification of the Social Security Number from the SSA.

B.   REFERRAL TO THE DEPARTMENT OF HOMELAND SECURITY

1.   If the AGENCY receives a tentative nonconfirmation issued by DHS, the AGENCY must print the E-Verify tentative nonconfirmation notice and promptly provide it to the referred worker so that the worker may determine whether he or she will contest the tentative nonconfirmation.

2.   If the AGENCY finds a photo non-match for an alien who provides a document for which the automated system has transmitted a photo, the AGENCY must print the E-Verify photo non- match tentative nonconfirmation notice and provide it to the referred worker so that the worker may determine whether he or she will contest the finding.

3.   The AGENCY agrees to refer individuals to DHS only when the referred worker chooses to contest a tentative nonconfirmation received from the DHS automated verification process or when the AGENCY issues a tentative nonconfirmation based upon a photo non-match. The AGENCY will determine whether the worker contests the tentative nonconfirmation as soon as possible after the AGENCY receives it.

4.   If the referred worker contests a tentative nonconfirmation issued by DHS, the AGENCY will promptly provide the worker with the E-Verify DHS referral letter and instruct the worker to contact the Department through its toll-free hotline listed on the referral letter within 8 Federal Government work days.

5.   If the referred worker contests a tentative nonconfirmation based upon a photo non-match, the AGENCY will promptly provide the worker with the E-Verify referral letter to DHS. DHS will electronically transmit the result of the referral to the AGENCY within 10 Federal Government work days of the referral unless it determines that more than 10 days is necessary.

6.   The AGENCY agrees that if a referred worker contests a tentative nonconfirmation based upon a photo non-match, the AGENCY will send a copy of the worker's Form I-551 or Form I-766 to DHS for review by:

x   Scanning and uploading the document, or
x   Sending a photocopy of the document by an express mail account (furnished and paid for by DHS).

7.   The AGENCY understands that if it cannot determine whether there is a photo match/non- match, the AGENCY is required to forward the referred worker's documentation to DHS by scanning and uploading, or by sending the document as described in the preceding paragraph, and resolving the case as specified by the Immigration Services Verifier at DHS who will determine the photo match or non-match.

ARTICLE IV SERVICE PROVISIONS

The SSA and DHS will not charge the AGENCY for verification services performed under this MOU. The AGENCY is responsible for providing equipment needed to make inquiries. To access the E-Verify System, AGENCY will need a personal computer with Internet access.

ARTICLE V PARTIES

1.   This MOU is effective upon the signature of all parties, and shall continue in effect for as long as the SSA and DHS conduct the E-Verify program unless modified in writing by the mutual consent of all parties, or terminated by any party upon 30 days prior written notice to the others. Any and all system enhancements to the E-Verify program by DHS or SSA, including but not limited to the E-Verify checking against additional data sources and instituting new verification procedures, will be covered under this MOU and will not cause the need for a supplemental MOU that outlines these changes. DHS agrees to train the AGENCY on all changes made to E-Verify through the use of mandatory refresher tutorials and updates to the E-Verify manual. Even without changes to E-Verify, DHS reserves the right to require the AGENCY to take mandatory refresher tutorials.

2.   Termination by any party shall terminate the MOU as to all parties. The SSA or DHS may terminate this MOU without prior notice if deemed necessary because of the requirements of law or policy, or upon a determination by SSA or DHS that there has been a breach of system integrity or security by the AGENCY, or a failure on the part of the AGENCY to comply with established procedures or legal requirements. Some or all SSA and DHS responsibilities under this MOU may be performed by contractor(s), and SSA and DHS may adjust verification responsibilities between each other as they may determine.

3.   Nothing in this MOU is intended, or should be construed, to create any right or benefit, substantive or procedural, enforceable at law by any third party against the United States, its agencies, officers, or employees, or against the AGENCY, its agents, officers, or employees.

4.   Each party shall be solely responsible for defending any claim or action against it arising out of or related to E-Verify or this MOU, whether civil or criminal, and for any liability wherefrom, including (but not limited to) any dispute between the AGENCY and any other person or entity regarding the applicability of Section 403(d) of IIRIRA to any action taken or allegedly taken by the AGENCY.

5.   The AGENCY understands that the fact of its participation in E-Verify is not confidential information and may be disclosed as authorized or required by law and DHS or SSA policy, including but not limited to, Congressional oversight, E-Verify publicity and media inquiries, and responses to inquiries under the Freedom of Information Act (FOIA).

6.   The foregoing constitutes the full agreement on this subject among the SSA, DHS, and the SWA. This agreement is not intended to displace or modify any agreement between SSA and DHS regarding reimbursement to SSA for E-Verify-related work.

7.   The individuals whose signatures appear below represent that they are authorized to enter into this MOU on behalf of the AGENCY, SSA and DHS, respectively. The SSA has agreed that DHS's signature to the MOU shall also constitute SSA's agreement to its terms and conditions.

Please only sign the AGENCY's Section of the signature page. You must provide a telephone number and valid email address in the event we need to contact you. If you have any questions, contact E-Verify at: 888-464-4218.

APPENDIX F

CASE MANAGEMENT AND ELECTRONIC FILING SYSTEMS VENDORS

The companies listed below are primarily electronic I-9 and immigration case management providers. This is not meant as an endorsement of any company. There are many companies, such as Maximus, Vibe HCM, Inc. (formerly Electronic Commerce, Inc.), and Hire Right LLC, that provide electronic I-9 services as part of the employee onboarding process.

Guardian
by Lawlogix, a Division of Hyland

3111 N. Central Avenue
Phoenix, AZ 85012
Phone: 877-725-4355   ext. 1
Email: I9sales@lawlogix.com
Website: www.lawlogix.com

Tracker I-9
by Tracker Corp.

559 Sutter Street
San Francisco, CA 94102
Phone: 888-411-8757
Email: sales@trackercorp.com
Website: www.trackercorp.com

Form I-9 Compliance, LLC

24 Corporate Plaza
Suite 190
Newport Beach, CA 92660
Phone: 866-359-4949
Website: www.formi9.com

Lookout Services

4950 Bluebonnet Drive
Suite 102
Stafford, TX 77477
Phone: 713-364-9983
Website: www.lookoutservices.net

i9Advantage

21220 Kelly Road
Eastpointe, MI 48021
Phone: 800-724-8546
Email: sales@i9advantage.com
Website: http://i9advantage.com/

i9Check

18760 E. Amar Rd. #150
Walnut, CA 91789
Phone: 626-678-0804
Email: sales@i9check.com
Website: http://i9check.com/

I-9Zoom
by INSZoom

2603 Camino Ramon
Suite 375
San Ramon, CA 94583
Phone: 925-244-0600
Email: sales@inszoom.com
Website: www.inszoom.com

APPENDIX G

WORKSITE ENFORCEMENT OPERATIONS

Pizzarias, LLC

3/21/2017

Florida

- Reached a settlement with the IER (formerly OSC) to pay $140,000 in civil penalties for allegations of document abuse

Paragon Bldg. Maintenance

3/13/2017

California

- IER (formerly OSC) and company resolved allegations of document abuse by agreeing to $115,000 penalty and $30,000 in back pay

Metropolitan Enterprises

3/6/2017

Brooklyn, NY

- OCAHO reduced ICE's proposed penalties from $195,649 to $151,200 because ICE failed to prove 20 allegations - it did not show the 20 employees were employed during the audit period

Waterstone Grill

1/19/2017

Hamburg, NY

- OCAHO reduced penalties from $46,657 to $33,725 for a variety of reasons

J.E.T. Holding Co.

1/17/2017

CNMI

- Reached a settlement with IER (formerly OSC) to pay $12,000 in civil penalties and $40,000 in back pay to resolve allegations over whether discriminated against U.S. citizens

Pegasus Family Restaurant

12/22/2016

Hamburg, NY

- OCAHO reduced penalties sought by ICE from $96,398 to $58,850 for 107 substantive viola-

405

tions including 31 violations for failure to prepare I-9 forms

International Packaging, Inc.

11/30/2016

Minneapolis, MN

- OCAHO reduced penalties sought by ICE from $88,825 to $38,050 due to good faith reliance on attorney's advice, which lead to failure to provide I-9 supporting documentation & the company's financial problems

Aldine, Texas Ind. School District

11/22/2016

Aldine, TX

- Reached a settlement with the OSC to pay $140,000 civil penalty to resolve allegations of discrimination against non–U.S. citizens related to documentation

Spectrum Technical Staffing and Personnel Plus

11/10/2016

St. Paul, MN

- OCAHO found Personnel Plus was not liable for $1.4 million in penalties because it was not a corporate successor

DOJ v. Nebraska Beef, Ltd.

11/9/2016

Omaha, NE

- District Court ruled Nebraska Beef breached settlement agreement and ordered it to pay $200,000 in civil penalties, per agreement

Ideal Transportation

11/7/2016

Massachusetts

- OCAHO reduced penalties from $11,200 to $2,700 because even though employer did not present any timely prepared I-9 forms, the employees possessed TWIC cards proving work-authorized status

American Cleaning

10/17/2016

Brighton, MA

- Company reached a settlement with OSC to pay $195,000 in civil penalties to resolve allegations of discrimination against non–U.S. citizens

Frimmel Management

10/14/2016

Maricopa County, AZ

- OCAHO ordered company to pay fine of $347,000 for hundreds of I-9 violations; OCAHO declined to find ICE's investigation was "fruit of the poisonous tree" from Sheriff's criminal investigation

St. Croix Personnel Services

9/30/2016

Minnesota

- OCAHO reduced penalties from $16,690 to $5,450 because 8 of the alleged I-9 violations were timeliness violations barred by five-year statute of limitations

Solutions Group

9/20/2016

Beverly Hills, CA

- OCAHO reduced penalties from $86,394 to $56,150 for I-9 violations because of company's small size and inability to pay the penalty

Eastridge Workforce Solutions

8/15/2016

Mira Mesa, CA

- OSC and employer reached settlement where employer agreed to pay $175,000 in civil penalties for document abuse

Para Tacos La Chilanga

8/15/2016

Pharr, TX

- OCAHO found employer violated Act and ordered to pay over $33,000 for failure to prepare any I-9 forms

Employer Solutions Staffing v. OCAHO (5th Cir. 2016)

8/11/2016

Edina, MN

- Fifth Circuit vacated $226,000 civil penalty because employer did not have fair notice that a corporate attestation was insufficient as opposed to a personal certification

Mary's Gone Crackers

7/22/2016

Gridley, CA

- Inferred into a non-prosecution agreement to pay $1.5 million for retaining undocumented workers after informing ICE they had been fired

Crookham Company

6/27/2016

Caldwell, ID

- Reached a settlement with OSC to pay $200,000 civil penalty to resolve allegations that the company discriminated against work-authorized non–US citizens

Powerstaffing, Inc.

6/23/2016

Edison, NJ

- Reached a settlement with OSC to pay $153,000 civil penalty to resolve similar allegations as made in Crookham

East Coast Foods d/b/a Roscoe's House of Chicken + Waffles

6/8/2016

Pasadena, CA

- OCAHO assessed a penalty of $18,350, down from $38,708 sought by ICE to resolve substantive I-9 violations

DJ Drywall, Inc. and David Jones, owner

6/3/2016

Seattle, WA

- Pled guilty to knowingly encouraging an undocumented worker to reside in United States; owner forfeited $25,000 and received two years' probation while company paid $75,000 fine with five-year probation

Cawoods Produce

6/2/2016

Texas

- OCAHO reduced penalties from $36,465 to $14,575 for a variety of substantive violations, including failure to prepare I-9 forms for nine employees

Villa Rancho Bernardo Care Center

5/31/2016

San Diego, CA

- Reached a settlement with OSC to pay $24,000 civil penalty for allegedly discriminating against non–U.S. citizens

Net Jets Services, Inc.

5/13/2016

Columbus, OH

- Reached a settlement with OSC to pay $41,480 civil penalty for allegedly discriminating against work-authorized immigrants

Muniz Concrete & Contracting

4/29/2016

Texas

- OCAHO found company committed 32 violations plus assessed a $16,275 civil penalty (ICE sought $19,989)

Golden Employment Group

4/1/2016

Minnesota

- OCAHO assessed a fine of $209,600 for 465 Form I-9 violations, including failure to prepare or present 390 Form I-9s (ICE sought $305,525)

Barrios Street Realty

3/21/2016

Lockport. LA

- OSC reached a settlement wherein the company created a backpay fund of $115,000 and paid a $30,000 civil penalty by preferring foreign workers over U.S. workers under the H-2B visa program

Safe-Air of Illinois

3/10/2016

Chicago, IL

- OCAHO found the company committed 39 Form I-9 substantive violations but reduced the civil penalty from $34,969 to $18,450

Hair U Wear

2/18/2016

Buffalo, NY

- OCAHO found six I-9s had substantive violations and assessed a $4,776 civil penalty, which was reduced by 10 percent because of two mitigating factors

Golden Farm Market

2/18/2016

Buffalo, NY

- OCAHO found the company violated the law by not timely preparing I-9 forms and upheld the civil penalty of $7,106

SKZ Harvesting, Inc.

2/4/2016

Montana

- OCAHO reduced the sought civil penalty of $74,587 to $29,600 in part because ICE failed to prove some employees were undocumented

Sunny Grove Landscaping

11/23/2015

Ft. Meyers, FL

- OSC and company settled case where it was alleged LPRs were required to produce their green cards; assessed $7,500 civil penalty

Buffalo Transportation

10/23/2015

Buffalo, NY

- OCAHO assessed $75,600 in civil penalties for 100 percent error rate- mainly failure to prepare I-9 forms
- ICE sought $110,000

Miami-Dale County Public Schools

10/22/2015

Miami, FL

- OSC and company settled matter where it was claimed non–U.S. citizens had to present specific documents but not U.S. citizens; assessed $90,000 civil penalty and $125,000 backpay fund

Yellow Checker Star Transportation Co.

10/20/2015

Las Vegas, NV

- OSC and taxicab companies settled case, which alleged non–U.S. citizens had to present additional and unnecessary documents but not U.S. citizens; assessed $445,000 civil penalty

North American Shipbuilding, LLC

10/15/2015

Larose, LA

- OSC and company settled a retaliation claim with payment of $15,000 in back pay and $1,750 civil penalty

7-Eleven

9/1/2015

New York

- OCAHO found franchise had 100 percent error rate on I-9 forms not prepared, untimely prepared, back-dated and incomplete; assessed $15,450 in civil penalties
- ICE sought $34,408

Louisiana Crane & Construction

8/31/2015

Eunice, LA

- OSC and company settled case where allegedly company required non–U.S. citizens to produce only DHS-issued documents; company agreed to pay $165,000 in civil penalties and establish $50,000 backpay fund

Beyond Cleaning Services

8/14/2015

New Orleans, LA

- OCAHO found six workers were independent contractors; thus, no I-9 forms were required

City of Eugene

8/4/2015

Eugene, OR

- OSC and city settled case where city sought to restrict job applicants for policemen to U.S. citizens; agreed to pay $3,000 civil penalty

Hartmann Studios

7/8/2015

Richmond, CA & Atlanta, GA

- OCAHO found Hartmann committed 800 violations with about 50 percent re: a self-created I-9 form that was not signed by a company rep; assessed $605,000 in civil penalties

- ICE sought $812,000

Double Dragon Restaurant & owners

6/30/2015

Rio Rancho, NM

- Owners of restaurants were convicted of harboring undocumented workers and had to forfeit property of $120,000

PM Packaging

6/26/2015

Compton, CA

- OCAHO found ICE did not pierce corporate veil but still found 28 substantive I-9 violations; assessed $27,200 in civil penalties
- ICE sought $53,762

Abercrombie & Fitch

6/25/2015

Nationwide

- OSC and company settled claim of discrimination against a non–U.S. citizen; company agreed to establish backpay fund of $154,000 and pay a civil penalty of $1,100

Broetje Orchards

6/4/2015

Prescott, WA

- Company agreed to pay $2.25 million fine to avoid criminal prosecution for knowingly employing 950 undocumented workers

Luis Esparza Services

5/27/2015

Bakersfield, CA

- OSC and company settled case where allegations of citizenship status discrimination; non–U.S. citizens had to produce certain documents; assessed civil penalty of $320,000

Homestead Metal Recycling Corp

5/19/2015

Homestead, FL

- OCAHO found two owners did not have meaningful control; thus, they were treated as employees who must complete I-9 forms; assessed penalty of $2,450

Niche

5/13/2015

New Bedford, MA

- OCAHO found company committed 177 Form I-9 violations, mostly failure to complete Section 1 or 2 correctly; assessed $63,850 civil penalty

Horno MSJ, Ltd.

5/4/2015

San Antonio, TX

- OCAHO found numerous substantive I-9 violations for failing to complete I-9 forms and failure to prepare I-9 forms; assessed $14,600 in civil penalties

McPeek Racing Stables

4/21/2015

Kentucky

- OCAHO found approximately 100 violations with 60 percent for failure to prepare an I-9 form; assessed $35,900

Liberty Packaging

2/24/2015

Unknown location

- OCAHO found violations for backdating I-9 forms and assessed $11,700 in civil penalties

Overland Park Hotels and Rhonda Bridge

2/16/2015

Overland Park, KS

- Hotel owner sentenced to 21 months in prison for employing undocumented workers and filing false reports to state government

Speedy Gonzales Construction

2/4/2015

Glendale, AZ

- OCAHO found company committed 179 violations; over half for failure to prepare an I-9 form; assessed civil penalty of $97,000
- ICE sought $187,000

ESSG

1/20/2015

Edina, MN

- OCAHO found company committed 292 violations by wrong person signing employer certification and assessed $227,000 in civil penalties; Fifth Circuit reversed and found no violations

U.S. Service Industries

1/15/2015

Washington, D.C. and Virginia

- OSC and company settled claim that company demanded more documentation for non–U.S. citizens than U.S. citizens; agreed to pay $132,000 in civil penalties and $50,000 in back pay

Foothill Packing

1/13/2015

Somerton, AZ

- OCAHO dismissed 337 of the 381 alleged I-9 violations because original auditor didn't ask for supporting documentation; assessed $19,360 in civil penalties
- ICE sought $168,455

Dr. Robert Schaus, DDS

12/30/2014

Clarence, NY

- OCAHO found company liable for failing to prepare/present 10 Form I-9s; fined $5,400
- ICE sought $10,030

Raymond Vincent & RSV Pools

12/28/2014

Gaithersburg, MD

- Owner pled guilty to knowingly employing undocumented workers and ordered to pay $36,000 fine, forfeit $42,262, and serve two days in jail

Life Generations Healthcare

12/4/2014

California, Nevada and Arizona

- After OCAHO found violations of discrimination, OSC and company settled for $119,313 in back pay to two individuals and $88,687 in civil penalties

La Farine Bakery

11/25/2014

San Francisco

- OSC and bakery reached settlement on discriminatory document practices, where bakery agreed to pay $26,000 in back pay

Danny Hendon and Danny's Family Car Wash

11/20/2014

Arizona

- Company owner sentenced one year in prison for engaging in identity theft to employ unauthorized workers; company ordered to forfeit $156,000

Omnibus Express

9/26/2014

Houston, TX

- OSC and company entered into settlement agreement for $208,000 in back pay and $37,800 in civil penalties; company discriminat-

ed against U.S. citizens and permanent residents by favoring H-2B visa hold

Mott Thoroughbred Stables

9/26/2014

New York

- OCAHO found company violated INA by failing to ensure completion of 70 Form I-9s; OCAHO assessed $33,500 in civil penalties
- ICE sought $68,161

Romans Racing Stables

9/24/2014

Kentucky

- OCAHO found company violated INA by failing to prepare I-9 forms for 117 employees and assessed $76,100 in civil penalties   ICE sought $150,000 in civil penalties

Continental Airlines

9/23/2014

Nationwide

- OSC and airline reached settlement where Continental agreed to pay $215,000 in civil penalties and $55,000 back pay for placing additional documentary burdens on work-authorized LPRs

Durable, Inc.

9/23/2014

Wheeling, IL

- OCAHO agreed with ICE and assessed $330,000 in civil penalties for over 300 substantive violations; Durable was found to be a repeat violator based on prior case over 20 years before

7-Eleven

9/22/2014

Long Island & Virginia

- Five franchisees pled guilty to wire fraud and harboring undocumented workers; forfeited rights to franchises and $1.3 million

Grand America Hotels and Resorts

9/9/2014

Utah and other states

- Company agreed to forfeit $1.95 million for knowingly hiring undocumented workers after ICE had found company kept workers who had been found to be undocumented

Cullinaire International

9/2/2014

Houston, TX

- OSC and company resolved claim of citizenship status discrimination by establishment of $40,000 backpay fund and $20,460 in civil penalties

Jalisco's Bar and Grill

6/27/2014

El Centro, CA

- OCAHO fined company $13,000 for knowingly hiring unauthorized workers and 24 counts of untimely prepared I-9s
- ICE sought over $26,000

Desert Canyon Golf

6/13/2014

Scottsdale, AZ

- OCAHO fined company $57,650 for I-9 violations; company failed to provide any information in Section 2 for 93 employees

Senox Corporation

6/3/2014

Austin, TX

- Committed 68 violations, including 54 violations for failure to prepare I-9s; fined $44,800 by OCAHO
- ICE sought fine of $66,759

Century Hotels Corp.

5/27/2014

- OCAHO fined company $25,500 for failure to timely prepare I-9s for 19 employees and 40 violations re: Sections 1, 2 or 3
- ICE sought $55,000

Master Clean Janitorial

5/1/2014

Denver, CO

- Settled case with OSC concerning citizenship discrimination; paid $75,000 in civil penalties

El Rancho

4/1/2014

Texas

- Settled case with OSC involving document abuse, requiring LPRs to present new documentation when their LPR cards expired; paid $43,000 in civil penalties
- Also set-up payback fund to compensate all individuals discriminated against

Potter Concrete

4/1/2014

Dallas, TX

- Settled case with OSC for requiring non–U.S. citizens to provide specific documentation issued by DHS while U.S. citizens were allowed to show their choice of documentation; paid $115,000 in civil penalties

M&D Masonry

3/11/2014

Barnsville, GA

- Fined $228,000 for numerous I-9 violations, including 87 instances of failing to prepare/present I-9s and 277 instances of failing to ensure proper completion of Section 1 or failing to complete Section 2

Minerva Indian Cuisine

2/6/2014

Alpharetta, GA

- Fined $77,000 for failing to prepare I-9s for 82 employees

Peppers Mexican Grill & Cantina

2/1/2014

Jacksonville, FL

- Owner of company fined $10,000 for engaging in a pattern of hiring undocumented workers
- Criminal violation

Premier Parking

2/1/2014

Denver, CO

- Sentenced in federal court to forfeit $185,000 for criminal practice of hiring undocumented workers; owner fined $10,000
- 2nd violation involving hiring undocumented workers; previously fined $11,000 by ICE

Advantage Framing Systems

1/29/2014

Kansas City, KS

- Three owners of company sentenced to one year in prison for harboring undocumented workers

SD Staffing

1/23/2014

Methuen, MA

- Settled with OSC for $10,500 in civil penalties, undetermined back pay for discrimination in I-9 documents required

Two for Seven LLC

1/15/2014

Rochester, NY

- Fined $88,700 by OCAHO for I-9 violations, including failure to prepare/present I-9s for 18 employees
- ICE sought $264,605

Infosys Limited

10/30/2013

Plano, TX

- Settled with DOJ and other agencies for $34 million for alleged visa fraud and I-9 violations
- Infosys used B-1 visas for computer programmers to enter United States and work; no I-9 forms for many workers and failed to re-verify many workers

Huber Industries

9/26/2013

Manheim, PA

- Settled with OSC for preferring to hire H-2A visa holders; paid $59,617 in back pay and $2,250 in civil penalties

IBM

9/26/2013

Nationwide

- Settled with OSC for preferring H-1B visa holders; paid $44,000 in civil penalties

Platinum Builders of Central Fla.

8/20/2013

Port Charlotte, FL

- Fined $23,700 by OCAHO for numerous I-9 violations, including failure to present I-9s for 15 employees and failure to ensure proper completion of Section 1 and/or failure to properly complete Section 2 for 54 employees
- ICE sought $71,000 in penalties

Red Coach Restaurant

8/7/2013

Niagara Falls, NY

- OCAHO reduced penalties from $37,730 to $16,300 because company under new management

Ketchikan Drywall Services

8/6/2013

Washington

- OCAHO adopted Ninth Circuit's decision fining the company $173,250 for numerous I-9 violations, including no status box checked or multiple boxes checked; no employee and/or employer signatures; unacceptable documents; and failure to record any data in Lists A, B or C
- ICE sought fine of $286,624

Monadnock Mt, Spring Water

8/1/2013

Wilton, NH

- OCAHO gave employer the option of paying lump sum of $10,500 or $14,630 over three years

Pharaoh's Gentleman's Club

7/18/2013

Cheektowaga, NY

- OCAHO fined company $17,500 for 40 substantive violations; ICE sought fine of $38,325

Macy's

6/27/2013

Nationwide

- Settled case with OSC for $175,000 in civil penalties and $100,000 for back pay

A&J Kyoto Japanese Restaurant

6/13/2013

Amherst, NY

- Committed 91 substantive violations, including no I-9s for nine employees and no Section 2 attestation for 82 employees; fined $30,475 by OCAHO
- ICE sought fine of $80,000

Anodizing Industries

5/24/2013

Los Angeles, CA

- OCAHO fined company $15,600 for 26 instances of failure to timely prepare I-9s
- ICE sought $25,525

Subway #37616

5/2/2013

Lumberton, NC

- Company fined $9,600 by Oahu for failing to timely prepare I-9 forms and then backdating them
- ICE sought $49,368

H&Y Staffing

4/26/2013

Scranton, PA

- Operator of illegal alien employment business sentenced to a year

Modern Disposal

3/28/2013

Model City, NY

- Fined $33,275 by OCAHO for I-9 violations, including failure to prepare/present I-9s for 55 employees
- No reduction in amount sought by ICE

GPX/GXP

3/12/2013

Williamsport, PA

- Company found guilty of harboring and transporting illegal aliens and fined $50,000 plus forfeited $250,000

Black and Blue Steak and Crab-Buffalo

3/1/2013

Williamsville, NY

- Fined $32,850 by OCAHO for 73 violations for failing to ensure proper completion of Section 1 and/or failing to complete Section 2

- ICE sought $44,165

Fowler Equipment

2/20/2013

Union, NJ

- OCAHO fined company $41,400 for I-9 violations, including failure to prepare/present I-9s for 18 employees

Occupational Resource Management

1/23/2013

Seattle, WA

- Fined $108,000 by OCAHO for I-9 violations, including constructive knowledge of undocumented workers
- ICE sought fine of $188,000

Centerplate, Inc.

1/7/2013

Spartanburg, SC

- Settled with OSC for fine of $250,000 for engaging in pattern or practice of document abuse

Demoulas Super Markets

1/2/2013

Ashland, MA

- Settled case with ICE for I-9 violations; paid $38,491 in penalties

Pureview LLC

1/2/2013

Chelsea, MA

- Settled case with ICE for I-9 violations, including failure to present/prepare I-9s for 107 employees; paid $30,000 in penalties

Amex

11/14/2012

East Boston, MA

- Settled with ICE with fine of $70,000 for I-9 violations

NORBEL

11/14/2012

New Bedford, MA

- Settled with ICE with fine of $151,200 for I-9 violations

March Construction

11/13/2012

San Antonio, TX

- Fined $17,120 by OCAHO for failure to present I-9s for 10 employees and violations in Section 1 and 2 of I-9 form
- ICE sought $87,000

Advantage Health Care

10/25/2012

Hackensack, NJ

- Settled with OSC for $46,525 in penalties for citizenship discrimination

Tuscany Hotel and Casino

10/10/2012

Las Vegas, NV

- Settled with OSC for $49,000 in penalties for citizenship discrimination

Brake Landscaping and Lawn care

9/13/2012

St. Louis, MO

- Found guilty of visa fraud and ordered to forfeit $145,000

Santiago's Repacking

8/24/2012

Nogales, AZ

- Fined $20,000 by OCAHO for failure to pre-pare/present I-9s for 54 individuals. ICE sought $52,528
- 1/3 owner of company didn't need I-9

Infinite Visions

8/8/2012

Newark, NJ

- Settled with ICE for fine of $625,000 for hiring undocumented workers

Stanford Sign and Awning

6/21/2012

- OCAHO fined company $9,600 for 18 substantive violations. Failure to properly complete Sections 1, 2 or 3

Whiz International

5/30/2012

Jersey City, NJ

- Settled with OSC for $22,000 in back pay for terminating employee in retaliation for expressing opposition to company preference for foreign nationals

ABC Professional Tree Services

5/18/2012

Houston, TX

- Forfeited $2 million in revenue, amount it earned through use of about 750 undocumented workers
- Avoided criminal prosecution

Imagine Schools

5/7/2012

Groveport, OH

- Settled with OSC for $20,000 in back pay for terminating employee for failing to re-verify his green card

HerbCo

5/1/2012

Seattle, WA

- Fined $1 million for harboring and concealing 25 undocumented workers

LTCI

4/6/2012

Syracuse, NY

- Two executives of company forfeited $223,000 based on unlawful employment of illegal aliens and tax evasion

Sun Drywall & Stucco

4/4/2012

Tucson, AZ

- President of company forfeited $225,000 for knowingly employing undocumented workers

Onward Healthcare

3/28/2012

Wilton, CT

- Settled case with OSC for $100,000 in civil penalties for posting jobs requiring U.S. citizenship

Atlanta Meat Company

2/22/2012

Atlanta, GA

- Three owners of company sentenced to three to five years in prison for immigration and tax fraud

ACSI

1/24/2012

Houston, TX

- Forfeited $2 million based on constructive knowledge of undocumented workers

Atrium Companies

1/24/2012

Houston, TX

- Forfeited $2 million in revenue - based on pattern and practice of knowingly hiring undocumented workers

J&J Industrial

1/17/2012

St. Louis, MO

- Forfeited $150,000 for employment of more than 10 illegal aliens

Pegasus Restaurant

1/5/2012

Castle Rock, CO

- Fined $47,427 by OCAHO for numerous I-9 violations, including 134 instances of failure to prepare/present I-9s for employees
- ICE sought $131,554 in penalties

UC-S.D. Medical Center

1/4/2012

San Diego, CA

- Settled a case with OSC for $115,000 in civil penalties for citizenship discrimination

Balboa Ambulance

1/2/2012

San Diego, CA

- Settled with ICE for $50,000 fine for I-9 violations

Calabro Cheese

1/2/2012

East Haven, CT

- Settled with ICE with fine of $45,000 for I-9 violations

Impact Plastics

1/2/2012

Putnam, CT

- Settled with ICE with fine of $34,000 for I-9 violations

Mexicali Chicken & Salad

1/2/2012

San Diego, CA

- Settled with ICE for $21,500 for I-9 violations

BAE Systems

12/28/2011

Virginia

- Settled case with OSC for $53,000 for document abuse

French Gourmet

12/22/2011

La Jolla, CA

- Company ordered to forfeit $109,000 and pay fine of $277,000 for employing more than 10 illegal aliens
- Owner sentenced to five years' probation and $396,575 fine

Aquila Farms

11/8/2011

Bad Axe, MI

- Company and Owner fined $2.7 million for employment of 78 undocumented workers

Ice Castles Daycare

9/22/2011

El Paso, TX

- OCAHO fined company $18,500 for failure to prepare I-9s for 74 employees
- ICE sought over $55,000

Eurofresh

8/26/2011

Tucson, AZ

- Ordered to forfeit $600,000 for knowingly employing more than 10 undocumented workers

Kinro Mfg.

8/26/2011

Goshen, IN

- Settled case with OSC for $25,000 in penalties and $10,000 in back pay for discrimination against non–U.S. Citizens

Farmland Foods

8/22/2011

Kansas City, MO

- Settled case with OSC for $290,400 in penalties for imposing excessive documentary requirements on non–U.S. citizens and foreign-born U.S. citizens

Alyn Industries

8/17/2011

Van Nuys, CA

- OCAHO assessed penalties at $43,000 for I-9 violations, including 59 instances of not properly completing section 2
- ICE sought $63,000

Dunkin Donuts

8/3/2011

Portland, ME

- Manager fined $64,000 for hiring illegal aliens

Commercial Cleaning Services

7/21/2011

Allston, MA

- Settled with ICE for fine of $100,000 for I-9 violations

Brand Energy and Industrial Services

7/21/2011

Prairieville, LA

- Settled case with OSC for $43,560 in civil penalties and $7,200 in back pay for termination of employee due to citizenship discrimination

Jasper Wyman & Son

7/21/2011

Milbridge, MA

- Settled with ICE for fine of $118,000 for I-9 violations

China Buffet

3/22/2011

Poplar Bluff, MO

- Manager of restaurant sentenced to one year in prison for hiring and harboring illegal aliens

Howard Industries

2/25/2011

Laurel, MS

- Guilty of conspiracy to induce illegal aliens to work at plant; paid $2.5 million fine

Collins Mgmt Corp.

12/29/2010

Oregon

- Settled case with OSC for $15,000 in back pay and $600 in penalties for citizenship discrimination

Snack Attack Deli

12/22/2010

Fayetteville, NC

- OCAHO reduced penalties from $111,000 to $27,150 for numerous I-9 violations due to inability to pay and small size

Daniel Builders

12/14/2010

Miami, FL

- Executives sentenced to 1 1/2 to two years in prison and fines and restitution of approximately $200,000 due to conspiracy to induce illegal aliens to remain in United States for commercial gain.

Hoover, Inc.

11/10/2010

Glenwillow, OH

- Settled case with OSC for $10,200 in penalties for requiring green-card holders to re-verify when their cards expired

Catholic Healthcare West

10/19/2010

California, Nevada and Arizona

- Settled case with OSC concerning document abuse for $257,000 in civil penalties

Abercrombie & Fitch

9/28/2010

Michigan

- Settled with ICE for fine of $1.05 million for I-9 violations

Amador Poultry Contracting

7/20/2010

Fort Smith, AR

- Four owners sentenced to between one year and 2 1/2 years in prison for harboring and employing illegal aliens; forfeited $1.87 million in cash and property

DJ Drywall

7/14/2010

- OCAHO fined company $32,316 for 66 Form I-9 violations - increase of $1,000 for penalties sought by ICE

New China Buffet

5/27/2010

- OCAHO reduced fine from $6,545 to $3,150 due to small size and inability to pay

Koch Foods

2/12/2010

Cincinnati, OH

- Settled with ICE for $536,000 fine for employment of undocumented workers

Taylor-Made Roofing

2/3/2010

Bolivar, MO

- Owner sentenced to forfeiture and fine of $220,000 for knowingly hiring, contracting, and sub-contracting to hire illegal aliens

INDEX

F

I

V

W

Made in the USA
Lexington, KY
12 March 2019